# Inspiration for Leaders and Learners

Karen Kettle & Dr. Spencer Kagan

***Kagan Publishing***
P.O. Box 72008
San Clemente, CA 92673-2008
**1(800) 933-2667**
**www.KaganOnline.com**

ISBN: 978-1-879097-89-6

# Table of Contents

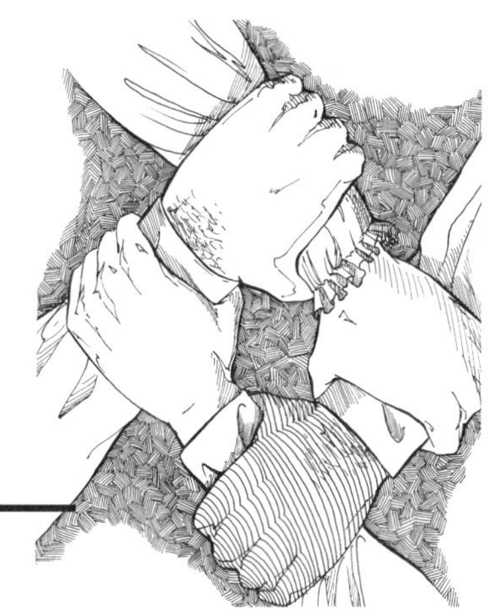

## Inspirational Quotations

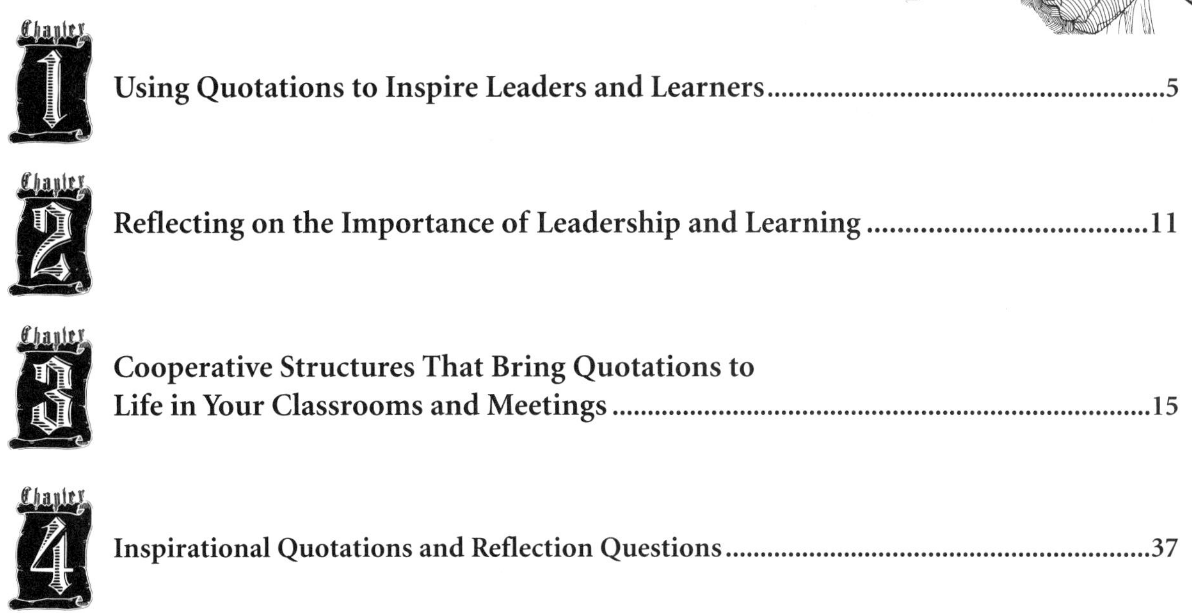


Chapter 1 Using Quotations to Inspire Leaders and Learners ........ 5

Chapter 2 Reflecting on the Importance of Leadership and Learning ........ 11

Chapter 3 Cooperative Structures That Bring Quotations to Life in Your Classrooms and Meetings ........ 15

Chapter 4 Inspirational Quotations and Reflection Questions ........ 37


## Inspirational Topics


- Attitude ........ 39
- Challenge ........ 51
- Change ........ 61
- Character ........ 75
- Communication ........ 87
- Conflict ........ 97
- Creativity ........ 107
- Decision Making ........ 119
- Diversity ........ 131
- Education ........ 141
- Emotional Intelligence ........ 153
- Experience ........ 165
- Humor ........ 177
- Interconnectedness ........ 187
- Leadership ........ 199
- Learning ........ 211
- Opportunity ........ 225
- Perseverance ........ 235
- Risk ........ 245
- Service and Love ........ 255
- Success and Failure ........ 267
- Teaching ........ 279
- Vision and Goals ........ 295

# Preface

I fell in love with the power of quotations as a kid at summer camp. Quotations were in all the important places. The day began with a poignant morning thought that gave us more to chew on than the rubbery toast that was central to the breakfast routine. The honor of reading the morning thought circulated from cabin to cabin and I can remember trembling in my sneakers the first time it became my responsibility. It was one of my first leadership experiences. Quotations accompanied us on canoe trips. The more inspirational they were the longer, hotter, steeper, and mosquito infested the portage was that loomed ahead of us. We loved them anyway. Quotations were woven into closing campfires. Carefully selected to capture the moment, they helped us to relive cherished camp adventures and prepare to reenter the outside world. I was hooked. So are a lot of other people. I keep finding them. I returned to camp as an adult and worked its summer magic with other leaders to sculpt "aha" moments, pump kids up to face a challenge, or reflect to shed a heartfelt tear. Quotations were part of the enchantment. I've learned from teachers who used quotations to frame lessons and articles and much to my surprise I joined their ranks. I've supported student leaders in the development of a school leadership camp and watched them use the wisdom of quotations in ingenious ways. I continue to learn from them. I want to thank everyone who has shared their favorite quotations with me throughout the years. Leading and learning are part of our lives.

***—Karen***

Unlike Karen, I can't remember the time I first fell in love with quotes. I do remember the affair was in advanced stages by the time I took a speed-reading course in high school. Near the end of the course, the instructor proudly showed me my graphs. I had much more than doubled my reading speed and increased my retention. She asked if I would like to take advanced speed-reading. I declined, saying I would much rather spend an hour on fifteen good words than read a whole novel in fifteen minutes.

I have always been a slow processor but don't regret it. I would rather be touched one time deeply than many times superficially.

Karen and I discovered our common love for quotes as we worked on our *Cooperative Meetings* book, a book designed for leaders and learners. As we dug from our collections to sprinkle the pages of that book with quotes, we realized our need to share our quotes exceeded the room in that book. It was Karen who suggested a book of quotes. Thus began a work of love, combining our collections and then selecting, verifying, categorizing, and organizing. Our intent: to provide a useful source of quotations for leaders and learners on the topics most relevant to those who desire to inspire others and who, given the hard work of generating positive change, can from time to time use a dose of re-inspiration.

Look up the word *inspiration* in the dictionary. You find two apparently disparate meanings: 1) draw in air; 2) fill with revolutionary ideas. But in fact the ideas converge. When we take a deep breath we fill our lungs with oxygen, much of which goes directly to the brain where it energizes our thinking. When there is revolution in the air, when we breathe in revolutionary ideas, our thinking is in the same way energized. We are inspired.

A good quote is a breath of fresh, revolutionary air. It causes us to see things differently. Of course different quotes change our vision and our energy in different ways. Some quotes reaffirm or refine our thinking; some are signposts, pointing toward a different path of thinking; some simply make us muse. But all of them, like a good deep breath of fresh air leave us changed, energized, exalted.

Our hope is that as a leader and learner you will not only return again and again to these pages as a resource in your work of inspiring others, but also a personal resource in your process of continual renewal.

***—Dr. Spencer Kagan***


## Appreciations

We are indebted to Toni Swagler whose drawings enliven these pages. His lines are a compliment to those who originally penned the lines we have chosen. Erin Kant with her gift for the whimsical created the cover. Miguel Kagan provided his sure guidance with book design and production. Alex Core created and implemented the terrific design for this book. Of course, our greatest debt and appreciation is to all of the authors of these inspirational quotes; their insights and visions spark the imagination and provide renewed energy for each generation.

# Chapter 1

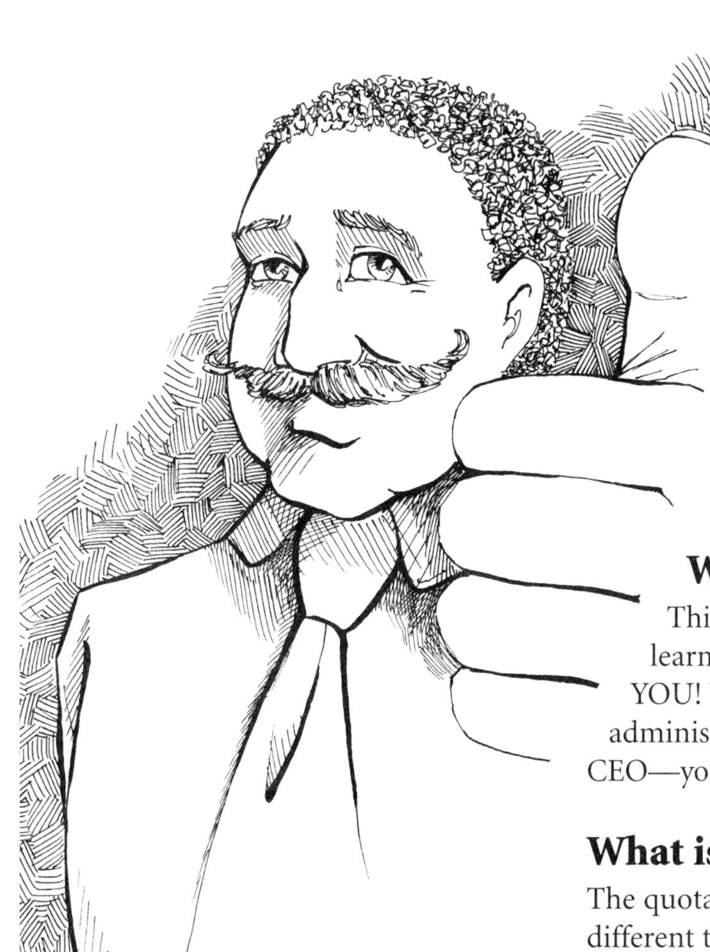

# Using Quotations to Inspire Leaders and Learners

## Who will use this book?

This book was created for leaders and learners of all ages and stages. That includes YOU! Whether you're a student, teacher, administrator, parent, community member, or CEO—you'll find inspiration between these covers.

## What is included within the book?

The quotations in this book explore twenty-three different themes connected to leadership and learning. We've chosen quotations that represent men and women across cultures and time to provide a diversity of ideas and role models.

Three introductory chapters stand between you and the quotations. Chapter 1 provides an overview to answer all of your *who, what, why, when, and where* questions! Chapter 2 stretches from the practical to the theoretical to reflect on the importance of leadership and learning within the context of school. Chapter 3 provides you with ten well-tested cooperative structures and sample activities. While the examples reflect educational settings, the themes are equally valuable for any organization in the community—church, service club, youth group, business—that values the connection between

***Colors fade, temples crumble, empires fall, but wise words remain.***
***—Thorndike***

leadership and learning. We want you to bring the quotations in this book to life—to interact with them in your communications, classrooms, and meetings. You can select quotations and easily create activities with your own goals in mind.

At the back of the book you will find an index to help you locate quotations by specific authors.

## Why use quotations?

Everyone reading this book has a favorite quotation. We may not remember the exact words but we treasure the moment we encountered them for the first time. This powerful attraction may emerge from one or more of the following qualities:

**Quotations stand the test of time.** Proverbs are handed down over and over again until their source has long since been forgotten. Their wise words provide maxims for living well.

**Quotations resonate with personal experience.** We connect to what is being said because we've been there. The words echo with meaning from our own lives.

**Quotations challenge and inspire us.** They make us think and dare us to see things in new ways. They awaken new possibilities.

**Quotations capture a much broader story.** They cause a shiver to run up our spines because they evoke the spirit of a specific event or era of history. The words trigger our memories—the sights, the sounds, the feelings—of the larger experience.

**Quotations rekindle dreams.** They provide affirmation. They tap into our idealism of what could be and allow us to rise above everyday events to see the big picture of what we would like to achieve.

**Quotations connect us to people we admire.** Ideas are often important because of their source. Quotations connect us to eminent individuals that we respect because of their courage, intellect, endurance, creativity, or contributions to society. They also connect us to unsung heroes—grandparents, teachers, friends. In repeating the words we keep all that the person stood for alive in our hearts and minds.

**Quotations connect us to the wisdom of other times and places.** They remind us of the universality of the human condition. We are interconnected across cultures, throughout time, and to the universe as a whole.

**Quotations make us laugh.** Last, but not least, the wit and wordplay in quotations often makes us smile.

Finding just the right quotation at just the right time will NOT solve problems, settle conflicts, build relationships, create vision, or achieve goals. All of these things represent the hard work that members of your organization, school, or classroom community must engage in person to person. Quotations, if used effectively, can be part of the process. They are useful tools for leaders and learners because they focus attention and energy that can then be used to:

- **Spark debate,**
- **Clarify positions,**
- **Identify signposts on a journey,**
- **Frame a presentation, speech, or essay,**

- **Grab attention,**
- **Refocus on the big picture,**
- **Shift perspectives,**
- **Provide comic relief,**
- **Create identity,**
- **Motivate and inspire,**
- **Affirm, and**
- **Celebrate.**

## When and where can quotations be used?

Here are some ideas on how to put the quotations in this book to work for you.

### Communication Applications

• **Newsletters:** Newsletters are often an important communication link between school and home. Quotations quickly capture the spirit of the exchange and focus the reader's attention.

• **Websites:** Websites are the newsletters of the 21st century. Many schools have websites that publicize coming events, celebrate achievements, provide information to families, and connect alumni.

• **Hallway Inspiration:** The advertising industry recognizes that it's almost impossible to walk by a billboard without reading it. Students can be invited to identify meaningful quotations that represent the creativity and character of the disciplines they are studying. Paint is cheap. Contributing to the atmosphere of the school by painting inspirational quotations in the hallways provides a huge payoff in ownership. Everyone who walks by is reminded of what is important. Hallway inspirations can be updated regularly so that they always belong to the students currently in the school.

• **Affirmations of Learning:** Displaying quotations about perseverance and learning adds to a positive classroom environment. Quotations provide encouragement, remind students that failure leads to success, and affirm the importance of effort.

• **Proverbs in Action:** Proverbs can be brought to life. A different maxim for living can be posted on a bulletin board at the beginning of each month and students who embody its wisdom can be celebrated with a picture and a brief description of their achievements. The diversity of insights that proverbs provide ensures a wide variety of students and contributions are recognized.

### Classroom Applications

• **Grab Attention:** Some quotations naturally grab the attention of students. They can be provocative, poignant, or humorous. At times the message has a surprising messenger.

• **Make Personal Connections:** Quotations provide rich territory for personal reflection. Students can be asked to explore the wisdom within a quotation before connecting the concept to the curriculum.

• **Review or Preview:** Thought provoking quotations and guiding questions can be used as a preview to determine students' prior knowledge. Quotations that represent key ideas can be used to check understanding and raise unanswered questions during a review.

• **Jumpstart Writing:** Quotations can be used to spark ideas for creative writing. When combined with an idea generating activity a team of students can build on each other's imaginations to brainstorm oodles of creative options before beginning to write.

• **Frame a Presentation, Speech or Essay:** Authors and speakers often use quotations to frame their work. Students can learn how to use this literary device.

• **Clarify Positions:** Quotations that state strong positions can be used to help students clarify their opinions and take a stand on the continuum from agreement to disagreement.

• **Supply Evidence:** Students are often asked to find quotations to supply evidence that the knowledge claim they are making is valid.

• **Spark Debate:** Quotations can form the resolution under consideration in a formal debate. This type of activity can be tightly tied to curriculum by quoting the individuals whose contributions are being studied.

• **Recognize Eminent Individuals and Historical Eras:** Content is often presented without context. Students don't know anything about the person whose work they are studying or the social or historical era in which it was created. Quotations can be used to provide background insights.

• **Provide Inspiration:** A carefully selected "Thought for the Day" can be used to provide whatever inspiration or understanding students need to discuss to handle the situation at hand.

**Meeting Applications**

• **Frame a Presentation:** Quotations are a helpful tool for presenters to use to focus their audience.

• **Review or Preview:** Thought provoking quotations and guiding questions can be used to find out what people know about a topic, check their understanding, and raise questions or concerns.

• **Make Personal Connections:** Considering the connections between a quotation and professional experience helps to prepare people before they enter into a dialogue with their peers.

• **Identify Signposts on a Journey:** Change initiatives and major decision making processes are journeys that a faculty takes together. Quotations can be used to recognize each stage of the journey and stand as signposts along the way.

• **Focus on the Big Picture:** Sometimes meetings bog down in details and administrivia. Quotations can be used to remind people of the importance of the big picture of student learning.

• **Shift Perspectives:** Quotations can remind people of absent voices or different points of view. They can help people to step into someone else's shoes and see the world anew.

• **Clarify Positions:** Quotations that state strong positions can be used to help people explore potential alternatives. This type of activity can be tightly tied to the larger purpose of the meeting.

• **Diffuse Emotional Situations:** Quotations capture a range of emotions. Discussing the quotations and their connection to the situation at hand provides an outlet for people to articulate their feelings.

• **Provide Comic Relief:** Professional development often occurs after school. People are tired. Laughing and seeing the humor in life lightens the moment and generates positive energy.

• **Recognize Educational Researchers:** Attaching educational research to quotations from the authors grounds the concepts and provides a connection for people who want to find out more on their own.

• **Provide Inspiration:** A carefully selected "Thought for the Day" provides proof that the leader understands current challenges and is in touch with the nature of the inspiration or understanding that people are seeking.

# Chapter 

# Reflecting on the Importance of Leadership and Learning

## People Love to Learn

Our capacity to learn sets us apart from all the other species that share our planet. It's so important to us that we've created schools to ensure that our children learn what they need to know, be able to do, and value as contributing members of society. Learning is hard work and an extremely personal endeavor. It's also so engaging that people continue to do it throughout their lives.

Students learn in many different ways. The more they know about learning the more able they are to marshal the personal resources and perseverance they need to be successful in and beyond school. Learning how to learn empowers students. Every magnificent mind and creative soul in history germinated within a child who was curious about the world.

***Leadership and learning are indispensable to each other.***
***—John F. Kennedy***

Great teachers love to learn. They keep up with discoveries in their favorite subject areas, consume research on learning, and continue to improve their classroom practice. Teachers who value professional learning are eager to share ideas with colleagues and learn from the experiences of others—including their students. They thrive on the complexity of their profession. There is always something new to learn.

Innovative administrators are always on the lookout for new ideas and resources. They make time for their own professional development and facilitate the professional learning of their faculty. They create the frameworks and climate necessary for the ongoing improvement of student learning.

## Leaders are Everywhere

There are abundant leadership opportunities at school. At first glance it might seem that leadership resides mainly in the principal's office. The principal plays a critical role that extends far beyond the managerial workings of creating schedules and maintaining order. He or she sets the tone for the school community and directly or indirectly facilitates everything that happens within the building. Anyone who has stepped into the principal's role knows that to do it well you cannot do it alone. You need to rely on the expertise of others and build the capacity for leadership throughout the faculty, the student population, and the school-community council. The principal is a leadership role model. How he or she goes about building relationships, creating vision, supporting learning, and involving others in important school decisions affects everyone.

Teachers are leaders. They make thousands of decisions daily in the process of designing curriculum, supporting student learning, interacting with young people, mentoring less experienced peers, and communicating with parents. Students see teachers in leadership roles far beyond the classroom—supervising the playground, coaching teams, directing the school play, and organizing special school events. Teachers are leadership role models. What they do is important and the way they do it is even more significant. Students are paying attention. While they may not always be attuned to the lesson at hand, they notice if teachers value learning, communicate effectively, celebrate diversity, solve conflicts in a constructive way, interact with generosity, and embrace change.

Students are learning to be leaders. School provides them with formal opportunities to develop their leadership abilities. They are required to work in cooperation with others, communicate information and ideas, and accept responsibility for classroom routines. Extracurricular activities abound with leadership opportunities—student council executive, team captain, first clarinet, safety patroller, or peer tutor. Informal opportunities to lead arise everyday as young people develop self-understanding and learn how to influence others. Programs that develop student leaders broaden the leadership base within the school. Senior students can serve as important leadership role models for their younger peers. If students are welcomed into school leadership initiatives, they will rise to the challenge with energy and enthusiasm.

Leadership ability develops over time. It's a lifelong journey and everyone is at a different spot along the trail. Leadership is about finding new possibilities, stepping into new roles, and creating meaning. Everyone can develop the knowledge, skills, and attitudes necessary to imagine a better world and inspire their peers and community to do something about it.

## Leaders are Learners

The inseparable nature of leadership and learning is recognized in educational literature. Leadership is about embracing change. No one becomes a great leader by maintaining the status quo. Effective leaders change things for the better. Michael Fullan (2001) presents five components of leadership that interact to support positive change. Learning is highlighted throughout his model.

- *Moral purpose* captures the intention of making a positive difference in the lives of everyone who interacts with the school. Moral purpose provides the direction for decision making and change.
- *Understanding change* requires that the leader do his or her homework to learn about the complexity of the change process and articulate it to others.
- *Building relationships* honors the people involved in the change. People are emotional beings. They want to be known, feel that they belong, and have influence. Trusting relationships provide the mutual support required to celebrate and work with diverse ideas so that people can learn together.
- *Creating and sharing knowledge* calls for the leader to facilitate the social processes and interactions required for learning. People must work together to decide what they know and how they will apply their knowledge.
- *Making coherence* aligns change initiatives and creates a narrative story to show how the pieces fit together to create a big picture.

These five components exist within the energy, enthusiasm, and hope of the leader and the people involved in the change. As the five components interact, they generate commitment. The results are simple but profound, "more good things happen; fewer bad things happen." Educational leaders who thrive in a culture of change are avid learners who enjoy the complexity of ongoing improvement and seek to embed change within the culture and structure of their schools. Two educational models that bring this vision to life are Peter Senge's Learning Organization and Richard DuFour and Robert Eaker's Professional Learning Communities.

Peter Senge and his colleagues (2000) suggest that the key to school improvement is an orientation toward learning that builds on the strengths of everyone who has a stake in education (students, parents, teachers, administrators, business leaders, community members, union representatives). Leaders of Learning Organizations recognize the importance of personal mastery and vision. They invite people to examine the mental models that frame and sometimes limit their understanding of teaching and learning. Commitment and ownership develop from taking time for the sustained dialogue that is necessary to find common ground or a shared vision within a diverse set of hopes and dreams. The awareness of a common purpose provides a direction for team learning.

Learning turns like a wheel as teams observe what is happening in their school, reflect on the patterns they identify, decide what to do, do it, measure what happens, reflect, reconsider, reconnect, and reframe the problem. Leaders of Learning Organizations are aware of the complex, non-linear, and interconnected nature of systems and the messiness of change.

Richard DuFour and Robert Eaker paint a vivid picture of the benefits of schools that focus on student learning where:

- mission, vision, and values are shared,
- inquiry is conducted collectively,
- people work in collaborative teams,
- experimentation and action are valued,
- continuous improvement is expected, and
- improvement is based on observable results.

Three key questions frame the ongoing work of collaborative teams within these Professional Learning Communities:

1. What do we want students to learn?
2. How will we know what students have learned?
3. How will the school respond when students do not learn?

School leadership within a Professional Learning Community always returns to the prime directive—student learning.

Both of these models embed learning in the culture of the school and suggest systematic ways of gathering data, recognizing patterns, making adjustments, and continuing to improve. These processes require a collaborative and interactive form of leadership that fosters growth within individuals and builds capacity within the organization as a whole.

## References

DuFour, Richard & Eaker, Robert (1998). ***Professional Learning Communities at Work: Best Practices for Enhancing Student Achievement.*** National Educational Service: Bloomington, Indiana.

Fullan, Michael (2001). ***Leading in a Culture of Change.*** San Francisco: Jossey-Bass.

Senge, Peter, et al. (2000). ***Schools That Learn: A Fifth Discipline Fieldbook for Educators, Parents, and Everyone Who Cares About Education.*** New York: Doubleday.

# Chapter 3

# Cooperative Structures That Bring Quotations to Life in Your Classrooms and Meetings

You can bring quotations to life in your classroom or in your meetings in an interactive way. It's only when leaders and learners engage deeply with the content of the quotations that we internalize their wisdom and can transfer it to the context of our own lives. This chapter provides you with ten Cooperative Structures and examples of classroom and meeting activities. This is only the beginning. Cooperative Structures are content-free. You can add quotations that resonate with the purpose of your lesson or meeting and create your own activities. Let your imagination play.

***There is, in fact, no teaching without learning.***
***—Paolo Freire***

# Carousel Preview or Review

Carousel Preview or Review provides an opportunity to generate ideas, check understanding, and raise unanswered questions. Teams rotate from one poster to the next around the room at given intervals reading the quotations and responding to the guiding questions. They take time to comment on information written by previous teams. They may agree, disagree, or raise questions. Each time the team rotates, a different person becomes the recorder. If each team has a different colored marker, they become accountable for their contributions. Music can be used to increase energy and provide a cue to rotate between charts. The written record can be used to plan future activities, summarize the issues, or generate follow-up ideas around questions or misconceptions.

## Steps:

1. Quotations and guiding questions are posted around the room.
2. Teams each stand by a chart.
3. Teams have a given amount of time to record their ideas.
4. Teams select a new recorder and rotate to the next chart.
5. Teams read and discuss what previous teams have written.
6. Teams record additional information before rotating.

## Classroom Activity

Teachers can use this Carousel Preview activity at the beginning of the year. The following quotations and guiding questions have been selected to gather information about students' interests and learning preferences. Providing opportunities for students to influence their learning environment builds classroom community.

***"I have no special talents. I am only passionately curious."***
**—Albert Einstein**
What are you curious about?

***"You win some and you learn some."***
**—Barry Johnson**
What have you learned from mistakes?

***"I hear and I forget. I see and I remember. I do and I understand."***
**—Confucius**
What helps you learn?

***"To every answer you can find a new question."***
**—Yiddish proverb**
What questions would you like to have answered?

***"What we learn with pleasure we never forget."***
**—Louis Mercier**
What makes you enjoy learning?

***"When I got my library card, that's when my life began."***
**—Rita Mae Brown**
What are your favorite books?

# Meeting Activity

School leaders must create the systems and nurture the people that meet the wide-ranging needs of students. The following quotations and guiding questions for this Carousel Preview/Review activity are designed to generate ideas about diversity.

***"In diversity, there is strength."***
**—Maya Angelou**
In what ways do our differences make us stronger as a faculty?

***"The best hope of solving all our problems lies in harnessing the diversity, the energy and the creativity of all our people."***
**—Roger Wilkins**
How can we involve students, parents, community members, teachers, and administrators in improving student learning?

***"Culture is the widening of the mind and the spirit."***
**—Jawaharlal Nehru**
In what ways can we embrace the cultures of all of the students at our school?

***"One of the great strengths of caring as an ethic is that it does not assume that all students should be treated by some impartial standard of fairness. Some students need more attention than others."***
**—Nel Noddings**
How can we work together to meet the diverse needs of our students?

***"Freedom to think—which means nothing unless it means freedom to think differently—can be society's most precious gift to itself. The first duty of a school is to defend and cherish it."***
**—Arthur Bestor**
In what ways do we encourage our students to think for themselves?

***"The essence of our effort to see that every child has a chance must be to assure each an equal opportunity, not to become equal, but to become different—to realize whatever unique potential of body, mind and spirit he or she possesses."***
**—John Fischer**
How do we help students discover and develop their individual talents?

# Corners

In Corners, the leader announces a theme and posts quotations in the four corners of the room. It's important that everyone understands the content of the quotations. Students may require the leader to read each quotation to the class and facilitate a discussion to explore its meaning. Learners then select the quotation that is most significant to them and move to the corner representing their choice. They find a partner in their corner and share the reasons for their selections. Corners is designed to allow learners to create bonds with and support others who have made similar choices but may have very different rationales. It also acknowledges that a variety of positions are valid.

## Steps:

1. Leader announces corners.
2. Learners think and record their selection.
3. Learners go to the corners.
4. Pairs discuss.

## Classroom Activity

The following quotations all deal with courage. Students engage in this Corners activity to explore the nature of courage in a personal way before connecting the concept of courage to the curriculum. They are then asked to identify acts of courage within the content they are studying—a novel, historical period, social movement, artistic creation, academic discipline, or current event.

***"Courage is not the absence of fear, but rather the judgment that something else is more important than fear."***
**—Ambrose Redmoon**

***"Courage allows the successful person to fail—and to learn powerful lessons from the failure—so that in the end, it was not a failure at all."***
**—Maya Angelou**

***"To see what is right and not to do it is want of courage."***
**—Confucius**

***"Courage is what it takes to stand up and speak. Courage is also what it takes to sit down and listen."***
**—Winston Churchill**

## Meeting Activity

Communication is essential to leading and learning. The following quotations all discuss challenges that are inherent to effective communication. Participants are asked to select the quotation that represents a frustration that they've experienced or a challenge they'd like to overcome. This activity provides an opportunity for personal reflection and sharing to set the stage for professional development on how to provide effective feedback to students, parents, or teachers.

***"Truth is not everywhere the same, because language is not everywhere the same, and human existence is essentially linguistic and essentially historical."***
**—Richard Rorty**

***"The most important thing in communication is to hear what isn't being said."***
**—Peter Drucker**

***"The single biggest problem in communication is the illusion that it has taken place."***
**—George Bernard Shaw**

***"The genius of communication is the ability to be both totally honest and totally kind at the same time."***
**—John Powell**

# Jigsaw

Jigsaw provides an efficient and interactive way to share ideas. Jigsaw begins with a focus statement that clarifies the nature of the task ahead. Each home team member is assigned a number from one to four. Individuals leave their home team and form expert groups or expert pairs based on their numbers. Each expert group is provided with a different quotation and task. The expert groups read and discuss the quotation and collaborate to complete the task. They make sure that all expert group members can articulate their shared understanding. Group members then return to their home teams. Individuals interact using RoundRobin with the aim of presenting all four pieces of the puzzle to inform their team's understanding.

## Steps:

1. Learners number themselves 1 to 4 in home groups.
2. Expert groups are formed using the numbers.
3. Each expert group is presented with a different quotation.
4. Learners discuss the quotation in their expert group.
5. Learners return to their home group to share.

## Classroom Activity

This Jigsaw activity encourages students to explore the consequences of approaching life with a positive or negative attitude. They work in their expert groups or pairs to generate examples that illustrate the wisdom in the quotation. Examples may be drawn from history, literature, media, or everyday life. Students then return to their home teams to share and illustrate the meaning of the quotations in a RoundRobin discussion.

***"Attitude will take you further than talent."***
**—Ruthie Bolton-Holifield**

***"Life is what we make it; always has been, always will be."***
**—Grandma Moses**

***"I am a big believer that eventually everything comes back to you. You get back what you give out."***
**—Nancy Reagan**

***"No one can make you feel inferior without your consent."***
**—Eleanor Roosevelt**

## Meeting Activity

This Jigsaw activity is designed to focus a discussion on the complexity of teaching. Each expert team is asked to clarify the author's insights into teaching and make connections to best practice in their classrooms. In sharing best practices, teachers learn from their peers' experiences, celebrate their successes, and kindle each other's curiosity. They lead and they learn.

***"Teaching is an instinctual act, mindful of potential, craving of realizations, a pausing, seamless process, where one rehearses constantly while acting, sits as a spectator at a play one directs, engages every part in order to keep the choices open and the shape alive for the student, so that the student may enter in and begin to do what the teacher has done: make choices."***
**—A. Barlett Giamatti**

***"Human activity consists of action and reflection: it is praxis; it is transformation of the world. And as praxis, it requires theory to illuminate it. Human activity is theory and practice; it is reflection and action. It cannot be reduced to either verbalism or activism."***
**—Paolo Freire**

***"For good teaching rests neither in accumulating a shelf full of knowledge nor in developing a repertoire of skills. In the end, good teaching lies in a willingness to attend and care for what happens in our students, ourselves, and the space between us. Good teaching is a certain kind of stance, I think. It is a stance of receptivity, of attunement, of listening."***
**—Laurent A. Daloz**

***"As a teacher I possess tremendous power to make a child's life miserable or joyous. I can be a tool of torture or an instrument of inspiration. I can humiliate or humor, hurt or heal. In all situations it is my response that decides whether a crisis will be escalated or de-escalated, and a child is humanized or de-humanized."***
**—Haim Ginott**

# Journey Wall

A Journey Wall is a collaborative arrangement of artifacts that forms a timeline. Its purpose is to provide everyone with an opportunity to reflect on a process or on their learning—all of it—the highs and lows. A Journey Wall can be created with markers and mural paper, but it's fun to use art supplies, newspaper headlines, cartoons, clip art, magazine pictures and quotations. The leader prepares for this activity by collecting artifacts and art supplies. Quotations can be typed on colorful paper and laminated for reuse. The collection of quotations should be eclectic so that the learners can make connections that are meaningful to them. A long wall is required. The leader displays key artifacts and dates to anchor the timeline of the Journey Wall. It's essential to leave lots of space for additions. Each team is assigned a portion of the Journey Wall to illustrate. Teams discuss their section of the timeline and enhance it with their artistic creations. When the wall is finished, each team presents their portion. Everything that goes up on the Journey Wall must be explained. Music can be added to highlight the theme of each stage of the journey.

## Steps:

1. Display the artifacts.
2. Present the team with a collection of quotations.
3. Have teams add to the display.
4. Celebrate the journey.

## Classroom Activity

There are lots of opportunities within the curriculum where Journey Walls are an effective activity to consolidate student learning.

Students can create a timeline for a historical event or era. Teams represent the experiences of different countries or different social groups. The teacher chooses to provide students with a random collection of quotations, key quotations from the major historical players, or some of each.

The storyline of a novel can be mapped out on a Journey Wall. Major events anchor the display. Teams are responsible for different chapters or represent the encounters of different characters. Students illustrate their storyline by selecting key quotations from the text. They can even use in-class quotations from their peers' reactions to illustrate the journey.

The process involved in a major undertaking like the creation of a drama night, a science fair, or an open house can be illustrated with a Journey Wall. This reflective process helps students explore leadership roles, learn from mistakes, and celebrate their accomplishment.

## Meeting Activity

Journey Walls are great activities to develop a common understanding of a process or event while incorporating many different perspectives in an honest and open way. They capture the complexity of emotion. A key event can represent a joyful occasion for some while others face it with a sense of loss. All of the key players can be involved—students, parents, teachers, administrators, and community members. Journey Walls can represent:

- the history of the school,
- the timeline of a change,
- the implementation of an innovation,
- the creation of a school plan,
- a decision making process, or
- a major school event.

# Line-Ups

The leader reads a quotation to which learners may strongly agree or strongly disagree. Once the extremes of the line are established, participants line up in a place that represents their position. A number of techniques can then be used to provide partners for discussion.

a) Starting at one end of the line, learners may be paired to talk to someone with a similar view.
b) The line may be folded in half so that learners with extremely different values can meet and discuss. To do this, learners follow the leader at one end until everyone has a partner.
c) The line can be split in the middle. Half of the line takes three steps forward and turns and slides down so that everyone faces a partner. Participants who are in the middle are now faced with people from the ends.

Line-Ups is a convenient way to number pairs off to create new teams of four.

## Steps:

1. Leader describes the line.
2. Learners line up.
3. The line is split or folded to form pairs.
4. Pairs discuss.

## Classroom Activity

***"It's better to err on the side of daring than the side of caution."***
**—Alvin Toffler**

This quotation is a good selection for a Line Up activity because it presents students with clear choices. Do they think it is better to err on the side of daring, to err on the side of caution, or to consider the situation first? The teacher establishes the extreme ends of the line. Students select a place on the line that represents their position. Starting at one end of the line, learners are paired to talk to someone with a similar view. Pairs brainstorm as many situations as possible that support their position. Students who represent the middle position brainstorm situations where it is better to be daring and situations where caution is required. After students return to their seats, the teacher facilitates a general discussion and connects student ideas to the subject at hand.

## Meeting Activity

***"It's choice—not chance—that determines your destiny."***
**—Jean Nidetch**

Participants line up from strongly agree to strongly disagree. The line is split in the middle. Half of the line takes three steps forward and turns and slides down so that everyone shares their ideas with a partner who has a different perspective. Starting at one end of the double line, pairs join together to form teams of four for the remainder of the meeting. When teams sit down, they conduct a quick RoundRobin activity to get to know each other by explaining either a critical choice they made or something important that happened by chance in their lives that brought them to where they are today. This Line-Ups activity serves three functions in the meeting. It helps to build relationships as people share personal information. It forms new teams and it draws people into the main purpose of the meeting, which involves exploring choices before making an informed decision.

# RoundRobin

RoundRobin is a simple structure used to equalize participation and sharing in a team. Quotations selected for a RoundRobin activity should be complex enough to have a variety of interpretations or applications. A guiding question may be used to focus the response. The content of the quotation should be connected to the overall purpose of the lesson or the meeting. The leader announces the topic and indicates which team member will speak. The rest of the team listens attentively while their teammate speaks for the allotted amount of time. The leader then asks the next person to speak. This continues until all four team members have shared. If time permits a second round follows so that teammates can respond to each other's contributions. RoundRobin prevents individuals from dominating the group discussion.

## Steps:

1. Leader announces the topic.
2. Learners take turns talking.

## Classroom Activity

***"If I were given the opportunity to present a gift to the next generation, it would be the ability for each individual to learn to laugh at himself (herself)."***
**—Charles M. Schulz**
***(creator of the Peanuts cartoon)***
**If you could present a gift to the next generation what would it be? How would it make the world a better place?**

This RoundRobin discussion is designed as a prewriting activity. Students often have difficulty coming up with a creative idea when faced with a writing task. As the RoundRobin activity continues to circle around the table, students generate lots of ideas and build on each other's imaginations. Creative ideas usually appear after more obvious suggestions are voiced. By the time the activity is over, students have lots of options to write about.

## Meeting Activity

***"Six Critical Life Messages: I believe in you. I trust you. I know you can handle this. You are listened to. You are cared for. You are very important to me."***
**—Barbara Coloroso**
**How do we send these critical life messages to our students?**

The social and emotional well being of young people is an ongoing concern for educators. This quotation sparks a RoundRobin discussion because it frames a productive dialogue that explores curriculum, instruction, assessment, reporting, routines, and discipline. Teams can be asked to explore the quotation generally or the guiding question for each team can focus the discussion on a particular aspect of school life. After the RoundRobin, teams share their ideas with the larger group.

# Simultaneous RoundTable

Simultaneous RoundTable is a structure that allows individuals quiet moments of personal reflection to express themselves on paper before entering into a cooperative structure to share ideas. Each team member is given a different response sheet with a quotation at the top and a guiding question. He or she responds in writing. After several minutes, the facilitator indicates that it is time to rotate the sheets to the next team member. The process continues until all team members have responded to each of the questions. At this point another structure such as RoundRobin, can be used to share the ideas on the sheets. Simultaneous RoundTable can be used effectively in emotionally charged situations because it requires people to think and write before they speak.

## Steps:

1. A different quotation is given to each team member.
2. Each learner writes a response.
3. Response sheets are passed to the next person who also responds.
4. The process continues until all team members have responded to each sheet.

## Classroom Activity

Student leaders play an important role in the development of a positive school culture. This Simultaneous RoundTable activity urges students to consider the skills they need to be effective in leadership roles.

***"The art of communication is the language of leadership."***
**—James Humes**
**What communication skills do student leaders need to be successful?**

***"Leadership has a harder job to do than just choose sides. It must bring sides together."***
**—Jesse Jackson**
**What strategies can student leaders use to help people work together to achieve a goal?**

***"Example is not the main thing in influencing others. It is the only thing."***
**—Albert Schweitzer**
**In what ways are you a good example to those who see you as a student leader?**

***"I suppose leadership at one time meant muscles; but today it means getting along with people."***
**—Indira Gandhi**
**How can student leaders build relationships with peers, teachers, and administrators?**

## Meeting Activity

Change is an inevitable topic of discussion for leaders and learners. Effective leaders change things for the better. Successful learners change themselves. Change is always difficult—even for educators who are focused on the ongoing improvement of student learning. This Simultaneous RoundTable activity spotlights change.

***"It is change, continuing change, inevitable change; that is the dominant factor in society today. No sensible decision can be made any longer without taking into account not only the world as it is but the world as it will be."***
**—Isaac Asimov**
How can we prepare our students for the future?

***"In times of drastic change, it is the learners who inherit the future. The learned usually find themselves beautifully equipped to live in a world that no longer exists."***
**—Eric Hoffer**
What do we need to learn to increase student learning?

***"People will not venture into uncertainty unless they or others appreciate that difficulties are a natural part of any change scenario. And if people do not venture into uncertainty no significant change will occur."***
**—Michael Fullan**
What difficulties and emotions are we experiencing in this change?

***"Only in growth, reform and change, paradoxically enough is true security found."***
**—Anne Morrow Lindbergh**
What processes have we created that allow us to continue to grow and change as a faculty?

# Team Statements

The leader provides a topic related to the content of the lesson or the meeting. Quotations serve as model statements. Participants have 30 seconds to think before writing an individual answer. They then pair with a partner in their team, discuss the topic and synthesize and record their ideas. The two pairs in the team then compare statements. They synthesize their ideas to create a team statement that captures the essence of what was expressed in all of the individual statements. Teams share their statement with the entire group.

## Steps:

1. Leader presents topic.
2. Learners think and write individually.
3. Learners pair and share with partner.
4. Learners synthesize ideas with partners.
5. Pairs compare.
6. Team synthesizes ideas into a statement.

## Classroom Activity

Students are asked to create a concise statement that captures the essence of *success.* The following quotations are used as examples. In discussing the examples, students realize that success can be defined in many different ways. Their job is to create a statement that is meaningful to all team members. Once students reach consensus, they can read their statement in unison, write it on the blackboard, or construct a poster to display in the classroom.

***"Success is not the key to happiness. Happiness is the key to success."***
**—Albert Schweitzer**

***"Success is a little like wrestling a gorilla. You don't quit when you're tired—you quit when the gorilla is tired."***
**—Robert Strauss**

***"Success is to be measured not so much by the position that one has reached in life as by the obstacles which he (she) has overcome while trying to succeed."***
**—Booker T. Washington**

## Meeting Activity

Creativity may appear as a topic in a meeting that focuses on teaching creative thinking skills to students, taking the necessary risks to try a new instructional strategy, or coming up with a catchy theme for the annual school open house. The following quotations can be used as examples. Having teams engage in a creative activity as a warm-up prepares them to think "outside of the box" as they tackle the main task of the meeting.

***"Creativity is inventing, experimenting, growing, taking risks, breaking rules, making mistakes, and having fun."***
**—Mary Lou Cook**

***"Creativity is the power to connect the seemingly unconnected."***
**—William Plomer**

***"Creativity is piercing the mundane to find the marvelous."***
**—Bill Moyers**

# Timed Pair Share

Timed Pair Share is a simple structure that can be inserted at any time in order to engage learners actively in explaining their understanding. The leader reads a quotation. Learners are asked to pair with the person beside them (Shoulder Partner) or the person across the table (Face Partner). Partners label themselves A and B. The leader sets an appropriate amount of time. Person A speaks. The leader indicates that time is up and provides Person B with a strategy to thank his or her partner. Person B speaks for an equal amount of time. The leader indicates that time is up and provides Person A with a strategy to thank his or her partner.

## Steps:

1. Leader reads a quote for discussion.
2. Learners pair and label themselves A and B.
3. A shares his or her thinking for a set time.
4. B shares his or her thinking for a set time.

## Classroom Activity

***"When you have a great and difficult task, something perhaps almost impossible, if you only work a little at a time, every day a little, suddenly the work will finish itself."***
**—Isak Dinesen**

Timed Pair Share is so simple a structure that it can be used at a moment's notice. This quotation can be used to encourage students to think about a major assignment and break it down into tiny jobs to work on a little each day. Sharing with a partner provides everyone with strategies and support.

## Meeting Activity

***"Conflicts, even of long standing duration, can be resolved if people come out of their heads and stop criticizing and analyzing each other, and instead get in touch with their needs, and hear the needs of others, and realize the interdependence that we all have in relation to each other. We can't win at somebody else's expense. We can only fully be satisfied when the other person's needs are fulfilled as well as our own."***
**—Marshall B. Rosenberg**

People's attitudes as they approach a problem can affect the outcome. This quotation might be used in a Timed Pair Share activity to provide a positive mindset before the faculty tackles a thorny subject like a budget discussion. A quotation will not solve budget problems but it may serve as a reminder that relationships are involved.

# Three-Step Interview

In this structure, learners become interviewers, interviewees, and reporters. Learners form pairs within their teams and label themselves A and B. The leader reads a quotation for discussion and frames the discussion with a question or statement. In each pair, A is the interviewer and B is the subject. It is A's job to ask probing questions, listen carefully to B, and take notes to prepare to share the information with the team. After a given amount of time, the learners switch roles and B becomes the interviewer. The pairs join together to form a team of four, and each participant in turn reports what he or she has learned from his or her partner.

## Steps:

1. Leader reads a quotation and poses a question.
2. Learners pair and label themselves A and B.
3. A's interview B's.
4. B's interview A's.
5. RoundRobin share.

## Classroom Activity

***"Formulate and stamp indelibly on your mind a mental picture of yourself as succeeding. Hold this picture tenaciously. Never permit it to fade. Your mind will seek to develop the picture.... Do not build up obstacles in your imagination."***
**—Norman Vincent Peale**

The teacher reads the quotation and explains to students why it is important to have a clear picture of achieving a desired goal. Sports provide good examples. Skiers can be seen with their eyes shut at the top of the hill going through the entire run in their minds over and over again before stepping into the gates. The teacher then asks students to close their eyes and imagine themselves attaining a goal that it important to them. It could be something they wish to achieve that day or a long-term goal for the future. Students are asked to imagine what they have achieved, where they are, who they are with, and what it feels like to have succeeded. Once the guided imagery is complete, Three-Step Interview is used to structure student interaction as they explore and report on each other's future achievements.

## Meeting Activity

***"Educational practices should be gauged not only by the skills and knowledge they impart for present use but also by what they do to children's beliefs about their capabilities, which affects how they approach the future. Students who develop a strong sense of self-efficacy are well equipped to educate themselves when they have to rely on their own initiative."***
**—Albert Bandura**

Quotations that are used for Three-Step Interview must be complex enough to provide food for thought. If participants are unfamiliar with using Three-Step Interview as a structure, leaders may want to provide some guiding questions as well as the quotation.

**For example:**
**What strategies do you use to develop students' belief in their own capabilities?**

**How do you reach out to enfranchise students who find school learning difficult?**

**In what ways do you make the subject that you teach appealing so that students will want to interact with it again?**

**How do you know if your students are equipped to educate themselves?**

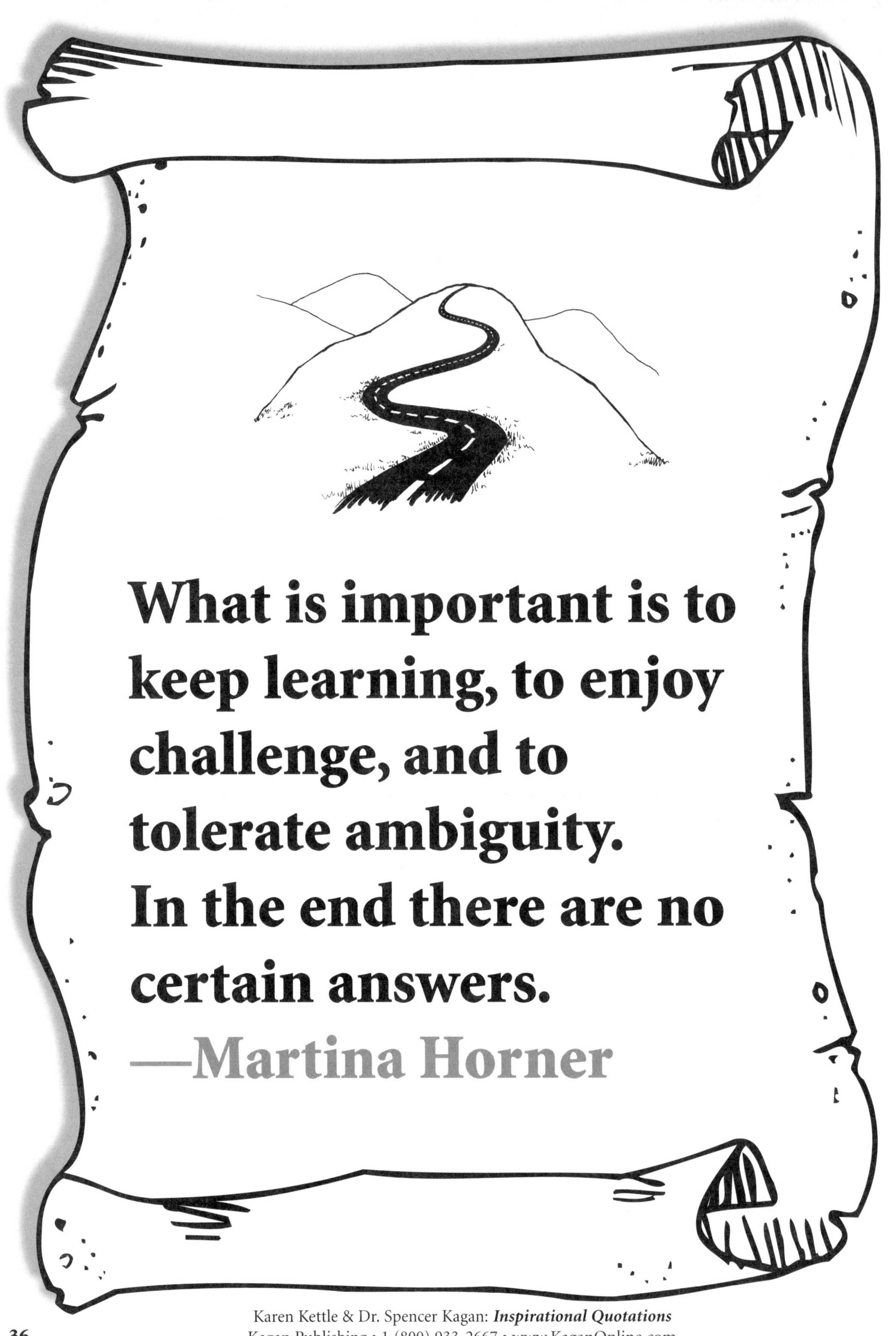
What is important is to keep learning, to enjoy challenge, and to tolerate ambiguity. In the end there are no certain answers.
—Martina Horner

# Chapter 4

# Inspirational Quotations and Reflection Questions

## Inspirational Topics


- Attitude.....39
- Challenge.....51
- Change.....61
- Character.....75
- Communication.....87
- Conflict.....97
- Creativity.....107
- Decision Making.....119
- Diversity.....131
- Education.....141
- Emotional Intelligence.....153
- Experience.....165
- Humor.....177
- Interconnectedness.....187
- Leadership.....199
- Learning.....211
- Opportunity.....225
- Perseverance.....235
- Risk.....245
- Service and Love.....255
- Success and Failure.....267
- Teaching.....279
- Vision and Goals.....295

Attitude Challenge Conflict Change

Character Communication

Creativity Decision Making

Diversity Education Experience

Emotional Intelligence

Interconnectedness Humor

Leadership Learning

Opportunity Perseverance

Risk Service & Love

Success & Failure

Attitude

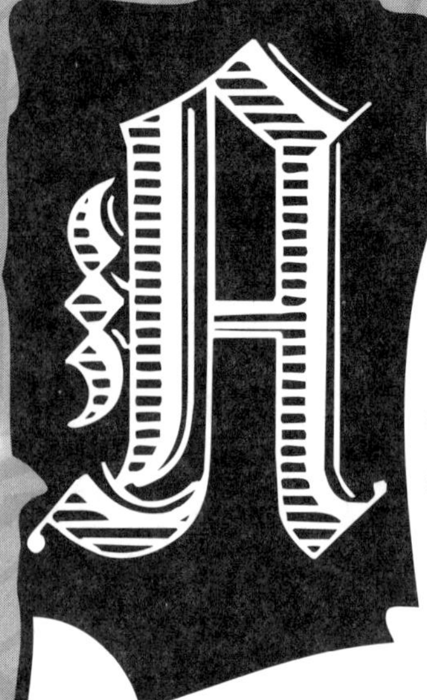

# Attitude

*Our attitude colors our world. It determines who we are, how we are seen, and ultimately whether or not we will be successful.*

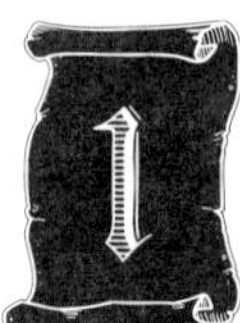

**This is the team. We're trying to go to the moon. If you can't put someone up, please don't put them down.**

*—NASA Motto*

Reflection Questions

- *Why are compliments more effective than put-downs?*
- *How can you improve a teammate's attitude?*
- *How do you express your attitude?*

**Even if I knew that tomorrow the world would go to pieces, I would still plant my apple tree.**

*—Martin Luther*

Reflection Questions

- *Why is it important to remain optimistic?*
- *Do you do good deeds for how good they make you feel or because they have good consequences?*
- *What attitude do you want the world to see?*

**If you want the rainbow, you gotta put up with the rain.**

*—Dolly Parton*

Reflection Questions

- *Why is hard work and practice necessary for success?*
- *What frustrates you? How do you deal with frustration?*
- *How do you motivate yourself to keep working toward a goal when the going gets tough?*

**Life is a one-way street. No matter how many detours you take, none of them leads back. And once you know and accept that, life becomes much simpler.**
*—Isabel Moore*

### Reflection Questions

- *Why do we sometimes worry about the past when we can't change it?*
- *If you have done something wrong in the past, what can you do to right it in the present?*
- *What kinds of detours do people take in their life journeys?*

**Think you can or think you can't—either way, you'll be right.**
*—Henry Ford*

### Reflection Questions

- *Who is responsible for your attitude?*
- *Why is believing that you can succeed the first step to becoming successful?*
- *How can you use "the little voice in your head" to convince yourself that you can succeed?*

# Attitude

◆ Your attitude about who you are and what you have is a very little thing that makes a very big difference.
**—Theodore Roosevelt**

◆ Attitude will take you further than talent.
**—Ruthie Bolton-Holifield**

◆ The only disability in life is a bad attitude.
**—Scott Hamilton**

◆ A chip on the shoulder is too heavy a piece of baggage to carry through life.
**—John Hancock**

◆ Life is what we make it; always has been, always will be.
**—Grandma Moses**

◆ The greatest part of our happiness depends on our dispositions, not our circumstances.
**—Martha Washington**

◆ I am a big believer that eventually everything comes back to you. You get back what you give out.
**—Nancy Reagan**

◆ The game of life is the game of boomerangs. Our thoughts, deeds and words return to us sooner or later, with astounding accuracy.
**—Florence Shinn**

◆ Most folks are about as happy as they make up their minds to be.
**—Abraham Lincoln**

◆ Life is a grindstone. Whether it grinds us down or polishes us up depends on us.
**—L. Thomas Holdcroft**

***One can never consent to creep when one has an impulse to soar.***
***—Helen Keller***

◆ The greatest revolution of our generation is the discovery that human beings, by changing the inner attitudes of their minds, can change the outer aspects of their lives.
**—William James**

◆ Being in control of the mind means that literally anything that can happen can be a source of joy.
**—Mihaly Csikszentmihalyi**

◆ There are those of us who are always about to live. We are waiting until things change, until there is more time, until we are less tired, until we get a promotion, until we settle down—until, until, until. It always seems as if there is some major event that must occur in our lives before we begin living.
**—George Sheehan**

◆ Believe in yourself and in everything you can be … not only will you be happy, but you will be able to appreciate the good qualities of the people around you.
**—James Garner**

◆ Believe that life is worth living, and your belief will help create the fact.
**—William James**

◆ Each day comes bearing its gifts. Untie the ribbons.
**—Ann Schabacker**

◆ Open your mind, open your heart, open your arms, take it all in.
**—Kobi Yamada**

◆ People are just as wonderful as sunsets if I can let them be. I don't try to control a sunset. I watch it with awe as it unfolds, and I like myself best when appreciating the unfolding of life.
**—Carl Rogers**

◆ Look at everything as if you were seeing it either for the first or last time. Then your time on earth will be filled with glory.
**—Betty Smith**

◆ Why wait? Life is not a dress rehearsal. Quit practicing what you're going to do, and just do it. In one bold stroke you can transform today.
**—Philip Markins**

◆ People who never get carried away should be.
**—Malcolm Forbes**

◆ There is so much in the world for us all if we only have the eyes to see it, and the heart to love it, and the hand to gather it to ourselves ...
**—Lucy Maud Montgomery**

◆ Find the good. It's all around you. Find it, show it to others, and you'll start believing in it.
**—Jesse Owens**

◆ The whole idea of living is to believe the best is yet to be.
**—Peter Ustinov**

◆ Choose to be happy. It is a way of being wise.
**—Colette**

◆ Happiness is not a station to arrive at, but a manner of traveling.
**—Margaret Lee Runbeck**

◆ Happiness is a thing to be practiced, like the violin.
**—John Lubbock**

◆ You are much happier when you are happy than when you ain't.
**—Ogden Nash**

◆ Optimism is essential to achievement and it is also the foundation of courage and of true progress.
**—Nicholas Murray Butler**

◆ Optimism is the faith that leads to achievement. Nothing can be done without hope and confidence.
**—Helen Keller**

◆ I studied the lives of great men and famous women, and I found that the men and women who got to the top were those who did the jobs they had in hand, with everything they had of energy and enthusiasm.
**—Henry Truman**

◆ You only lose energy when life becomes dull in your mind. You don't have to be tired and bored. Get interested in something. Get absolutely enthralled in something. Throw yourself into it with abandon.
**—Norman Vincent Peale**

◆ Act enthusiastic and you become enthusiastic.
**—Dale Carnegie**

***Enthusiasm is one of the most powerful engines of success. When you do a thing, do it with all your might. Put your whole soul into it. Stamp it with your own personality. Be active, be energetic, be enthusiastic and faithful and you will accomplish your object. Nothing great was ever achieved without enthusiasm.***
***—Ralph Waldo Emerson***

◆ Enthusiasm is the electric current that keeps the engine of life going at top speed. Enthusiasm is the very propeller of progress.
**—B. C. Forbes**

◆ No one keeps up his (her) enthusiasm automatically. Enthusiasm must be nourished with new actions, new aspirations, new efforts, new vision.
**—Papyrus**

◆ We act as though comfort and luxury were the chief requirements in life, when all that we need to make us really happy is something to be enthusiastic about.
**—Charles Kingsley**

◆ Every memorable act in the history of the world is a triumph of enthusiasm. Nothing great was ever achieved without it because it gives any challenge or any occupation, no matter how frightening or difficult, a new meaning. Without enthusiasm you are doomed to a life of mediocrity but with it you can accomplish miracles.
**—Og Mandino**

◆ Are you in earnest? Then seize this very minute. Whatever you can do, or dream you can do, begin it. Boldness has genius, power and magic in it. Only engage and then the mind grows heated; only begin, and then the goal will be completed.
**—Johann Wolfgang Von Goethe**

# Attitude

◆ Do you love life? Then do not squander time, for that's the stuff life is made of.
**—Benjamin Franklin**

◆ High expectations are the key to everything.
**—Sam Walton**

◆ Motivation is when your dreams put on work clothes.
**—Parkes Robinson**

◆ The more I want to get something done, the less I call it work.
**—Aristotle**

◆ Work is either fun or drudgery. It depends on your attitude. I like fun.
**—Colleen C. Barrett**

◆ When we accept tough jobs as a challenge and wade into them with enthusiasm, miracles can happen.
**—Arland Gilbert**

◆ Cushion the painful effects of hard blows by keeping the enthusiasm going strong, even if doing so requires struggle.
**—Norman Vincent Peale**

◆ Don't give up trying to do what you really want to do. Where there is love and inspiration I don't think you can go wrong.
**—Ella Fitzgerald**

◆ I long to accomplish a great and noble task, but it is my chief duty to accomplish small tasks as if they were great and noble.
**—Helen Keller**

◆ I'm never going to be a movie star. But then, in all probability, Liz Taylor is never going to teach first and second grade.
**—Mary J. Wilson**

◆ People who deal with life generously and large-heartedly go on multiplying relationships to the end.
**—Arthur Christopher Benson**

◆ A pessimist sees the difficulty in every opportunity; an optimist sees the opportunity in every difficulty.
**—Winston Churchill**

***I can be changed by what happens to me. I refuse to be reduced by it.***
***—Maya Angelou***

◆ Call on God, but row away from the rocks.
**—Indian proverb**

◆ A positive attitude may not solve all your problems, but it will annoy enough people to make it worth the effort.
**—Herm Albright**

◆ There is little difference in people, but that little difference makes a big difference. That little difference is attitude. The big difference is whether it is positive or negative.
**—Mark Twain**

◆ Nobody ever has it "all together." That's like trying to eat "once and for all."
**—Marilyn Grey**

◆ The difference between greatness and mediocrity is often how an individual views a mistake.
**—Nelson Boswell**

◆ We do not see things as they are. We see them as we are.
**—Talmud**

◆ Life is not the way it's supposed to be. It's the way it is. The way you cope with it is what makes the difference.
**—Virginia Satir**

◆ Do not seek to have events happen as you want them to, but instead want them to happen as they do happen, and your life will go well.
**—Epictetus**

◆ Things turn out best for the people who make the best of the way things turn out.
**—Art Linkletter**

◆ Life is a train of moods like a string of beads; and as we pass through them they prove to be many colored lenses, which paint the world their own hue, and each shows us only what lies in its own focus.
**—Ralph Waldo Emerson**

◆ I wanted a perfect ending. Now I've learned, the hard way, that some poems don't rhyme, and some stories don't have a clear beginning, middle, and end. Life is about not knowing, having to change, taking the moment and making the best of it, without knowing what is going to happen next.
**—Gilda Radner**

***No one can make you feel inferior without your consent.***
***—Eleanor Roosevelt***

◆ We can not tell what may happen to us in the strange medley of life. But we can decide what happens in us—how we take it, what we do with it—and that is what really counts in the end.
**—Joseph F. Newton**

◆ Finish each day and be done with it …, You have done what you could; some blunders and absurdities no doubt crept in; forget them as soon as you can. Tomorrow is a new day: you shall begin it well and serenely.
**—Ralph Waldo Emerson**

◆ Do not take life too seriously. You will never get out of it alive.
**—Elbert Hubbard**

In the long run, the pessimist may be proved right; but the optimist has a better time on the trip.
**—Daniel L. Reardon**

◆ No sense being pessimistic. It wouldn't work anyway!
**—Graffito**

◆ Hope is definitely not the same thing as optimism. It is not the conviction that something will turn out well, but the certainty that something makes sense, regardless of how it turns out. It is hope, above all, that gives us strength to live and to continually try new things, even in conditions that seem hopeless.
**—Vaclav Havel**

◆ The best day of your life is the one on which you decide your life is your own. No apologies or excuses. No one to lean on, rely on, or blame. The gift of life is yours; it is an amazing journey; and you alone are responsible for the quality of it.
**—Dan Zadra**

◆ The longer I live, the more I realize the impact of attitude on life. Attitude, to me, is more important than facts. It is more important than the past, than education, than money, than circumstances, than failures, than successes than what other people think or say or do. It is more important than appearance, than giftedness or skill. It will make or break a company … a church … a home. The remarkable thing is we have a choice every day regarding the attitude we will embrace for that day. We cannot change our past … we cannot change the fact that people will act a certain way. We cannot change the inevitable. The only thing we can do is play on the one thing we have, and that is our attitude. I am convinced that life is 10% what happens to me and 90% how I react to it. And so it is with you …. we are in charge of our attitudes.
**—Charles Swindonoll**

◆ We who lived in concentration camps can remember the men who walked throughout the huts comforting others, giving away their last piece of bread …. Everything can be taken away from a man but one thing: the last of human freedoms—to choose one's attitude in any given set of circumstances, to choose one's own way.
**—Viktor Frankl**

◆ Act as if it were impossible to fail.
**—Dorothea Brande**

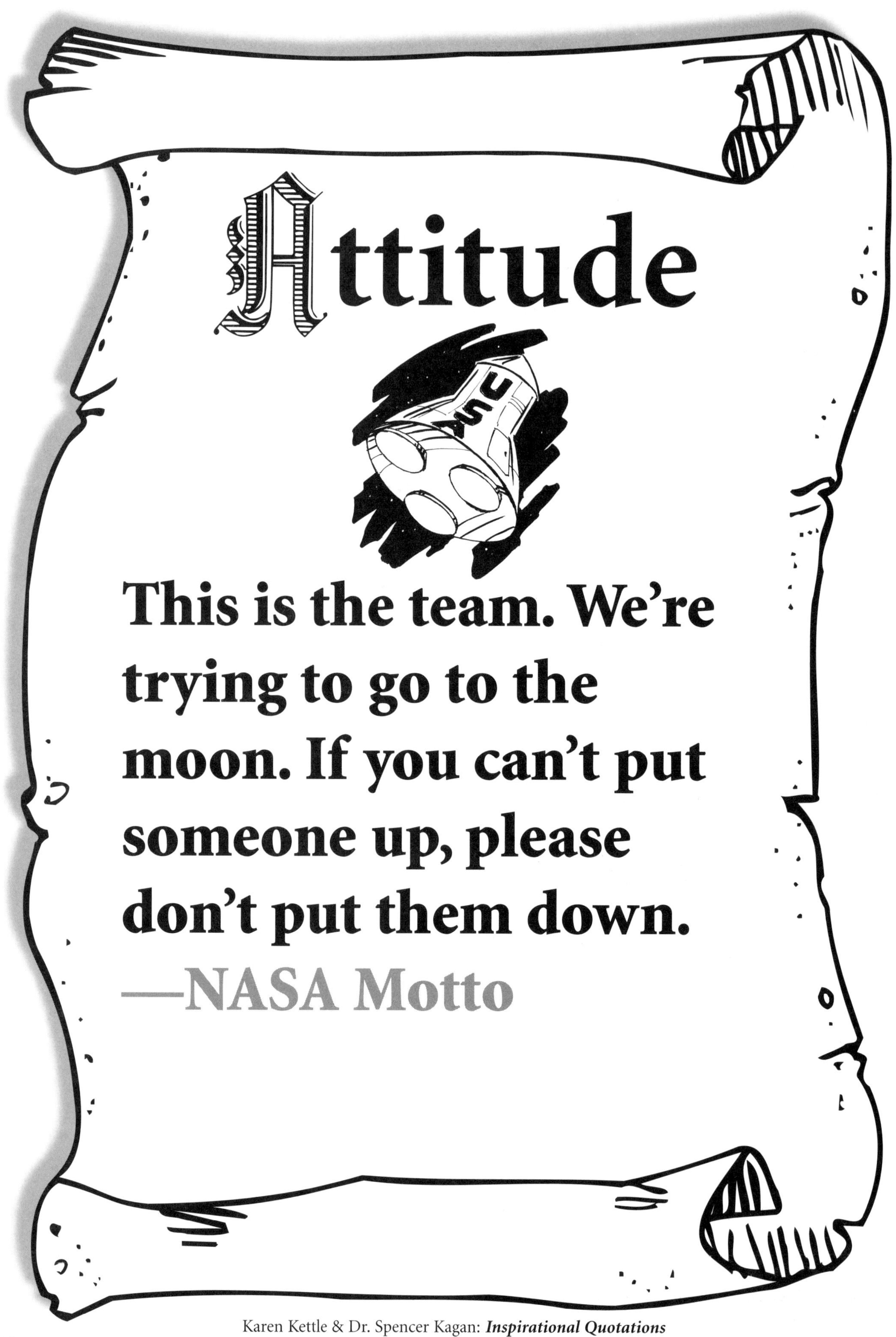

# Attitude

**This is the team. We're trying to go to the moon. If you can't put someone up, please don't put them down.**

**—NASA Motto**



Karen Kettle & Dr. Spencer Kagan: ***Inspirational Quotations***
Kagan Publishing • 1 (800) 933-2667 • www.KaganOnline.com

# Attitude

**Even if I knew that tomorrow the world would go to pieces, I would still plant my apple tree.**

**—Martin Luther**

Attitude
If you want the rainbow, you gotta put up with the rain.
—Dolly Parton

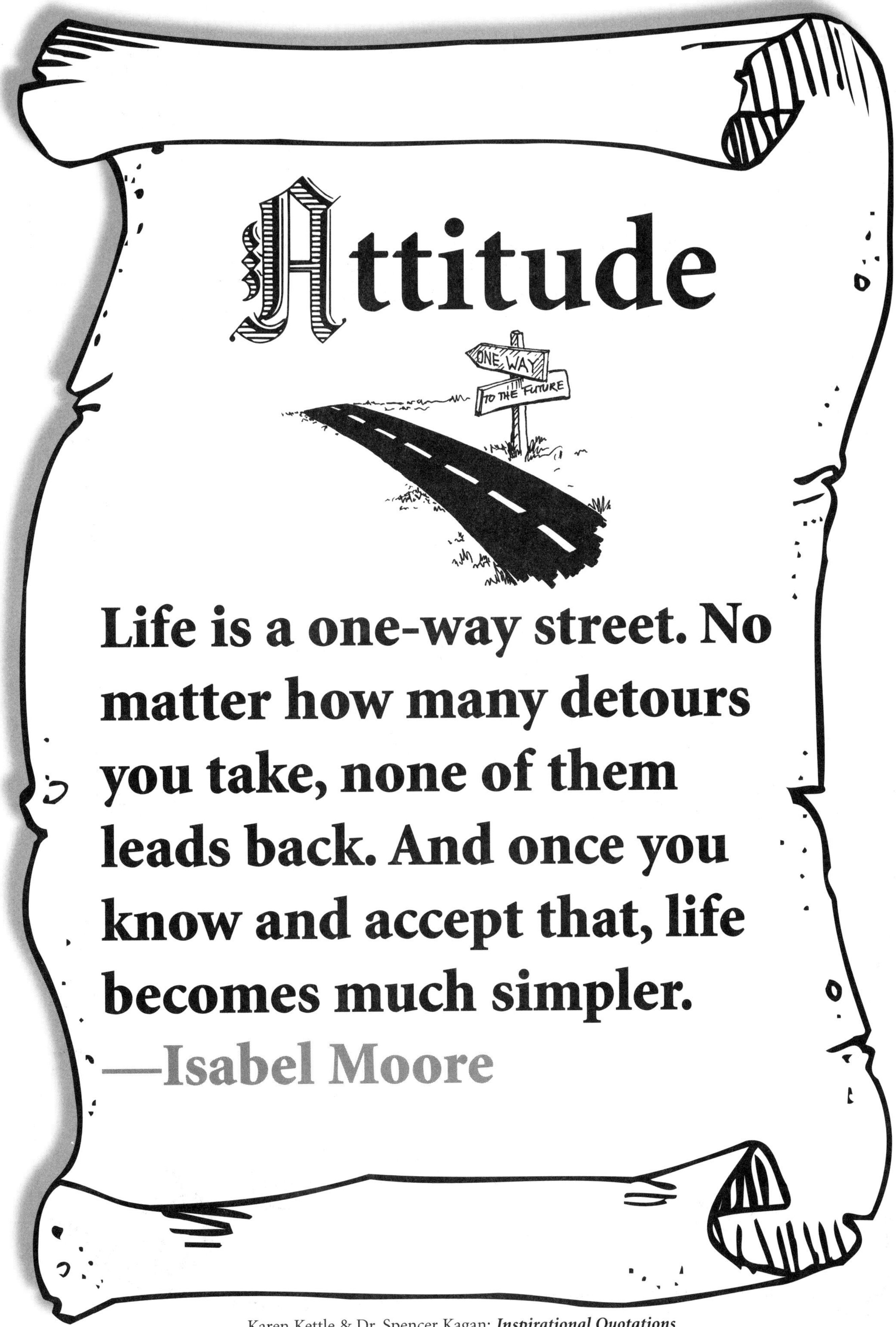
Attitude
ONE WAY
TO THE FUTURE
Life is a one-way street. No matter how many detours you take, none of them leads back. And once you know and accept that, life becomes much simpler.
—Isabel Moore

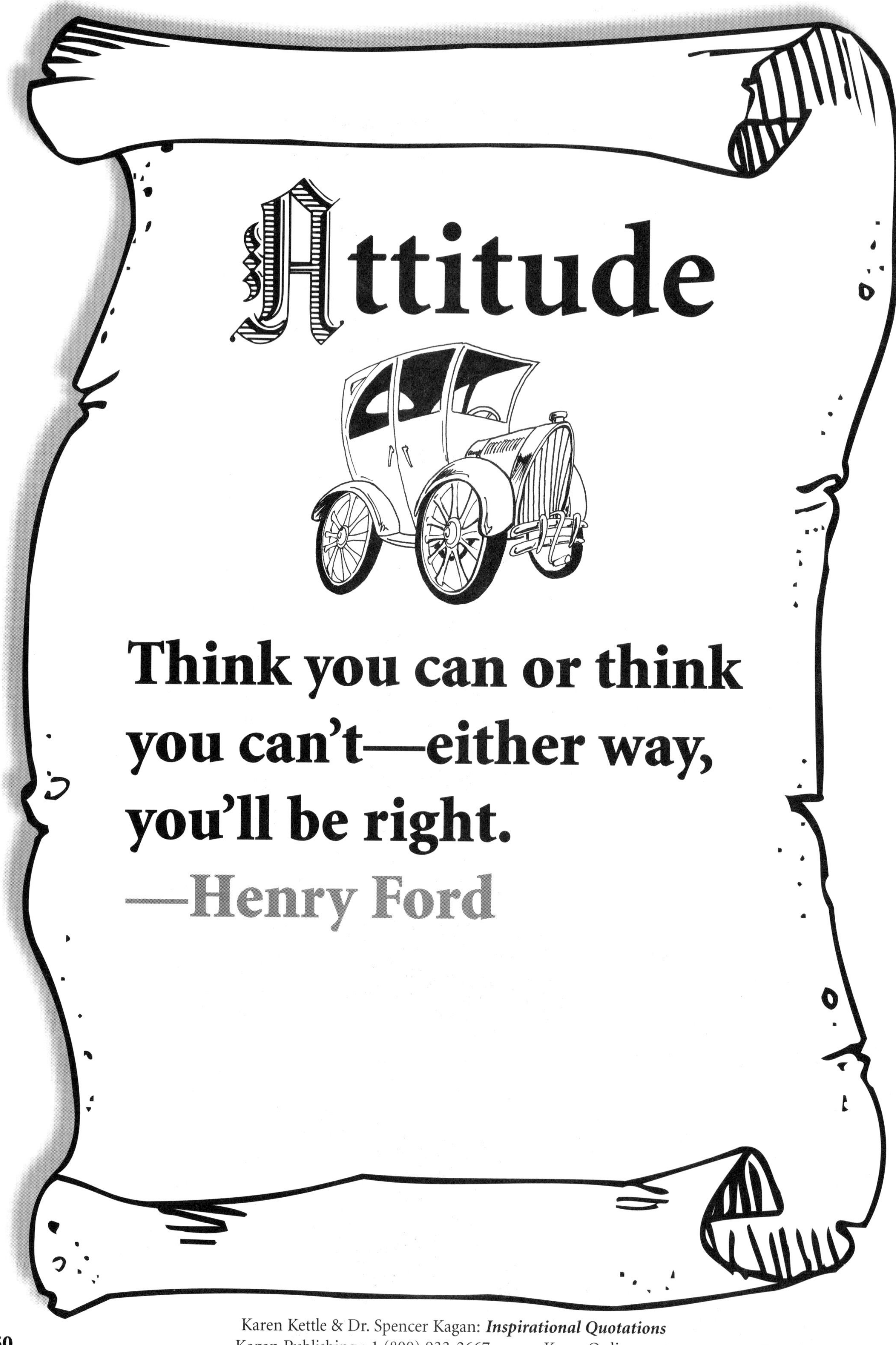
Attitude
Think you can or think you can't—either way, you'll be right.
—Henry Ford

Karen Kettle & Dr. Spencer Kagan: *Inspirational Quotations*
Kagan Publishing • 1 (800) 933-2667 • www.KaganOnline.com

# Challenge

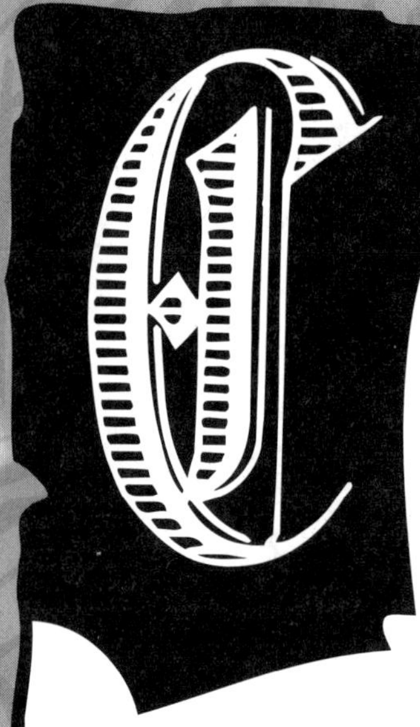

# Challenge

*Life presents us with one challenge after another. Rising to meet our challenges stretches us toward growth and wisdom.*

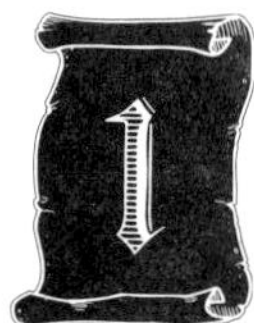

**You never know how a horse will pull until you hook him to a heavy load.**

*—Bear Bryant*

### Reflection Questions

- *What kinds of challenges do you seek out in life?*
- *What kinds of challenges do you have to meet that are not of your choosing?*
- *Is it harder to accept challenges you choose or those that arrive on their own?*

**Challenge is a dragon with a gift in its mouth …. Tame the dragon and the gift is yours.**

*—Noela Evans*

### Reflection Questions

- *Anxiety is a "dragon" that might accompany a challenge. What other dragons do challenges bring?*
- *What do you learn about yourself by overcoming a challenge?*
- *How is that self-knowledge a gift for you to use in the future?*

**Challenges are gifts that force us to search for a new center of gravity. Don't fight them. Just find a different way to stand.**

*—Oprah Winfrey*

### Reflection Questions

- *Why do new challenges make you feel off balance?*
- *How do you regain your balance as you work through a challenge?*
- *How do you select the challenges you want to meet?*

**The greater the obstacle, the more glory in overcoming it.**

*—David Hume*

Reflection Questions

- *What do you gain from always trying to do your best?*
- *What obstacles are you proud to have overcome?*
- *Why is there more satisfaction in succeeding at something difficult than something that was easy?*

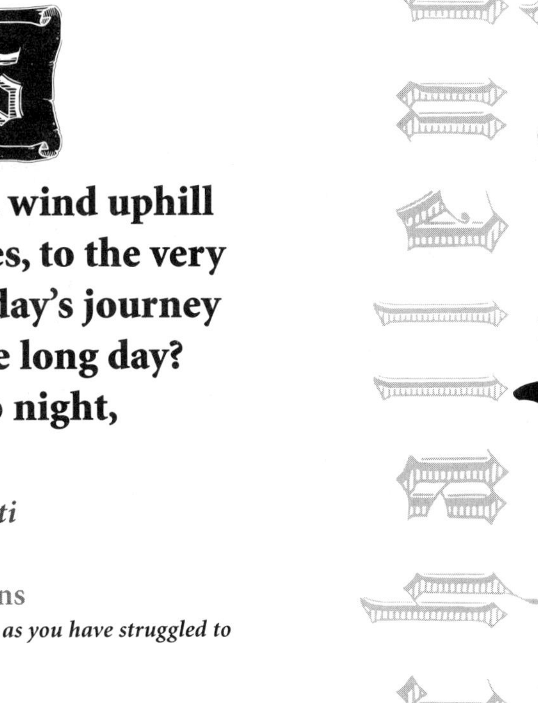

**Does the road wind uphill all the way? Yes, to the very end. Will the day's journey take the whole long day? From morn to night, my friend.**

*—Christina Rossetti*

Reflection Questions

- *Who has supported you as you have struggled to overcome a challenge?*
- *How did their support help you succeed?*
- *Why is it important to meet challenges one day at a time?*

# Challenge

◆ All adventures, especially into new territory, are scary.
**—Sally Ride**

◆ Face a challenge and find joy in the capacity to meet it.
**—Ayn Rand**

◆ All adversity is really an opportunity for our souls to grow.
**—John Gray**

◆ One who gains strength by overcoming obstacles possesses the only strength which can overcome adversity.
**—Albert Schweitzer**

◆ There is no excellence uncoupled with difficulties.
**—Ovid**

◆ It is surmounting difficulties that makes heroes.
**—Louis Kossuth**

◆ Problems are messages.
**—Shakti Gawain**

◆ Can it be that man is essentially a being who loves to conquer difficulties? The creature whose function is to solve problems?
**—Gorham Munson**

◆ Conquering any difficulty always gives one a secret joy, for it means pushing back a boundary-line and adding to one's liberty.
**—Henri Frédéric Amiel**

◆ One day, who knows? Even these hardships will be grand things to look back on.
**—Virgil**

***In times of stress and adversity, it's always best to keep busy, to plow your anger and your energy into something quite positive.***
***—Lee Iacocca***

◆ It's a good thing to have all the props pulled out from under us occasionally. It gives us some sense of what is rock under our feet, and what is sand.
**—Madeleine L'Engle**

◆ Difficulties mastered are opportunities won.
**—Winston Churchill**

◆ Golf without bunkers and hazards would be tame and monotonous. So would life.
**—B. C. Forbes**

◆ God gives every bird its food, but he does not throw it into its nest.
**—J. G. Holland**

◆ The only thing that ever sat its way to success was a hen.
**—Sarah Brown**

◆ When the going gets tough, the tough get going.
**—Dr. Robert H. Schuller**

◆ Whenever you are asked if you can do a job, tell them, "Certainly I can!" Then get busy and find out how to do it.
**—Theodore Roosevelt**

◆ Bite off more than you can chew, then chew it.
**—Ella Williams**

◆ Aerodynamically the bumblebee shouldn't be able to fly, but the bumblebee doesn't know that so it goes on flying anyway.
**—Mary Kay Ash**

◆ What ought one to say then as each hardship comes? I was practicing for this, I was training for this.
**—Epictetus**

◆ There are two ways of meeting difficulties. You alter the difficulties or you alter yourself to meet them.
**—Phyllis Bottome**

◆ The difficulties, hardships and trials of life, the obstacles … are positive blessings. They knit the muscles more firmly, and teach self-reliance.
**—William Matthews**

◆ Adversity not only draws people together but brings forth that beautiful inward friendship, just as the cold winter forms ice-figures on the window panes which the warmth of the sun effaces.
**—Søren Kierkegaard**

◆ It is not because things are difficult that we do not dare; it is because we do not dare that they are difficult.
**—Lucius Annaeus Seneca**

◆ Great things are not done by impulse but by a series of small things brought together.
**—Vincent van Gogh**

◆ When you have a great and difficult task, something perhaps almost impossible, if you only work a little at a time, every day a little, suddenly the work will finish itself.
**—Isak Dinesen**

◆ When we long for life without difficulties, remind us that oaks grow strong in contrary winds and diamonds are made under pressure.
**—Peter Marshall**

***Far better to dare mighty things, to win glorious triumphs, even though checkered by failure, than to take rank with those poor spirits who neither enjoy much nor suffer much, because they live in the gray twilight that knows not victory nor defeat.***
***—Theodore Roosevelt***

◆ The difficult is that which can be done immediately; the impossible is that which takes a little longer.
**—George Santayana**

◆ If all difficulties were known at the outset of a long journey, most of us would never start out at all.
**—Dan Rather**

◆ Anyone can carry his (her) burden, however hard, until nightfall. Anyone can do his (her) work, however hard, for one day.
**—Robert Louis Stevenson**

◆ One may go a long way after one is tired.
**—French proverb**

◆ You've got to love what you're doing. If you love it, you can overcome any handicap or the soreness or all the aches and pains and continue to play for a long, long time.
**—Gordie Howe**

◆ Energy is the power that drives every human being. It is not lost by exertion but maintained by it.
**—Germaine Greer**

◆ I learned early in life that the richness in life is found in adventure. Adventure calls on all the faculties of mind and spirit. It develops self-reliance and independence. Life then teams with excitement.
**—William O. Douglas**

◆ Our energy is in proportion to the resistance it meets. We attempt nothing great, but from a sense of the difficulties we have to encounter; we persevere in nothing great but from a pride in overcoming them.
**—William Hazlitt**

◆ They sicken of the calm who know the storm.
**—Dorothy Parker**

◆ There is no finer sensation in life than that which comes with victory over one's self. It feels good to go fronting into a hard wind, winning against its power; but it feels a thousand times better to go forward to a goal of inward achievement, brushing aside all your internal enemies as you advance.
**—Vash Young**

◆ You gain strength, courage, and confidence by every experience in which you really stop to look fear in the face. You are able to say to yourself, "I lived through this horror. I can take the next thing that comes along." … you must do the thing you think you cannot do.
**—Eleanor Roosevelt**

◆ So many of our dreams at first seem impossible, then they seem improbable and then, when we summon the will, they soon become inevitable.
**—Christopher Reeve**

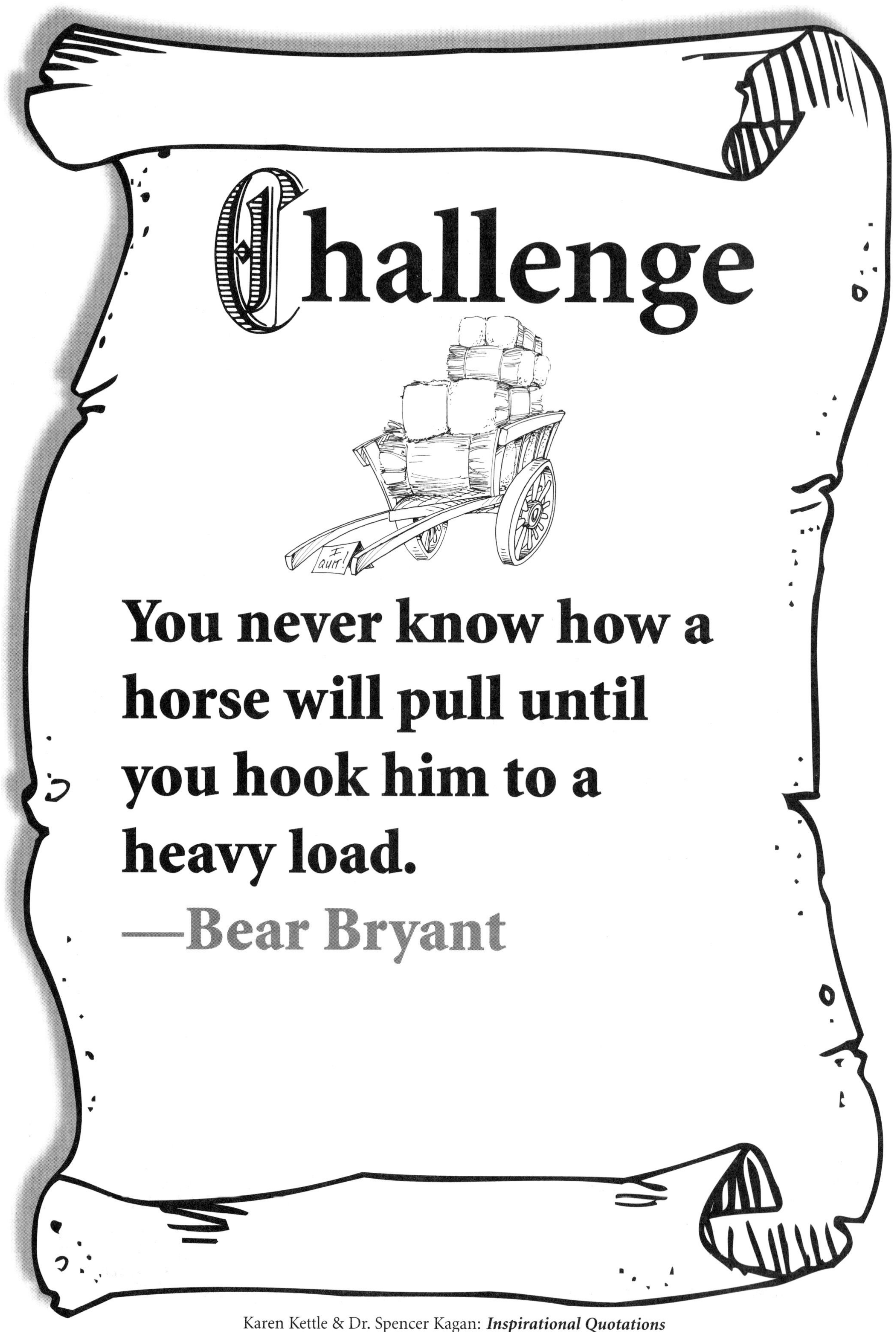
Challenge
I QUIT!
You never know how a horse will pull until you hook him to a heavy load.
—Bear Bryant

# Challenge

Challenge is a dragon with a gift in its mouth …. Tame the dragon and the gift is yours.

—Noela Evans

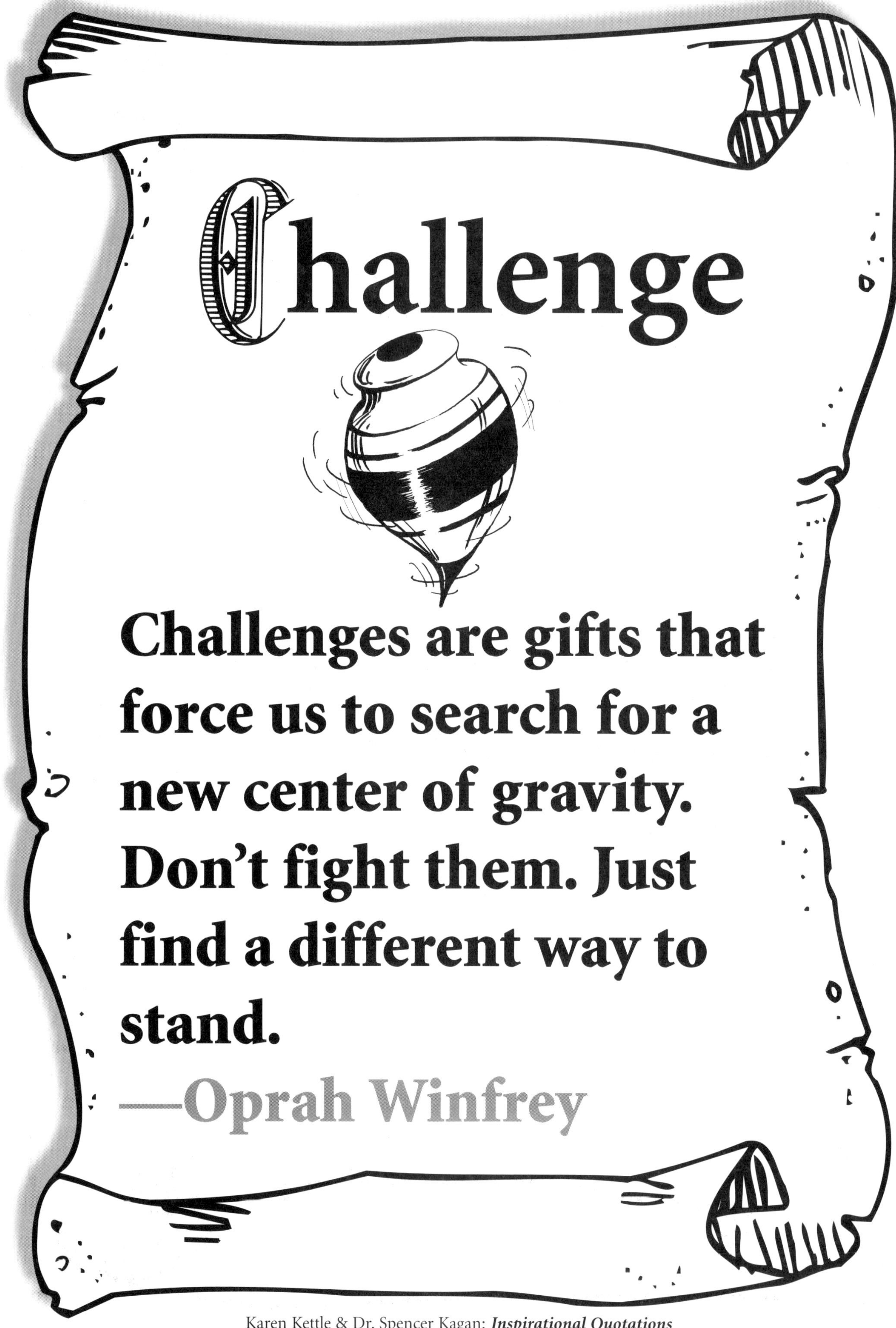

Challenge
Challenges are gifts that force us to search for a new center of gravity. Don't fight them. Just find a different way to stand.
—Oprah Winfrey

Karen Kettle & Dr. Spencer Kagan: *Inspirational Quotations*
Kagan Publishing • 1 (800) 933-2667 • www.KaganOnline.com

# Challenge

**The greater the obstacle, the more glory in overcoming it.**

**—David Hume**

# Challenge

**Does the road wind uphill all the way? Yes, to the very end. Will the day's journey take the whole long day? From morn to night, my friend.**

**—Christina Rossetti**



Karen Kettle & Dr. Spencer Kagan: *Inspirational Quotations*
Kagan Publishing • 1 (800) 933-2667 • www.KaganOnline.com

Change

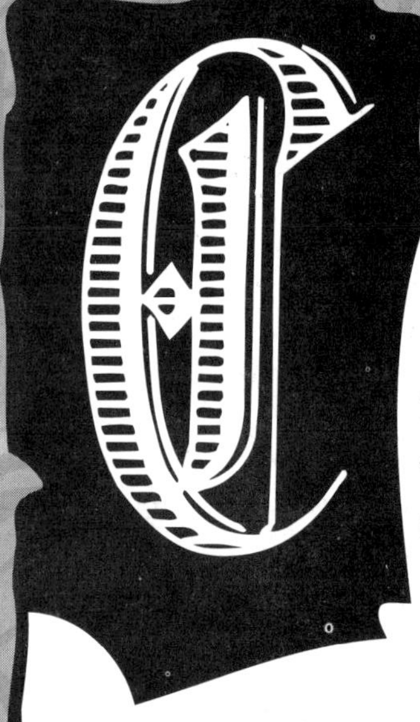

# hange

*The universe changes every second. To live fully in the world we must overcome our fear of the unknown and continue to change as well. We are unfinished creations.*

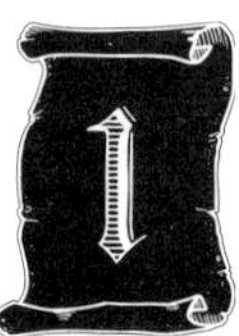

**It's not so much that we're afraid of change or so in love with the old ways, but it's that place in between that we fear .... It's like being between trapezes. It's Linus when his blanket is in the dryer. There is nothing to hold on to.**

*—Marilyn Ferguson*

### Reflection Questions

- *Why is change scary?*
- *What do you do to find comfort when things around you are changing?*
- *How do you decide if a change is good or bad?*

**The need for change bulldozed a road down the center of my mind.**

*—Maya Angelou*

### Reflection Questions

- *What injustice in the world would you like to change?*
- *Who has changed the world for the better? How did they make change happen?*
- *How have you been a positive agent for change?*

**Change happens one conversation at a time.**

*—Margaret Wheatley*

### Reflection Questions

- *What changes are regular, orderly parts of how our world works?*
- *What would the world be like if nothing changed?*
- *What would you like to change?*

**In times of drastic change, it is the learners who inherit the future. The learned usually find themselves beautifully equipped to live in a world that no longer exists.**

*—Eric Hoffer*

Reflection Questions

- *What has been the biggest change in the world in the past ten years?*
- *What skills that were important in the past are now rarely used?*
- *What new skills do you think we will need in the future?*

**Change involves abandoning an old steady me in favor of a shaky new me. Profound change is to die a bit—and to be reborn.**

*—Spencer Kagan*

Reflection Questions

- *What changes in life are you looking forward to?*
- *Why do changes allow you to re-invent yourself?*
- *Why do changing and learning go hand in hand?*

# Change

◆ Nothing is permanent except change.
**—Heraclitus**

◆ The world is inherently orderly. And fluctuation and change are a part of the very process by which order is created.
**—Margaret Wheatley**

◆ The only constant in life is change. Learn to love it and be comfortable with it. The people who succeed in the future are those who learn to walk on quicksand and dance with electrons.
**—Frank Ogden**

◆ Change alone is eternal, perpetual, immortal.
**—Arthur Schopenhauer**

◆ Change is inevitable, except from a vending machine.
**—Robert C. Gallagher**

◆ Change is the constant, the signal for rebirth, the egg of the phoenix.
**—Christina Baldwin**

◆ It is change, continuing change, inevitable change; that is the dominant factor in society today. No sensible decision can be made any longer without taking into account not only the world as it is, but the world as it will be.
**—Isaac Asimov**

◆ Our moral responsibility is not to stop the future, but to shape it … to channel our destiny into humane directions and to ease the trauma of transition.
**—Alvin Toffler**

◆ Since we are capable of change and modifications, the future will be in many ways only as good as we have the courage to make it.
**—June Tapp**

◆ As we face accelerating change, our knowledge is not as important as our ongoing re-thinking. Our success, our very survival, depends not on what we know, but on what we can learn.
**—Spencer Kagan**

◆ It is not necessary to change. Survival is not mandatory.
**—W. Edwards Denning**

◆ If we don't change direction soon, we'll end up where we're going.
**—Irwin Corey**

***It is not the strongest of the species that survives, nor the most intelligent, but the most responsive to change.***
***—Charles Darwin***

◆ What is the use of running when we are not on the right road.
**—German proverb**

◆ Life is change. Growth is optional. Choose wisely.
**—Karen Kaiser Clark**

◆ To exist is to change, to change is to mature, to mature is to go on creating oneself endlessly.
**—Henri Bergson**

◆ Only in growth, reform and change, paradoxically enough is true security found.
**—Anne Morrow Lindbergh**

◆ It takes a lot of courage to release the familiar and seemingly secure, to embrace the new. But there is no real security in what is no longer meaningful. There is more security in the adventurous and exciting, for in movement there is life, and in change there is power.
**—Alan Cohen**

◆ If you don't like the road you're walking, start paving another one.
**—Dolly Parton**

◆ Be not afraid of growing slowly, be afraid only of standing still.
**—Chinese proverb**

◆ We must always change, renew, rejuvenate ourselves; otherwise we harden.
**—Johann Wolfgang Von Goethe**

◆ We cannot become what we need to be by remaining what we are.
**—Max De Pree**

◆ Insanity: doing the same thing over and over again and expecting different results.
**—Albert Einstein**

◆ When you are through changing, you're through.
**—Bruce Barton**

◆ A finished person is a boring person.
**—Anna Quindlen**

◆ Consistency is the last refuge of the unimaginative.
**—Oscar Wilde**

◆ All conservatism is based upon the idea that if you leave things alone you leave them as they are. But you do not. If you leave a thing alone you leave it to a torrent of change.
**—G. K. Chesterton**

◆ Disconnecting from change does not recapture the past. It loses the future.
**—Kathleen Norris**

◆ Change is the law of life. And those who look only to past or present are certain to miss the future.
**—John F. Kennedy**

◆ Change is one thing, progress is another. "Change" is scientific, "progress" is ethical: change is indubitable, whereas progress is a matter of controversy.
**—Bertrand Russell**

◆ All change is not growth; all movement is not forward.
**—Ellen Glasgow**

◆ It's hard for me to get used to these changing times. I can remember when the air was clean and sex was dirty.
**—George Burns**

***Reasonable people adapt themselves to the world. Unreasonable people attempt to adapt the world to themselves. All progress, therefore, depends on unreasonable people.***
***—George Bernard Shaw***

◆ Just because everything's different doesn't mean anything's changed.
**—Irene Porter**

◆ The art of progress is to preserve order amid change and to preserve change amid order.
**—Alfred North Whitehead**

◆ Although change is unpredictable, you can set up conditions that help to guide the process.
**—Michael Fullan**

◆ The charm of history and its enigmatic lessons consist in the fact that, from age to age, nothing changes and yet everything is completely different.
**—Aldous Huxley**

◆ If the rate of change outside your organization is greater than the rate of change inside your organization, then the end is in sight.
**—Jack Welch**

◆ Once a new technology rolls over you, if you're not part of the steamroller, you're part of the road.
**—Stewart Brand**

◆ If you want to make enemies, try to change something.
**—Woodrow Wilson**

◆ Nobody told me how hard and lonely change is.
**—Joan Gilbertson**

◆ The world is round and the place which may seem like the end may also be the beginning.
**—Ivy Baker Priest**

◆ Each time we begin, we begin anew, alone, afraid.
**—Jan Phillips**

◆ The world fears a new experience more than it fears anything. Because a new experience displaces so many old experiences … The world doesn't fear a new idea. It can pigeon-hole any idea. But it can't pigeon-hole a real new experience.
**—D. H. Lawrence**

# Change

◆ People will not venture into uncertainty unless they or others appreciate that difficulties are a natural part of any change scenario. And if people do not venture into uncertainty no significant change will occur.
**—Michael Fullan**

◆ There is no way to make people like change. You can only make them feel less threatened by it.
**—Frederick Hayes**

◆ All changes, even the most longed for, have their melancholy; for what we leave behind us is a part of ourselves; we must die to one life before we can enter another.
**—Anatole France**

◆ It seems necessary to completely shed the old skin before the new, brighter, stronger, more beautiful one can emerge …. I never thought I'd be getting a life lesson from a snake!
**—Julie Ridge**

◆ Every beginning is a consequence. Every beginning ends something.
**—Paul Valery**

◆ Any real change implies the breakup of the world as one has always know it, the loss of all that gave one an identity, the end of safety.
**—James Baldwin**

◆ There is a certain relief in change, even though it be from bad to worse! As I have often found in travelling in a stagecoach, that it is often a comfort to shift one's position, and be bruised in a new place.
**—Washington Irving**

◆ Change can either challenge or threaten us. Your beliefs pave your way to success or block you.
**—Marsha Sinctar**

***Usually when people are sad, they don't do anything. They just cry over their condition. But when they get angry, they bring about change.***
***—Malcolm X***

◆ Change has a considerable psychological impact on the human mind. To the fearful it is threatening because it means that things may get worse. To the hopeful it is encouraging because things may get better. To the confident it is inspiring because the challenge exists to make things better.
**—King Whitney Jr.**

◆ The world hates change, yet it is the only thing that has brought progress.
**—Charles Kettering**

◆ Change is not made without inconvenience, even from worse to better.
**—Richard Hooker**

◆ Changes for the better are often resented. Old boots were once new—and hated.
**—George Iles**

◆ The nature of change includes fear of loss and obsolescence and feelings of awkwardness.
**—Michael Fullan**

◆ I have accepted fear as part of life—specifically the fear of change. I have gone ahead despite the pounding in the heart that says turn back.
**—Erica Jong**

◆ Against change of fortune set a brave heart.
**—French proverb**

◆ Greatness, in the last analysis, is largely bravery—courage in escaping from old ideas and old standards and respectable ways of doing things.
**—James Harvey Robinson**

◆ Grant me the serenity to accept the things I cannot change, the courage to change the things I can and the wisdom to know the difference.
**—Reinhold Niebuhr**

◆ Wisdom means keeping a sense of the fallibility of all our views and opinions, and of the uncertainty and instability of the things we most count on.
**—Gerald Brenan**

◆ The philosophies of one age have become the absurdities of the next, the foolishness of yesterday has become the wisdom of tomorrow.
**—Sir William Osler**

◆ It is well for people who think to change their minds occasionally in order to keep them clean.
**—Luther Burbank**

◆ We have to live today by what truth we can get today and be ready tomorrow to call it falsehood.
**—William James**

◆ I have found over and over again that the acceptance of a new point of view … has much less to do with the validity of that point of view than with readiness to consider any alternatives whatsoever.
**—Edgar Schein**

◆ It's not that some people have willpower and some don't. It's that some people are ready to change and others are not.
**—James Gordon**

◆ When we become conditioned to perceived truth and closed to new possibilities, the following happens: We see what we expect to see, not what we can see. We hear what we expect to hear, not what we can hear. We think what we expect to think, not what we can think.
**—John Maxwell**

◆ The only difference between a rut and a grave is their dimensions.
**—Ellen Glasgow**

◆ The greatest difficulty in the world is not for people to accept new ideas but to make them forget about their old ideas.
**—John Maynard Keynes**

◆ Persistence melts resistance.
**—Spencer Kagan**

◆ Give wind and tide a chance to change.
**—Richard E. Byrd**

***Habits can't be thrown out the upstairs window. They have to be coaxed down the stairs one step at a time.***
***—Mark Twain***

◆ In the choice between changing one's mind and proving there's no need to do so most people get busy on the proof.
**—John Kenneth Galbraith**

◆ The foolish and the dead alone never change their opinions.
**—James R. Lowell**

◆ For three days after death, hair and fingernails continue to grow, but phone calls taper off.
**—Johnny Carson**

◆ All truth passes through three stages. First it is ridiculed. Second it is violently opposed. Third it is accepted as being self-evident.
**—Arthur Schopenhauer**

◆ A new scientific truth does not triumph by convincing its opponents and making them see the light, but rather because its opponents eventually die, and a new generation grows up that is familiar with it.
**—Max Planck**

◆ The most damaging phrase in the language is: "It's always been done that way."
**—Grace Murray Hopper**

◆ Not to change is impossible. We are reborn each instant. The only question: How shall I change? Shall I dig the rut deeper, or choose to blaze a new trail.
**—Spencer Kagan**

◆ When you discover you are riding a dead horse, the best strategy is to dismount.
**—Sioux proverb**

◆ Not everything that is faced can be changed but nothing can be changed until it is faced.
**—James Baldwin**

◆ You have to stop in order to change direction.
**—Erich Fromm**

◆ Change starts when someone sees the next step.
**—William Drayton**

◆ To change what you get, you must change who you are.
**—Vernon Howard**

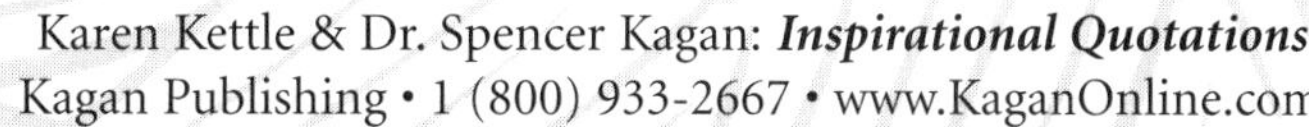

# Change

◆ Only I can change my life. No one can do it for me.
**—Carol Burnett**

◆ The curious paradox is that when I accept myself just as I am, then I can change.
**—Carl Rogers**

◆ The important thing is this: to be able at any moment to sacrifice what we are for what we could become.
**—Charles Du Bos**

◆ You may have habits that weaken you. The secret of change is to focus all your energy, not on fighting the old, but on building the new.
**—Socrates**

◆ Change—real change—comes from the inside out.
**—Stephen Covey**

◆ Change your thoughts and you change your world.
**—Norman Vincent Peale**

◆ There are things I can't force. I must adjust. There are times when the greatest change needed is a change of my viewpoint.
**—C. M. Ward**

◆ As a change agent, the power you've got is the power of new ideas.
**—Clive Meanwell**

◆ Every now and then go away, have a little relaxation for when you come back to your work your judgment will be surer. Go some distance away because then the work appears smaller and more of it can be taken in at a glance and a lack of harmony and proportion is more readily seen.
**—Leonardo da Vinci**

◆ Lasting change is a series of compromises. And compromise is all right, as long as your values don't change.
**—Jane Goodall**

◆ Living with change means simultaneously letting go and reining in.
**—Michael Fullan**

◆ The only way to make sense out of change is to plunge into it, move with it, and join the dance.
**—Alan Watts**

◆ We cannot wait for the world to turn, for times to change that we might change with them, for the revolution to come and carry us around in its new course. We are the future. We are the revolution.
**—Beatrice Brueau**

***If the wind will not serve, take to the oars.***
***—Latin proverb***

◆ One of the greatest pains to human nature is the pain of a new idea.
**—Walter Bagehot**

◆ All the significant breakthroughs were breaks with old ways of thinking.
**—Thomas Kuhn**

◆ There is only one admirable form of the imagination: the imagination that is so intense that it creates a new reality, that it makes things happen.
**—Sean O'Faolain**

◆ The best way to predict the future is to invent it.
**—Allan Kay**

◆ We are not creatures of circumstance; we are creators of circumstance.
**—Benjamin Disraeli**

◆ From the pain comes the dream. From the dream comes the vision. From the vision come the people. From the people comes the power. From this power comes the change.
**—Peter Gabriel**

◆ The world will change for the better when people decide that they are sick and tired of being sick and tired of the way the world is, and decide to change themselves.
**—Sidney Madwed**

◆ Once in awhile it really hits people that they don't have to experience the world in the way they have been told to.
**—Alan Keightley**

◆ Most of today's problems are not solved by experience. The further we advance into the modern age, the less important experience will become. It's much more important to have the necessary adaptability with which to face and solve new problems.
**—Pierre E. Trudeau**

◆ To cope with a changing world, any entity must develop the capability of shifting and changing—of developing new skills and attitudes: in short, the capability of learning.
**—A. De Gues**

◆ There is nothing more powerful than an idea whose time has come.
**—Victor Hugo**

◆ If you don't like the way the world is, you change it. You have an obligation to change it. You just do it one step at a time.
**—Marian Wright Edelman**

◆ Never doubt that a small group of thoughtful, committed citizens can change the world. Indeed, it's the only thing that ever has.
**—Margaret Mead**

◆ They always say that time changes things, but you actually have to change them yourself.
**—Andy Warhol**

◆ Both tears and sweat are salty, but they render a different result. Tears will get you sympathy; sweat will get you change.
**—Jesse Jackson**

◆ If we recognize that change and uncertainty are basic principles, we can greet the future and the transformation we are undergoing with the understanding that we do not know enough to be pessimistic.
**—Hazel Henderson**

◆ At any time, about half of the persons needed to pursue a solution are getting married or divorced; tending to a sick or well relative; going bankrupt or coming into money; just starting, getting ready to leave, or near retirement; taking care of babies or putting children through college; making up or breaking up; getting sick, getting well; getting chronic or dying.
**—Tom Bird**

◆ There is a new science of complexity which says that the link between cause and effect is increasingly difficult to trace; that change (planned or otherwise) unfolds in non-linear ways; that paradoxes and contradictions abound; and that creative solutions arise out of diversity, uncertainty and chaos.
**—Andy Hargreaves and Michael Fullan**

***You must be the change you wish to see in the world.***
***—Mahatma Gandhi***

◆ Life is like an ever-shifting kaleidoscope—a slight change, and all patterns alter.
**—Sharon Salzberg**

◆ Confusion is a word we have invented for an order which is not yet understood.
**—Henry Miller**

◆ Life affords no higher pleasure than that of surmounting difficulties, passing from one stage of success to another, forming new wishes and seeing them gratified.
**—Samuel Johnson**

◆ If everything's under control, you're going too slow.
**—Mario Andretti**

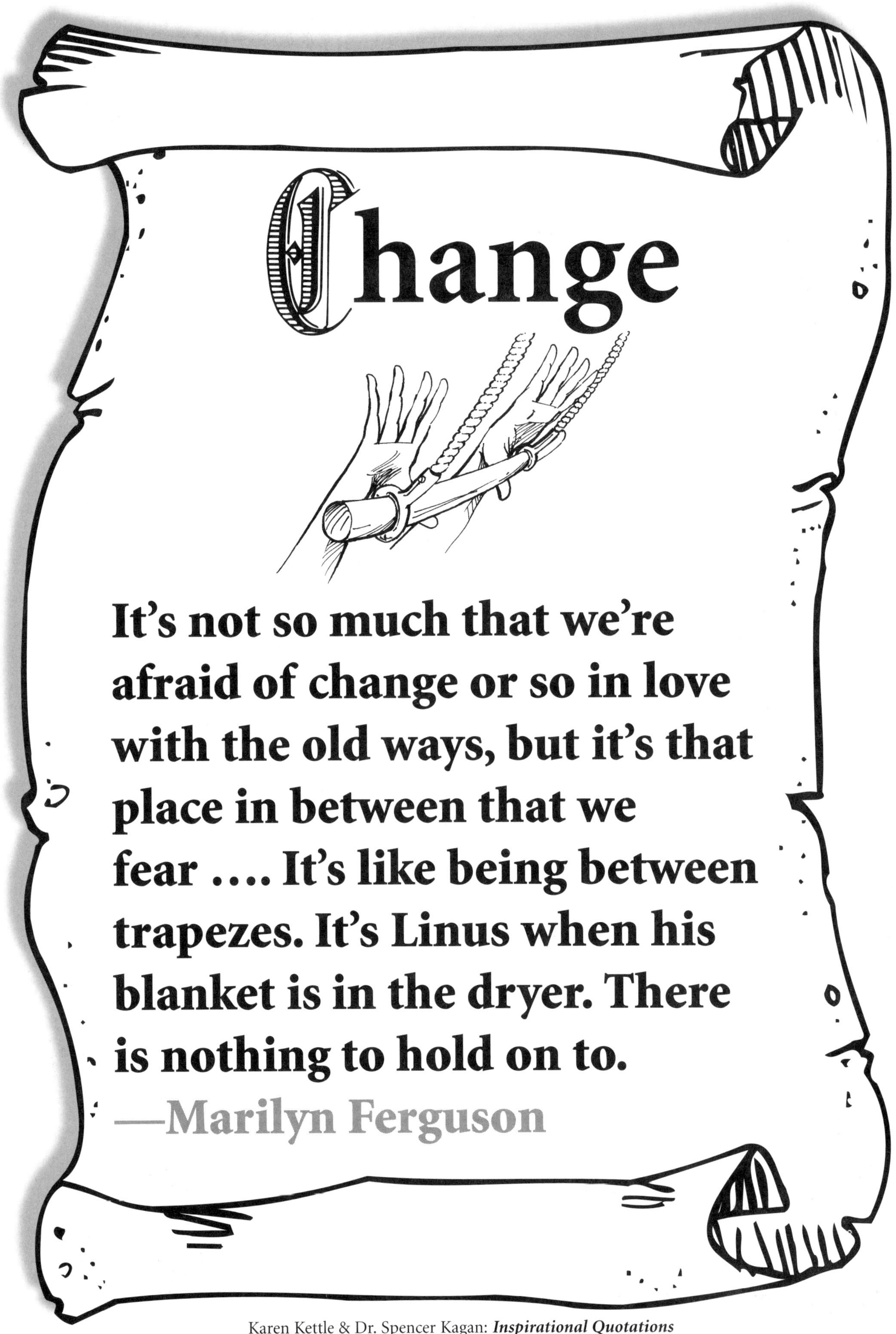

# Change

It's not so much that we're afraid of change or so in love with the old ways, but it's that place in between that we fear …. It's like being between trapezes. It's Linus when his blanket is in the dryer. There is nothing to hold on to.

—Marilyn Ferguson

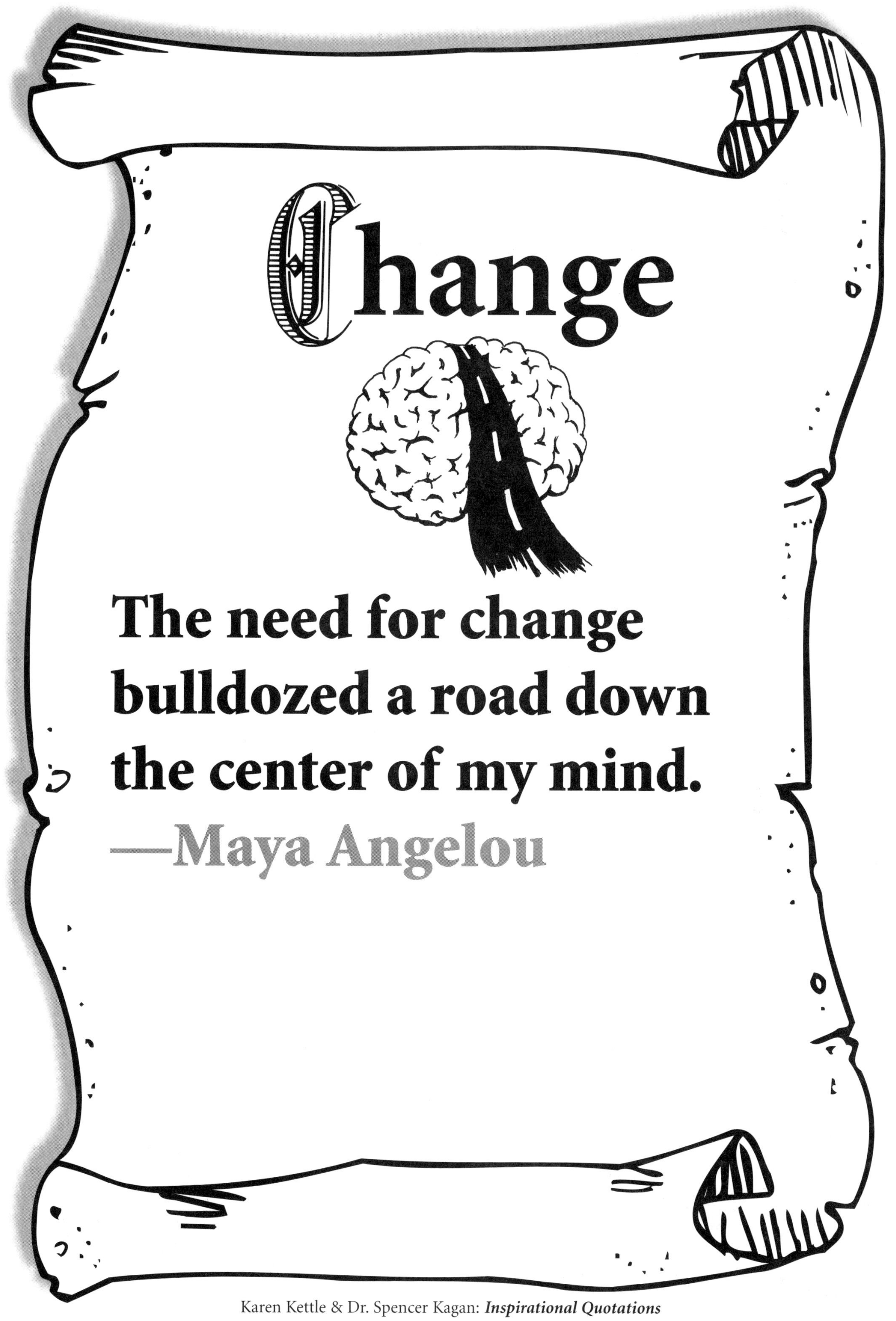
Change

The need for change bulldozed a road down the center of my mind.
—Maya Angelou

Change
Change happens one conversation at a time.
—Margaret Wheatley

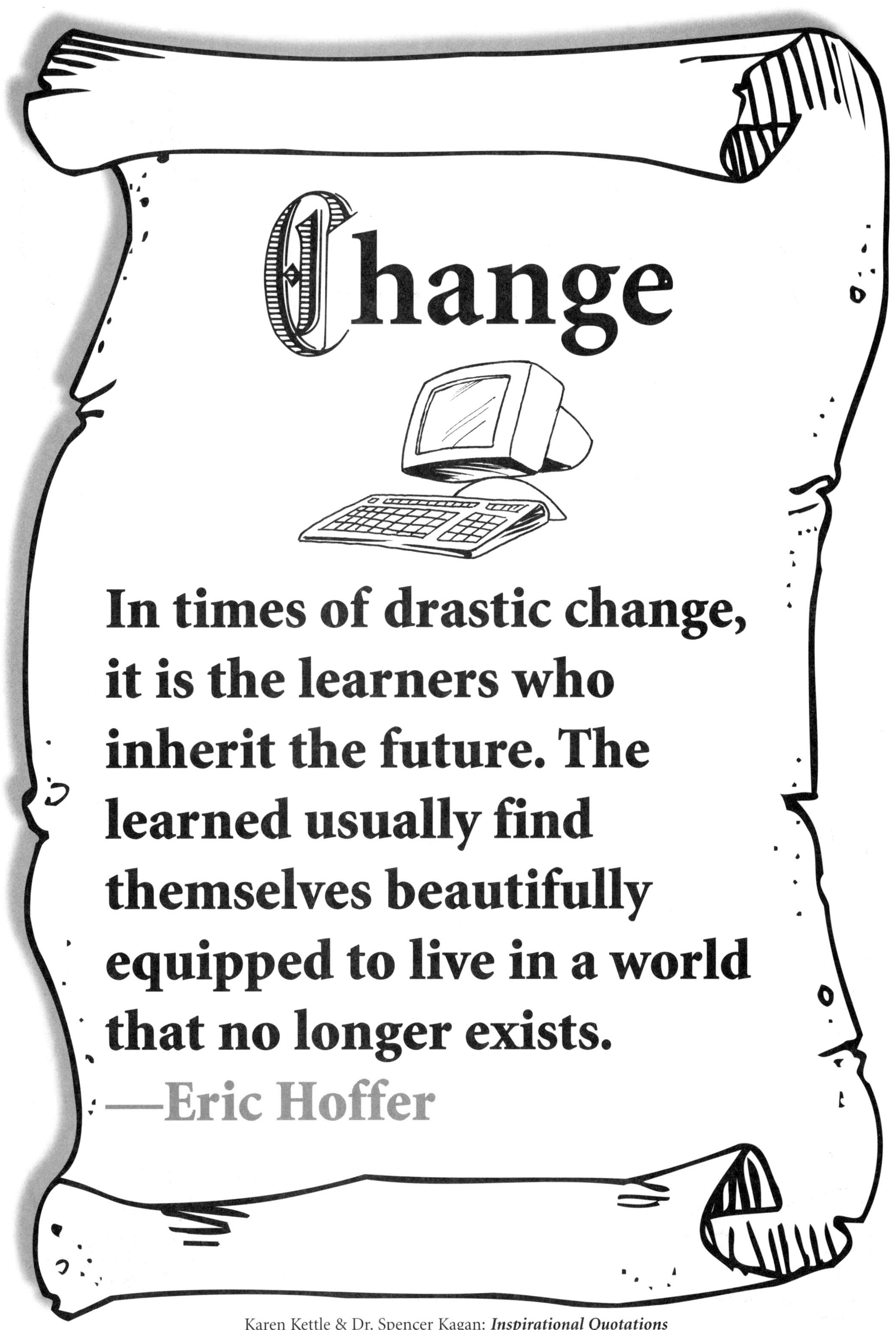
Change
In times of drastic change,
it is the learners who
inherit the future. The
learned usually find
themselves beautifully
equipped to live in a world
that no longer exists.
—Eric Hoffer

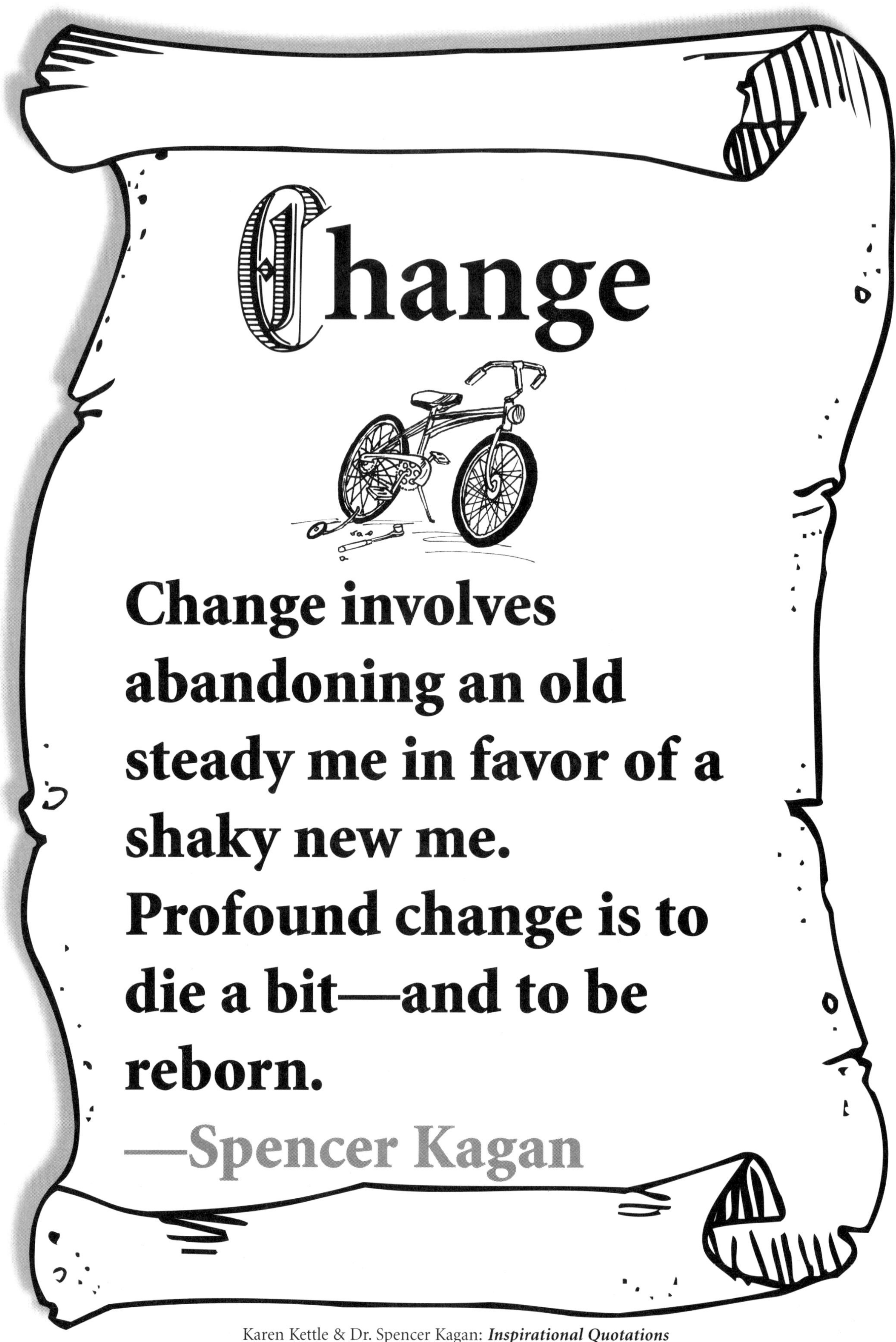

Change

Change involves abandoning an old steady me in favor of a shaky new me. Profound change is to die a bit—and to be reborn.

—Spencer Kagan

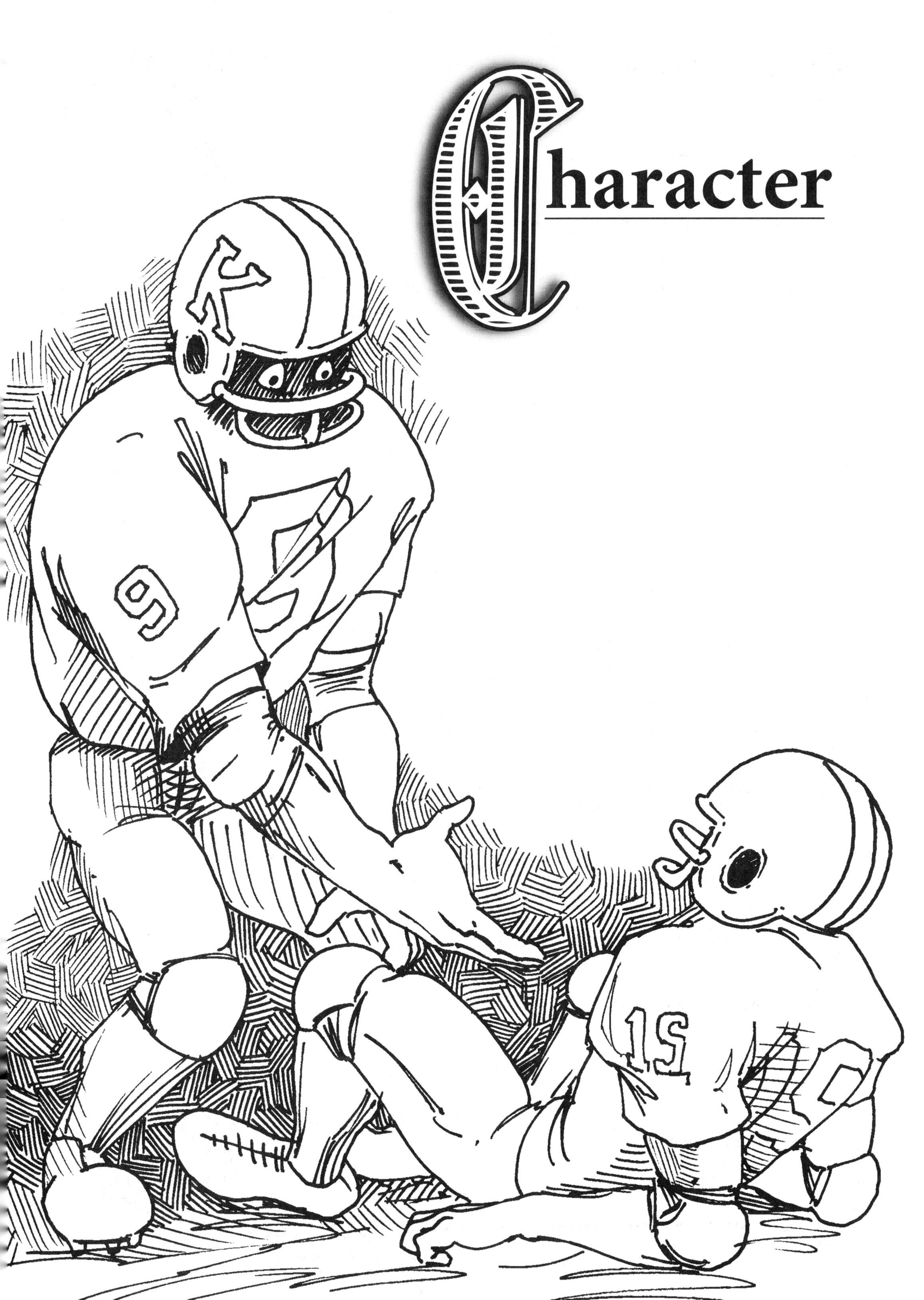

# Character

# haracter

*Our character is one of the few things in life that we control. Sculpting an honorable character is the surest way to bring trust, courage, and understanding to the world.*

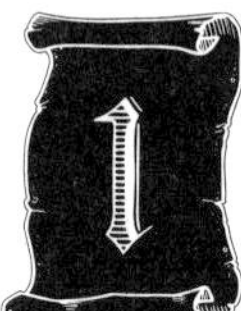

**Our lives begin to end the day we become silent about things that matter.**

*—Martin Luther King Jr.*

Reflection Questions

- *How does it feel to keep something inside that you really want to say?*
- *Why is it important to speak up when you see something wrong?*
- *How have you been true to your character in a tough situation?*

**There's only one corner of the universe you can be certain of improving and that's your own self.**

*—Aldous Huxley*

Reflection Questions

- *What part of yourself are you working to improve?*
- *Why is it difficult to break bad habits?*
- *What resources are available to help you make a positive change in your life?*

**What is honored in a country will be cultivated there.**

*—Plato*

Reflection Questions

- *What does our school value? How do you know?*
- *What do you value? How do you share what you value with other people?*
- *How do your choices in life reflect your character?*

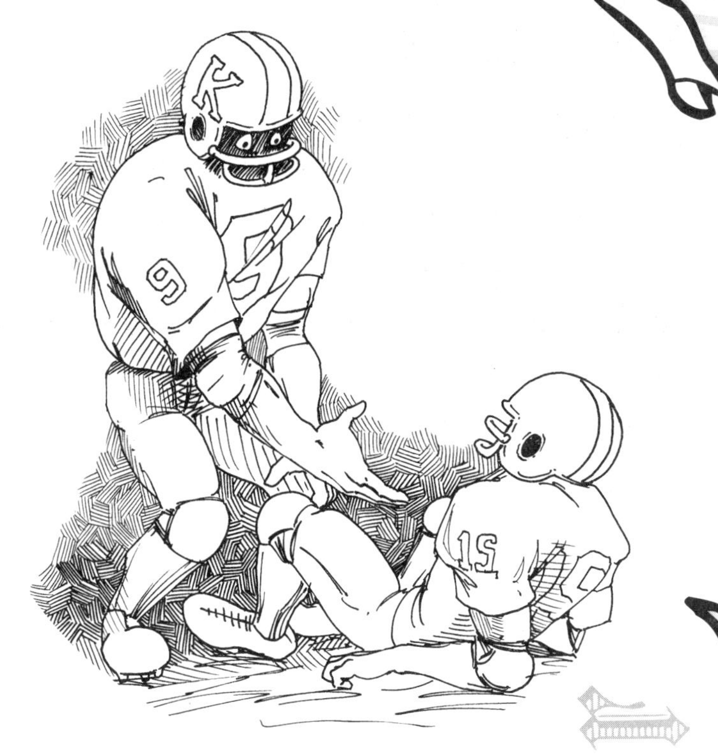

**Hard work spotlights the character of people: some turn up their sleeves, some turn up their noses, and some don't turn up at all.**

*—Sam Ewig*

Reflection Questions

- *What have you done that is hard work?*
- *What characteristics make a dependable friend or teammate?*
- *Why is it important to be worthy of trust?*

**We are what we pretend to be, so we must be careful what we pretend to be.**

*—Kurt Vonnegut*

Reflection Questions

- *The heroes we honor tell us what we admire. Who are your heroes?*
- *Why do you sometimes have to pretend to be brave before you feel it inside?*
- *Why is it dangerous to pretend to be someone else just to fit into a group?*

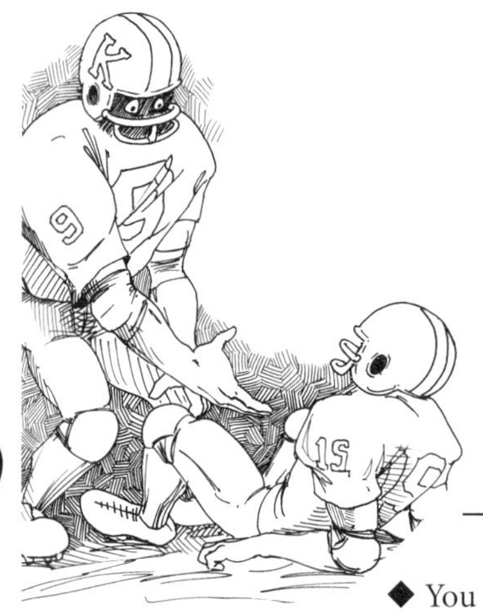

# Character

◆ Character is destiny.
**—Heraclitus**

◆ You cannot dream yourself into a character; you must hammer and forge yourself one.
**—James A. Froude**

◆ Six essential qualities that are key to success: Sincerity, personal integrity, humility, courtesy, wisdom, charity.
**—William Menninger**

◆ Good character is more to be praised than outstanding talent. Most talents are to some extent a gift. Good character, by contrast, is not given to us. We have to build it piece by piece—by thought, choice, courage and determination.
**—John Luther**

◆ Thoughts lead on to purposes; purposes go forth in action; actions form habits; habits decide character and character fixes our destiny.
**—Tyron Edwards**

◆ Character is the sum and total of a person's choices.
**—P. B. Fitzwater**

◆ I look for the day when the only criterion of excellence or position shall be the ability and character of the individual; and this time will come.
**—Susan B. Anthony**

◆ Talent builds itself in stillness, character in the stream of the world.
**—Johann Wolfgang Von Goethe**

◆ The turning point in the process of growing up is when you discover the core strength within you that survives all hurt.
**—Max Lerner**

***You can never be what you ought to be until I am what I ought to be.***
***—Martin Luther King Jr.***

◆ Character cannot be developed in ease and quiet. Only through experiences of trial and suffering can the soul be strengthened, vision cleared, ambition inspired and success achieved.
**—Helen Keller**

◆ Do we pay a price for our character? Absolutely. But one way or another we all pay the price—either we pay for our character, or we pay with our character.
**—Tom Selleck**

◆ It is not in the still calm of life, or the repose of a pacific station, that great characters are formed .... The habits of a vigorous mind are formed in contending with difficulties .... Great necessities call out great virtues.
**—Abigail Adams**

◆ There is no single royal road to character—a variety of routes will always need to be used. The development of right character in youth is too important to risk disregarding any promising line of attack.
**—Frank Cody**

◆ Character consists of what you do on the third and fourth tries.
**—James A. Michener**

◆ There is more in us than we know. If we can be made to see it, perhaps for the rest of our lives, we will be unwilling to settle for less.
**—Kurt Hahn**

◆ People are like stained-glass windows. They sparkle and shine when the sun is out, but when the darkness sets in, their true beauty is revealed only if there is a light from within.
**—Elisabeth Kubler-Ross**

◆ Long is the life that is fully lived: it is fulfilled only when the mind supplies its own good qualities and empowers itself from within.
**—Seneca saying**

◆ Do not think of your faults; still less of other's faults. Look for what is good and strong and try to imitate it. Your faults will drop off like dead leaves when their time comes.
**—John Ruskin**

◆ Nothing splendid has ever been achieved except by those who dared believe that something inside them was superior to circumstance.
**—Bruce Barton**

◆ The place to improve the world is first in one's own heart and head and hands, and then work outward from there.
**—Robert M. Pirsig**

◆ To be nobody but yourself in a world that's doing its best to make you somebody else is to fight the hardest battle you are ever going to fight. Never stop fighting.
**—e.e. cummings**

◆ Lean on no one. Find your own centre and live in it, surrendering it to no person or thing.
**—Emily Murphy**

◆ Live so that when your children think of fairness, caring and integrity, they think of you.
**—H. Jackson Brown Jr.**

◆ The foundations of character are built not by lecture, but by bricks of good example, laid day by day.
**—Leo Blessing**

◆ Never grow a wishbone … where your backbone ought to be.
**—Clementine Paddleford**

◆ Don't compromise yourself. You are all you've got.
**—Janis Joplin**

◆ It's never too late to be what you might have been.
**—George Eliot**

◆ Be like a postage stamp. Stick to something until you get there.
**—John Noe**

◆ Happiness is when what you think, what you say, and what you do are in harmony.
**—Mahatma Gandhi**

***In matters of principle, stand like a rock.***
***—Thomas Jefferson***

◆ Whenever you are to do a thing, though it can never be known but to yourself, ask yourself how you would act were all the world looking at you, and act accordingly.
**—Thomas Jefferson**

◆ Character is like a tree and reputation like its shadow. The shadow is what we think of it; the tree is the real thing.
**—Abraham Lincoln**

◆ Change your opinions, keep to your principles; change your leaves, keep intact your roots.
**—Victor Hugo**

◆ Have the courage to say no. Have the courage to face the truth. Do the right thing because it is right. These are the magic keys to living your life with integrity.
**—Mark Twain**

◆ Back of every noble life there are principles that have fashioned it.
**—George H. Lorimer**

◆ Character is the foundation stone upon which one must build to win respect. Just as no worthy building can be erected on a weak foundation, so no lasting reputation worthy of respect can be built on a weak character.
**—R. C. Samsel**

◆ Character is the real foundation of all worthwhile success.
**—John Hays Hammond**

◆ Whatever is hurtful to you, do not do to any other person.
**—Moses**

◆ Character is easier kept than recovered.
**—English proverb**

◆ Do not throw the arrow which will return against you.
**—Kurdish proverb**

◆ Whoever gossips to you will gossip about you.
**—Spanish proverb**

◆ If you scatter thorns, don't go barefoot.
**—Italian proverb**

# Character

◆ What you do not want done to yourself, do not do to others.
—**Confucius**

◆ Without courage, we cannot practice any other virtue consistently.
—**Maya Angelou**

◆ Life shrinks or expands according to one's courage.
—**Anais Nin**

◆ Courage is not the absence of fear, but rather the judgment that something else is more important than fear.
—**Ambrose Redmoon**

◆ To see what is right and not to do it is want of courage.
—**Confucius**

***The only way you can truly control how you're seen is by being honest all the time.***
***—Tom Hanks***

◆ It is curious that physical courage should be so common and moral courage so rare.
—**Mark Twain**

◆ I knew someone had to take the first step and I made up my mind not to move.
—**Rosa Parks**

◆ Courage is not the towering oak that sees storms come and go; it is the fragile blossom that opens in the snow.
—**Alice Mackenzie Swaim**

◆ Compassion leads to courage.
—**Lao-tzu**

◆ I learned that it is the weak who are cruel, and that gentleness is to be expected only from the strong.
—**Leo Rosten**

◆ Courage is being scared to death—and saddling up anyway.
—**John Wayne**

◆ The will to do, the tenacity to overcome all obstacles and to finish the course, the strength to cling to inexorable ideals, are all rooted in courage.
—**J. Edgar Hoover**

◆ We could never learn to be brave and patient if there were only joy in the world.
—**Helen Keller**

◆ I take the good with the bad, and I try to face them both with as much calm and dignity as I can muster.
—**Arthur Ashe**

◆ It is very strange that the years teach us patience—that the shorter our time, the greater our capacity for waiting.
—**Elizabeth Taylor**

◆ I hope I shall possess firmness and virtue enough to maintain what I consider the most enviable of all titles, the character of an honest man.
—**George Washington**

◆ You have to be honest with people. You have to have great respect for yourself. If you see something that is not right, you must do something about it.
—**Annie Wauneka**

◆ If you tell the truth, you don't have to remember anything.
—**Mark Twain**

◆ To be persuasive we must be believable; to be believable we must be credible; to be credible, we must be truthful.
—**Edward R. Murrow**

◆ The one quality that all successful people have is the ability to take on responsibility.
—**Michael Korda**

◆ Hold yourself responsible for a higher standard than anybody expects of you. Never excuse yourself.
—**Henry Ward Beecher**

◆ Responsibility breeds maturity.
—**Kurt Hahn**

◆ Few things help individuals more than to place responsibility on them, and to let them know that you trust them.
—**Booker T. Washington**

◆ Honors and rewards fall to those who show their good qualities in action.
—**Aristotle**

◆ Our deeds determine us as much as we determine our deeds.
—**George Eliot**

◆ Give to the world the best you have and the best will come back to you.
—**Madeline Bridges**

◆ The roots of true achievement lie in the will to become the best that you can be.
—**Harold Taylor**

◆ The world is full of willing people, some willing to work, the rest willing to let them.
—**Robert Frost**

◆ There are two kinds of people in the world: those who make excuses and those who get results. An excuse person will find any excuse for why a job was not done, and a results person will find any reason why it can be done. Be a creator, not a reactor.
—**Alan Cohen**

◆ Progress results only from the fact that there are some men and women who refuse to believe that what they know to be right cannot be done.
—**Russell Davenport**

◆ It is not who is right, but what is right, that is of importance.
—**Thomas H. Huxley**

***Courage is what it takes to stand up and speak. Courage is also what it takes to sit down and listen.***
***—Winston Churchill***

◆ The shortest and surest way to live with honor in the world, is to be in reality what we would appear to be; all human virtues increase and strengthen themselves by the practice and experience of them.
—**Socrates**

◆ Be honorable if you wish to associate with honorable people.
—**Welsh proverb**

◆ Tell me your friends, and I'll tell you who you are.
—**Assyrian proverb**

◆ People seem not to see that their opinion of the world is also a confession of character.
—**Ralph Waldo Emerson**

◆ Time does not change us. It just unfolds us.
—**Max Frisch**

◆ There is something in every one of you that waits and listens for the sound of the genuine in yourself.
—**Howard Thurman**

◆ The true test of character is not how much we know how to do, but how we behave when we don't know what to do.
—**John Holt**

◆ It is more useful to watch a man in times of peril, and in adversity to discern what kind of man he is; for then, at last, words of truth are drawn from the depths of his heart and the mask is torn off, reality remains.
—**Lucretius**

◆ The ultimate measure of a man is not where he stands in moments of comfort and convenience, but where he stands during challenge and controversy.
—**Martin Luther King Jr.**

◆ Your life is your message.
—**Mahatma Gandhi**

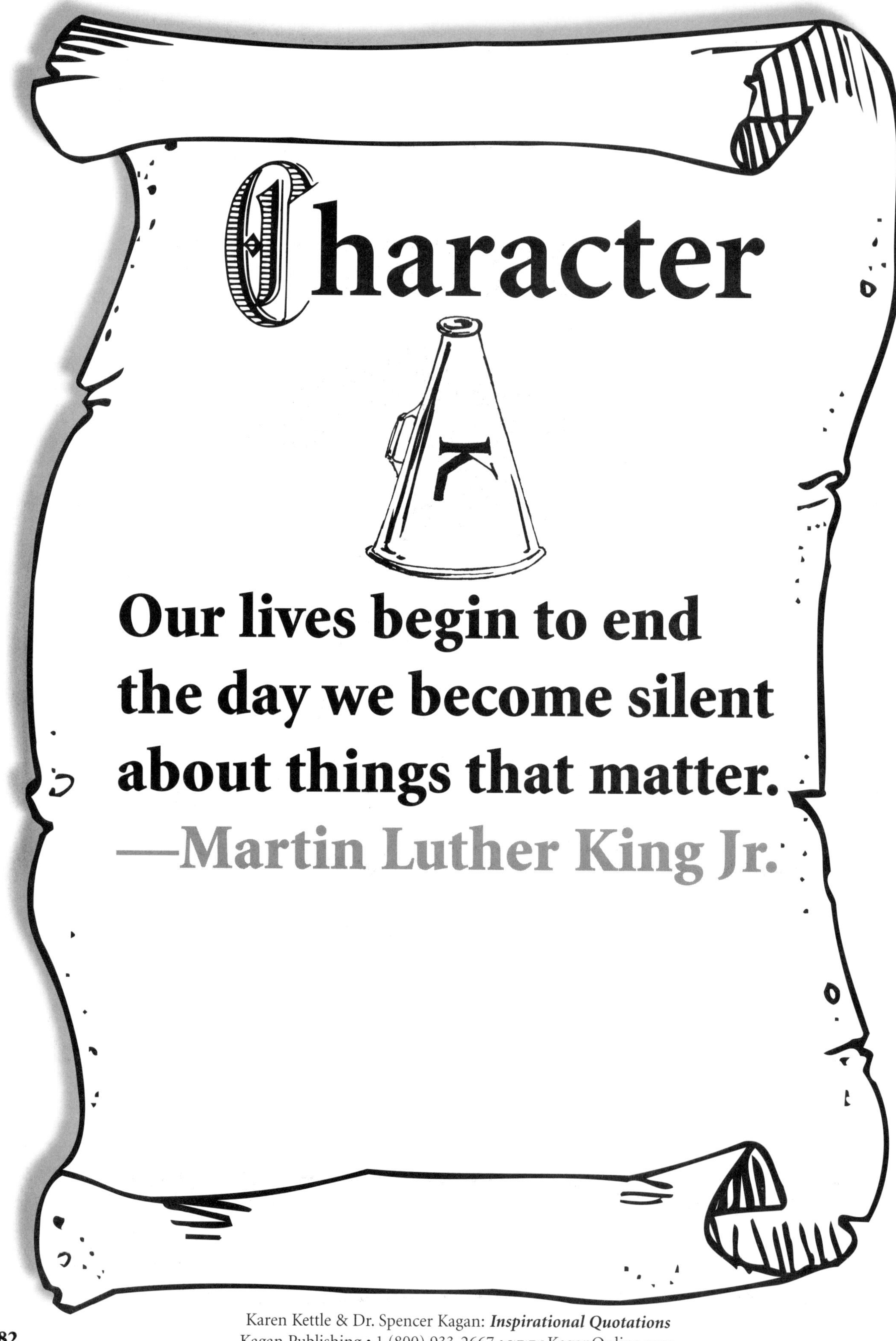
Character
K
Our lives begin to end
the day we become silent
about things that matter.
—Martin Luther King Jr.

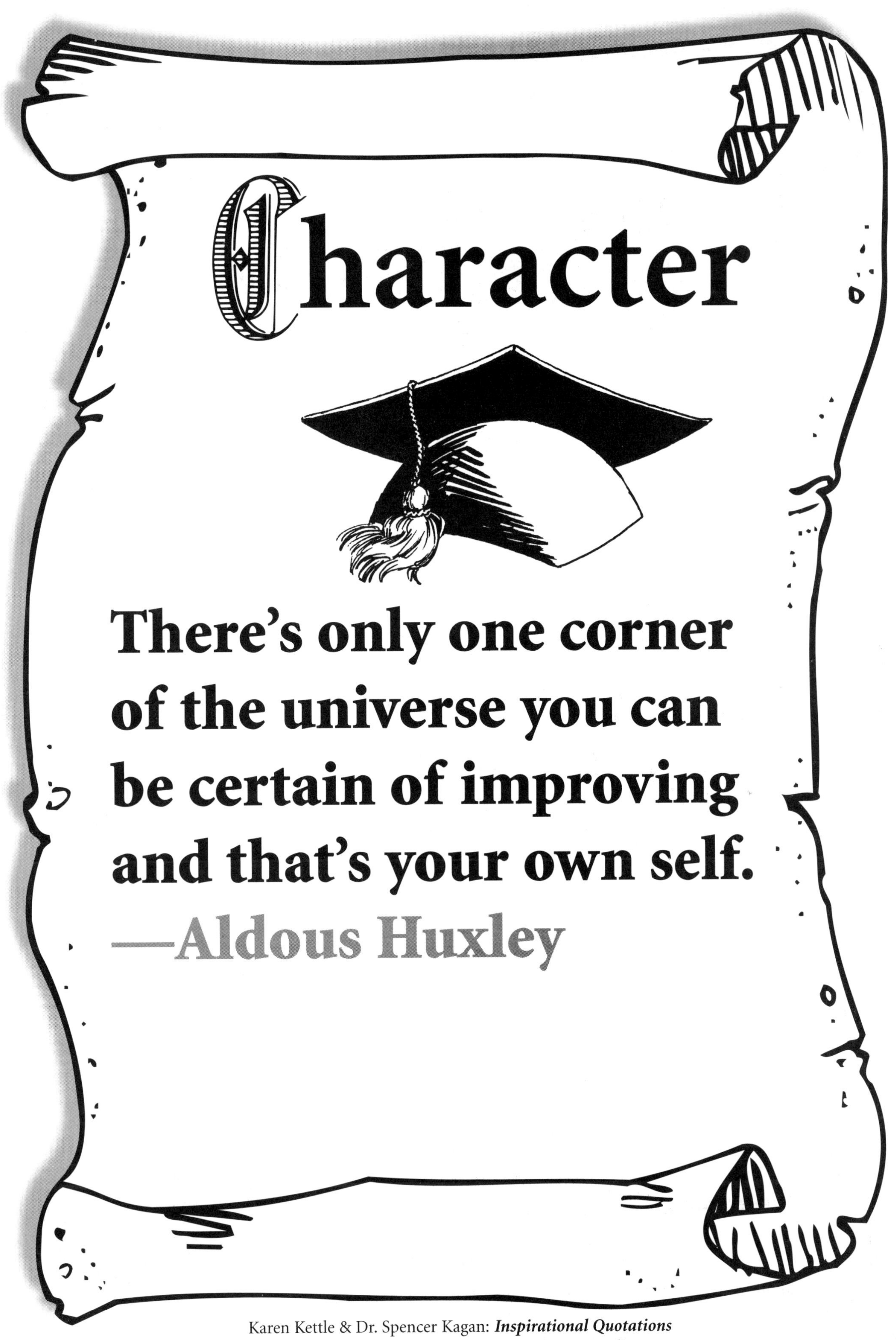
Character
There's only one corner of the universe you can be certain of improving and that's your own self.
—Aldous Huxley

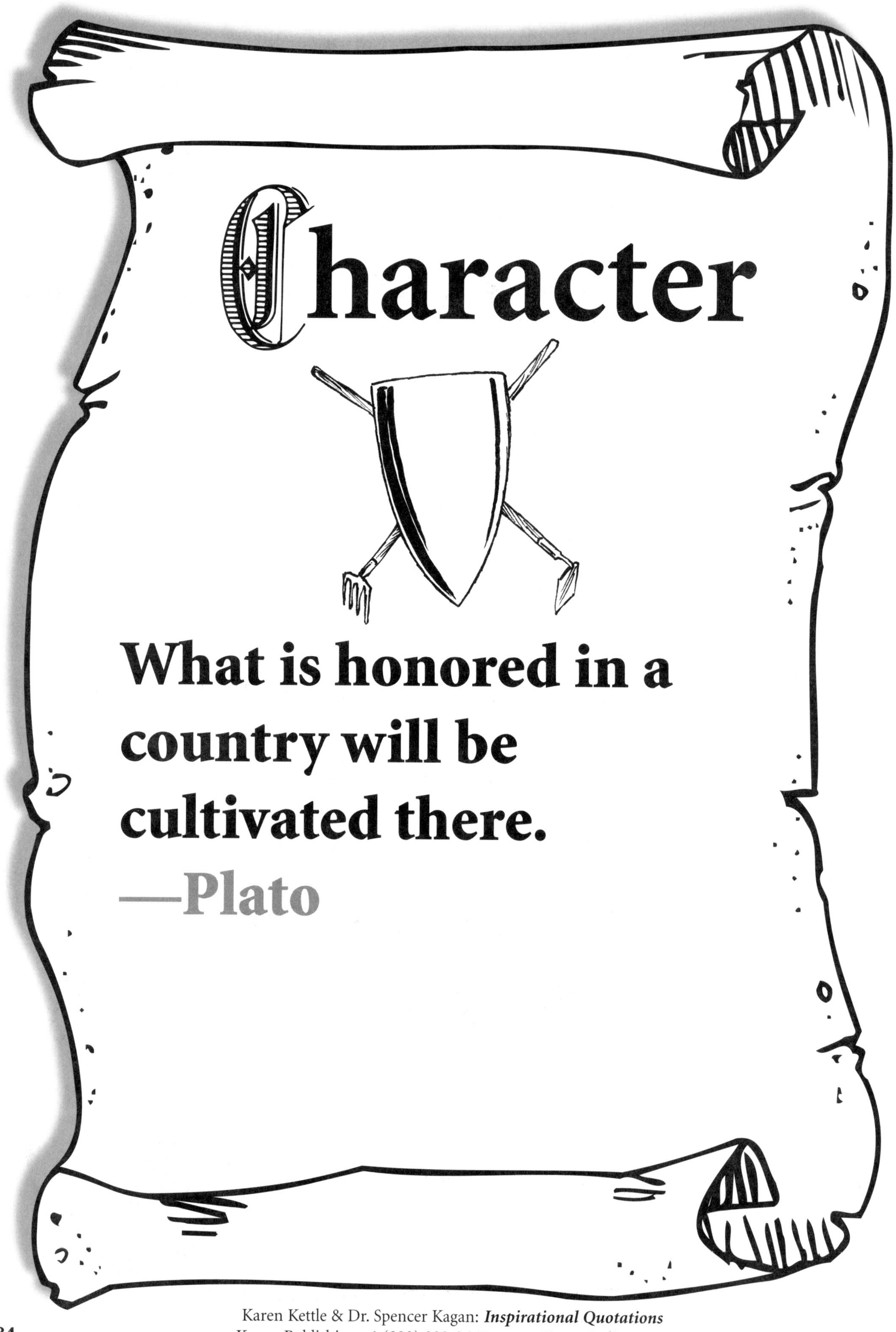
Character
What is honored in a
country will be
cultivated there.
—Plato

Character
Hard work spotlights the character of people: some turn up their sleeves, some turn up their noses, and some don't turn up at all.
—Sam Ewig

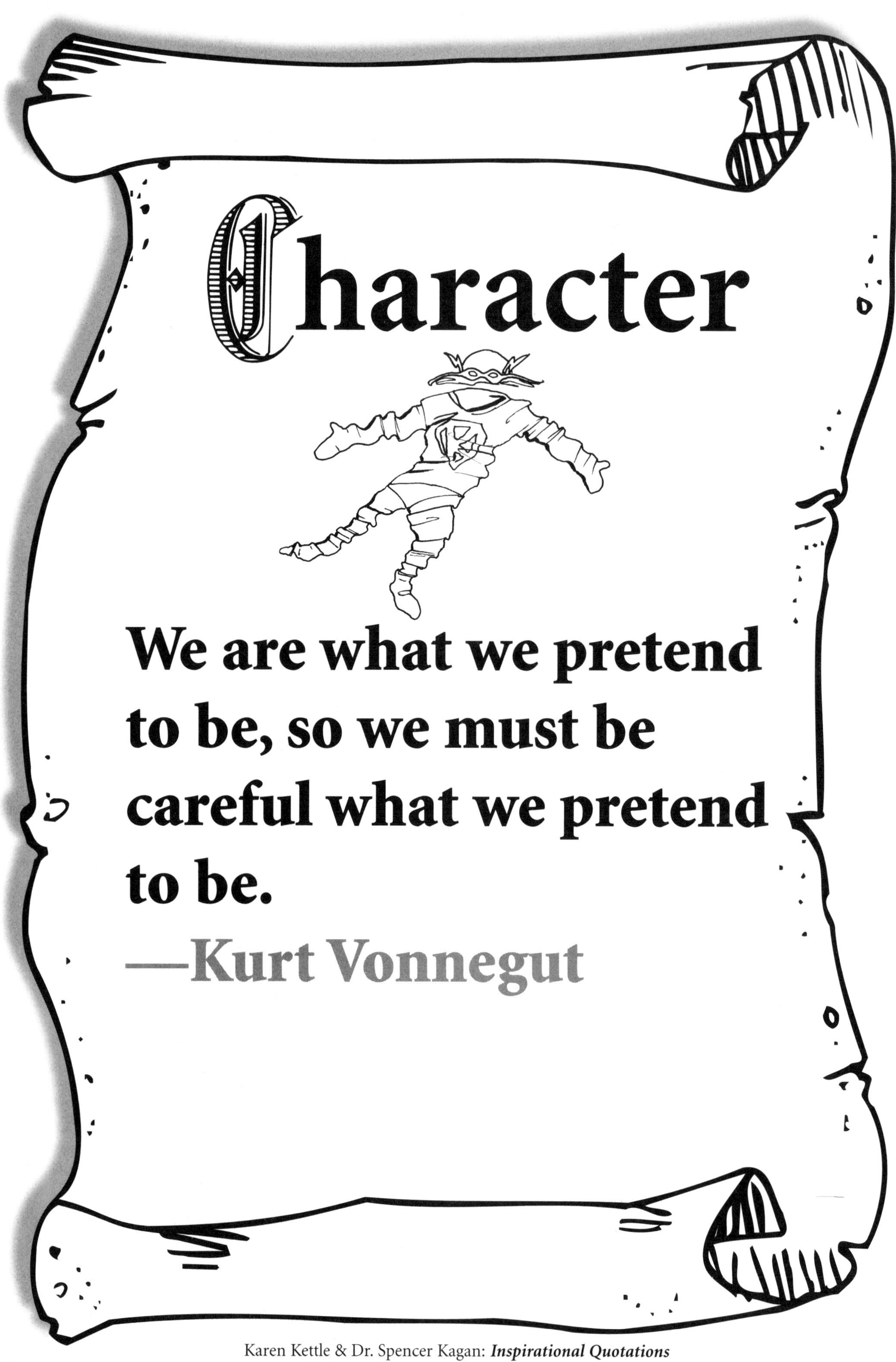

Character

We are what we pretend to be, so we must be careful what we pretend to be.

—Kurt Vonnegut

Karen Kettle & Dr. Spencer Kagan: *Inspirational Quotations*
Kagan Publishing • 1 (800) 933-2667 • www.KaganOnline.com

Communication

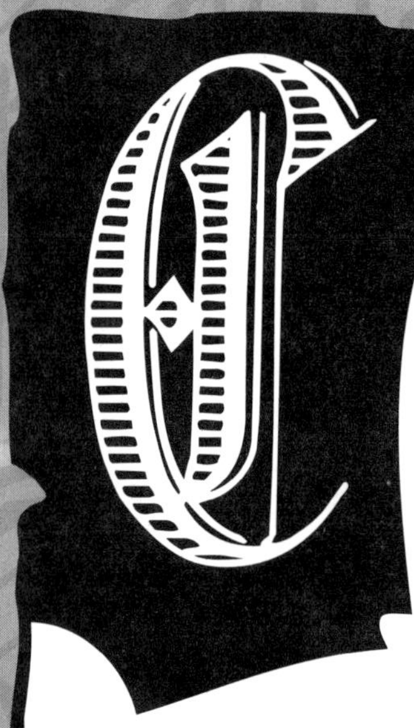

# Communication

*Our ability to communicate with others connects us to humanity. If we don't communicate we face the world alone.*

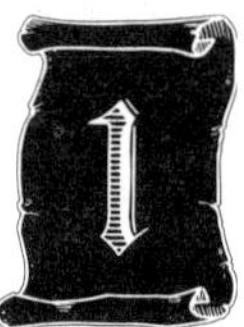

**The quality of our lives improves immensely when there is at least one other person who is willing to listen to our troubles.**

*—Mihaly Csikszentmihalyi*

Reflection Questions

- *Who do you go to when you need someone to listen?*
- *What does it take to listen deeply with your heart and mind?*
- *Who do you listen to?*

**The universe is made up of stories not atoms.**

*—Muriel Rukeyser*

Reflection Questions

- *What happens in your favorite story?*
- *If you were to write the most important story in the world, what would it be about?*
- *What would you pick as a theme for your "life story"?*

**If we are to live and work together, we have to talk to each other.**

*—Eleanor Roosevelt*

Reflection Questions

- *If you could talk to anyone past or present who would you choose? What would you talk about?*
- *Why are some people harder to talk to than others?*
- *What strategies can you use to start a conversation?*

**Good communication is as stimulating as black coffee, and just as hard to sleep after.**
*—Anne Morrow Lindbergh*

Reflection Questions
- *What exciting ideas keep you awake at night?*
- *Why does some of our best thinking happen just before we fall asleep or just after we wake up?*
- *Why are some conversations difficult but worth having?*

**Whatever words we utter should be chosen with care for people will hear them and be influenced by them for good or ill.**
*—Buddha*

Reflection Questions
- *How does gossip hurt people?*
- *Have you ever said anything you wish you could take back? How did it make you feel?*
- *Why does everyone benefit when you speak well of others?*

# Communication

◆ Only through communication can human life hold meaning.
**—Paolo Freire**

◆ Communication leads to community, that is, to understanding, intimacy and mutual valuing.
**—Rollo May**

◆ If you don't know the kind of person I am, and if I don't know the kind of person you are, a pattern that others made may prevail in the world—and we may miss our star.
**—William Stafford**

◆ We don't all speak a common language, even when we seem to use the same words.
**—Jami Bernard**

◆ Truth is not everywhere the same, because language is not everywhere the same, and human existence is essentially linguistic and essentially historical.
**—Richard Rorty**

◆ Language exerts hidden power, like the moon on tides.
**—Rita Mae Brown**

◆ If I do not speak in a language that can be understood there is little chance for a dialogue.
**—bell hooks**

◆ Nothing is so simple that it cannot be misunderstood.
**—Junior Teague**

◆ What we've got here is a failure to communicate.
**—Frank R. Pierson**

◆ If you want to know what you are thinking, put your thoughts into words.
**—John Stuart Mill**

◆ You can have brilliant ideas, but if you can't get them across, your ideas won't get you anywhere.
**—Lee Iacocca**

◆ If you can't explain it simply, you don't understand it well enough.
**—Albert Einstein**

◆ You don't have to be loud. If you know what you want, people respect that.
**—Sophia Coppola**

◆ A good message will always find a messenger.
**—Amelia E. Barr**

***It is better to keep your mouth closed and let people think you are a fool than to open it and remove all doubt.***
***—Mark Twain***

◆ The finest expression of respect is not praise or status, but a willingness to talk openly to a person.
**—Less Bittle**

◆ In order to have a conversation with someone you must reveal yourself.
**—James Baldwin**

◆ Free and fair discussion will ever by found the firmest friend to truth.
**—G. Campbell**

◆ For me, words are a form of action, capable of influencing change.
**—Ingrid Bengis**

◆ In Maine, we have a saying that there's no point in speaking unless you can improve on silence.
**—Edmund Muskie**

◆ Be silent or let thy word be worth more than silence.
**—Pythagoras**

◆ The words of the tongue should have three gatekeepers: Is it true? Is it kind? Is it necessary?
**—Arabian proverb**

◆ Make sure you have finished speaking before your audience has finished listening.
**—Dorothy Sarnoff**

◆ Trust must be reciprocal—to be sincere, speakers must trust their listeners.
**—Frank Pajares**

◆ The greatest compliment that was ever paid to me was when someone asked me what I thought, and attended to my answer.
**—Henry David Thoreau**

◆ To listen closely and reply well is the highest perfection we are able to attain in the art of conversation.
**— Francois de La Rochefoucauld**

◆ When people talk, listen completely. Most people never listen.
**—Ernest Hemingway**

◆ Most conversations are monologues delivered in the presence of a witness.
**—Margaret Miller**

◆ Listening is love in action.
**—Leo Buscaglia**

◆ An essential part of true listening is the discipline of bracketing, the temporary giving up or setting aside of one's own prejudices, frames of reference and desires so as to experience as far as possible the speaker's world from the inside.
**—M. Scott Peck**

◆ We have two ears and one mouth so that we can listen twice as much as we speak.
**—Epictetus**

◆ The word *listen* contains the same letters as the word *silent.*
**—Alfred Brendel**

◆ One of the best ways to persuade others is with your ears.
**—Dean Rusk**

◆ There is a craft and a power to listening.
**—Glenn Gould**

◆ Listen long enough and the person will generally come up with an adequate solution.
**—Mary Kay Ash**

◆ Be a good listener. Your ears will never get you in trouble.
**—Frank Tyger**

◆ It takes wisdom to listen to others.
**—Oliver Wendell Holmes**

◆ What you do speaks so loudly, they can't hear what you say.
**—Ralph Waldo Emerson**

◆ Kind words can be short and easy to speak, but their echoes are truly endless.
**—Mother Teresa**

***The single biggest problem in communication is the illusion that it has taken place.***
***—George Bernard Shaw***

◆ Appreciative words are the most powerful force for good on earth!
**—George W. Crane**

◆ Feeling gratitude and not expressing it is like wrapping a present and not giving it.
**—William Arthur Ward**

◆ Few things in the world are more powerful than a positive push. A smile. A word of optimism and hope. A "you can do it" when things are tough.
**—Richard M. Devos**

◆ The most important thing in communication is to hear what isn't being said.
**—Peter Drucker**

◆ The genius of communication is the ability to be both totally honest and totally kind at the same time.
**—John Powell**

◆ When ... someone really hears you without passing judgment on you, without trying to take responsibility for you, without trying to mold you, it feels good.
**—Carl Rogers**

◆ If we all discovered that we had only five minutes left to say all that we wanted to say, every telephone booth would be occupied by people calling other people to tell them that they loved them.
**—Christopher Morely**

# Communication

**The quality of our lives improves immensely when there is at least one other person who is willing to listen to our troubles.**

**—Mihaly Csikszentmihalyi**

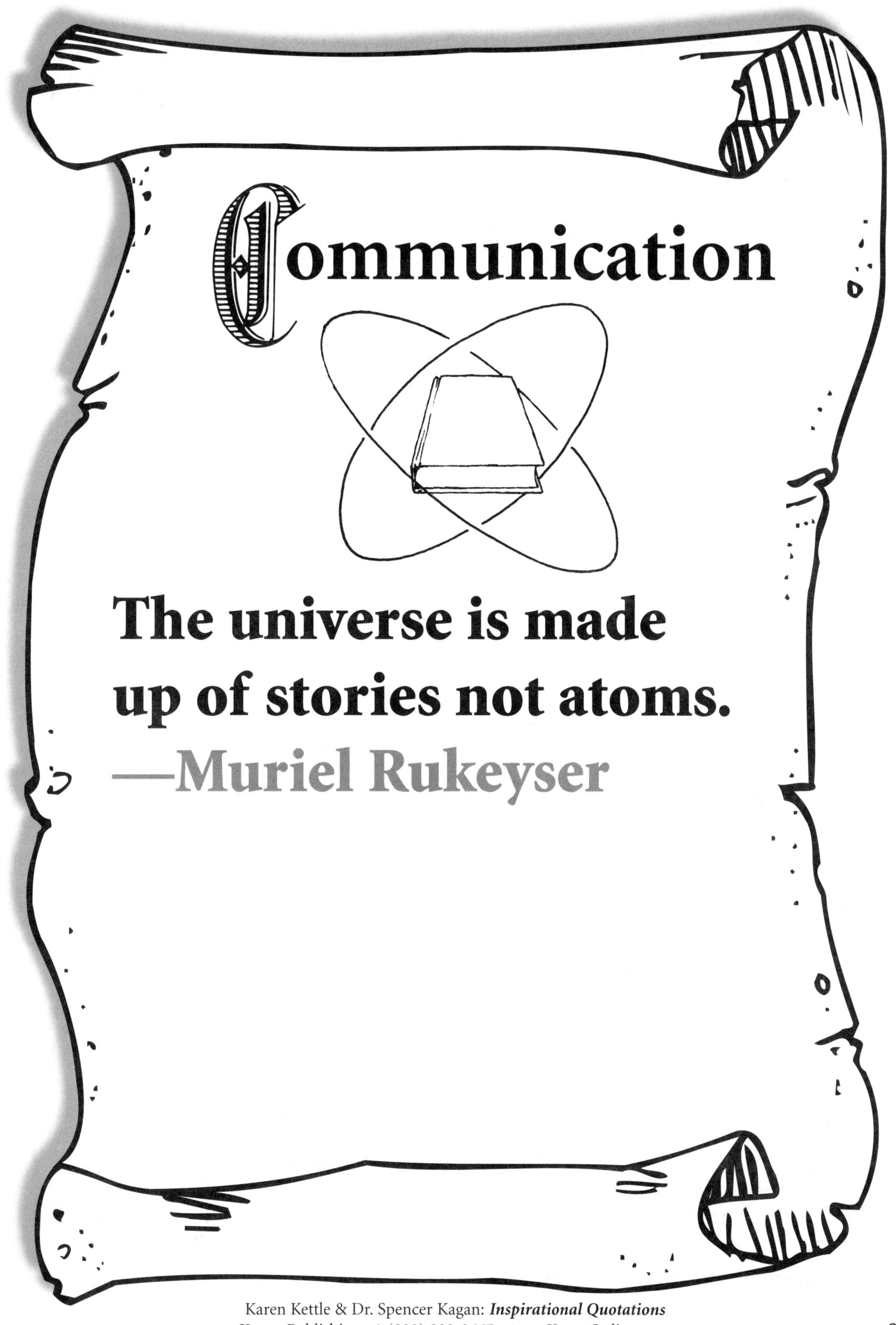

# Communication

The universe is made up of stories not atoms.

—Muriel Rukeyser

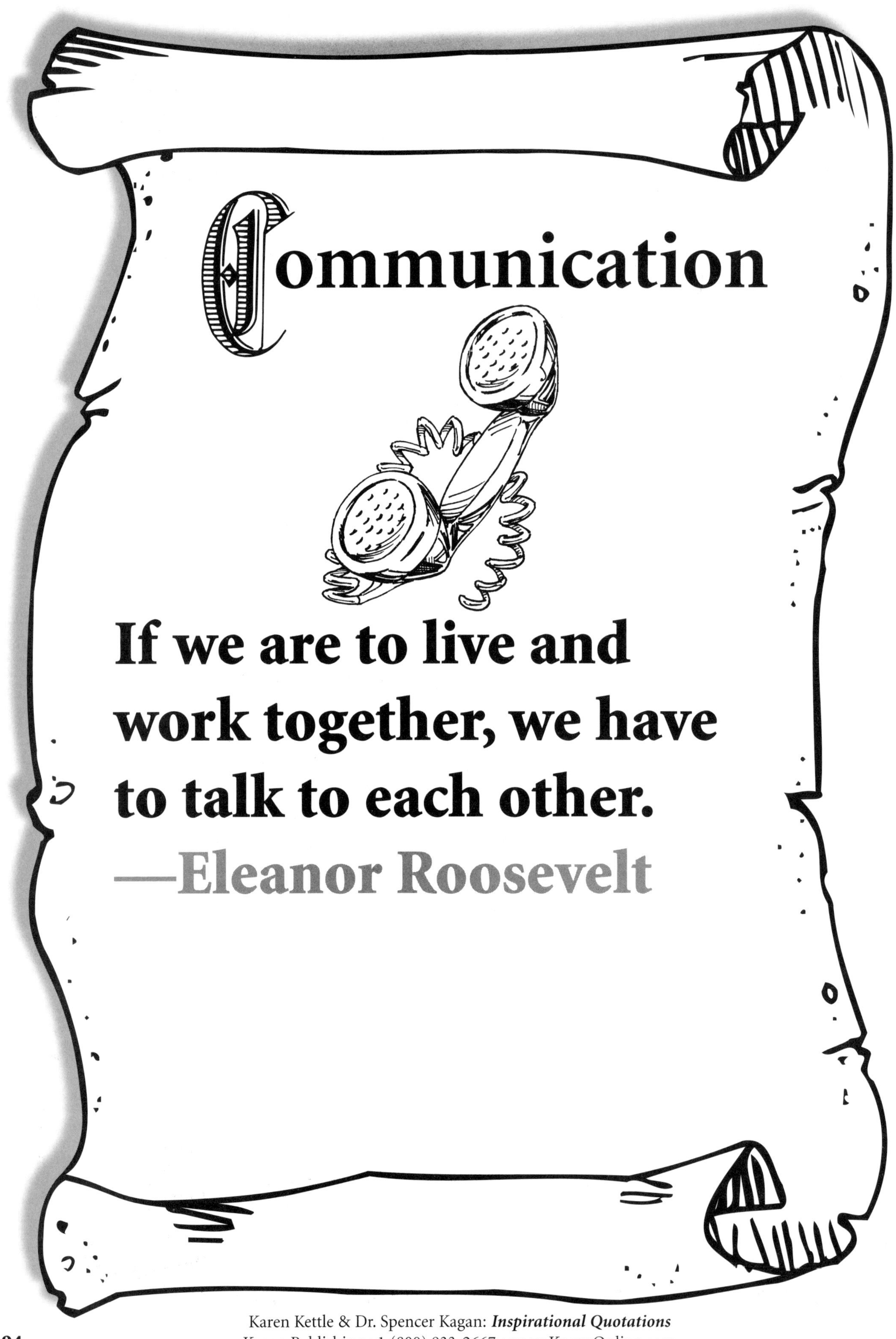

# Communication

**If we are to live and work together, we have to talk to each other.**

**—Eleanor Roosevelt**

# Communication

**Good communication is as stimulating as black coffee, and just as hard to sleep after.**

**—Anne Morrow Lindbergh**

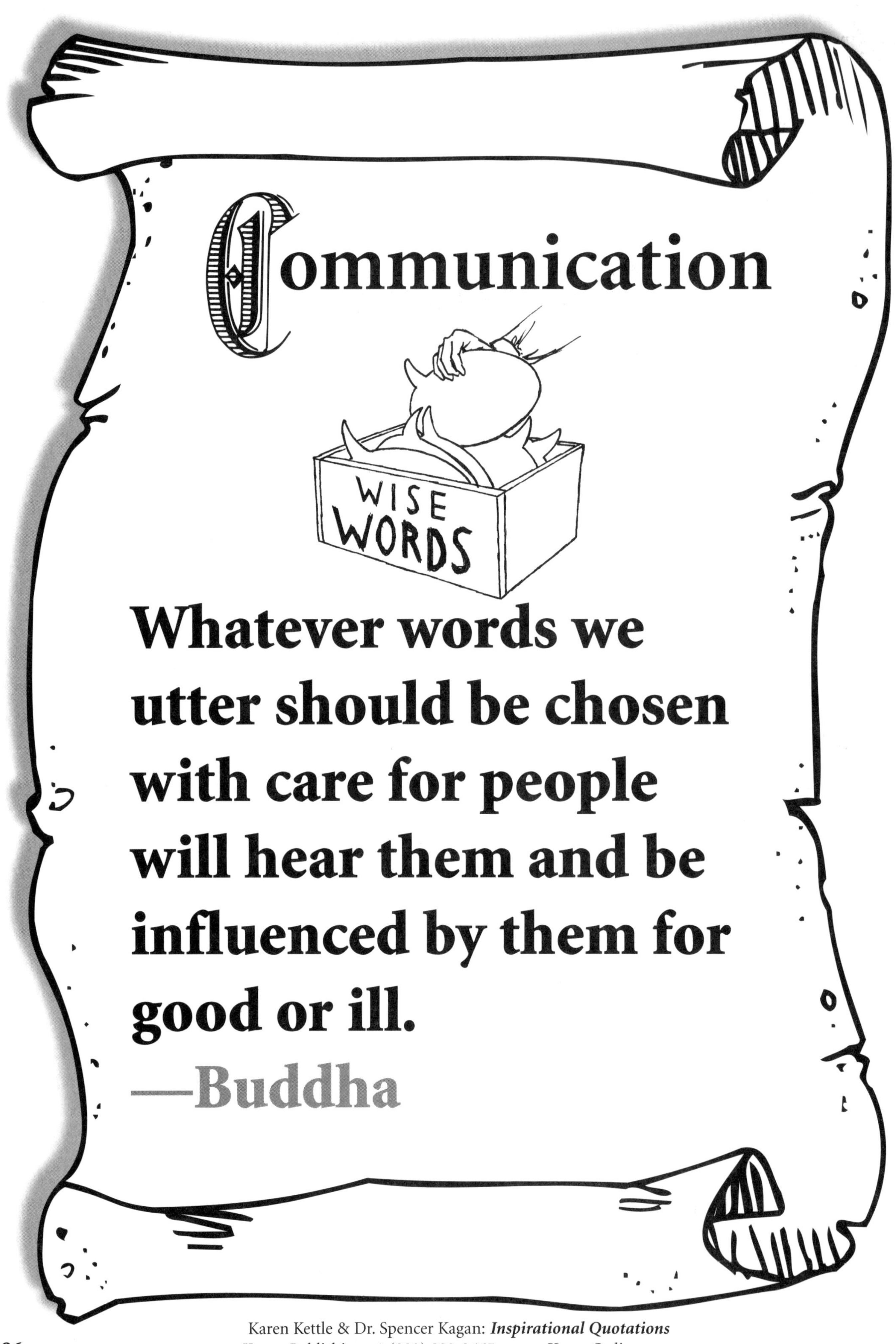


# Communication

**Whatever words we utter should be chosen with care for people will hear them and be influenced by them for good or ill.**

**—Buddha**

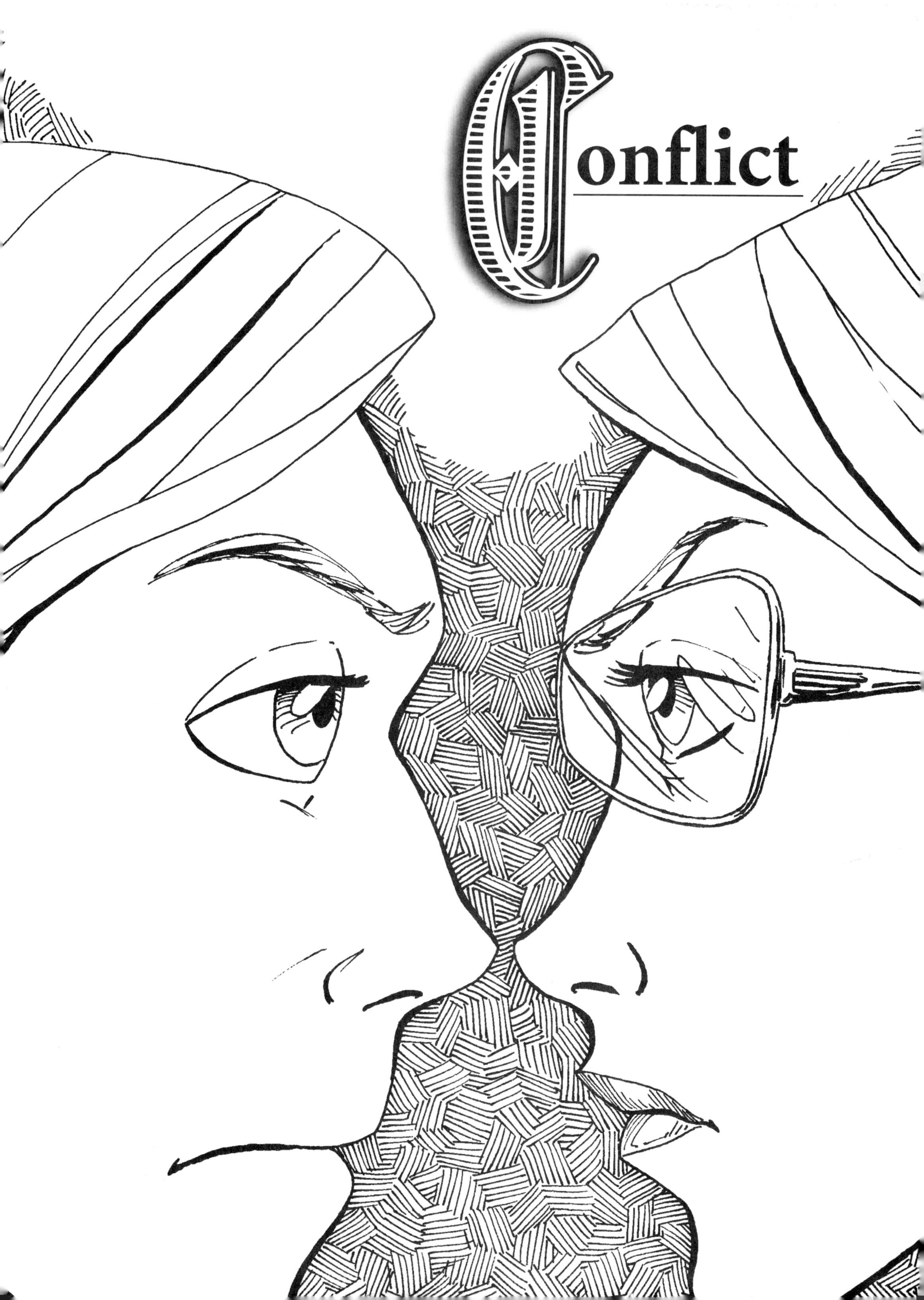
Conflict

# Conflict

***Conflict crystallizes our differences. Faced with a conflict, we can choose to learn and create. How we respond to conflict determines the quality of our relationships and the type of world we build.***

1

**Always keep your composure. You can't score from the penalty box; and to win, you have to score.**

*—Bobby Hull*

Reflection Questions

- *What does it feel like to be angry?*
- *What are productive ways to express your anger?*
- *When you feel angry, what can you do to make sure you act in an appropriate way?*

**A certain amount of opposition is good for a team. Kites don't rise with the wind, but against it.**

*—Doris Pickert*

Reflection Questions

- *Why do kites rise against the wind?*
- *What makes a team rise to the occasion and give its best effort?*
- *What situations make you give your best effort? Why?*

**Change means movement. Movement means friction. Only in the frictionless vacuum of a nonexistent abstract world can movement or change occur without the abrasive friction of conflict.**

*—Saul Alinsky*

Reflection Questions

- *Why do people see the world differently?*
- *What important lesson have you learned from someone you disagreed with at the beginning?*
- *How do you manage conflict in a positive manner in order to maintain relationships?*

**If we have no peace, it is because we have forgotten that we belong to each other.**

*—Mother Teresa*

### Reflection Questions

- *Who do you have conflicts with that you care about?*
- *What can you do to live peacefully?*
- *What strategies can you use to be a peacemaker with others?*

**You cannot shake hands with a clenched fist.**

*—Indira Ghandi*

### Reflection Questions

- *How can people agree to disagree?*
- *Why is it important to be willing to admit that you are wrong?*
- *What do you have to do to get over a disagreement and work together?*

# Conflict

◆ To fly, we have to have resistance.
—**Maya Lin**

◆ Turbulence is life force. It is opportunity. Let's love turbulence and use if for change.
—**Ramsay Clark**

◆ The greater the tension, the greater the potential. Great energy springs from a correspondingly great tension of opposites.
—**Carl Jung**

◆ I learned there are troubles of more than one kind. Some come from ahead and some from behind.
—**Dr. Seuss**

◆ Difficulties are meant to rouse, not discourage. The human spirit is to grow strong by conflict.
—**William Ellery Channing**

◆ What used to be conflict is now a synergy.
—**Jack B. Grubman**

◆ Conflict is the gadfly of thought. It stirs us to observation and memory. It instigates to invention. It shocks us out of sheeplike passivity, and sets us at noting and contriving.
—**John Dewey**

◆ Put the argument into a concrete shape, into an image, some hard phrase, round and solid as a ball, which they can see and handle and carry home with them, and the cause is half won.
—**Ralph Waldo Emerson**

◆ Too much agreement kills a chat.
—**Eldridge Cleaver**

◆ Conflict is the alchemical soup that transforms raw emotion and instinct into pure gold.
—**Harville Hendrix**

***Storms make oaks take deeper root.***
***—George Herbert***

◆ Far from being necessarily dysfunctional, a certain degree of conflict is an essential element in group formation and the persistence of group life.
—**Lewis A. Coser**

◆ There are some things you can learn best in calm, and some in storm.
—**Willa Cather**

◆ The bamboo which bends is stronger than the oak which resists.
—**Japanese proverb**

◆ The greatest conflicts are not between two people but between one person and himself (herself).
—**Garth Brooks**

◆ Since the general or prevailing opinion on any subject is rarely or never the whole truth, it is only by the collision of adverse opinion that the remainder of the truth has a chance of being supplied.
—**John Stuart Mill**

◆ When the power of love overcomes the love of power the world will know peace.
—**Jimi Hendrix**

◆ Difference of opinion leads to inquiry, and inquiry to truth.
—**Thomas Jefferson**

◆ To think is to differ.
—**Clarence Darrow**

◆ Often those who resist have something important to tell us. We can be influenced by them. People resist for what they view as good reasons. They may see alternatives we never dreamed of.
—**R. Maurer**

◆ Convincing yourself does not win an argument.
—**Robert Half**

◆ Have you learned lessons only of those who admired you, and were tender with you, and stood aside for you? Have you not learned great lessons from those who braced themselves against you, and disputed the passage with you?
**—Walt Whitman**

◆ Life is confrontation, and vigilance, and a fierce struggle against any threat of intrusion or death. We are unworthy of our ideal if we are not ready to defend, as we would life itself, the only roads to change that respect the human person.
**—Pierre E. Trudeau**

◆ Washing one's hands of the conflict between the powerful and the powerless means to side with the powerful, not to be neutral.
**—Paulo Freire**

◆ You have not converted a man because you have silenced him.
**—John Manley**

◆ Those convinced against their will are of the same opinion still.
**—Dale Carnegie**

◆ The old law of "an eye for an eye" leaves everybody blind.
**—Martin Luther King Jr.**

◆ Fear not those who argue but those who dodge.
**—Marie Von Ebner-Eschenbach**

◆ It is not necessary to understand things in order to argue about them.
**—Pierre Beaumarchais**

◆ In quarreling, the truth is always lost.
**—Publius Syrus**

◆ There is no squabbling so violent as that between people who accepted an idea yesterday and those who will accept the same idea tomorrow.
**—Christopher Morley**

◆ The test of a first-rate intelligence is the ability to hold two opposed ideas in the mind at the same time, and still retain the ability to function.
**—F. Scott Fitzgerald**

◆ There is no greater mistake than the hasty conclusion that opinions are worthless because they are badly argued.
**—Thomas H. Huxley**

◆ To repeat what others have said, requires education; to challenge it, requires brains.
**—Mary Pettibone Poole**

◆ It takes two to make a quarrel, but only one to end it.
**—Spanish proverb**

◆ I may disagree with what you have to say, but I shall defend to the death your right to say it.
**—Voltaire**

◆ People need to see how much agreement is possible between seemingly intractable opponents.
**—Robert Redford**

◆ Let the past drift away with the water.
**—Japanese proverb**

◆ By blending the breath of the sun and the shade, true harmony comes into the world.
**—Tao Te Ching**

◆ What a world this would be if we just built bridges instead of walls.
**—Carlos Ramirez**

***Honest disagreement is often a good sign of progress.***
***—Mahatma Gandhi***

◆ Whenever you're in conflict with someone, there is one factor that can make the difference between damaging your relationship and deepening it. That factor is attitude.
**—Timothy Bentley**

◆ Diplomacy is letting someone else have your way.
**—Lester B. Pearson**

◆ The ultimate test of a relationship is to disagree but to hold hands.
**—Alexandria Penney**

◆ If civilization is to survive, we must cultivate the science of human relationships—the ability of all peoples, of all kinds, to live together, in the same world at peace.
**—Franklin D. Roosevelt**

# Conflict

**Always keep your composure. You can't score from the penalty box; and to win, you have to score.**

**—Bobby Hull**

Conflict
A certain amount of opposition is good for a team. Kites don't rise with the wind, but against it.
—Doris Pickert

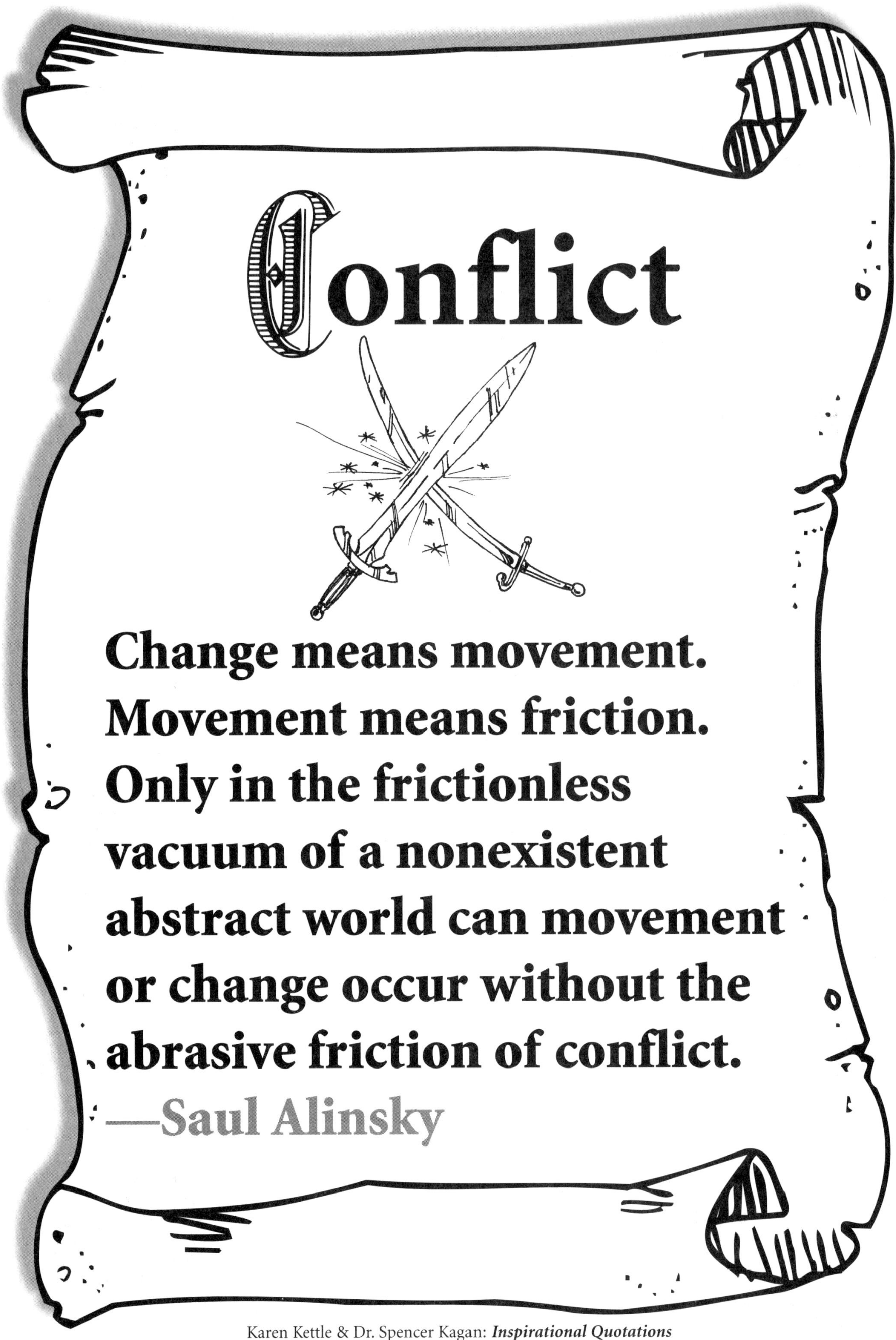

# Conflict

**Change means movement. Movement means friction. Only in the frictionless vacuum of a nonexistent abstract world can movement or change occur without the abrasive friction of conflict.**

**—Saul Alinsky**

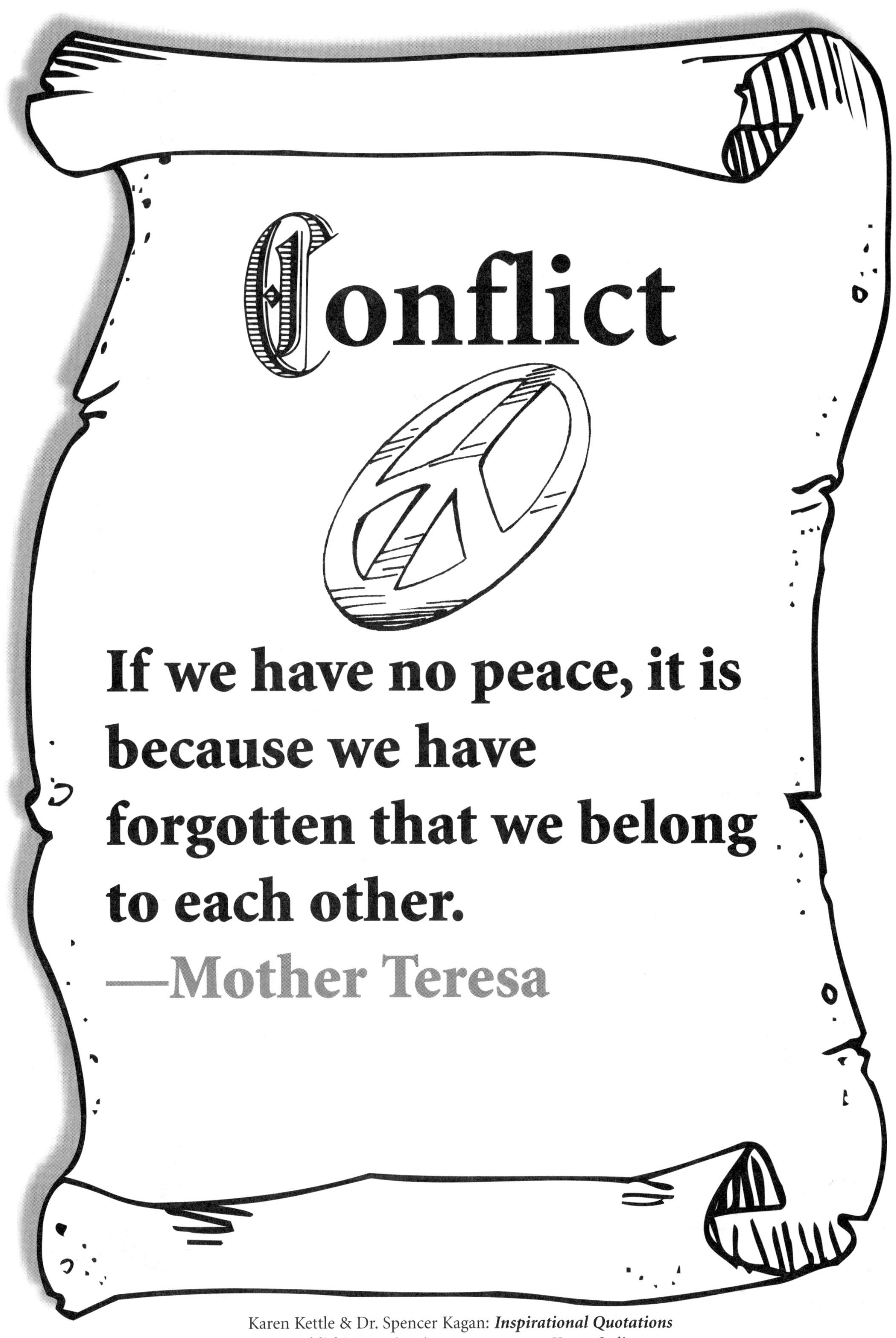
Conflict
If we have no peace, it is because we have forgotten that we belong to each other.
—Mother Teresa

Conflict
You cannot shake hands
with a clenched fist.
—Indira Ghandi

Creativity

# Creativity

*Creativity is a lifestyle. It is a way of exploring the world, developing talents, inventing a unique identity, and making a personal contribution.*

**Ideas, like wind-blown seeds, have a way of crossing boundaries and appearing in unlikely places.**
*—William Irving Thompson*

Reflection Questions

- *Where do ideas come from?*
- *Why is it exciting to come up with a new idea?*
- *Why is it important to have an open mind and look for new ideas everywhere?*

**The way to get good ideas is to get lots of ideas and throw the bad ones away.**
*—Linus Pauling*

Reflection Questions

- *What strategies do creative people use to generate lots and lots of ideas?*
- *How do you decide if an idea is worth keeping?*
- *How does writing a journal help creative people keep track of good ideas?*

**Innovation is simply group intelligence having fun.**
*—Michael Nolan*

Reflection Questions

- *How do we build on the ideas of others?*
- *What have you created that was fun?*
- *What could we put together to create a zany new product?*

**Use the talents you possess, for the woods would be very silent if no birds sang except the best.**

*—Henry Van Dyke*

Reflection Questions

- *What talents do you have that you like to use?*
- *How can you live creatively regardless of your natural talents?*
- *What would school be like if we valued creativity as much as academic achievement?*

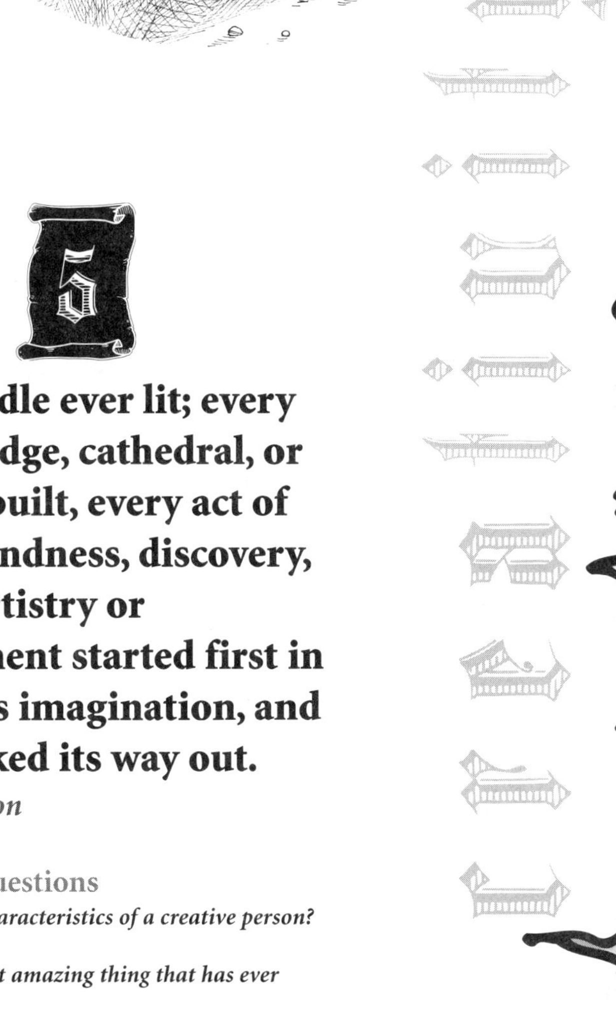

**Every candle ever lit; every home, bridge, cathedral, or city ever built, every act of human kindness, discovery, daring, artistry or advancement started first in someone's imagination, and then worked its way out.**

*—Gil Atkinson*

Reflection Questions

- *What are the characteristics of a creative person?*
- *What is the most amazing thing that has ever been invented?*
- *If you could invent anything, what would it be?*

# Creativity

◆ Sometimes I think creativity is magic; it's not a matter of finding an idea, but allowing the idea to find you.
**—Maya Lin**

◆ The most potent muse is our own inner child.
**—Stephen Nachmanovitch**

◆ When you think at the moment that it is possible—then the magic starts.
**—Siegfried**

◆ Creativity involves breaking out of established patterns in order to look at things in a different way.
**—Edward De Bono**

◆ Creativity is the power to connect the seemingly unconnected.
**—William Plomer**

◆ Creativity is one of those words, or concepts, which seems plain enough, even simple, till you start fixing your eye on it. Then, like innocence or internationalism or love, it begins to swell up like a cloud into something that fills the whole sky of meaning, and darkens it, and comes to signify everything or nothing.
**—Earle Birney**

◆ Creativity does not happen inside people's heads, but in the interaction between a person's thoughts and the sociocultural context.
**—Mihaly Csikszentmihalyi**

◆ Creativity requires the courage to let go of certainties.
**—Erich Fromm**

◆ Creativity is allowing yourself to make mistakes. Art is knowing which ones to keep.
**—Scott Adams**

◆ Creativity is piercing the mundane to find the marvelous.
**—Bill Moyers**

***Creativity is inventing, experimenting, growing, taking risks, breaking rules, making mistakes, and having fun.***
***—Mary Lou Cook***

◆ There is no greater agony than bearing an untold story inside you.
**—Maya Angelou**

◆ Creative courage is the discovering of new forms, new symbols, new patterns on which a new society can be built.
**—Rollo May**

◆ There's words enough, paint and brushes enough, and thoughts enough. The whole difficulty seems to be getting the thoughts clear enough, making them stand still long enough to be fitted with words and paint. They are so elusive, like wild birds singing above your head, twittering close beside you, chortling in front of you, but gone the moment you put out your hand.
**—Emily Carr**

◆ Self-expression must pass into communication for its fulfillment.
**—Pearl S. Buck**

◆ It is the uncontemporary spirit that is the genius of discovery and art and invention.
**—Bliss Carman**

◆ Even without success, creative persons find joy in a job well done. Learning for its own sake is rewarding.
**—Mihaly Csikszentmihalyi**

◆ Creativity is a type of learning process where the teacher and pupil are located in the same individual.
**—Arthur Koestler**

◆ It is the tension between creativity and skepticism that has produced the stunning and unexpected findings of science.
**—Carl Sagan**

◆ Creativity arises out of the tension between spontaneity and limitations, the latter (like the river banks) forcing the spontaneity into the various forms which are essential to the work of art or poem.
**—Rollo May**

◆ Why, sometimes I've believed as many as six impossible things before breakfast.
**—Lewis Carroll**

◆ Always use the word *impossible* with the greatest caution.
**—Werner von Braun**

◆ To live a creative life, we must lose our fear of being wrong.
**—Joseph Chilton Pearce**

◆ It is better to have enough ideas for some of them to be wrong, than to be always right by having no ideas at all.
**—Edward De Bono**

◆ Every great advance has issued from a new audacity of imagination.
**—John Dewey**

◆ Every creator painfully experiences the chasm between his (her) inner vision and its ultimate expression.
**—Isaac Singer**

◆ Beginnings are always messy.
**—John Galsworth**

◆ Creativity comes from trust. Trust your instincts. And never hope more than you work.
**—Rita Mae Brown**

◆ I will master something, then the creativity will come.
**—Japanese proverb**

◆ It is worth mentioning, for future reference, that the creative power which bubbles so pleasantly in beginning a new book quiets down after a time, and one goes on more steadily. Doubts creep in. Then one becomes resigned. Determination not to give in, and the sense of an impending shape keep one at it more than anything.
**—Virginia Woolf**

◆ In my dream, the angel shrugged and said if we fail this time, it will be a failure of imagination. And then she placed the world gently in the palm of my hand.
**—Brian Andreas**

***Inspiration usually comes during work, rather than before it.***
***—Madeleine L'Engle***

◆ Be brave enough to live creatively. The creative is the place where no one else has ever been. You have to leave the city of your comfort and go into the wilderness of your intuition. You can't get there by bus, only by hard work, risking, and by not quite knowing what you're doing. What you'll discover will be wonderful: yourself.
**—Alan Alda**

◆ The life of the creative man (woman) is lead, directed and controlled by boredom. Avoiding boredom is one of our most important purposes.
**—Saul Steinberg**

◆ Creative life is a dynamic bridge between opposites.
**—Lawren Harris**

◆ I learned to make my mind large, as the universe is large, so there is room for paradoxes.
**—Maxine Hong Kingston**

◆ The reverse side also has a reverse side.
**—Japanese proverb**

◆ Discovery is seeing what everybody else has seen, and thinking what nobody else has thought.
**—Albert Szent-Gyorgyi**

◆ Originality is the essence of true scholarship. Creativity is the soul of the true scholar.
**—Nnamdi Azikiwe**

◆ It is by logic that we prove, but by intuition that we discover.
**—Henri Poincare**

◆ The creation of something new is not accomplished by the intellect but by the play instinct acting from inner necessity. The creative mind plays with the objects it loves.
**—Carl Jung**

◆ If order appeals to the intellect, then disorder titillates the imagination.
**—Paul Claudel**

◆ One of the advantages of being disorderly is that one is constantly making exciting discoveries.
**—A. A. Milne**

◆ A hunch is creativity trying to tell you something. It's the voice of invention calling you forward.
**—Frank Capra**

◆ A moment's insight is sometimes worth a life's experience.
**—Oliver Wendell Holmes**

◆ When inspiration does not come to me, I go halfway to meet it.
**—Sigmund Freud**

◆ Conditions for creativity are to be puzzled; to concentrate; to accept conflict and tension; to be born everyday; to feel a sense of self.
**—Erich Fromm**

◆ The problem is not that there are problems. The problem is expecting otherwise and thinking that having problems is a problem.
**—Theodore Isaac Rubin**

◆ You do not get out of a problem by using the same consciousness that got you into it.
**—Albert Einstein**

◆ Creativity can solve almost any problem. The creative act, the defeat of habit by originality, overcomes everything.
**—George Lois**

◆ The capacity to be puzzled is … the premise of all creation, be it in art or in science.
**—Erich Fromm**

◆ When I am working on a problem I never think about beauty. I only think about how to solve the problem. But when I have finished, if the solution is not beautiful, I know it is wrong.
**—R. Buckminster Fuller**

◆ When I am … entirely alone … or during the night when I cannot sleep, it is on such occasions that my ideas flow best and most abundantly. Whence and how these come I know not nor can I force them.
**—Wolfgang Amadeus Mozart**

◆ We lay there and looked up at the night sky and she told me about stars called blue squares and red swirls and I told her I'd never heard of them …. Of course not, she said, the really important stuff they never tell you. You have to imagine it on your own.
**—Brian Andreas**

◆ Ideas won't keep. Something must be done with them.
**—Alfred North Whitehead**

***The cure for boredom is curiosity. There is no cure for curiosity.***
***—Ellen Parr***

◆ To break through creativity, we must defer judgment. That is, learn to accept all ideas, without prejudice, and examine them each in turn.
**—Scott Isaksen**

◆ The "silly question" is the first intimation of some totally new development.
**—Alfred North Whitehead**

◆ A new idea is delicate. It can be killed by a sneer or a yawn; it can be stabbed to death by a joke or worried to death by a frown on the right person's brow.
**—Charles Bower**

◆ Whenever I'm stuck in traffic, I can't help but wonder, "Where did the creator of *The Jetsons* go, and why hasn't he done something about this?"
**—Jimmy Fallon**

◆ The dynamic principle of fantasy is play, which belongs also to the child, and as such it appears to be inconsistent with the principle of serious work. But without fantasy no creative work has ever yet come to birth. The debt we owe to the play of imagination is incalculable.
**—Carl Jung**

◆ Creative work is play. It is free speculation using materials of one's chosen form.
**—Stephen Nachmanovitch**

◆ When I examine myself and my methods of thought, I come to the conclusion that the gift of fantasy has meant more to me than any talent for abstract, positive thinking.
**—Albert Einstein**

◆ You can't use up creativity. The more you use, the more you have. Sadly, too often, creativity is smothered rather than nurtured. There has to be a climate in which new ways of thinking, perceiving, questioning are encouraged.
**—Maya Angelou**

◆ Creativity is a drug I cannot live without.
**—Cecil B. DeMille**

◆ So you see, imagination needs moodling—long, inefficient, happy idling, dawdling and puttering.
**—Brenda Ueland**

◆ I learned three important things in college—to use the library, to memorize quickly and visually, to drop asleep at any time given a horizontal surface and fifteen minutes. What I could not learn was to think creatively on schedule.
**—Agnes De Mille**

◆ We all need an occasional whack on the side of the head to shake us out of routine patterns, force us to rethink problems, and stimulate us to ask new questions that may lead to other right answers.
**—Roger von Oech**

◆ Arrange whatever pieces come your way.
**—Virginia Woolf**

◆ There are precious few Einsteins among us. Most brilliance arises from ordinary people working together in extraordinary ways.
**—Roger von Oech**

◆ The things we fear most in organizations—fluctuations, disturbances, imbalances—are the primary sources of creativity.
**—Margaret Wheatley**

***It's kind of fun to do the impossible.***
***—Walt Disney***

◆ Synergy—the bonus that is achieved when things work together harmoniously.
**—Mark Twain**

◆ What we have to do is to be forever curiously testing new opinions and courting new impressions.
**—Walter Pater**

◆ I am imagination. I can see what the eyes cannot see. I can hear what the ears cannot hear. I can feel what the heart cannot feel.
**—Peter Nivio Zarlenga**

◆ Imagination is new reality in the process of being created. It represents the part of the existing order that can still grow.
**—Nancy Hale**

◆ Imagination will often carry us to worlds that never were. But without it we go nowhere.
**—Carl Sagan**

◆ Imagination is the living power and prime agent of all human perception.
**—Samuel Taylor Coleridge**

◆ The world is but a canvas to the imagination.
**—Henry David Thoreau**

◆ Chaos is the soul of creation. It plows the ground of intuition. Without chaos, nothing will grow.
**—Michell Cassou**

◆ We live in a rainbow of chaos.
**—Paul Cezanne**

◆ We adore chaos because we love to produce order.
**—M. C. Escher**

◆ From the glow of enthusiasm I let the melody escape. I pursue it. Breathless I catch up with it. It flies again, it disappears, it plunges into chaos of diverse emotions. I catch it again, I seize it, I embrace it with delight … I multiply it by modulations, and at last I triumph in the first theme. There is the whole symphony.
**—Beethoven**

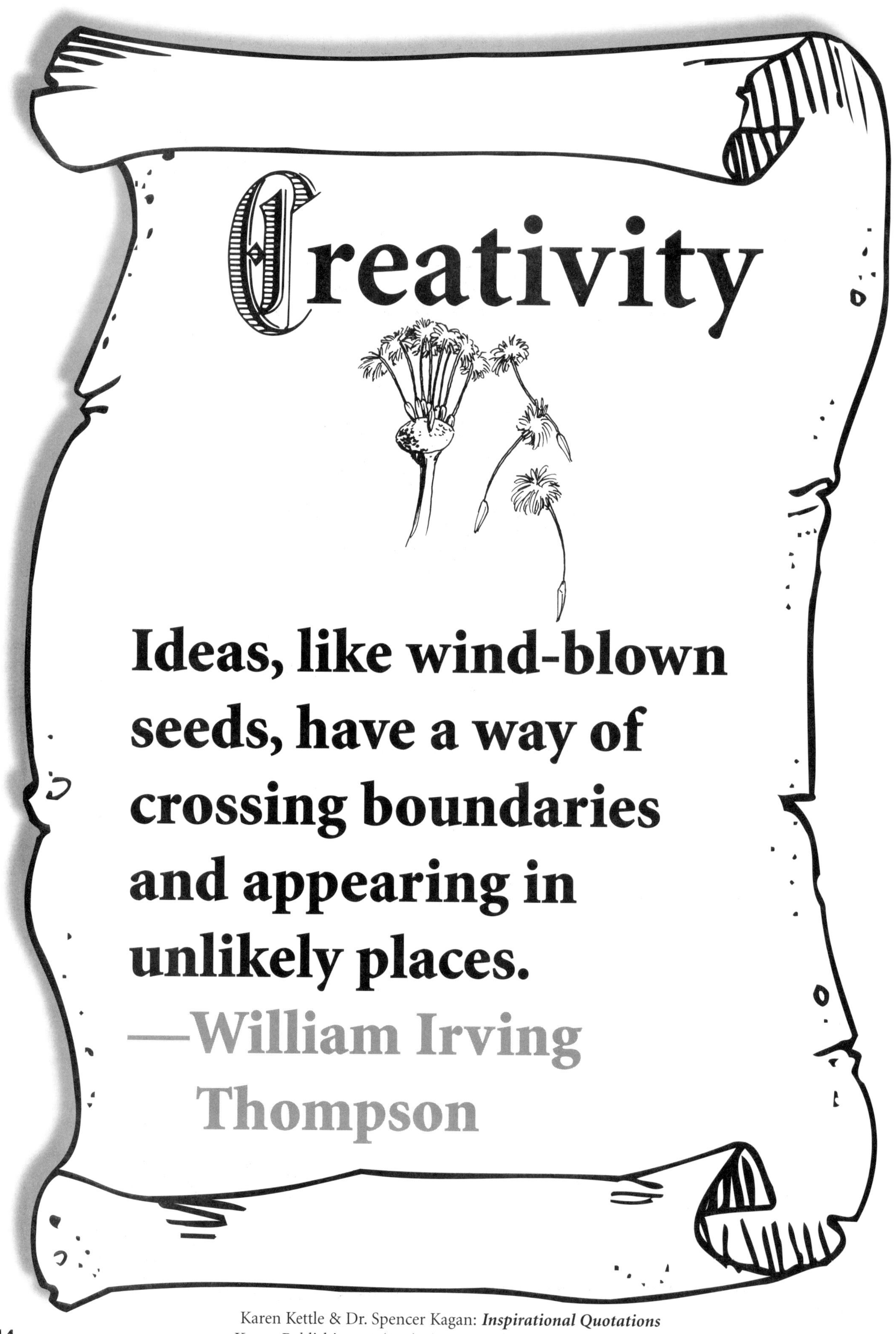

# Creativity

**Ideas, like wind-blown seeds, have a way of crossing boundaries and appearing in unlikely places.**

**—William Irving Thompson**



Karen Kettle & Dr. Spencer Kagan: *Inspirational Quotations*
Kagan Publishing • 1 (800) 933-2667 • www.KaganOnline.com

Creativity
The way to get good ideas is to get lots of ideas and throw the bad ones away.
—Linus Pauling

Creativity
Innovation is simply group intelligence having fun.
—Michael Nolan

Creativity
Use the talents you possess, for the woods would be very silent if no birds sang except the best.
—Henry Van Dyke

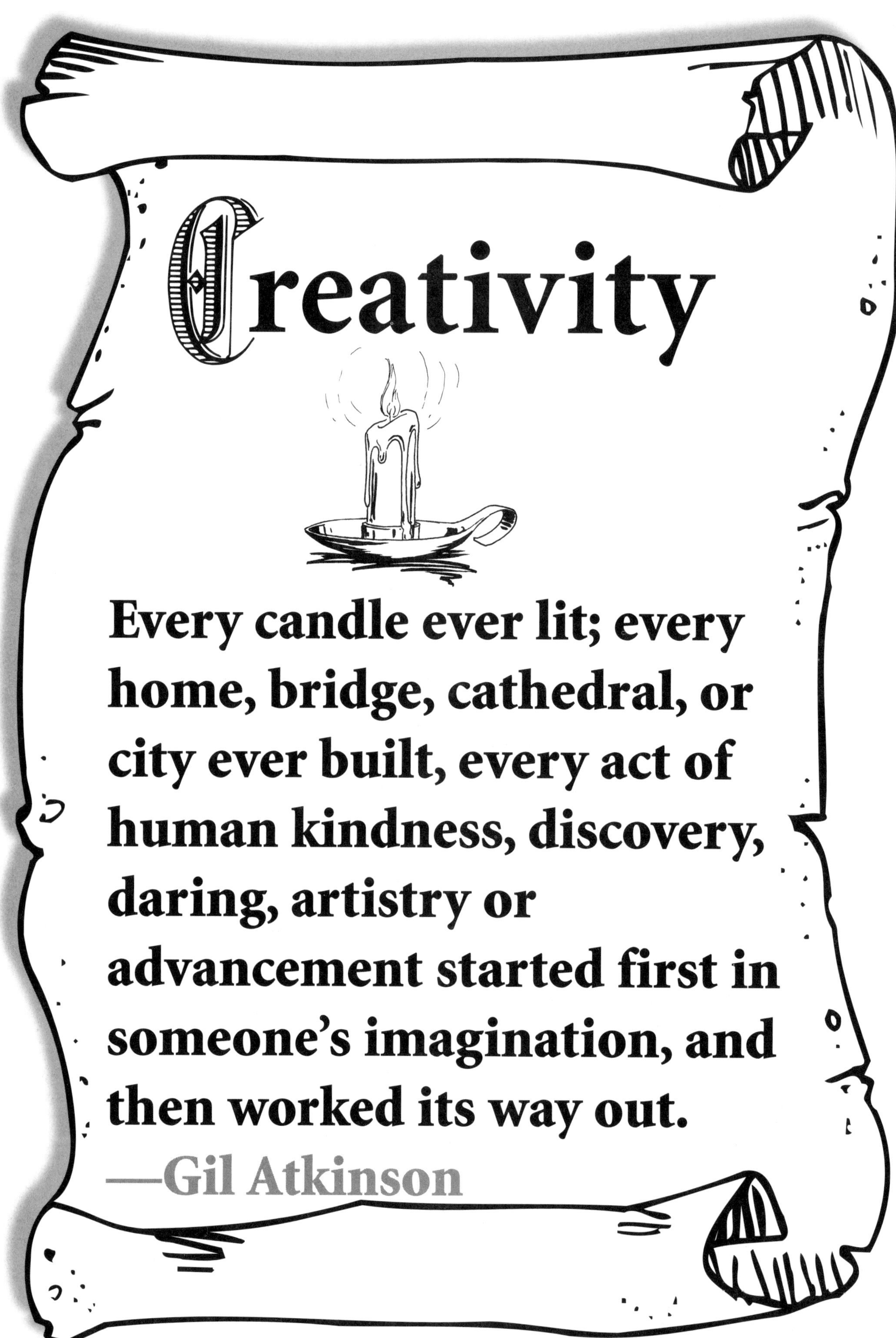
Creativity
Every candle ever lit; every home, bridge, cathedral, or city ever built, every act of human kindness, discovery, daring, artistry or advancement started first in someone's imagination, and then worked its way out.
—Gil Atkinson

Karen Kettle & Dr. Spencer Kagan: *Inspirational Quotations*
Kagan Publishing • 1 (800) 933-2667 • www.KaganOnline.com

# Decision Making

# Decision Making

*Decisions are crossroads. Our choices determine our future.*

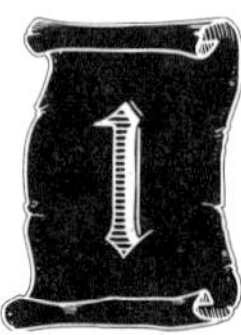

**Don't be afraid to take a big step if one is indicated. You can't cross a chasm in two small jumps.**

*—David Lloyd George*

Reflection Questions

- *What does it feel like to make an important decision?*
- *Who do you talk to when you are trying to decide?*
- *What strategies can you use to help you to decide?*

**Some of the best deals are the ones you don't make.**

*—Bill Veeck*

Reflection Questions

- *How do you say no when you don't want to get involved?*
- *What can you do if you find yourself in a bad situation?*
- *Who can you call for help?*

**Every great decision creates ripples—like a huge boulder dropped in a lake. The ripples merge, rebound off the banks in unforeseeable ways. The heavier the decision, the larger the waves, the more uncertain the consequences.**

*—Ben Aaronovitch*

Reflection Questions

- *How does the decision to always try your best ripple through your life?*
- *What consequences stem from your choice of friends?*
- *What conclusions can you draw from this quotation about the importance of making good choices?*

4

**The doors we open and close each day decide the lives we live.**

*—Flora Whittemore*

### Reflection Questions

- *What actions do people take that limit their options for the future?*
- *What doors are you keeping open for your future?*
- *What can you do today that will have a positive effect on your future?*

**Either you decide to stay in the shallow end of the pool or you go out in the ocean.**

*—Christopher Reeve*

### Reflection Questions

- *How can you compare staying in the shallow end of the pool to always making the safest choice?*
- *What do you gain from staying in the shallow end? What do you lose?*
- *As you venture into unfamiliar waters what strategies can you use to take care of yourself?*

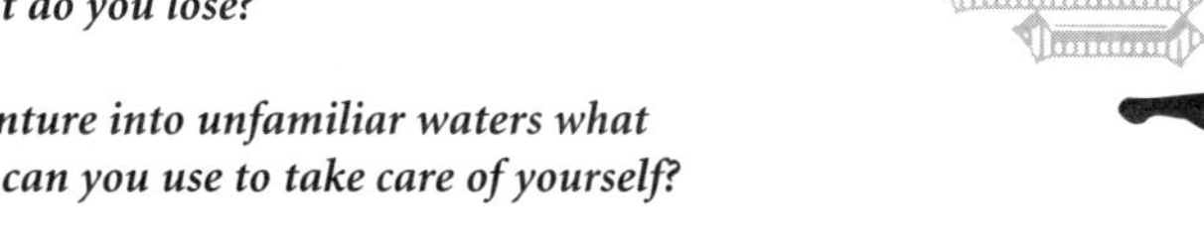

# Decision Making

◆ Decision is a risk rooted in the courage of being free.
**—Paul Tillich**

◆ Liberty, taking the word in its concrete sense, consists in the ability to choose.
**—Simone Weil**

◆ We make our decisions, and then our decisions turn around and make us.
**—R. W. Boreham**

◆ To decide, to be at the level of choice, is to take responsibility for your life and to be in control of your life.
**—Abbie M. Dale**

◆ I believe that we are solely responsible for our choices, and we have to accept the consequences of every deed, word, and thought throughout our lifetime.
**—Elisabeth Kubler-Ross**

◆ My will shall shape the future. Whether I fail or succeed shall be no one's doing but my own. I am the force; I can clear any obstacle before me or I can be lost in the maze. My choice; my responsibility; win or lose, only I hold the key to my destiny.
**—Elaine Maxwell**

◆ Choose well. Your choice is brief, and yet endless.
**—Johann Wolfgang Von Goethe**

◆ A president's hardest task is not to do what is right, but to know what is right.
**—Lyndon B. Johnson**

◆ It's choice—not chance—that determines your destiny.
**—Jean Nidetch**

***The self is not something ready-made, but something in continuous formation through choice of action.***
***—John Dewey***

◆ The strongest principle of growth lies in human choice.
**—George Eliot**

◆ Never take anything for granted.
**—Benjamin Disraeli**

◆ We are our choices.
**—Jean-Paul Sartre**

◆ A small decision now can change all your tomorrows.
**—Dr. Robert H. Schuller**

◆ A journey of a thousand miles begins with a single step.
**—Chinese proverb**

◆ A truly happy person is one who can enjoy the scenery on a detour.
**—Phil Humbert**

◆ Your life is the sum result of all the choices you make, both consciously and unconsciously. If you can control the process of choosing, you can take control of all aspects of your life. You can find the freedom that comes from being in charge of yourself.
**—Robert Bennett**

◆ No trumpets sound when the important decisions of our life are made. Destiny is made known silently.
**—Agnes De Mille**

◆ At every moment we decide: We choose to focus on what we want to express or on what the other person is trying to get across; on our feelings or on theirs; on what is inside or what is outside; what the other person has done right or how they did not measure up; on the weeds or on the flowers. And these decisions, multiplied by all the moments we are given, determine the meaning of our lives.
**—Spencer Kagan**

◆ In every success story, you find someone has made a courageous decision.
**—Peter Drucker**

◆ It is a sheer waste of time to imagine what I would do if things were different. They are not different.
**—Frank Crane**

◆ Again and again the impossible problem is solved when we see that the problem is only a tough decision waiting to be made.
**—Dr. Robert H. Schuller**

◆ Remember that yesterday's answer may have nothing to do with today's problem.
**—Don Ward**

◆ Nothing is more difficult, and therefore more precious, than to be able to decide.
**—Napoleon**

◆ It does not take much strength to do things, but it requires great strength to decide on what to do.
**—Elbert Hubbard**

◆ *Yes* and *no* are the oldest and simplest words, but they require the most thought.
**—Pythagoras**

◆ The art of leadership is saying no, not yes. It is very easy to say yes.
**—Tony Blair**

◆ You, too, can determine what you want. You can decide on your major objectives, targets, aims and destination.
**—Clement Stone**

◆ Consciously or unconsciously we all strive to make the kind of a world we like.
**—Oliver Wendell Holmes**

◆ Truth and life are all around you. What matters is where and when you decide to put your focus.
**—Roger von Oech**

◆ Don't agonize, organize.
**—Florynce Kennedy**

◆ Quality is never an accident, it is always the result of high intention, sincere effort, intelligent direction and skillful execution; it represents the wise choice of many alternatives.
**—Willa A. Foster**

◆ Win-win is a belief in the Third Alternative. It's not your way or my way; it's a better way.
**—Stephen Covey**

◆ Things which matter most must never be at the mercy of things which matter least.
**—Johann Wolfgang Von Goethe**

◆ What it lies in our power to do, it lies in our power not to do.
**—Aristotle**

***Whenever you find yourself on the side of the majority, it is time to pause and reflect.***
***—Mark Twain***

◆ If you limit your choices only to what seems possible or reasonable, you disconnect yourself from what you truly want, and all that is left is compromise.
**—Robert Fritz**

◆ Decide what you want, decide what you are willing to exchange for it. Establish your priorities and go to work.
**—H. L. Hunt**

◆ Pick battles big enough to matter, small enough to win.
**—Jonathan Kozol**

◆ Leadership is not mobilizing others to solve problems we already know how to solve, but helping them confront problems that have not yet been addressed successfully.
**—Michael Fullan**

◆ True genius resides in the capacity for evaluation of uncertain, hazardous, and conflicting information.
**—Winston Churchill**

◆ Some problems are so complex that you have to be highly intelligent and well informed just to be undecided about them.
**—Laurence J. Peter**

◆ If you are not confused, you're not paying attention.
**—Tom Peters**

◆ The whole problem with the world is that fools and fanatics are always so certain of themselves, but wiser people so full of doubts.
**—Bertrand Russell**

◆ He (she) who insists on seeing with perfect clearness before he (she) decides, never decides.
**—Henri Frédéric Amiel**

◆ In any moment of decision, the best thing you can do is the right thing, the next best thing is the wrong thing, and the worst thing you can do is nothing.
**—Theodore Roosevelt**

◆ Look at a day when you are supremely satisfied at the end. It's not a day when you lounge around doing nothing. It's when you've had everything to do, and you've done it.
**—Margaret Thatcher**

◆ Nothing will ever be attempted if all possible objections must first be overcome.
**—Samuel Johnson**

◆ As far as I can judge, not much good can be done without disturbing something or somebody.
**—Edward Blake**

◆ Take time to deliberate, but when the time for action arrives, stop thinking and go on in.
**—Andrew Jackson**

◆ What you always do before you make a decision is consult. The best public policy is made when you are listening to people who are going to be impacted. Then, once policy is determined, you call on them to help you sell it.
**—Elizabeth Dole**

◆ The leaders who work most effectively, it seems to me, never say "I." And that's not because they have trained themselves not to say "I." They don't think "I." They think "we"; they think "team." They understand their job is to make the team function. They accept responsibility and don't sidestep it, but "we" gets the credit .... This is what creates trust, what enables you to get the task done.
**—Peter Drucker**

***Deliberate with caution, but act with decision; and yield with graciousness, or oppose with firmness.***
***—Charles Caleb Colton***

◆ No matter how deep a study you make. What you really have to rely on is your own intuition and when it comes down to it, you really don't know what's going to happen until you do it.
**—Konosuke Matsushita**

◆ I make most decisions with my heart; my head simply looks after the administrative details.
**—Richard J. Needham**

◆ The heart makes better decisions than the head and it doesn't keep you awake at night doing it—just announces one day what the decision is.
**—Miles Morland**

◆ Trust your instinct to the end, though you can render no reason.
**—Ralph Waldo Emerson**

◆ Making a decision, even a bad one, is better than making no decision at all.
**—Jesse Aweida**

◆ If one does not decide when one should, one will suffer the consequences.
**—Chinese proverb**

◆ Making a wrong decision is understandable. Refusing to search continually for learning is not.
**—Philip Crosby**

◆ Organizations transform when they can establish mechanisms for learning in daily organizational life.
**—Michael Fullan**

◆ No matter how far you have gone on a wrong road, turn back.
**—Turkish proverb**

◆ There is a time when we must firmly choose the course we will follow, or the relentless drift of events will make the decision.
**—Herbert V. Prochnow**

◆ The person who does not make a choice, makes a choice.
**—Jewish proverb**

◆ I must have a prodigious quantity of mind; it takes me as much as a week sometimes to make it up.
**—Mark Twain**

◆ It is a common experience that a problem difficult at night is resolved in the morning after the committee of sleep has worked on it.
**—John Steinbeck**

◆ Decide not rashly. The decision made can never be recalled.
**—Longfellow**

◆ Avoid making irrevocable decisions while tired or hungry.
**—Robert Heinlein**

◆ I have learned, and it's been a hard lesson, that the more I take time to be still, sometimes introspective, or just to catch my breath, the better my next task is completed. I get better results when I make the pauses as meaningful as the battle.
**—Jonathon Lazear**

◆ The moment you commit and quit holding back, all sorts of unforeseen incidents, meetings and material assistance will rise up to help you. The simple act of commitment is a powerful magnet for help.
**—Napoleon Hill**

◆ We must be fully committed, but we must also be aware at the same time that we might possibly be wrong.
**—Rollo May**

◆ When you cannot make up your mind which of two evenly balanced courses of action you should take—choose the bolder one.
**—W. J. Slim**

◆ It is better to err on the side of daring than the side of caution.
**—Alvin Toffler**

◆ You will never stub your toe standing still. The faster you go, the more chance there is of stubbing your toe, but the more chance you have of getting somewhere.
**—Charles Kettering**

◆ Make up your mind to act decidedly and take the consequences. No good is ever done in this world by hesitation.
**—Thomas H. Huxley**

◆ Destiny is not a matter of chance, it is a matter of choice; it is not a thing to be waited for, it is a thing to be achieved.
**—William Jennings Bryan**

◆ I don't agonize over decisions as much these days. The criteria of what's important to me is clear.
**—John Cusack**

◆ Then and there I invented this rule for myself to be applied to every decision I might have to make in the future. I would sort out all the arguments and see which belonged to fear and which to creativeness, and other things being equal I would make the decision which had the larger number of creative reasons on its side. I think it must be a rule something like this that makes jonquils and crocuses come pushing through the cold mud.
**—Katherine Butler Hathaway**

◆ Two roads diverged in a wood, and I—I took the one less traveled by, and that has made all the difference.
**—Robert Frost**

◆ As you grow older you'll find the only things you regret are the things you didn't do.
**—Zachary Scott**

◆ The beginning is always today.
**—Mary Wollstoncraft**

***The manager asks how and when; the leader asks what and why.***
***—Warren Bennis***

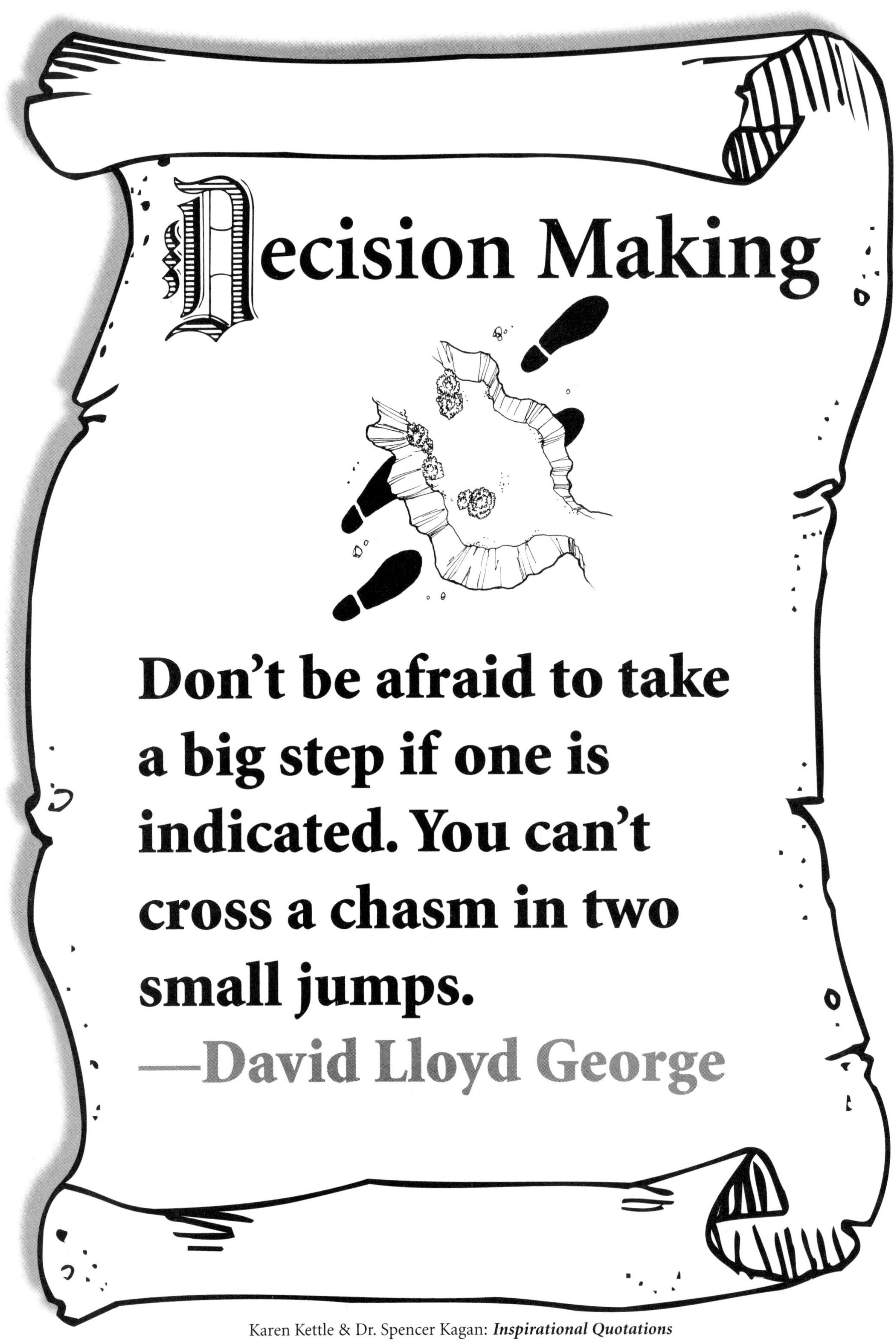

# Decision Making

**Don't be afraid to take a big step if one is indicated. You can't cross a chasm in two small jumps.**

**—David Lloyd George**

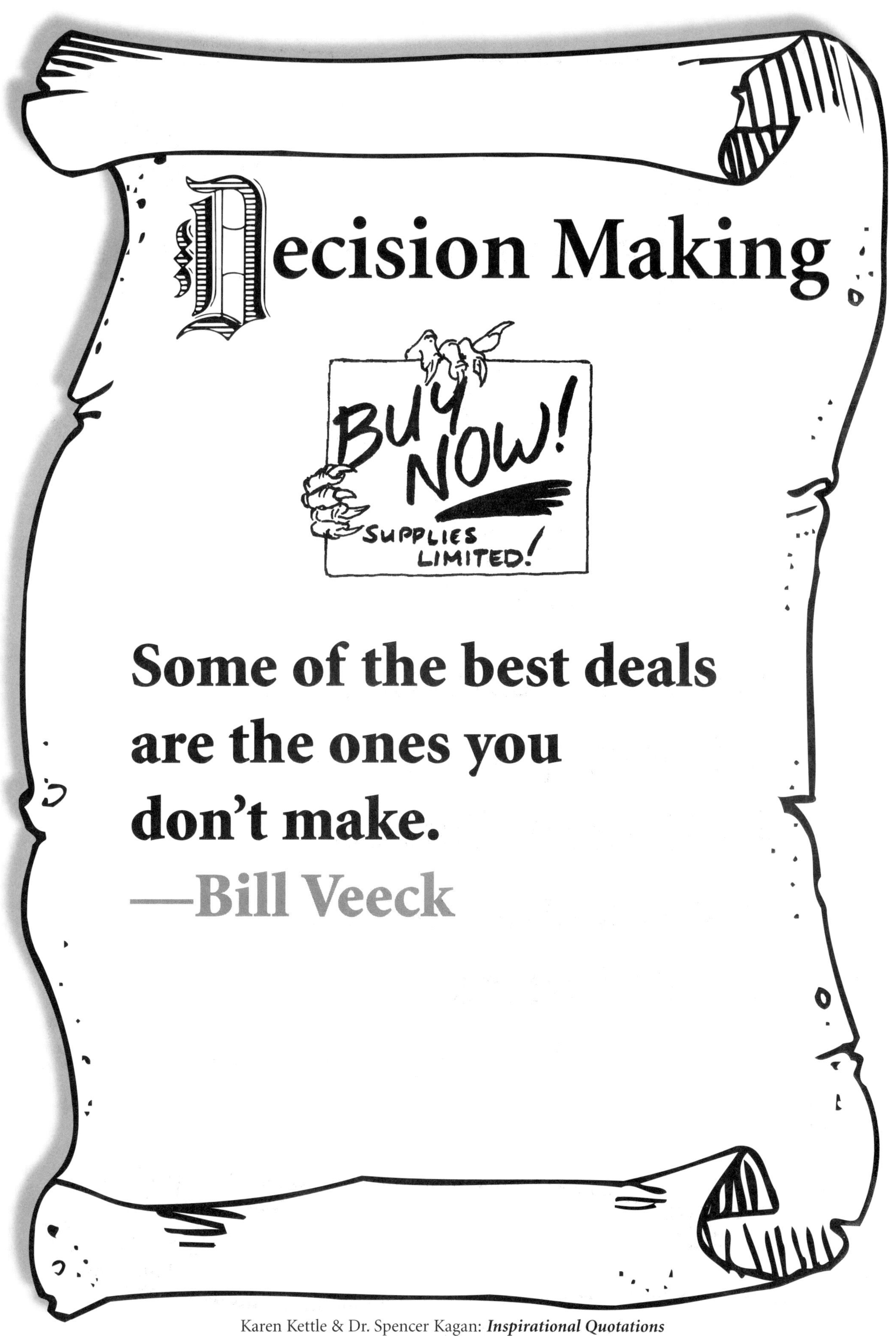

Decision Making
BUY NOW!
SUPPLIES LIMITED!
Some of the best deals are the ones you don't make.
—Bill Veeck

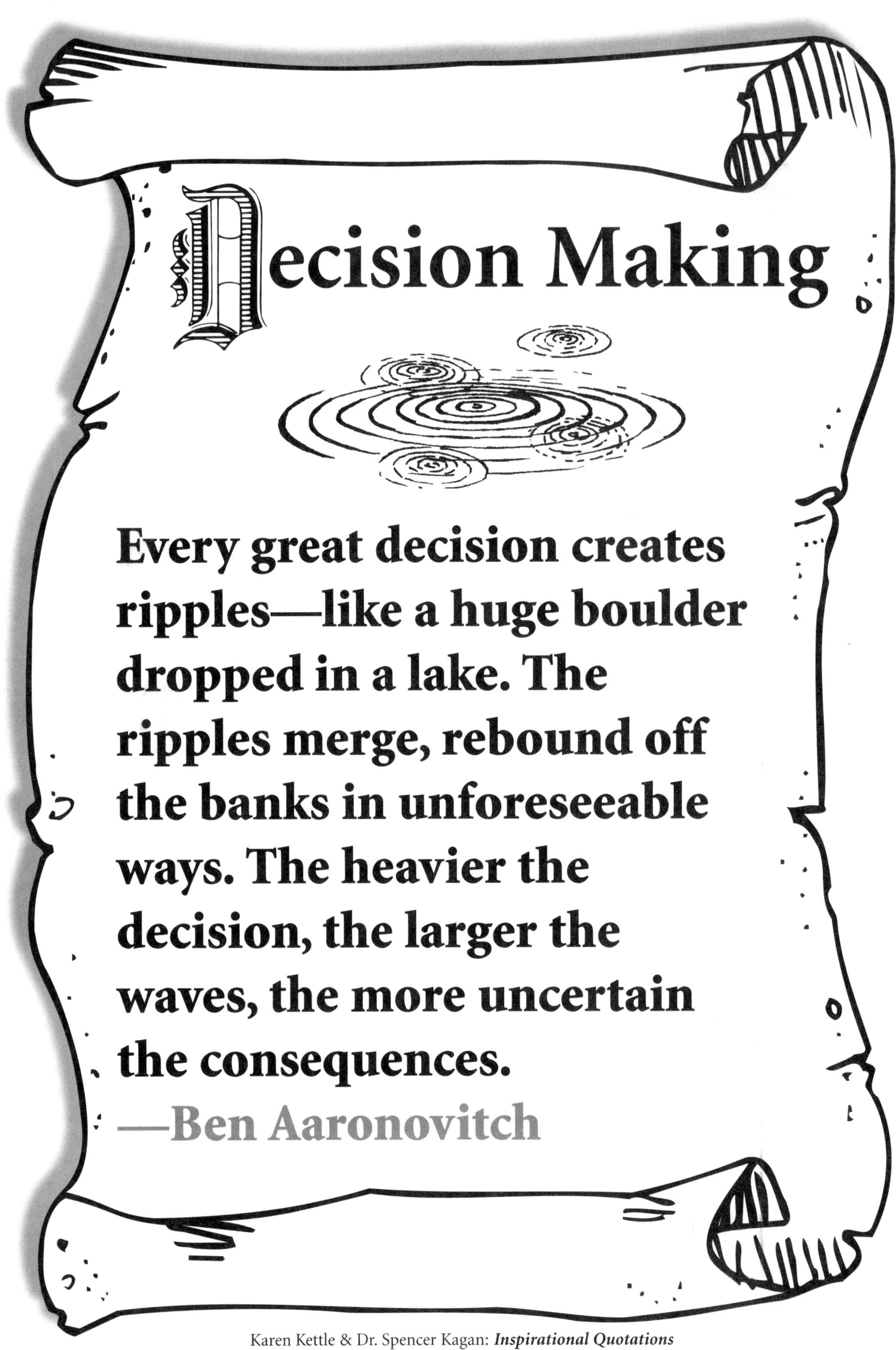

# Decision Making

**Every great decision creates ripples—like a huge boulder dropped in a lake. The ripples merge, rebound off the banks in unforeseeable ways. The heavier the decision, the larger the waves, the more uncertain the consequences.**

**—Ben Aaronovitch**

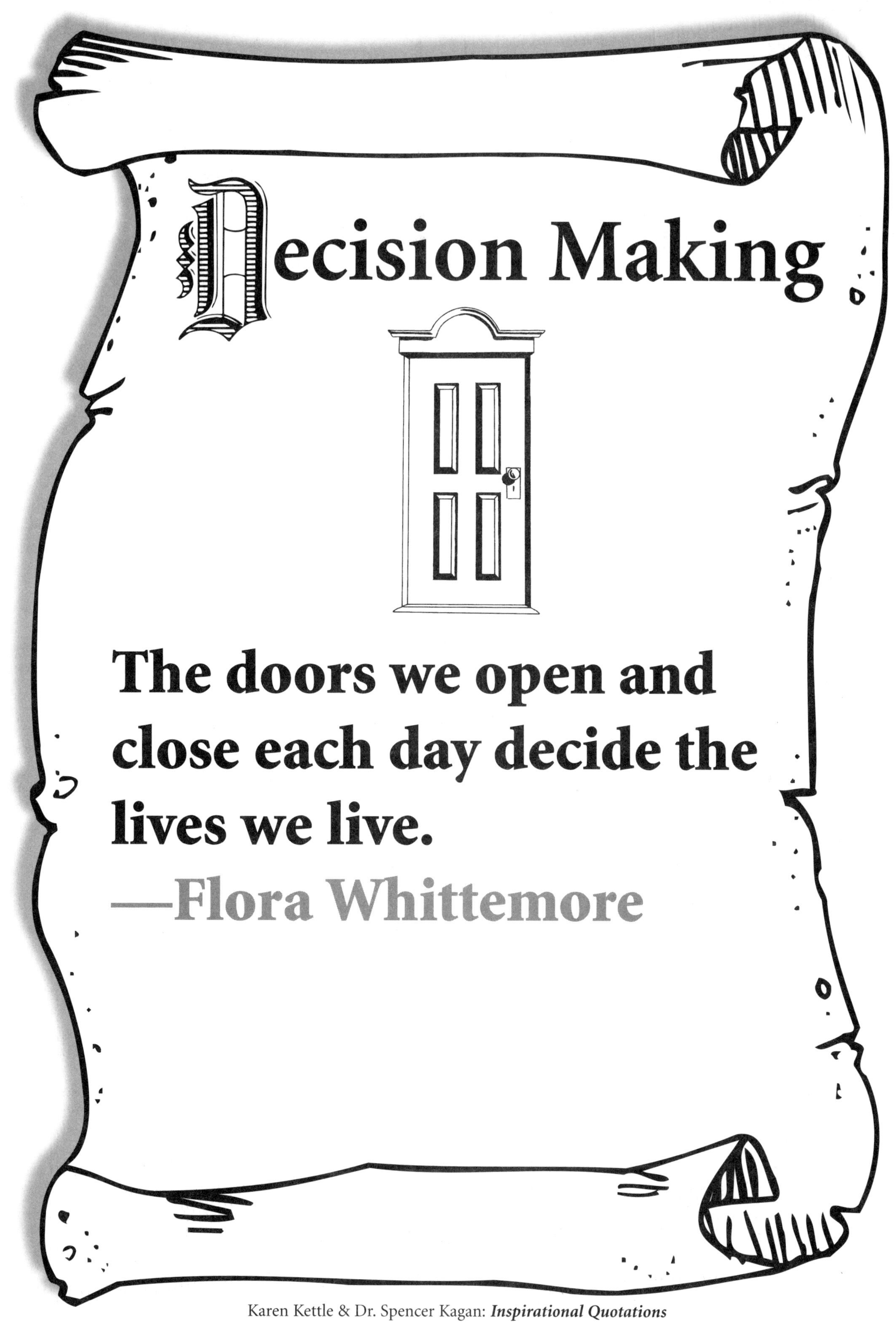
Decision Making
The doors we open and
close each day decide the
lives we live.
—Flora Whittemore

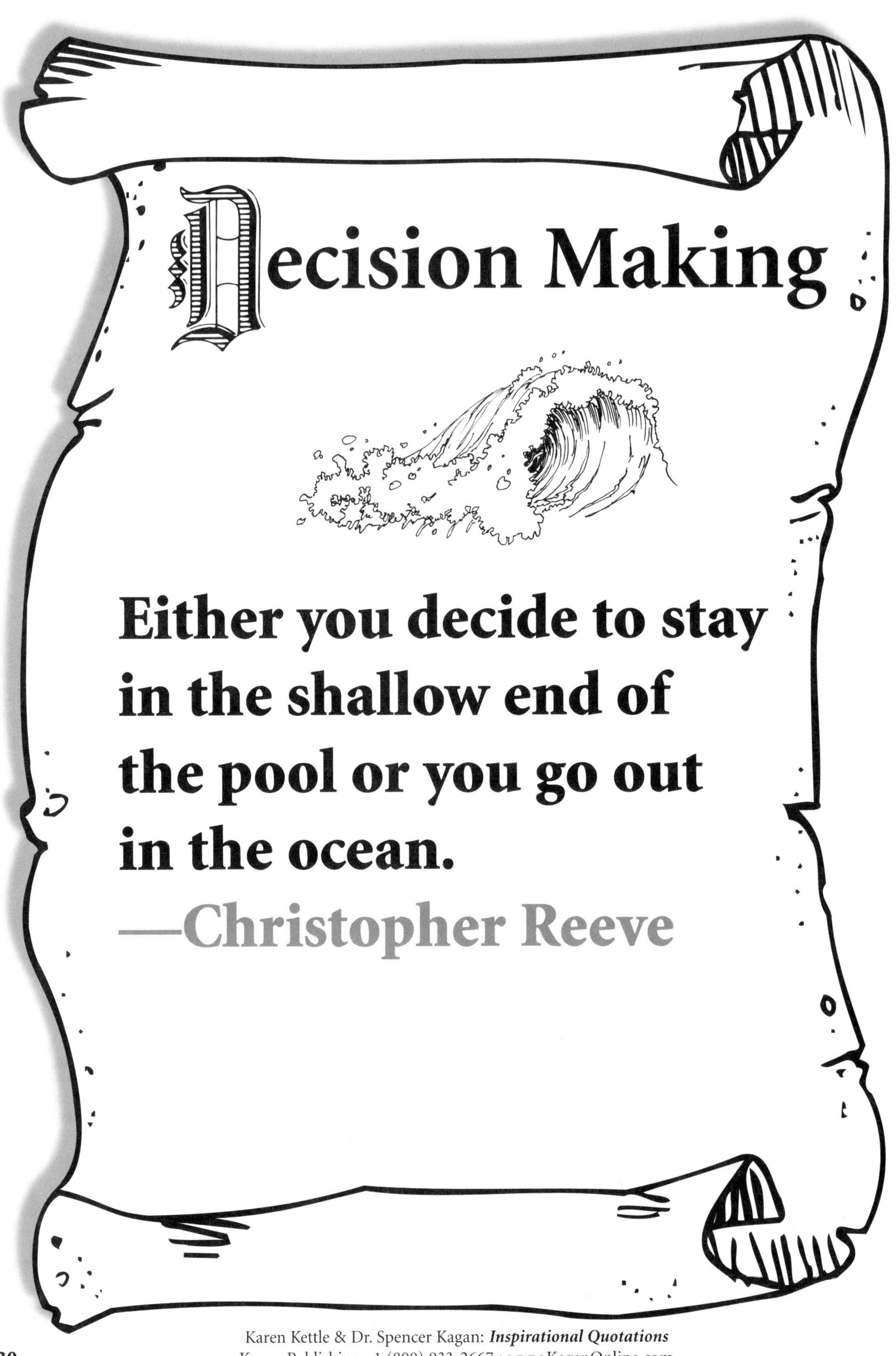

# Decision Making

**Either you decide to stay in the shallow end of the pool or you go out in the ocean.**

**—Christopher Reeve**



Karen Kettle & Dr. Spencer Kagan: ***Inspirational Quotations***
Kagan Publishing • 1 (800) 933-2667 • www.KaganOnline.com

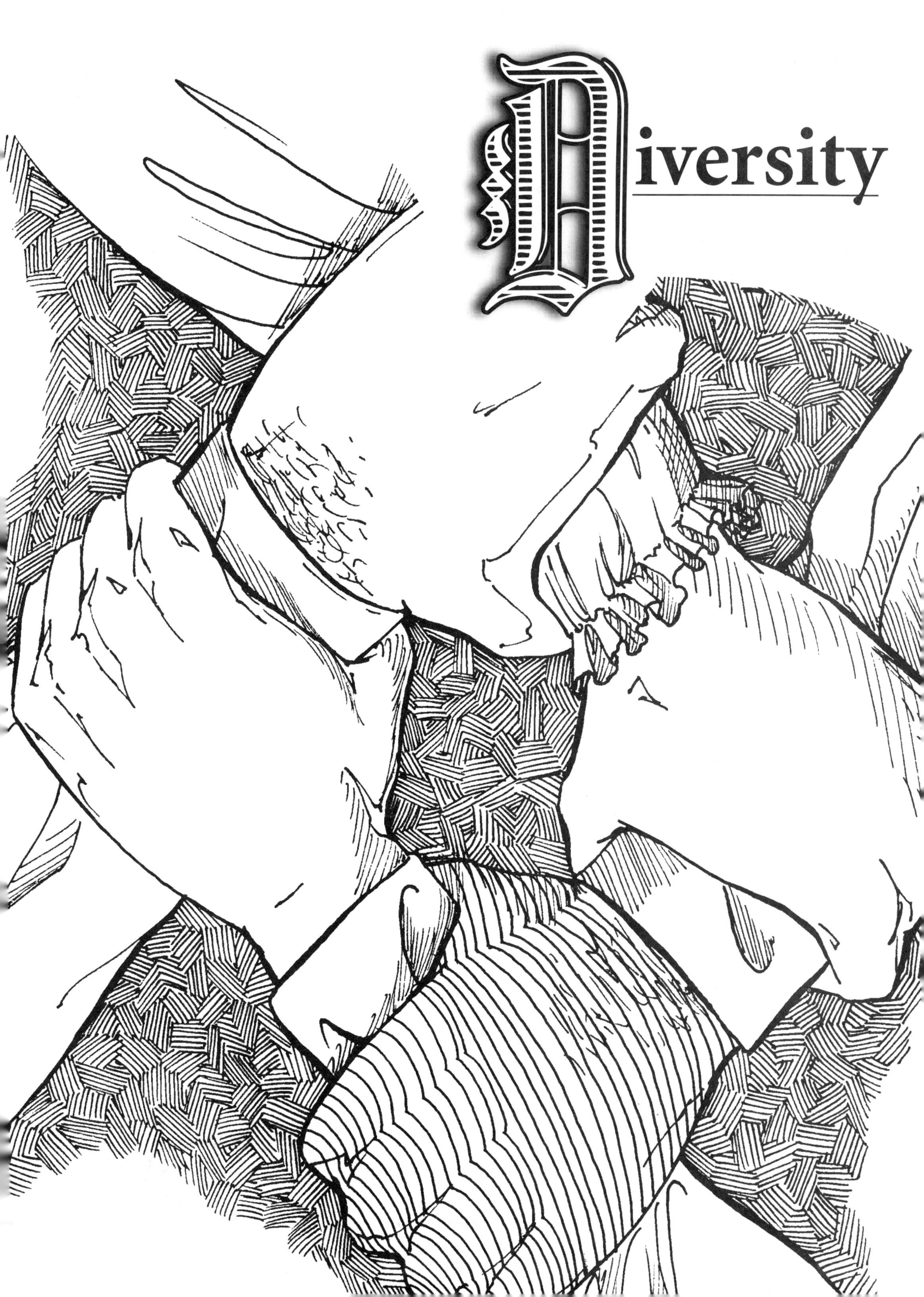
Diversity

# Diversity

*Celebrating the diversity of others opens the door for them to acknowledge and embrace our differences.*

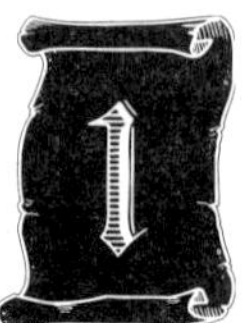

**We are more alike, my friend, than we are unalike.**

*—Maya Angelou*

### Reflection Questions

- *When was a time that you felt different and wanted to fit in?*
- *What feelings do all of the people in the world experience?*
- *Why do people care about each other?*

**I do not want my house to be walled in on all sides and my windows to be stuffed. I want the culture of all lands to be blown about my house as freely as possible. But I refuse to be blown off my feet by any.**

*—Mahatma Gandhi*

### Reflection Questions

- *How do you benefit from learning about other cultures?*
- *What customs do you celebrate as a family?*
- *Why is it important to be proud of your heritage?*

**We may have all come on different ships, but we're in the same boat now.**

*—Martin Luther King Jr.*

### Reflection Questions

- *When have you had the opportunity to get to know someone from a very different background?*
- *Why do you have to work a little harder to get to know someone who seems different?*
- *Why is that extra effort worthwhile?*

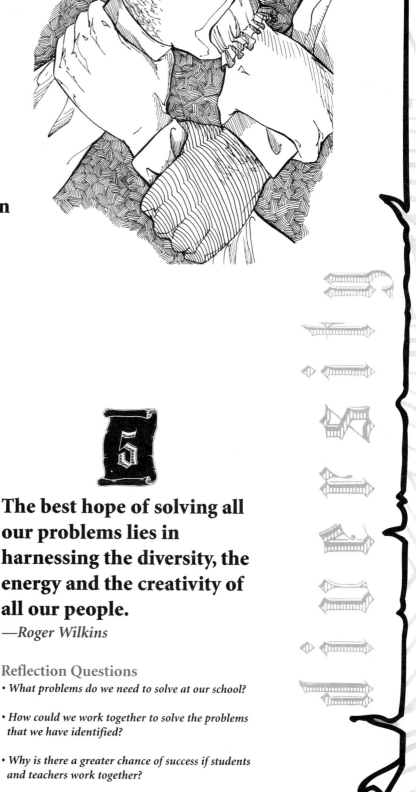

**No one can be the best at everything. But when we combine our talents, we can and will be the best at virtually anything.**

*—Dan Zadra*

Reflection Questions

- *What talents do you admire in others?*
- *What talents can you share with your team?*
- *Why are the best teams made up of people with different talents?*

5

**The best hope of solving all our problems lies in harnessing the diversity, the energy and the creativity of all our people.**

*—Roger Wilkins*

Reflection Questions

- *What problems do we need to solve at our school?*
- *How could we work together to solve the problems that we have identified?*
- *Why is there a greater chance of success if students and teachers work together?*

# Diversity

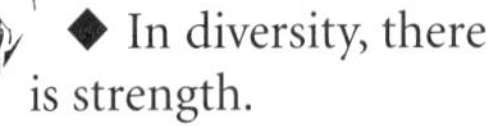

◆ In diversity, there is strength.
**—Maya Angelou**

◆ The price of the democratic way of life is a growing appreciation of people's differences, not merely as tolerable, but as the essence of a rich and rewarding human experience.
**—Jerome Nathanson**

◆ There never were, in the world, two opinions alike, no more than two hairs, or two grains; the most universal quality is diversity.
**—Michael de Montaigne**

◆ Civilization is a method of living and an attitude of equal respect for all people.
**—Jane Addams**

◆ If we are to achieve a richer culture, rich in contrasting values, we must recognize the whole gamut of human potentialities, and so weave a less arbitrary social fabric, one in which each diverse human gift will find a fitting place.
**—Margaret Mead**

◆ Culture is the widening of the mind and the spirit.
**—Jawaharlal Nehru**

◆ It takes a whole village to educate a child.
**—Nigerian proverb**

◆ We become not a melting pot but a beautiful mosaic. Different people, different beliefs, different yearnings, different hopes, different dreams.
**—Jimmy Carter**

◆ Everyone is ignorant, only on different subjects.
**—Will Rogers**

◆ What we have to do … is to find a way to celebrate our diversity and debate our differences without fracturing our communities.
**—Hillary Rodham Clinton**

◆ Fear makes strangers out of people who should be friends.
**—Shirley MacLaine**

◆ Fear of difference is fear of life itself.
**—Mary Parker Follett**

◆ Individuality of expression is the beginning and end of art.
**—Johann Wolfgang Von Goethe**

***We are, of course, a nation of differences. Those differences don't make us weak. They're the source of our strength.***
***—Jimmy Carter***

◆ Be who you are and say what you feel, because those who mind don't matter and those who matter don't mind.
**—Dr. Seuss**

◆ Every tale can be told a different way.
**—Greek proverb**

◆ Freedom to think—which means nothing unless it means freedom to think differently—can be society's most precious gift to itself. The first duty of a school is to defend and cherish it.
**—Arthur Bestor**

◆ People can collaborate to do the wrong things as well as the right things and by collaborating too closely they can miss danger signals and growth opportunities.
**—Michael Fullan**

◆ Where all think alike, no one thinks very much.
**—Walter Lippmann**

◆ When we lose the right to be different, we lose the privilege to go free.
**—Charles Evans Hughes**

◆ Especially now when views are becoming more polarized, we must work to understand each other across political, religious and national boundaries.
**—Jane Goodall**

◆ As long as the differences and diversities of mankind exist, democracy must allow for compromise, for accommodation, and for recognition of differences.
**—Eugene McCarthy**

◆ Human diversity makes tolerance more than a virtue; it makes it a requirement for survival.
**—Rene Dubos**

◆ Don't tolerate me as different. Accept me as part of the spectrum of normalcy.
**—Ann Northrop**

◆ Mankind will endure when the world appreciates the logic of diversity.
**—Indira Gandhi**

◆ Diversity: the art of thinking independently together.
**—Malcolm Forbes**

◆ If we want a beloved community, we must stand for justice, have recognition for difference without attaching difference to privilege.
**—bell hooks**

◆ There is no such thing as a weird human being. It's just that some people require more understanding than others do.
**—Tom Robbins**

◆ One of the great strengths of caring as an ethic is that it does not assume that all students should be treated by some impartial standard of fairness. Some students need more attention than others.
**—Nel Noddings**

◆ The essence of our effort to see that every child has a chance must be to assure each an equal opportunity, not to become equal, but to become different—to realize whatever unique potential of body, mind and spirit he or she possesses.
**—John Fischer**

***You are one of a kind; therefore, no one can really predict to what heights you might soar. Even you will not know until you spread your wings.***
***—Gil Atkinson***

◆ Remember that you are unique. If that is not fulfilled, then something wonderful has been lost.
**—Martha Graham**

◆ There are billions of people in the world, and every one of them is special. No one else in the world is like you.
**—Muhammad Ali**

◆ You are a child of the universe, no less than the trees and the stars; you have a right to be here. And whether or not it is clear to you, no doubt the universe is unfolding as it should.
**—Max Ehrmann**

◆ Do not compare yourself with others, for you are a unique and wonderful creation. Make your own beautiful footprints in the snow.
**—Barbara Kimball**

◆ Just imagine how boring life would be if we were all the same. My idea of a perfect world is one in which we really appreciated each other's differences: Short, tall; Democrat, Republican; black, white; gay, straight—a world in which all of us are equal, but definitely not the same.
**—Barbara Streisand**

◆ I feel we are all islands … in a common sea.
**—Anne Morrow Lindbergh**

◆ Unity in variety is the plan of the universe.
**—Swami Vivekananda**

◆ We all live with the objective of being happy; our lives are all different and yet the same.
**—Anne Frank**

◆ All human cultures have infinitely more in common … hidden somewhere deep in their sources and foundations.
**—Vaclav Havel**

◆ If you approach each new person you meet in a spirit of adventure you will find yourself endlessly fascinated by the new channels of thought and experience and personality that you encounter.
**—Eleanor Roosevelt**

Diversity
We are more alike, my
friend, than we
are unalike.
—Maya Angelou

Karen Kettle & Dr. Spencer Kagan: *Inspirational Quotations*
Kagan Publishing • 1 (800) 933-2667 • www.KaganOnline.com

# Diversity

**I do not want my house to be walled in on all sides and my windows to be stuffed. I want the culture of all lands to be blown about my house as freely as possible. But I refuse to be blown off my feet by any.**

**—Mahatma Gandhi**

Diversity
We may have all come on different ships, but we're in the same boat now.
—Martin Luther King Jr.

Diversity
No one can be the best at everything. But when we combine our talents, we can and will be the best at virtually anything.
—Dan Zadra

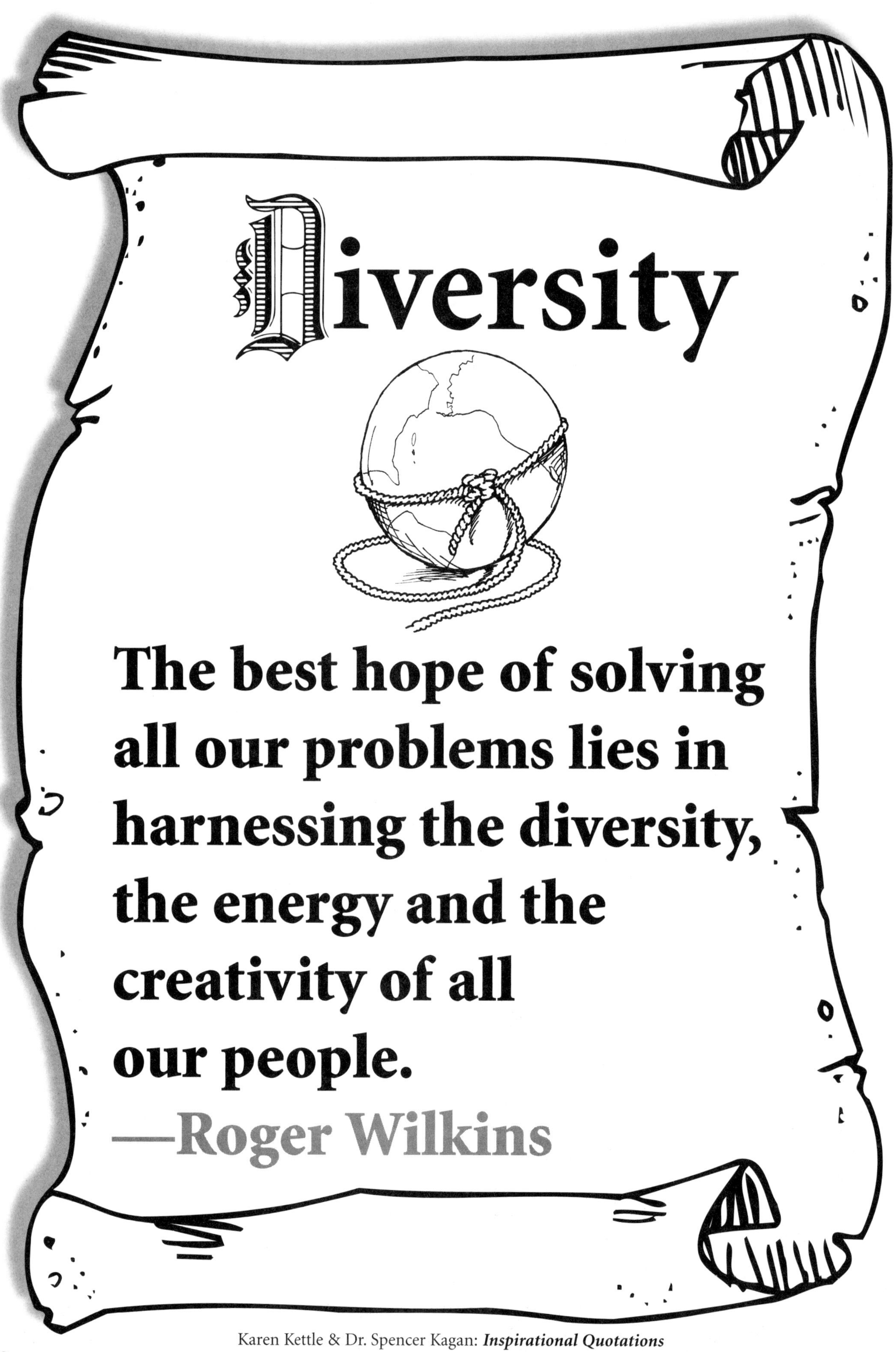
Diversity
The best hope of solving all our problems lies in harnessing the diversity, the energy and the creativity of all our people.
—Roger Wilkins

# Education

# Education

*Education is a gift that society gives its children.*

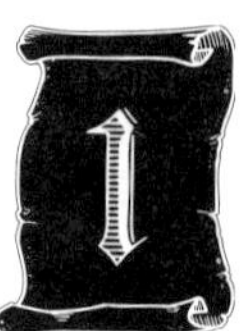

**Our fundamental task as human beings is to seek out connections—to exercise our imaginations. It follows, then, that the basic task of education is the care and feeding of the imagination.**

*—Katherine Paterson*

Reflection Questions

- *Who feeds your imagination?*
- *What exercises your imagination the most—movies, books, conversation, music, nature, quiet time, etc.?*
- *How regularly do you give your imagination a workout? Is it in good shape?*

**Education is not preparation for life, education is life itself.**

*—John Dewey*

Reflection Questions

- *What life lessons do you learn at school?*
- *How does school life help you understand the world?*
- *What are the ups and downs of life at school?*

**When I got my library card, that's when my life began.**

*—Rita Mae Brown*

Reflection Questions

- *What was the first book about that you remember reading on your own?*
- *What would happen if you could step into your favorite story?*
- *How do books educate and entertain us?*

**Curiosity is the very basis of education and if you tell me that curiosity killed the cat, I say only the cat died nobly.**

*—Arnold Edinborough*

Reflection Questions

- *What is curiosity? What does it feel like?*
- *What are you curious about?*
- *Can curiosity be dangerous? Explain.*

**All education springs from some image of the future. If the image of the future held by a society is grossly inaccurate, its education system will betray its youth.**

*—Alvin Toffler*

Reflection Questions

- *If a time machine took you 100 years into the future, what would you see?*
- *What will students be learning in school 100 years from now?*
- *What is the purpose of school?*

# Education

◆ Education is the power to think clearly, the power to act well in the world's work, and the power to appreciate life.
**—Brigham Young**

◆ Education is the point at which we decide whether we love the world enough to assume responsibility for it.
**—Hannah Arendt**

◆ Education is the mother of leadership.
**—Wendell L. Wilkie**

◆ If your plan is for one year, plant rice; if your plan is for ten years, plant trees; if your plan is for 100 years, educate children.
**—Confucius**

◆ For me, education means to inspire people to live more abundantly, to learn to begin with life as they find it and make it better.
**—Carter G. Woodson**

◆ Upon the subject of education, I can only say that I view it as the most important subject which we as a people may be engaged in.
**—Abraham Lincoln**

◆ A good education is the next best thing to a pushy mother.
**—Charles M. Schulz**

◆ Education is all a matter of building bridges.
**—Ralph Ellison**

◆ Education is for improving the lives of others and for leaving your community and world better than you found it.
**—Marian Wright Edelman**

***No one has yet fully realized the wealth of sympathy, kindness and generosity hidden in the soul of a child. The effort of every true education should be to unlock that treasure.***
***—Emma Goldman***

◆ A good school is the price of peace in the community.
**—Ursula Franklin**

◆ Education is what survives when what has been learnt has been forgotten.
**—B. F. Skinner**

◆ Education is the ability to listen to almost anything without losing your temper or your self-confidence.
**—Robert Frost**

◆ It is the mark of an educated mind to entertain a thought without accepting it.
**—Aristotle**

◆ Education is light, lack of it darkness.
**—Russian proverb**

◆ Education is not the filling of the pail, but the lighting of a fire.
**—William Butler Yeats**

◆ Let us think of education as the means of developing our greatest abilities, because in each of us there is a private hope and dream which, fulfilled, can be translated into benefit for everyone and greater strength for our nation.
**—John F. Kennedy**

◆ I entered the classroom with the conviction that it was crucial for me and every other student to be an active participant, not a passive consumer … education as the practice of freedom … education that connects the will to know with the will to become. Learning is a place where paradise can be created.
**—bell hooks**

◆ Education in the broadest of truest sense, will make an individual seek to help all people, regardless of race, regardless of color, regardless of condition.
**—George Washington Carver**

◆ Poverty must not be a bar to learning and learning must offer an escape from poverty.
**—Lyndon B. Johnson**

◆ All of us do not have equal talent, but all of us should have an equal opportunity to develop our talents.
**—John F. Kennedy**

◆ Education is our passport to the future, for tomorrow belongs to the people who prepare for it today.
**—Malcolm X**

◆ Education is … hanging around until you've caught on.
**—Robert Frost**

◆ Education is a lifelong process of which schooling is only a small but necessary part. As long as one remains alive and healthy, learning can go on—and should.
**—Mortimer J. Adler**

◆ Genius without education is like silver in the mine.
**—Benjamin Franklin**

◆ The only person who is educated is the one who has learned how to learn and change.
**—Carl Rogers**

◆ A liberally educated person meets new ideas with curiosity and fascination. An illiberally educated person meets new ideas with fear.
**—James B. Stockdale**

◆ An education isn't how much you have committed to memory, or even how much you know. It's being able to differentiate between what you do know and what you don't.
**—Anatole France**

◆ Sixty years ago I knew everything; now I know nothing; education is a progressive discovery of our own ignorance.
**—Will Durant**

◆ Not to know is bad; not to wish to know is worse.
**—African proverb**

***Schools should be the most beautiful place in every town and village … so beautiful that the punishment for undutiful children should be to be barred from going to school the following day.***
***—Oscar Wilde***

◆ Among the many purposes of schooling, four stand out to us as having special moral value; to love and care, to serve, to empower and, of course to learn.
**—Andy Hargreaves and Michael Fullan**

◆ Education is not merely a means for earning a living or an instrument for the acquisition of wealth. It is an initiation into life of spirit, a training of the human soul in the pursuit of truth and the practice of virtue.
**—Vijaya Lakshmi Pandit**

◆ Education is simply the soul of a society as it passes from one generation to another.
**—G. K. Chesterton**

◆ Most people are mirrors, reflecting the moods and emotions of the times; few are windows, bringing light to bear on the dark corners where troubles fester. The whole purpose of education is to turn mirrors into windows.
**—Sydney J. Harris**

◆ The education and empowerment of women throughout the world cannot fail to result in a more caring, tolerant, just and peaceful life for all.
**—Aung San Suu Kyi**

◆ The highest result of education is tolerance.
**—Helen Keller**

◆ It has always seemed strange to me that in our endless discussions about education so little stress is laid on the pleasure of becoming an educated person, the enormous interest it adds to life. To be able to be caught up into the world of thought—that is to be educated.
**—Edith Hamilton**

◆ The proper aim of education is to promote significant learning. Significant learning entails development. Development means successively asking broader and deeper questions of the relationship between oneself and the world. This is as true for first graders as graduate students, for fledging artists and graying accountants.
**—Laurent A. Daloz**

# Education

◆ Each second we live in a new and unique moment of the universe, a moment that never was before and will never be again. And what do we teach our children in school? We teach them that two and two make four, and that Paris is the Capitol of France. When will we also teach them what they are? You should say to each of them: "Do you know what you are? You are unique. In all the world there is no other child exactly like you. In the millions of years that have passed there has never been a child like you. And look at your body—what a wonder it is! Your legs, your arms, your cunning fingers, the way you move! You may be a Shakespeare, a Michelangelo, a Beethoven. You have the capacity for anything. Yes, you are a marvel."
**—Pablo Casals**

***If you think education is expensive, try ignorance.***
***—Derek Bok***

◆ The conception of education as a social process and function has no definite meaning until we define the kind of society we have in mind.
**—John Dewey**

◆ The educational system is regarded simultaneously as the nation's scapegoat and savior.
**—Judith Groch**

◆ If there is anything education does not lack today, it is critics.
**—Nathan M. Pusey**

◆ The greatest crime that society commits is that of wasting money which it should use for children on things that will destroy them and society as well.
**—Maria Montessori**

◆ Jails and prisons are the complement of schools: so many less as you have of the latter, so many more must you have of the former.
**—Horace Mann**

◆ All of life is a constant education.
**—Eleanor Roosevelt**

◆ Education is a great shield against experience. It offers so much, ready made and from the best shops, that there's a temptation to miss your own life in pursuing the lives of your betters. It makes you wise in some ways, but it can make you a blindfolded fool in others.
**—Robertson Davies**

◆ I've never let my schooling interfere with my education.
**—Mark Twain**

◆ Few citizens really know what's going on in their schools. They settle for the familiar and ignore the substance.
**—Theodore R. Sizer**

◆ Education strays from reality when it divides its knowledge into separate compartments without due regard to the connection between them.
**—Frances Wosmek**

◆ Knowledge which is acquired under compulsion has no hold on the mind. Therefore do not use compulsion, but let early education be rather a sort of amusement; this will better enable you to find out the natural bent of the child.
**—Plato**

◆ To the mind, curiosity is its own reward. And the by-product of perpetual curiosity is wisdom.
**—Chip R. Bell**

◆ It is, in fact, nothing short of a miracle that the modern methods of instruction have not yet entirely strangled the holy curiosity of inquiry.
**—Albert Einstein**

◆ Education happens when hope exceeds expectation.
**—Andy Hargreaves and Michael Fullan**

◆ The secret of education is respecting the pupil.
**—Ralph Waldo Emerson**

◆ Those who trust us educate us.
**—George Eliot**

◆ Nine tenths of education is encouragement.
**—Anatole France**

◆ Praise youth and it will prosper.
**—Irish proverb**

◆ We cannot always build the future for our youth, but we can build our youth for the future.
**—Franklin D. Roosevelt**

◆ The essence of education is not to stuff you with facts but to help you discover your uniqueness, to teach you how to develop it, and then to show you how to give it away.
**—Leo Buscaglia**

◆ Since there is no single set of abilities running throughout human nature, there is no single curriculum which all should undergo. Rather, the schools should teach everything that anyone is interested in learning.
**—John Dewey**

***Why should society feel responsible only for the education of children, and not for the education of all adults of every age?***
***—Erich Fromm***

◆ Educational practices should be gauged not only by the skills and knowledge they impart for present use but also by what they do to children's beliefs about their capabilities, which affects how they approach the future. Students who develop a strong sense of self-efficacy are well equipped to educate themselves when they have to rely on their own initiative.
**—Albert Bandura**

◆ Education is discovering the brain, and that's about the best news there could be … anyone who does not have a thorough holistic grasp of the brain's architecture, purposes, and main ways of operating is as far behind the times as an automobile designer without a full understanding of engines.
**—Leslie Hart**

◆ In the wider sense, what I want to advocate is not to make education shorter, but to make it much longer —indeed to make it last as long as life itself.
**—Stephen Leacock**

◆ The purpose of learning is growth, and our minds, unlike our bodies, can continue growing as we continue to live.
**—Mortimer J. Adler**

◆ Human history becomes more and more a race between education and catastrophe.
**—H. G. Wells**

◆ Establishing lasting peace is the work of education; all politics can do is keep us out of war.
**—Maria Montessori**

◆ Remember that our nation's first great leaders were also our first great scholars.
**—John F. Kennedy**

◆ It is the responsibility of intellectuals to speak the truth and expose lies.
**—Noam Chomsky**

◆ Education makes a people easy to lead, but difficult to drive; easy to govern but impossible to enslave.
**—Lord Brougham**

◆ Liberty cannot be preserved without general knowledge among the people.
**—John Adams**

◆ Education is essential to change, for education creates both new wants and the ability to satisfy them.
**—Henry Steele Commager**

◆ Education is the most powerful weapon which you can use to change the world.
**—Nelson Mandela**

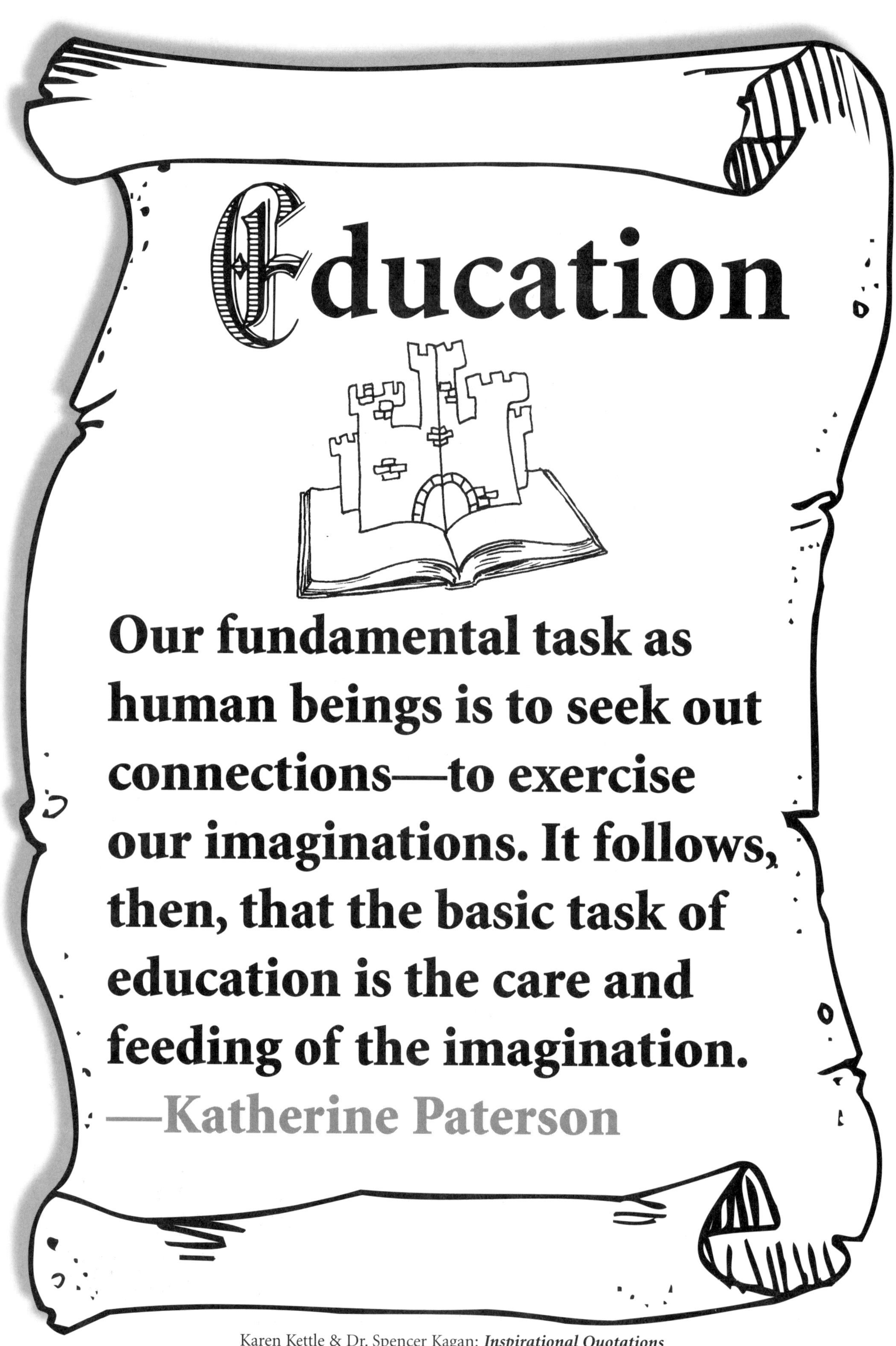

# Education

Our fundamental task as human beings is to seek out connections—to exercise our imaginations. It follows, then, that the basic task of education is the care and feeding of the imagination.

—Katherine Paterson

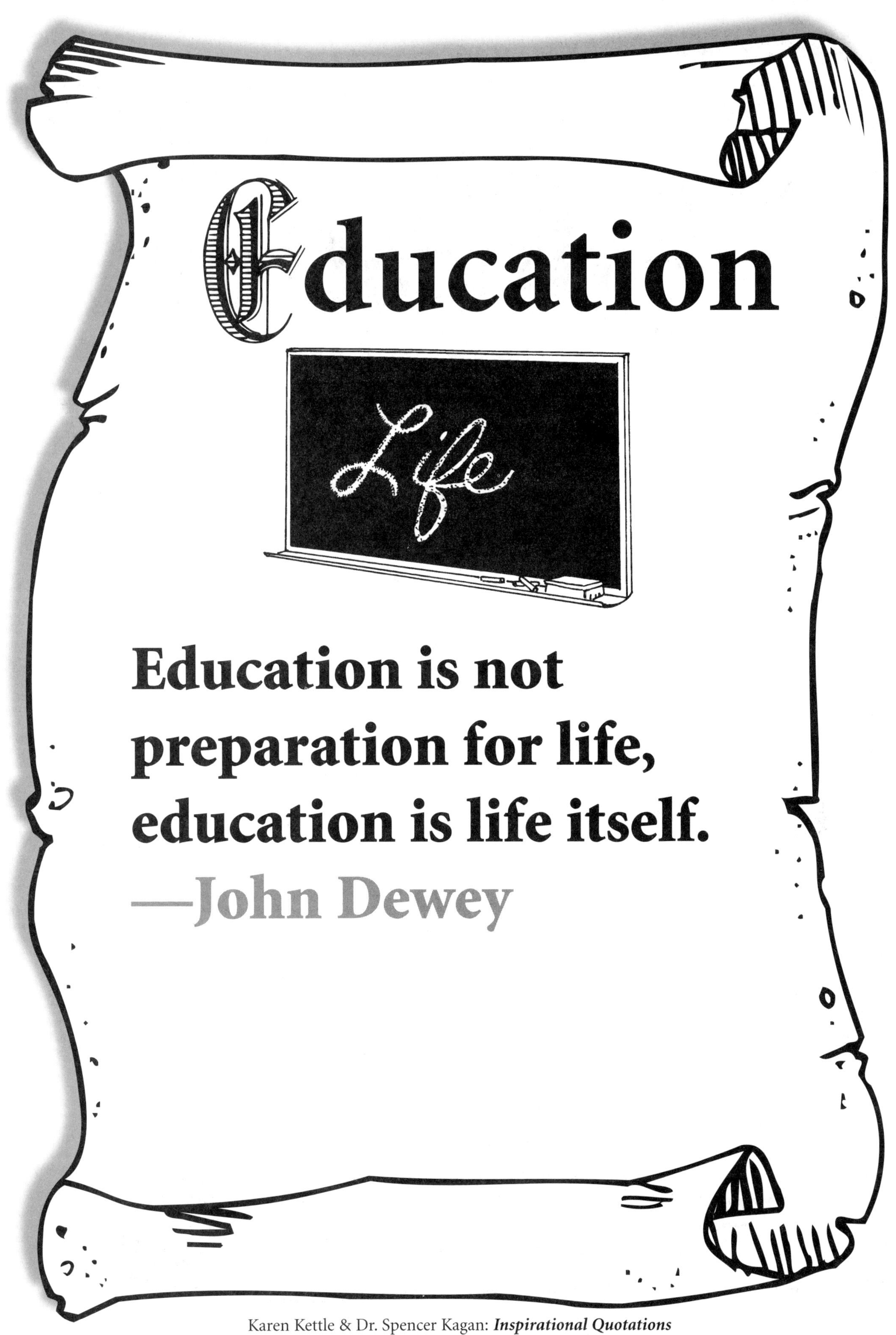
Education
Life
Education is not preparation for life, education is life itself.
—John Dewey

Education
When I got my library card, that's when my life began.
—Rita Mae Brown

Karen Kettle & Dr. Spencer Kagan: *Inspirational Quotations*
Kagan Publishing • 1 (800) 933-2667 • www.KaganOnline.com

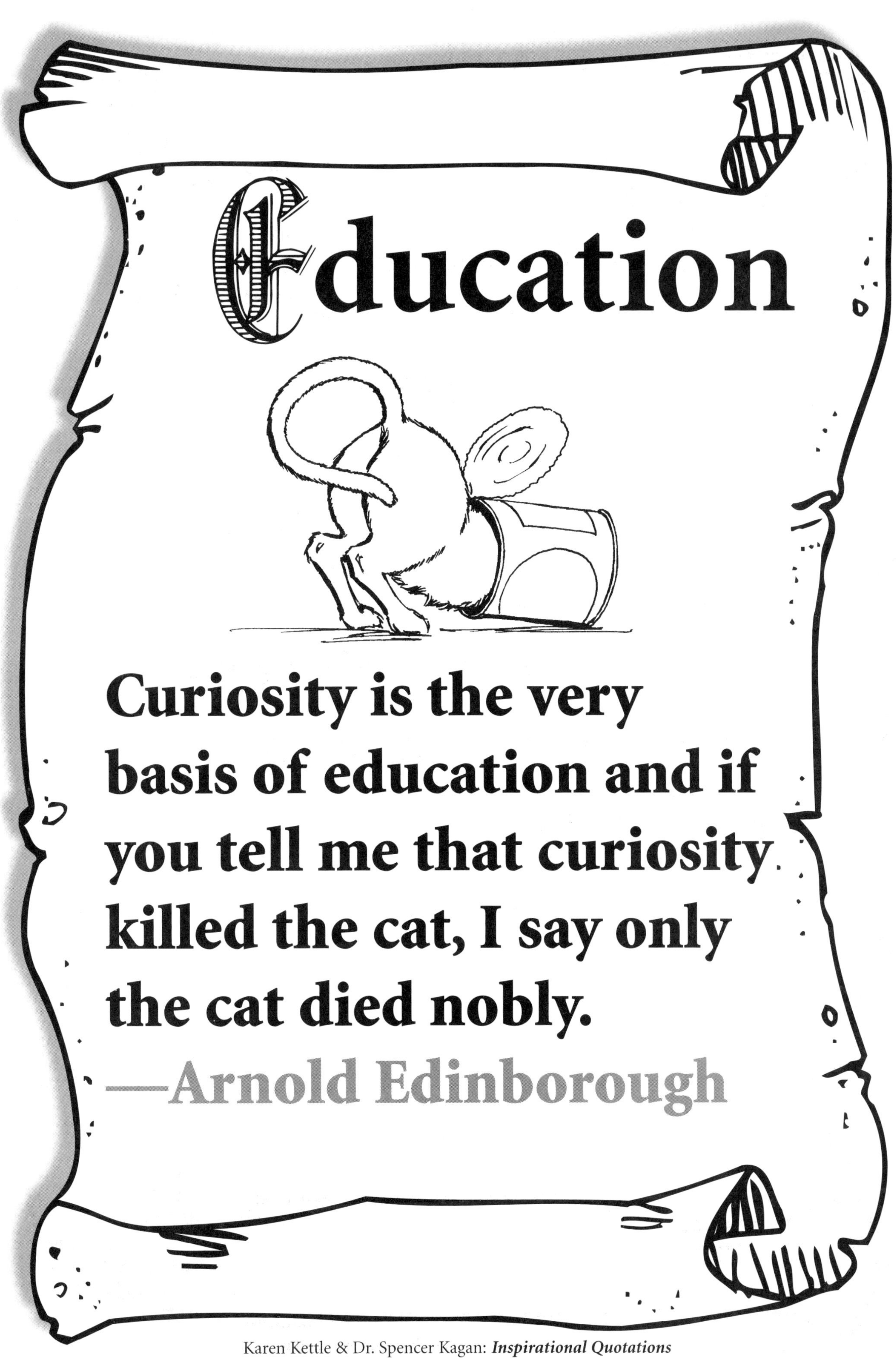
Education

Curiosity is the very basis of education and if you tell me that curiosity killed the cat, I say only the cat died nobly.
—Arnold Edinborough

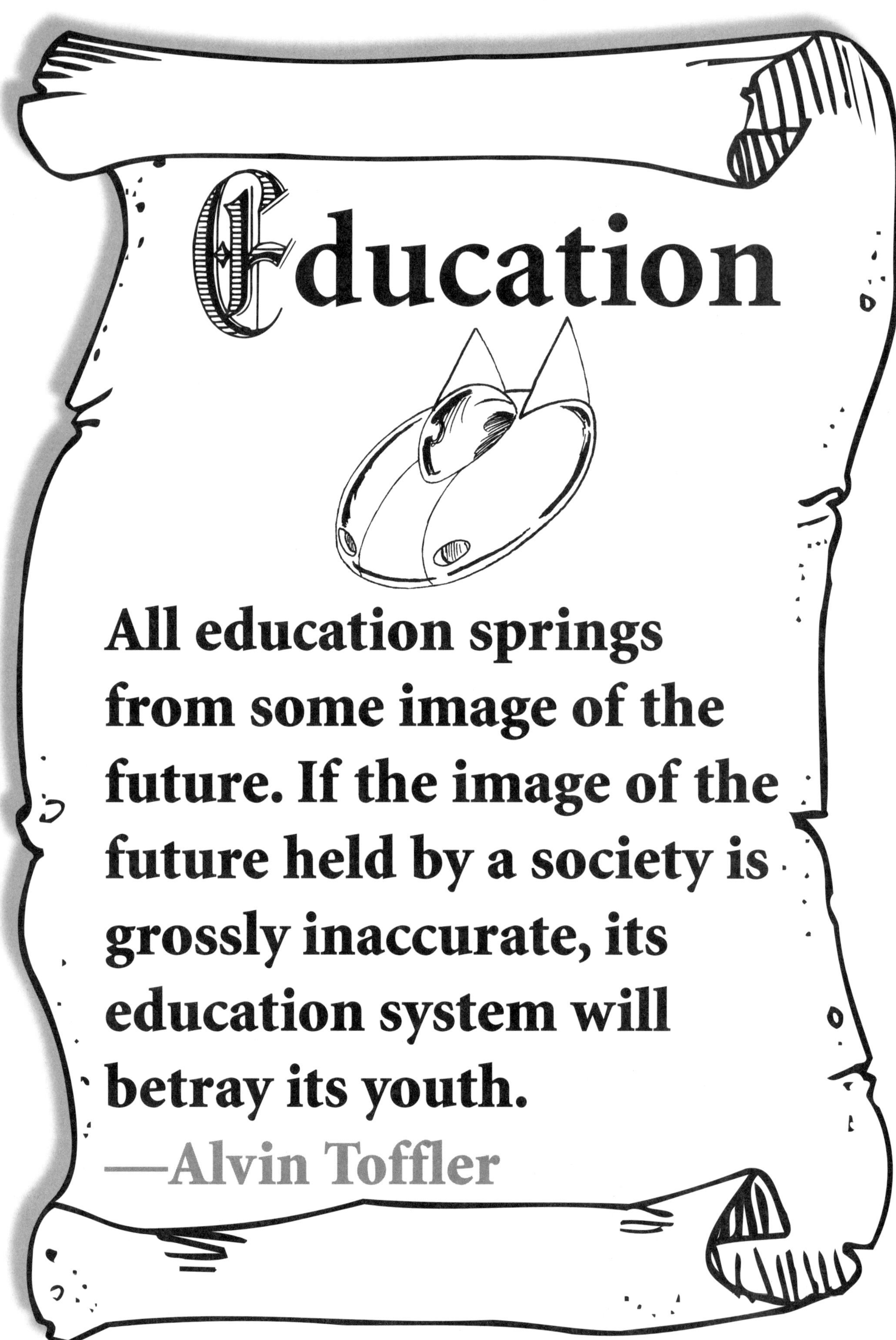

# Education

All education springs from some image of the future. If the image of the future held by a society is grossly inaccurate, its education system will betray its youth.

—Alvin Toffler



Karen Kettle & Dr. Spencer Kagan: *Inspirational Quotations*
Kagan Publishing • 1 (800) 933-2667 • www.KaganOnline.com

Emotional Intelligence

# Emotional Intelligence

*To develop the emotional mind, we must nurture self, awareness, management of feelings, empathy, and hope.*

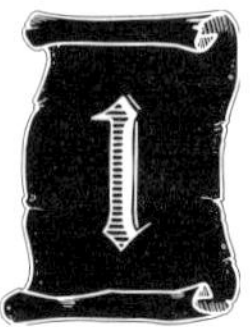

**Hope is the thing with feathers that perches in the soul and sings the tune without the words, and never stops at all ....**

*—Emily Dickinson*

Reflection Questions

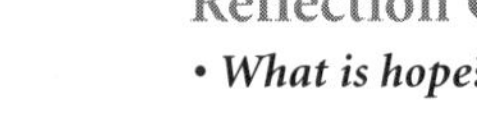

- *What is hope?*
- *How is a hope different than a dream or a goal?*
- *What does hope make possible?*

**If someone listens, or stretches out a hand, or whispers a kind word of encouragement, or attempts to understand, extraordinary things begin to happen.**

*—Loretta Girzartis*

Reflection Questions

- *How do you know when someone else is having a bad day?*
- *What do you do to encourage other people?*
- *What special kindness has made a difference in your life?*

**If you think you are too small to be effective, you have never been in bed with a mosquito.**

*—Betty Reese*

Reflection Questions

- *How does a mosquito keep you awake?*
- *Why do you have to be persistent to be effective?*
- *In what ways can small persistent efforts improve the world?*

## 4

**Patting the back knocks a chip off the shoulder.**

*—Muriel Solomon*

### Reflection Questions

- *Why do some people develop a chip on their shoulder?*
- *Why does patting someone on the back help them trust you?*
- *How many different ways can you think of to say, "Good for You"?*

**Some emotions don't make a lot of noise. It's hard to hear pride. Caring is real faint—like a heartbeat. And pure love—why some days it's so quiet, you don't even know it's there.**

*—Erma Bombeck*

### Reflection Questions

- *How do you know someone loves you?*
- *How do you let your friends know that you care about them?*
- *Why is it sometimes difficult to express emotion?*

# Emotional Intelligence

◆ You should be aware of the seeds of feelings in your heart and take care of them. And try to express the feeling sincerely and honestly.
—**Iizuka Shokansai**

◆ When you feel things deeply and you think about things a lot and you think about how you feel, you learn a lot about yourself.
—**Fiona Apple**

◆ By going along with feelings, you unify your emotional, mental and bodily states. When you try to fight or deny them, you divorce yourself from the reality of your being.
—**Jane Roberts**

◆ Bravery is about a willingness to show emotional need.
—**Richard Gere**

◆ There can be no transforming of darkness into light and of apathy into movement without emotion.
—**Carl Jung**

◆ Knowledge of the means to express our emotion is essential … and is acquired only after a very long experience.
—**Paul Cezanne**

◆ The longer I live, the less I trust ideas, the more I trust emotions.
—**Louis Malle**

◆ Better to be without logic than without feeling.
—**Charlotte Bronte**

◆ The wide discrepancy between reason and feeling may be unreal; it is not improbable that intellect is a high form of feeling—a specialized, intensive feeling about intuitions.
—**Susanna K. Langer**

◆ Never apologize for showing feeling. When you do so, you apologize for truth.
—**Benjamin Disraeli**

◆ We either make ourselves happy or miserable. The amount of work is the same.
—**Carlos Castaneda**

◆ We create our own feelings by the thoughts we choose to think. We have the ability to make different choices and create different experiences.
—**Louise Hay**

***Feelings are everywhere—be gentle.***
***—J. Masai***

◆ I try to see the dark and light in everything. This is my way of comforting myself when I am dealing with those emotions.
—**Francesca Lia Block**

◆ What others say and do may be the stimulus, but never the cause of our feelings. We see that our feelings result from how we choose to receive what others say and do, as well as our particular needs and expectations in that moment.
—**Marshall B. Rosenberg**

◆ Laughter and tears are both responses to frustration and exhaustion …. I myself prefer to laugh, since there is less cleaning up to do afterward.
—**Kurt Vonnegut Jr.**

◆ Feelings are untidy.
—**Esther Hautzig**

◆ You cannot make yourself feel something you do not feel, but you can make yourself do right in spite of your feelings.
—**Pearl S. Buck**

◆ There is no passion that so shakes the clarity of our judgment as anger. Things will truly seem different to us when we have quieted and cooled down.
—**Michel de Montaigne**

◆ Temper is the one thing you can't get rid of by losing it.
**—Jack Nicklaus**

◆ If you are patient in one moment of anger, you will escape a hundred days of sorrow.
**—Chinese proverb**

◆ How much more grievous are the consequences of anger than the causes of it.
**—Marcus Aurelius**

◆ When angry, count to ten before you speak; if very angry, count to a hundred.
**—Thomas Jefferson**

◆ Anger is momentary madness, so control your passion or it will control you.
**—Horace**

◆ A man's conquest of himself dwarfs the ascent of Everest.
**—Eli J. Schiefer**

***Anyone can become angry—that is easy. But to be angry with the right person, to the right degree, at the right time, for the right purpose, and in the right way—that is not easy.***
***—Aristotle***

◆ Remember not only to say the right thing in the right place, but far more difficult still, to leave unsaid the wrong thing at the tempting moment.
**—Benjamin Franklin**

◆ The benefits gained from learning how to manage conflict constructively far outweigh the costs of learning time lost by students being upset and angry.
**—Thomas J. Sergiovanni**

◆ The world needs anger. The world often continues to allow evil because it isn't angry enough.
**—Bede Jarrett**

◆ I was always looking outside myself for strength and confidence but it comes from within. It is there all the time.
**—Anna Freud**

◆ Patience is needed with everyone, but first of all with ourselves.
**—Saint Francis de Sales**

◆ If you believe in yourself, so will others.
**—Graham Greene**

◆ To have the sense of one's intrinsic worth which constitutes self-respect is potentially to have everything.
**—Joan Didion**

◆ Happiness is the sense that one matters.
**—Samuel Shoemaker**

◆ We need to live life with a burning passion. No fire, no heat—no heat, no life.
**—Rebecca Stuttelle**

◆ Thousands of candles can be lighted from a single candle, and the life of the candle will never be shortened. Happiness never ceases by being shared.
**—Chinese proverb**

◆ Believe that there's light at the end of the tunnel. Believe that you may be that light for someone else.
**—Kobi Yamada**

◆ Sometimes our light goes out but is blown into flame by another human being. Each of us owes deepest thanks to those who have rekindled this light.
**—Albert Schweitzer**

◆ People don't care how much you know until they know how much you care.
**—Mike McNight**

◆ Nobody has ever measured, not even poets, how much the heart can hold.
**—Zelda Fizgerald**

◆ What comes from the heart, goes to the heart.
**—Samuel Taylor Coleridge**

◆ Have a heart that never hardens, and a temper that never fires, and a touch that never hurts.
**—Charles Dickens**

◆ Sometimes when we are generous in small, barely detectable ways it can change someone else's life forever.
**—Margaret Cho**

◆ No act of kindness, no matter how small is ever wasted.
**—Aesop**

# motional Intelligence

◆ Kindness is more important than wisdom, and the recognition of this is the beginning of wisdom.
**—Theodore Isaac Rubin**

◆ Tenderness and kindness are not signs of weakness and despair, but manifestations of strength and resolution.
**—Kahlil Gibran**

◆ Constant kindness can accomplish much. As the sun makes ice melt, kindness causes misunderstanding, mistrust and hostility to evaporate.
**—Albert Schweitzer**

◆ The center of human nature is rooted in ten thousand ordinary acts of kindness that define our days.
**—Stephen Jay Gould**

◆ Because of their age-long training in human relations—for that is what feminine intuition real is—women have a special contribution to make to any group enterprise.
**—Margaret Mead**

◆ I expect to pass through life but once. If therefore, there be any kindness I can show, or any good thing I can do to any fellow being, let me do it now, and not defer or neglect it, as I shall not pass this way again.
**—William Penn**

◆ Never give up on anybody.
**—Hubert H. Humphrey**

◆ Invest in the human soul. Who knows, it might be a diamond in the rough.
**—Mary McLeod Bethune**

◆ The only justification we have to look down on someone is because we are about to pick him up.
**—Jesse Jackson**

***You can make more friends in two months by becoming really interested in other people than you can in two years by trying to get other people interested in you.***
***—Dale Carnegie***

◆ If you judge people, you have no time to love them.
**—Mother Teresa**

◆ See everything; overlook a great deal; correct a little.
**—Pope John XXIII**

◆ People who are brutally honest get more satisfaction out of the brutality than out of the honesty.
**—Richard J. Needham**

◆ Tact is the art of making a point without making an enemy.
**—Howard W. Newton**

◆ To speak ill of anyone is to speak ill of yourself.
**—Afghan proverb**

◆ A relationship is a living thing. It needs and benefits from the same attention to detail that an artist lavishes on his (her) art.
**—David Viscott**

◆ My lifetime listens to yours.
**—Margaret Peters**

◆ What is needed, rather than running away or controlling or suppressing or any other resistance, is understanding fear; that means, watch it, learn about it, come directly into contact with it. We are to learn about fear, not how to escape from it.
**—Jiddu Krishnamurti**

◆ Trouble is part of your life, and if you don't share it, you don't give the person who loves you a chance to love you enough.
**—Dinah Shore**

◆ For the most part, fear is nothing but an illusion. When you share it with someone else, it tends to disappear.
**—Marilyn C. Barrick**

◆ Worry is misuse of the imagination.
**—Mary Crowley**

◆ Worry often gives a small thing a big shadow.
**—Swedish proverb**

◆ Let go. Why cling to the pain and the wrongs of yesterday? Why hold on to the very things that keep you from hope and love?
**—Buddha**

◆ Don't ever be afraid to admit you were wrong. It's like saying you're wiser today than you were yesterday.
**—Robert Henry**

◆ When you make a mistake, admit it; learn from it and don't repeat it.
**—Bear Bryant**

◆ Two persons cannot long be friends if they cannot forgive each other's little failings.
**—Jean De La Bruyere**

◆ The practice of forgiveness is our most important contribution to the healing of the world.
**—Montel Williams**

◆ Those who are lifting the world upward and onward are those who encourage more than criticize.
**—Elizabeth Harrison**

◆ An ounce of motivation weighs more than a pound of rewards and punishments.
**—Spencer Kagan**

◆ Encourage each other to become the best you can be. Celebrate what you want to see more of.
**—Tom Peters**

◆ Most of us, swimming against tides of trouble the world knows nothing about, need only a bit of praise or encouragement—and we'll make the goal.
**—Jerome P. Fleishman**

◆ Deep in their roots, all flowers keep the light.
**—Theodore Roethke**

◆ Encouragement is oxygen to the soul.
**—George M. Adams**

◆ So when you are listening to somebody, completely, attentively, then you are listening not only to the words, but also to the feeling of what is being conveyed, to the whole of it, not part of it.
**—Jiddu Krishnamurti**

◆ Try and feel, in your heart's core, the reality of others.
**—Margaret Laurence**

◆ Empathy requires focusing full attention on the other person's message. We give to others the time and space they need to express themselves fully and to feel understood.
**—Marshall B. Rosenberg**

◆ Six Critical Life Messages: I believe in you. I trust you. I know you can handle this. You are listened to. You are cared for. You are very important to me.
**—Barbara Coloroso**

◆ Caring can be learned by all human beings, can be worked into the design of every life, meeting an individual need as well as a pervasive need in society.
**—Mary Catherine Bateson**

***The weak can never forgive. Forgiveness is the attribute of the strong.***
***—Mahatma Gandhi***

◆ When people feel there is a purpose and that they're needed, there's not much else to do except let them do the work.
**—Maya Angelou**

◆ Anxiety checks learning. An overall feeling of inferiority, a temporary humiliation, a fit of depression, defiance or anger, a sense of being rejected, and many other emotional disturbances affect the learning process. The reverse is true; a feeling of well-being and of being respected by others stimulates an alert mind, willingness to participate, and an attitude conducive to learning.
**—Eda LeShan**

◆ Children and adults alike share needs to be safe and secure; to belong and to be loved; to experience self-esteem through achievement, mastery, recognition, and respect; to be autonomous; and to experience self-actualization by pursuing one's inner abilities and finding intrinsic meaning and satisfaction in what one does.
**—Thomas J. Sergiovanni**

# Emotional Intelligence

**Hope is the thing with feathers that perches in the soul and sings the tune without the words, and never stops at all ….**

**—Emily Dickinson**

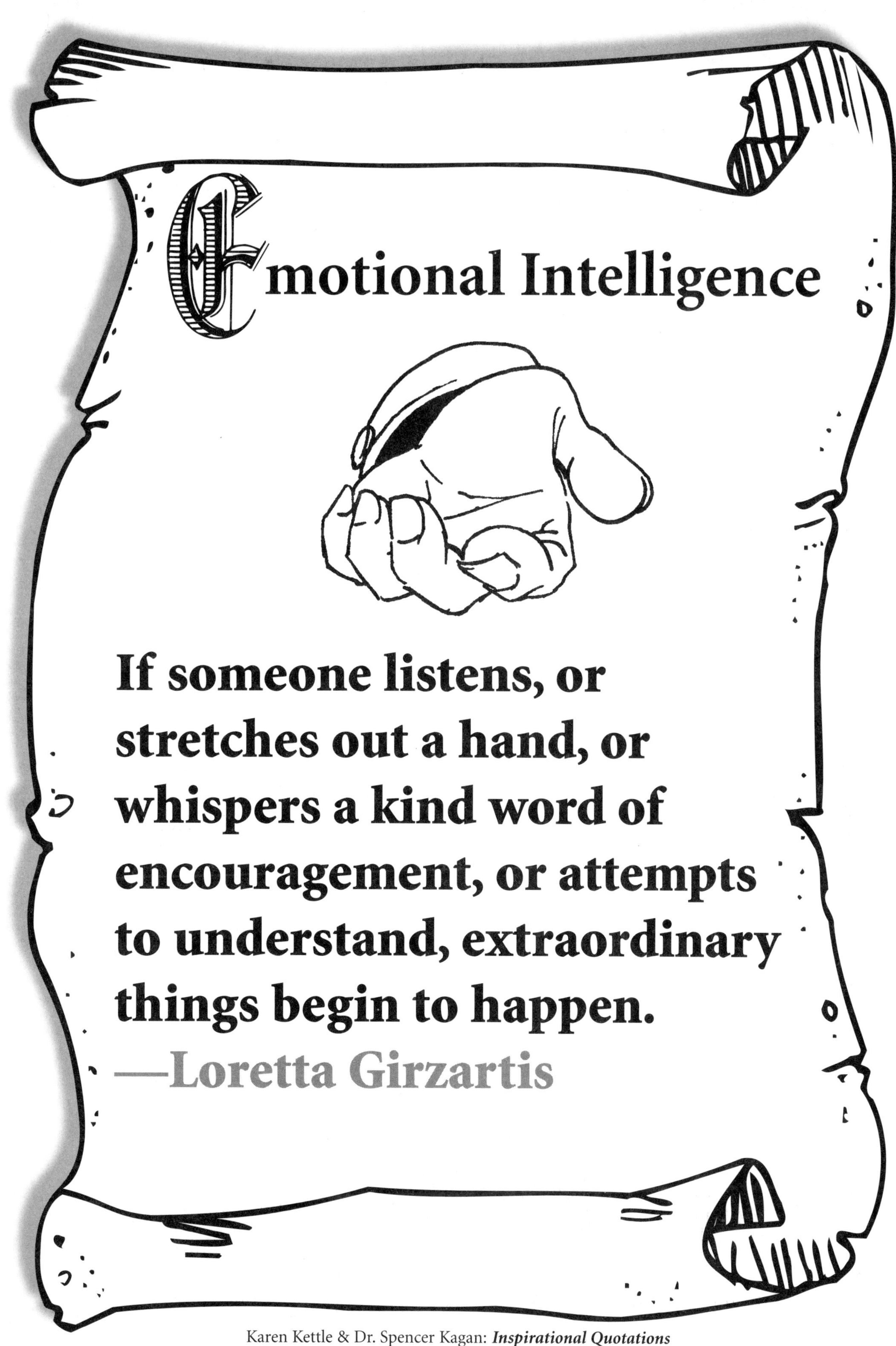
Emotional Intelligence
If someone listens, or stretches out a hand, or whispers a kind word of encouragement, or attempts to understand, extraordinary things begin to happen.
—Loretta Girzartis

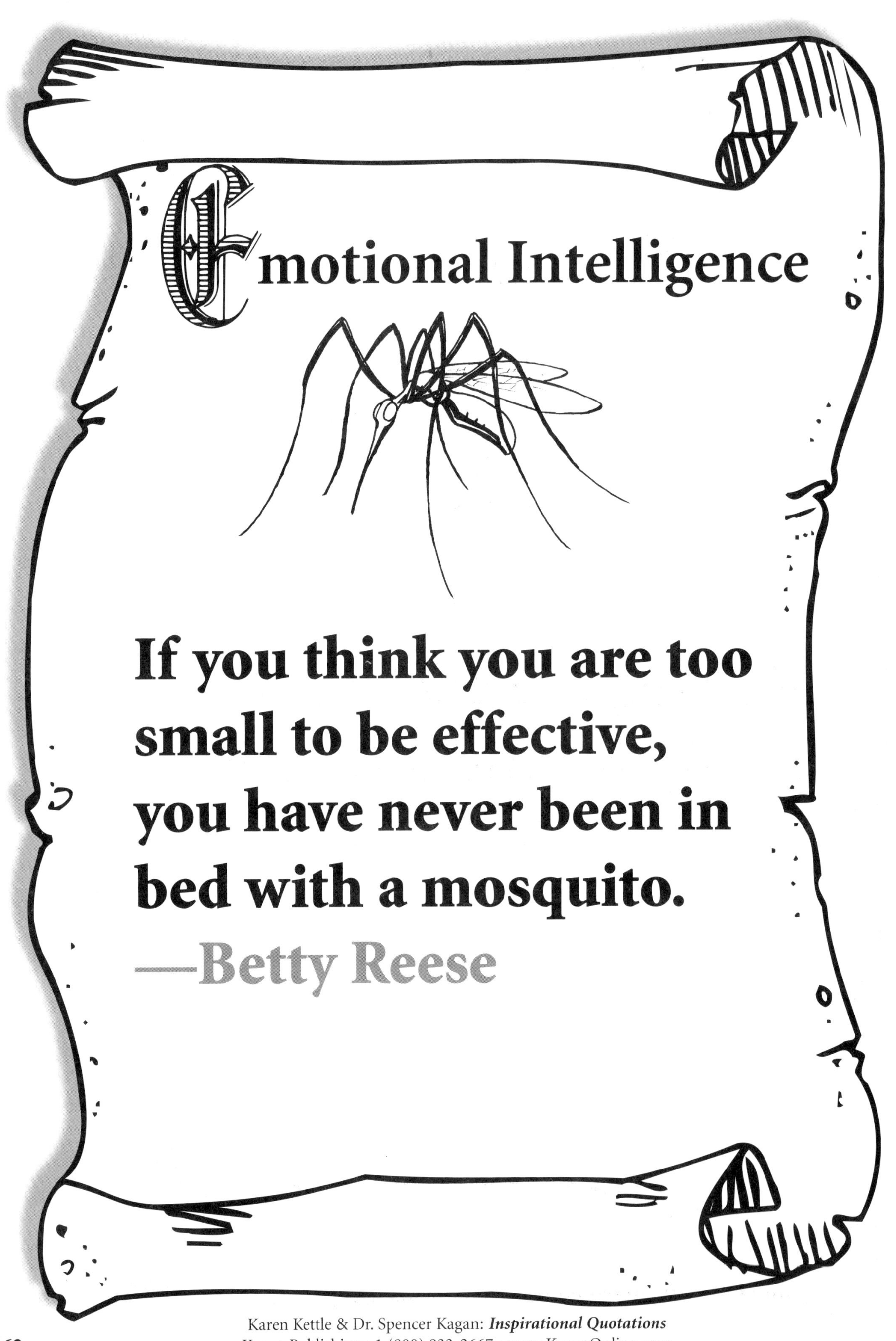

Emotional Intelligence
If you think you are too small to be effective, you have never been in bed with a mosquito.
—Betty Reese

Karen Kettle & Dr. Spencer Kagan: *Inspirational Quotations*
Kagan Publishing • 1 (800) 933-2667 • www.KaganOnline.com

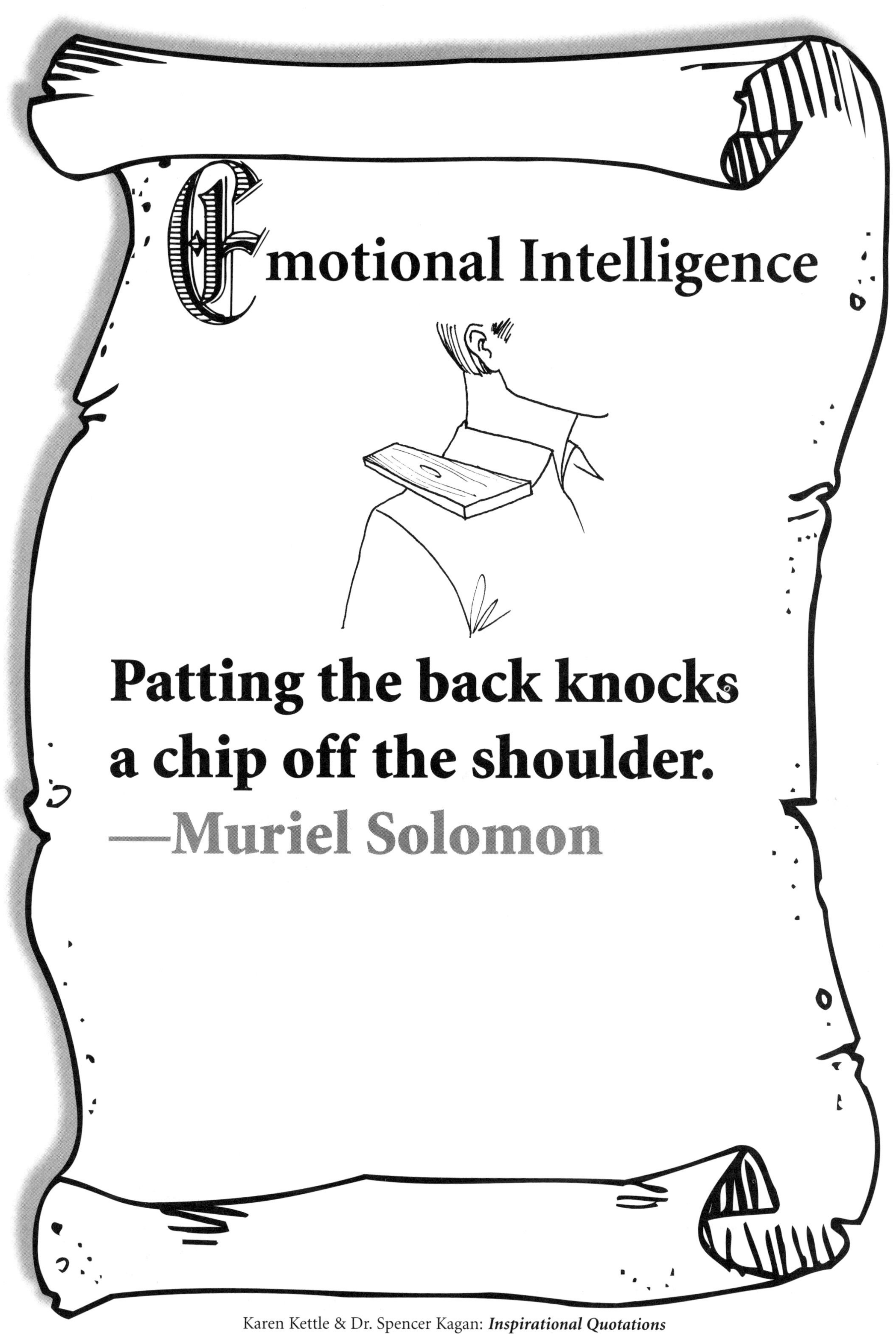
Emotional Intelligence
Patting the back knocks
a chip off the shoulder.
—Muriel Solomon

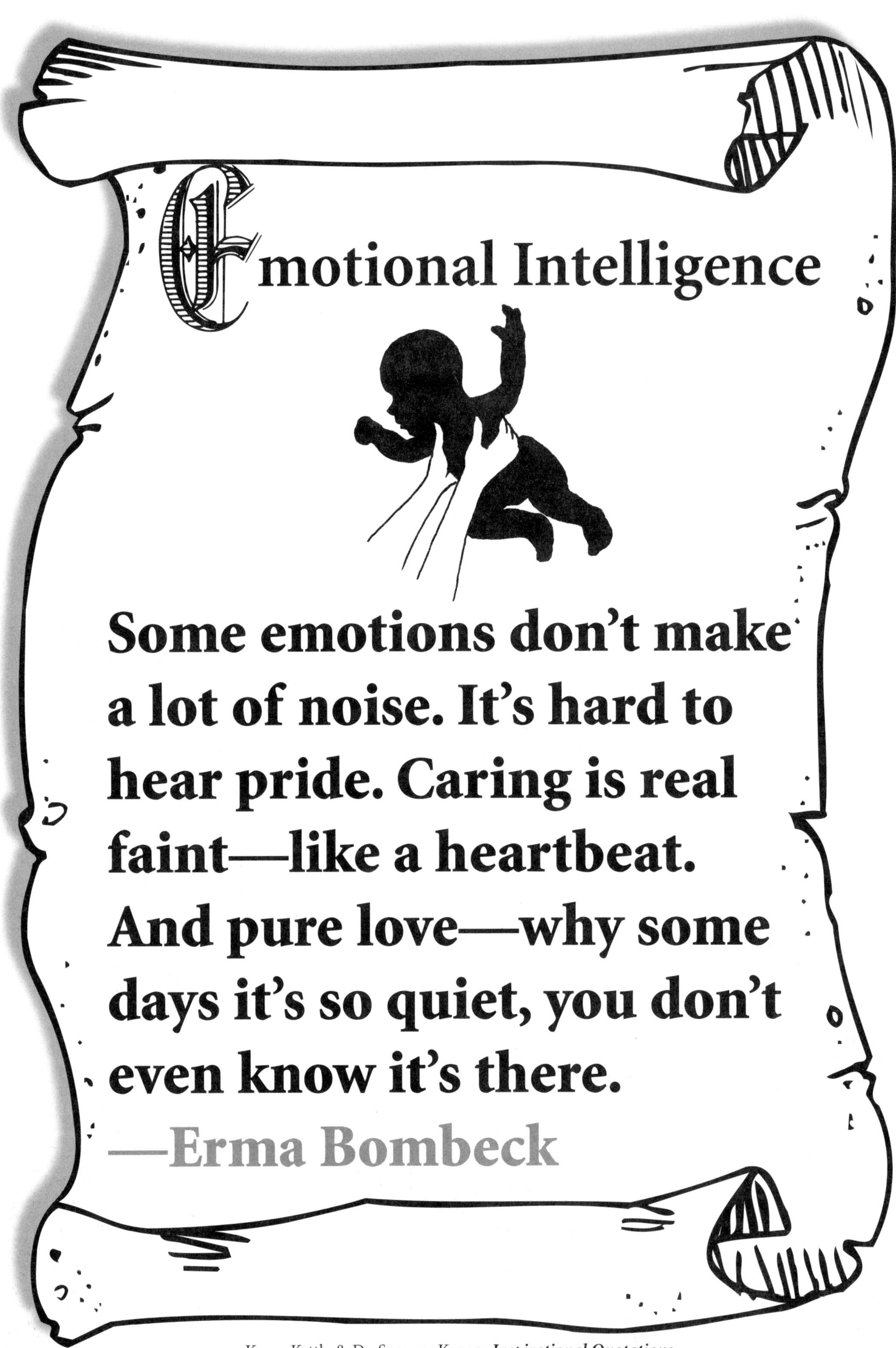

# Emotional Intelligence

**Some emotions don't make a lot of noise. It's hard to hear pride. Caring is real faint—like a heartbeat. And pure love—why some days it's so quiet, you don't even know it's there.**

**—Erma Bombeck**



Karen Kettle & Dr. Spencer Kagan: *Inspirational Quotations*
Kagan Publishing • 1 (800) 933-2667 • www.KaganOnline.com

Experience

# xperience

*Experience is everything—every sight, sound, taste, smell, feeling, vision, and memory. Every experience is a learning opportunity.*

**It is only in adventure that some people succeed in knowing themselves—in finding themselves.**

*—Andre Gide*

Reflection Questions

- *What comes to mind when you think about adventure?*
- *What adventures have you had?*
- *What have you learned about yourself from an adventure?*

**Life is like playing the violin solo in public and learning the instrument as you go along.**

*—Samuel Butler*

Reflection Questions

- *How is life like playing a violin in public?*
- *How does your first experience with something lead you toward or away from trying it again?*
- *Why does having an audience intensify your awareness of an experience?*

**Experience is something you don't get until just after you need it.**

*—Olivier*

Reflection Questions

- *What is something you would do differently now that you have more experience?*
- *What would happen if you could not learn from your experiences?*
- *Why do new experiences make you see the world from a different perspective?*

**We must get beyond textbooks, go out into the bypaths and untrodden depths of the wilderness and travel and explore and tell the world the glories of our journey.**

*—John Hope Franklin*

Reflection Questions

- *How is experiencing something different from learning about it from a book?*
- *What symbol best represents the wilderness?*
- *Should the wilderness be valued or feared? Why?*

**To know the road ahead, ask those coming back.**

*—Chinese proverb*

Reflection Questions

- *Who has given you good advice based on their experiences?*
- *Who could you provide with good advice? What would it be about?*
- *How do our experiences connect our past, present, and future choices?*

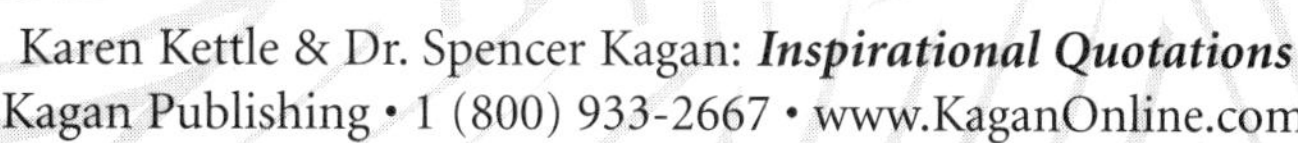

# Experience

◆ You cannot create experience. You must undergo it.
**—Albert Camus**

◆ Knowledge is experience. Everything else is just information.
**—Albert Einstein**

◆ Experience is never limited, and it is never complete; it is an immense sensibility, a kind of huge spider-web of the finest silken threads suspended in the chamber of consciousness, and catching every air-borne particle in its tissue.
**—Henry James**

***By far the best proof is experience.***
***—Sir Francis Bacon***

◆ Knowledge can only be got in one way, the way of experience, there is no other way to know.
**—Swami Vivekananda**

◆ It is wrong to coerce people into opinions, but it is a duty to impel them into experience.
**—Kurt Hahn**

◆ In brief, the function of knowledge is to make one experience freely available to other experiences.
**—John Dewey**

◆ Insight, I believe, refers to the depth of understanding that comes by setting experiences, yours and mine, familiar and exotic, new and old, side by side, learning by letting them speak to one another.
**—Mary Catherine Bateson**

◆ Few people even scratch the surface, much less exhaust the contemplation of their own experience.
**—Randolph Bourne**

◆ Life is the only real counselor. Wisdom unfiltered through personal experience does not become a part of the moral tissue.
**—Edith Wharton**

◆ Experience is not what happens to you, it is what you do with what happens to you.
**—Aldous Huxley**

◆ The value of experience is not in seeing much, but in seeing wisely.
**—Sir William Osler**

◆ Most people would say that what I am doing is "learning to play" the cello. But these words carry into our minds the strange idea that there exists two very different processes: 1) learning to play the cello; and 2) playing the cello .... We learn to do something by doing it. There is no other way.
**—John Holt**

◆ Experience is the child of thought, and thought is the child of action. We cannot learn from books.
**—Benjamin Disraeli**

◆ A little experience often upsets a lot of theory.
**—Cadman**

◆ Do you know the difference between education and experience? Education is when you read the fine print; experience is what you get when you don't.
**—Pete Seeger**

◆ Good judgment comes from experience, and experience … well, that comes from poor judgment.
**—Cousin Woodman**

◆ The hardest thing in life is to know which bridge to cross and which to burn.
**—David Russel**

◆ Experience is that marvelous thing that enables you to recognize a mistake when you make it again.
**—Franklin P. Jones**

◆ Mistakes are part of the dues one pays for a full life.
**—Sophia Loren**

◆ The truth is that our finest moments are most likely to occur when we are feeling deeply uncomfortable, unhappy, or unfulfilled. For it is only in such moments, propelled by our discomfort, that we are likely to step out of our ruts and start searching for different ways or truer answers.
**—M. Scott Peck**

◆ We should be careful to get out of an experience only the wisdom that is in it, and stop there, lest we be like the cat that sits down on a hot stove lid. She will never sit down on a hot stove lid again and that is well; but she will never sit down on a cold one either.
**—Mark Twain**

◆ You are wise to climb Mt. Fuji, but a fool to do it twice.
**—Japanese proverb**

◆ Some experiences are mis-educative. Any experience is mis-educative that has the effect of arresting or distorting the growth of further experience.
**—John Dewey**

***Experience is not always the kindest of teachers, but it is surely the best.***
***—Spanish proverb***

◆ Experience is the name everyone gives to their mistakes.
**—Oscar Wilde**

◆ Experience is a good school, but the fees are high.
**—Heinrich Heine**

◆ Experience teaches only the teachable.
**—Aldous Huxley**

◆ Experience is a hard teacher because she gives the test first, the lesson afterwards.
**—Vernon Sanders Law**

◆ Human beings, who are almost unique in having the ability to learn from the experience of others, are also remarkable for their apparent disinclination to do so.
**—Douglas Adams**

◆ If we could sell our experiences for what they cost us, we'd all be millionaires.
**—Abigail Van Buren**

◆ The desk is a dangerous place from which to watch the world.
**—John le Carre**

◆ Because of our routines we forget that life is an ongoing adventure.
**—Maya Angelou**

◆ The purpose of life, after all, is to live it, to taste experience to the utmost, to reach out eagerly and without fear for newer and richer experiences.
**—Eleanor Roosevelt**

◆ An adventure is only an inconvenience rightly understood. An inconvenience is only an adventure wrongly understood.
**—G. K. Chesterton**

◆ Adventure is worthwhile in itself.
**—Amelia Earhart**

◆ Rest not! Life is sweeping by; go and dare before you die.
**—Johann Wolfgang Von Goethe**

◆ There are periods when to dare is the highest wisdom.
**—William Ellery Channing**

◆ Life is either a daring adventure or nothing at all. Security is mostly a superstition. It does not exist in nature.
**—Helen Keller**

◆ Day after day, we discover our own lives. Because we never know what we will find, every discovery is an unexpected gift we give ourselves.
**—Barbara J. Esbensen**

◆ The moment when you first wake up in the morning is the most wonderful of the twenty-four hours. No matter how weary or dreary you may feel, you possess the certainty that, during the day that lies before you, absolutely anything can happen. And the fact that it practically always doesn't, matters not a jot. The possibility is always there.
**—Monica Baldwin**

◆ I went to the woods because I wished to live deliberately, to confront only the essential facts of life, and see, if I could not learn what it had to teach, and not, when I came to die, discover that I had not lived.
**—Henry David Thoreau**

◆ Life is a succession of lessons which must be lived in order to be understood.
**—Ralph Waldo Emerson**

# Experience

◆ You learn to speak by speaking, to study by studying, to run by running, to work by working; and just so, you learn to love by loving. All those who think to learn in any other way deceive themselves.
**—Saint Francis de Sales**

◆ Past experience, if not forgotten, is a guide to the future.
**—Chinese proverb**

◆ I had six hours to chop down a tree, I'd spend the first four sharpening the axe.
**—Abraham Lincoln**

◆ If you will call your troubles experiences, and remember that every experience develops some latent force within you, you will grow vigorous and happy, however adverse your circumstance may seem to be.
**—John R. Miller**

◆ Owing to the fact that all experience is a process, no point of view can ever be the last one.
**—William Jones**

◆ I learn by going where I have to go.
**—Theodore Roethke**

◆ I may not have gone where I intended to go, but I think I have ended up where I intended to be.
**—Douglas Adams**

◆ The voyage of discovery lies not in finding new landscapes, but in having new eyes.
**—Marcel Proust**

◆ I have discovered in life that there are ways of getting almost anywhere you want to go, if you really want to go.
**—Langston Hughes**

◆ I am a part of all that I have met.
**—Alfred Lord Tennyson**

***Nothing ever becomes real till it is experienced.***
***—John Keats***

◆ We travel to learn; and I have never been in any country where they did not do something better than we do it, think some thoughts better than we think, catch some inspiration from heights above our own.
**—Maria Mitchell**

◆ Officers wanted for hazardous journey. Small wages. Bitter cold. Long months of complete darkness. Constant danger. Safe return doubtful. Honour and recognition in case of success.
**—Ernest Shackleton**

◆ He who would learn to fly one day must first learn to stand and walk and run and climb and dance; one cannot fly into flying.
**—Friedrich Nietzsche**

◆ Every experience is a moving force. Its value can be judged only on the ground of what it moves toward and into.
**—John Dewey**

◆ Let us not look back in anger, nor forward in fear, but around in awareness.
**—James Thurber**

◆ You can't step into the same river twice.
**—Heraclitus**

◆ Don't throw away the old bucket until you know whether the new one holds water.
**—Swedish proverb**

◆ To finish the moment, to find the journey's end in every step of the road, to live the greatest number of good hours, is wisdom.
**—Ralph Waldo Emerson**

◆ Unless we live what we know, we do not even know it.
**—Thomas Menton**

◆ Do not follow where the path may lead. Go instead where there is no path and leave a trail.
**—Muriel Strode**

◆ Life's a pretty precious and wonderful thing. You can't sit down and let it lap around you … you have to plunge into it; you have to dive through it! And you can't save it, you can't store it up; you can't horde it in a vault. You've got to taste it; you've got to use it. The more you use the more you have … that's the miracle of it!
**—Lyle Samuel Crichton**

◆ The most beautiful thing we can experience is the mysterious. It is the source of all true art and all science. He to whom this emotion is a stranger, who can no longer pause to wonder and stand rapt in awe, is as good as dead: his eyes are closed.
**—Albert Einstein**

◆ What the caterpillar calls the end of the world, the master calls a butterfly.
**—Richard Bach**

◆ If we could see the miracle of a single flower clearly, our whole life would change.
**—Buddha**

◆ Let children walk with Nature, let them see the beautiful blendings and communions of death and life, their joyous inseparable unity, as taught in woods and meadows, plains and mountains and streams of our blessed star, and they will learn that death is stingless indeed, and as beautiful as life.
**—John Muir**

◆ Those who contemplate the beauty of the earth find reserves of strength that will endure as long as life lasts.
**—Rachel Carson**

◆ When I was young, I had to choose between the life of being and the life of doing. And I leapt at the later like a trout to a fly. But each deed you do, each act, binds you to itself and to its consequences, and makes you act again and yet again. Then very seldom do you come upon a space …between act and act when you may stop and simply be. Or wonder who, after all, you are.
**—Ursula K. LeGuin**

◆ I believe that only one person in a thousand knows the trick of really living in the present. Most of us spend fifty-nine minutes an hour living in the past, with regret for lost joys, or shame for things badly done (both utterly useless and weakening) or in a future which we either long for or dread. Yet the past is gone beyond a prayer, and every minute you spend in vain effort to anticipate the future is pressing against you at this minute. There is only one minute in which you are alive, this minute—here and now. The only way to live is by accepting each minute as an unrepeatable miracle. Which is exactly what it is.
**—Storm Jameson**

◆ Every year I live I am more convinced that the waste of life lies in the love we have not given, the powers we have not used, the selfish prudence which will risk nothing, and which, shirking pain, misses happiness as well.
**—Mary Cholomondeley**

***The journey is the reward.***
***—Taoist saying***

◆ Always in a big wood when you leave familiar ground and step off alone into a new place there will be, along with the feelings of curiosity and excitement, a little nagging of dread. It is the ancient fear of the unknown, and it is your first bond with the wilderness you are going into. What you are doing is exploring.
**—Wendell Berr**

◆ I embrace emerging experience. I participate in discovery. I am a butterfly. I am not a butterfly collector.
**—William Stafford**

◆ Life isn't about finding yourself. Life is about creating yourself.
**—George Bernard Shaw**

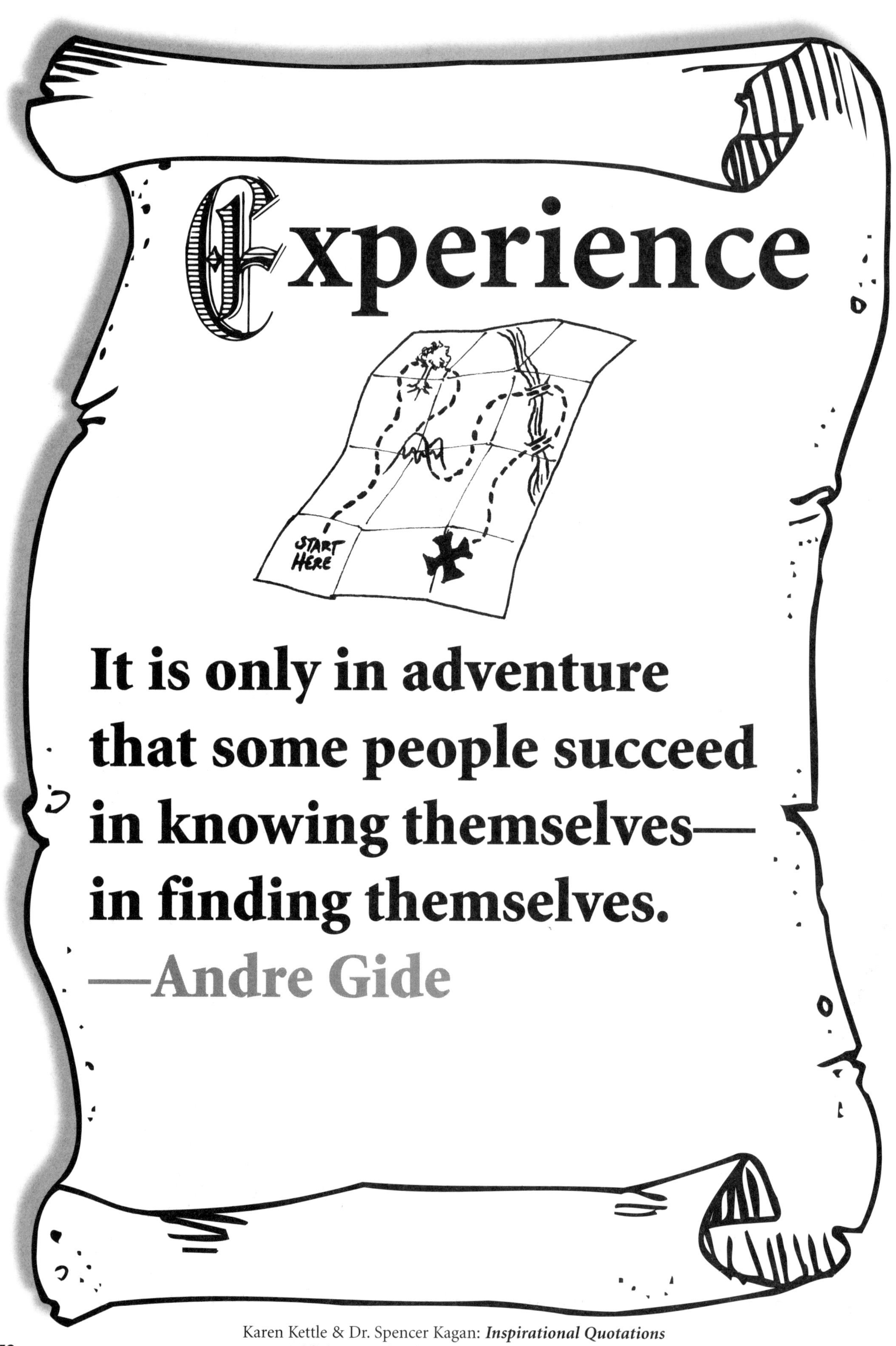


# Experience

**It is only in adventure that some people succeed in knowing themselves—in finding themselves.**

**—Andre Gide**



Karen Kettle & Dr. Spencer Kagan: *Inspirational Quotations*
Kagan Publishing • 1 (800) 933-2667 • www.KaganOnline.com

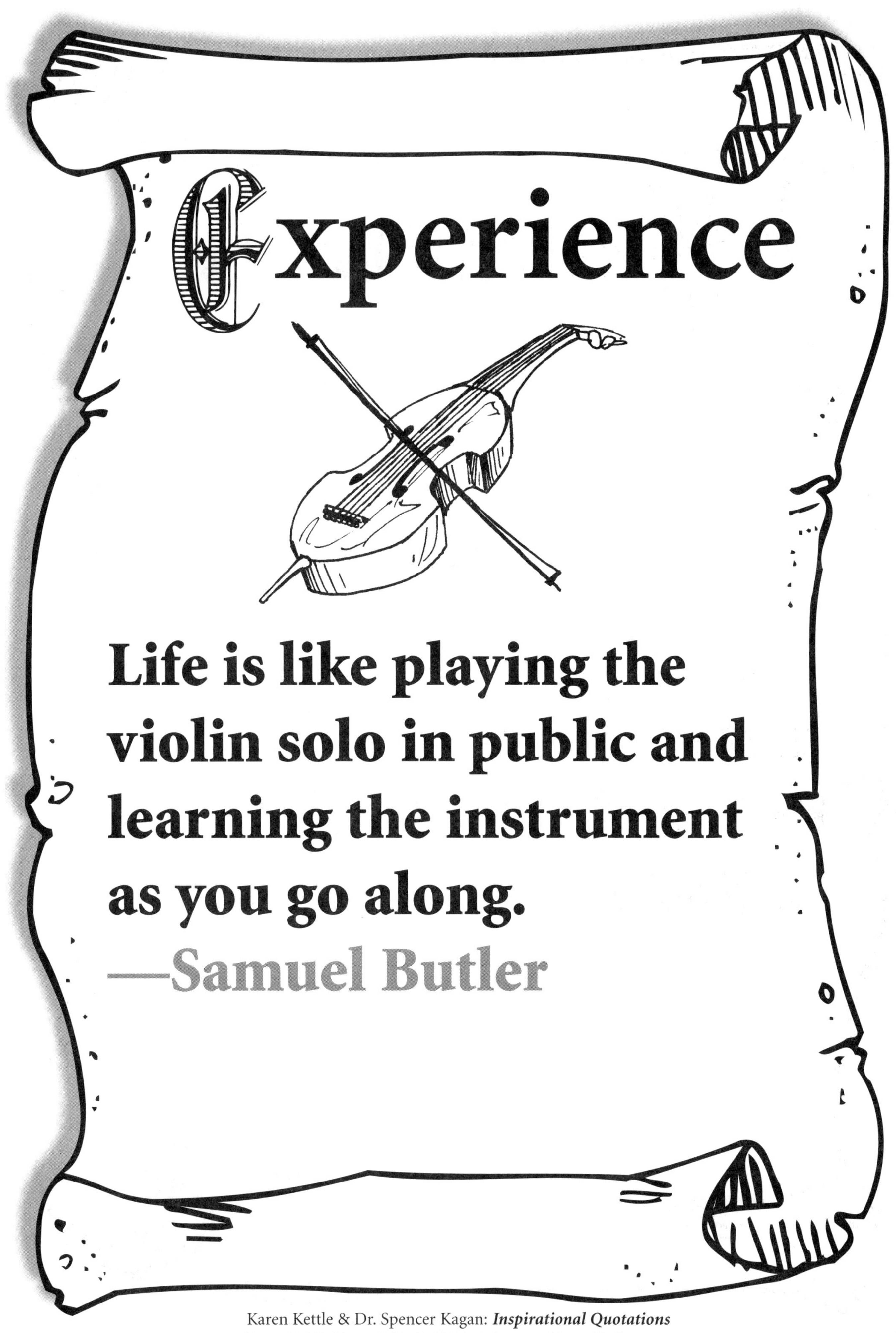
Experience
Life is like playing the violin solo in public and learning the instrument as you go along.
—Samuel Butler

# Experience

**Experience is something you don't get until just after you need it.**

**—Olivier**

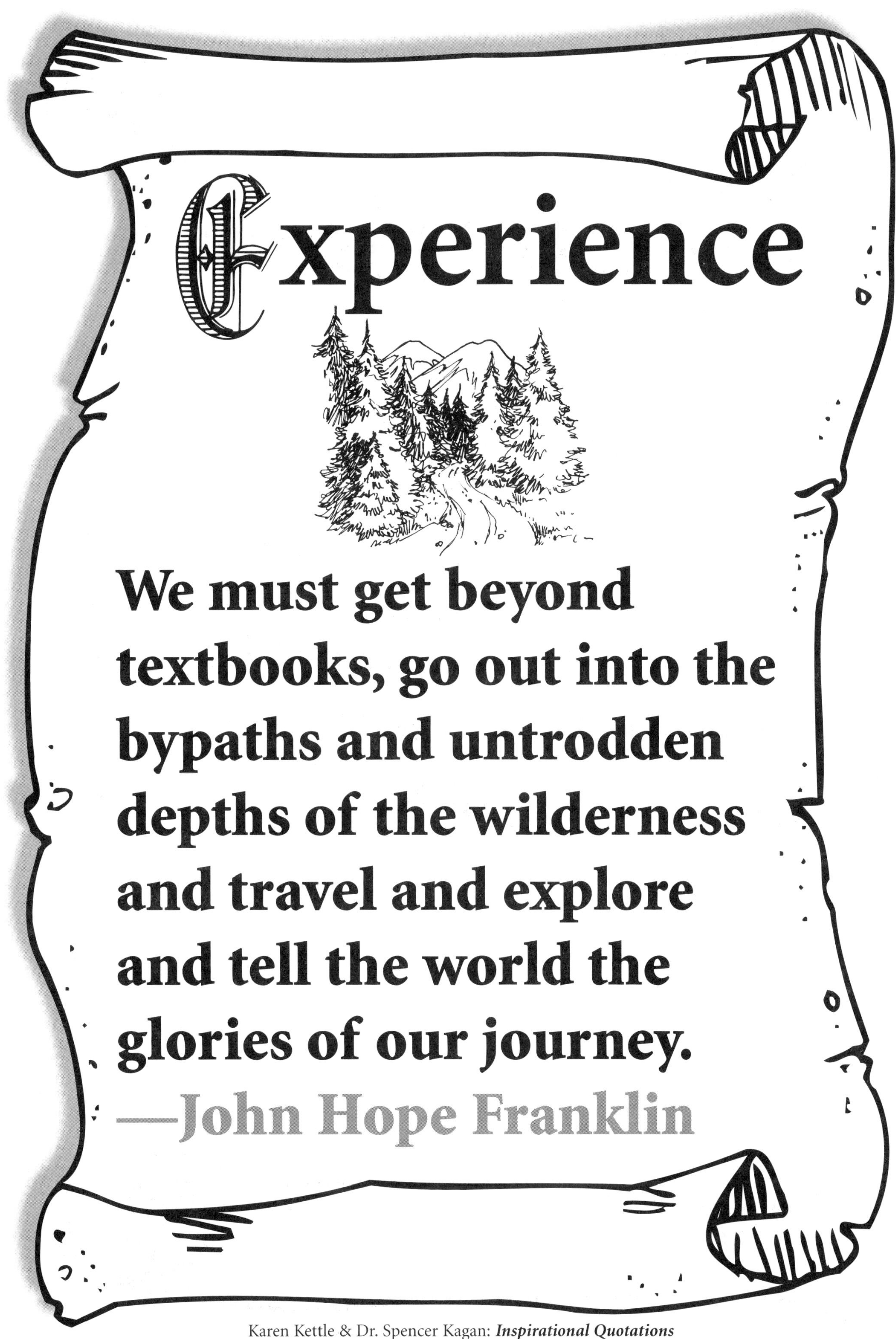
Experience
We must get beyond textbooks, go out into the bypaths and untrodden depths of the wilderness and travel and explore and tell the world the glories of our journey.
—John Hope Franklin

Experience
To know the road ahead,
ask those coming back.
—Chinese proverb

# Humor

# umor

*It is easier to thrive in a serious world if we appreciate the funny side of life.*

**Laughter is the shortest distance between two people.**

*—Victor Borge*

Reflection Questions

- *Why does laughing together make people feel connected?*
- *Who do you like to laugh with?*
- *What is the difference between laughing with someone and laughing at someone?*

**Take the time everyday to do something silly.**

*—Phillipa Walker*

Reflection Questions

- *What is the most ridiculous thing you have every done?*
- *When have you laughed at yourself?*
- *What makes something fun to do?*

**If you laugh a lot, when you grow older your wrinkles will be in the right places.**

*—Andrew Mason*

Reflection Questions

- *What kind of wrinkles do people get from smiling?*
- *Why does laughing help us live happier lives?*
- *What would the world be like without laughter?*

**Humor is a rubber sword—it allows you to make a point without drawing blood.**
*—Mary Hirsch*

Reflection Questions
- *How can you diffuse a tense situation with humor?*
- *When have you used humor to your advantage?*
- *Why do comedians poke fun at serious subjects?*

**A sense of humor is good for you. Have you ever heard of a laughing hyena with heartburn?**
*—Bob Hope*

Reflection Questions
- *What makes you laugh?*
- *How do you make other people laugh?*
- *What can you look back and laugh at now that seemed very serious at the time?*

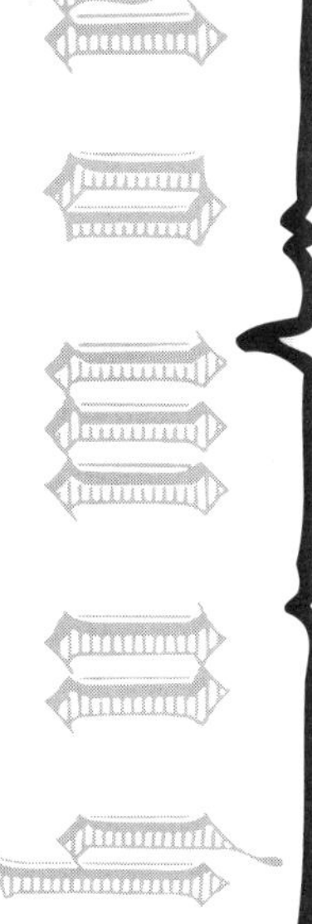

# Humor

◆ The most useless day is that in which we have not laughed.
**—Charles Field**

◆ Laughter is part of the human survival kit.
**—David Nathan**

◆ Laughter is the brush that sweeps away the cobwebs of the heart.
**—Mort Walker**

◆ What soap is to the body, laughter is to the soul.
**—Yiddish proverb**

◆ Laughter is an instant vacation.
**—Milton Berle**

◆ Laughter is a celebration of the human spirit.
**—Sabina White**

◆ Laughter is the best communion of all.
**—Robert Fulghum**

◆ Laughter prevents hardening of the attitudes.
**—Dunc Muncy**

◆ A smile starts on the lips,
A grin spreads to the eyes,
A chuckle comes from the belly;
But a good laugh bursts forth from the soul,
Overflows, and bubbles all around.
**—Carolyn Birmingham**

◆ A good laugh is sunshine in a house.
**—Thackeray**

◆ Always laugh when you can. It is cheap medicine.
**—Lord Byron**

◆ Laughter is the tranquilizer with no side effects.
**—Arnold Glasgow**

◆ Laughter can be more satisfying than honor; more precious than money.
**—Harriet Rochlin**

◆ If I were given the opportunity to present a gift to the next generation, it would be the ability for each individual to learn to laugh at himself (herself).
**—Charles M. Schulz**

◆ You grow up the day you have your first real laugh—at yourself.
**—Ethel Barrymore**

***Humor is by far the most significant activity of the human brain.***
***—Edward De Bono***

◆ Laugh at yourself first, before anyone else can.
**—Elsa Maxwell**

◆ If you are not allowed to laugh in heaven, I do not want to go there.
**—Martin Luther**

◆ Life isn't just the front page—it's in the comics too.
**—Jim Althoff**

◆ At the height of laughter, the universe is flung into a kaleidoscope of new possibilities.
**—Jean Houston**

◆ I realize that a sense of humor isn't for everyone. It's only for people who want to have fun, enjoy life, and feel alive.
**—Anne Wilson Schaef**

◆ The main point in the game of life is to have fun. We are afraid to have fun because somehow that makes life too easy.
**—Sammy Davis Jr.**

◆ Fun is FUNdamental.
**—Doug Hall**

◆ Life is playfulness .... We need to play so that we can discover the magic all around us.
**—Flora Colao**

◆ Live nutty. Just occasionally. Just once in a while. And see what happens. It brightens up the day.
**—Leo Buscaglia**

◆ Laughter is the lightning rod of play, the eroticism of conversation.
**—Eva Hoffman**

◆ That's what it's all about: If you can't have fun at it, there's no sense hanging around.
**—Joe Montana**

◆ From there to here, and here to there, funny things are everywhere.
**—Dr. Seuss**

◆ A person without a sense of humor is like a wagon without springs—jolted by every pebble in the road.
**—Henry Ward Beecher**

◆ Humor is the harmony of the heart.
**—Douglas Jerrold**

◆ Humor teaches tolerance.
**—W. Somerset Maugham**

◆ Among those whom I like or admire, I can find no common denominator, but among those whom I love, I can: all of them make me laugh.
**—W. H. Auden**

◆ We cannot really love anybody with whom we never laugh.
**—Agnes Repplier**

◆ You can't stay mad at somebody who makes you laugh.
**—Jay Leno**

◆ The wit makes fun of other persons; the satirist makes fun of the world; the humorist makes fun of himself (herself).
**—James Thurber**

◆ Inviting people to laugh with you while you are laughing at yourself is a good thing to do. You may be the fool, but you're the fool in charge.
**—Carl Reiner**

◆ Shared laughter creates a bond of friendship. When people laugh together, they cease to be young and old, teacher and pupils, worker and boss. They become a single group of human beings.
**—W. Lee Grant**

◆ Laughter gives us distance. It allows us to step back from an event, deal with it and then move on.
**—Bob Newhart**

◆ If we're going to be able to look back on something and laugh about it, we might as well laugh about it now.
**—Marie Osmond**

◆ Humor tells you where the trouble is.
**—Louise Bernikow**

◆ If you can laugh at it, you can survive it.
**—Bill Cosby**

***Wear your wit as a shield, not as a dagger.***
***—American proverb***

◆ Humor is just another defense against the universe.
**—Mel Brooks**

◆ I think the next best thing to solving a problem is finding some humor in it.
**—Frank Clark**

◆ If the world were a logical place, men would ride side-saddle.
**—Rita Mae Brown**

◆ When it's getting dark, you're miserable and the task at hand seems endless, then this is the time to dig your sense of humor out from the bottom of your pack, wear it on your spirit and lighten your load.
**—Carolyn Birmingham**

◆ Humor is the great thing, the saving thing. The minute it crops up, all our irritations and resentments slip away and a sunny spirit takes their place.
**—Mark Twain**

◆ That is the saving grace of humor, if you fail no one is laughing at you.
**—A. Whitney Brown**

◆ If you can tickle yourself, you can laugh when you like.
**—Chinese proverb**

◆ We don't stop laughing because we grow old—we grow old because we stop laughing.
**—Michael Pritchard**

◆ He (she) who laughs, lasts.
**—Mary Pettibone Poole**

Humor
HA HA HA HA HA HA HA HA HA
Laughter is the
shortest distance
between two people.
—Victor Borge

Humor
Take the time everyday
to do something silly.
—Phillipa Walker

Humor
If you laugh a lot, when you grow older your wrinkles will be in the right places.
—Andrew Mason

Humor
Humor is a rubber
sword—it allows you to
make a point without
drawing blood.
—Mary Hirsch

Humor
A sense of humor is
good for you. Have you
ever heard of a laughing
hyena with heartburn?
—Bob Hope

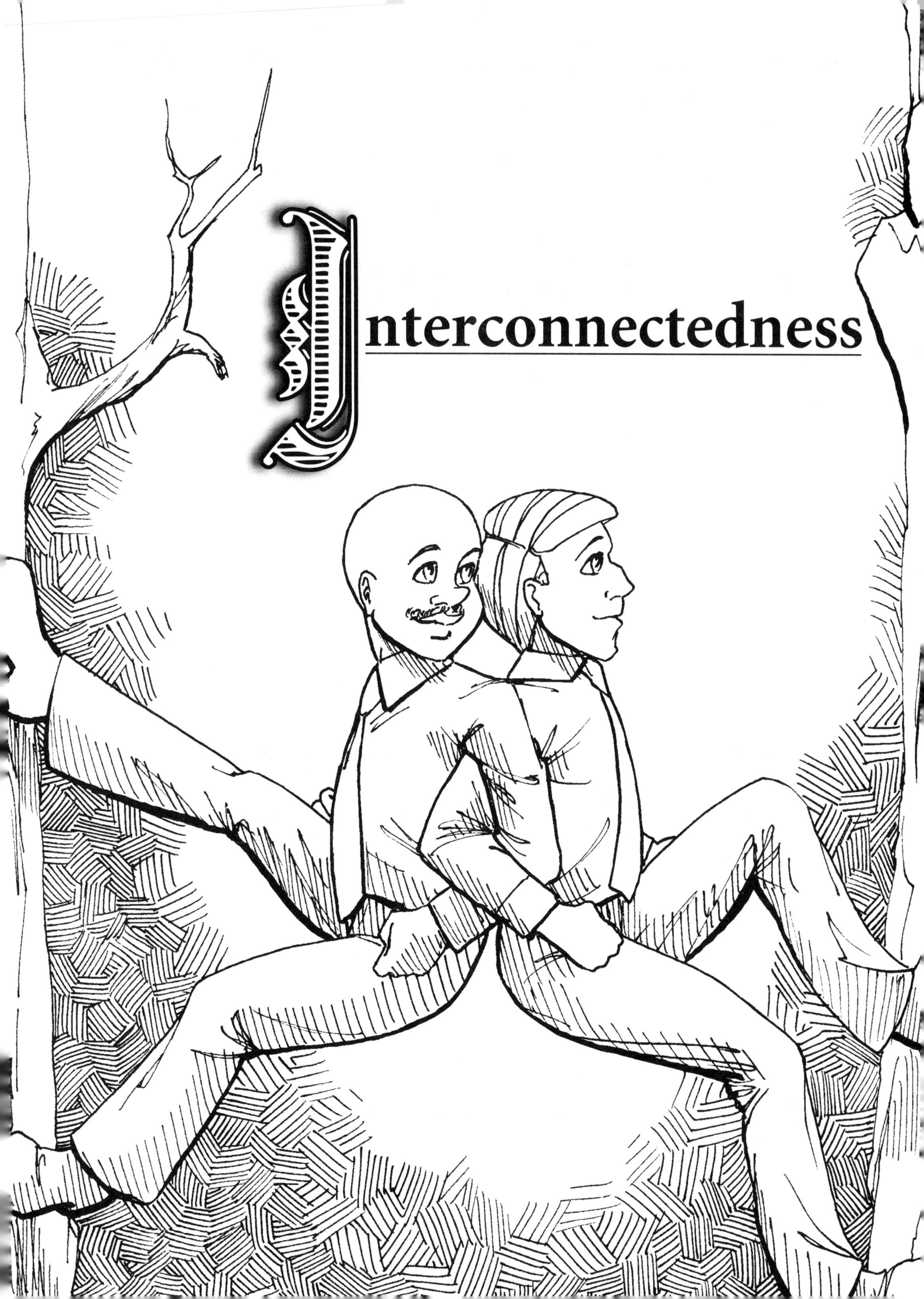
Interconnectedness

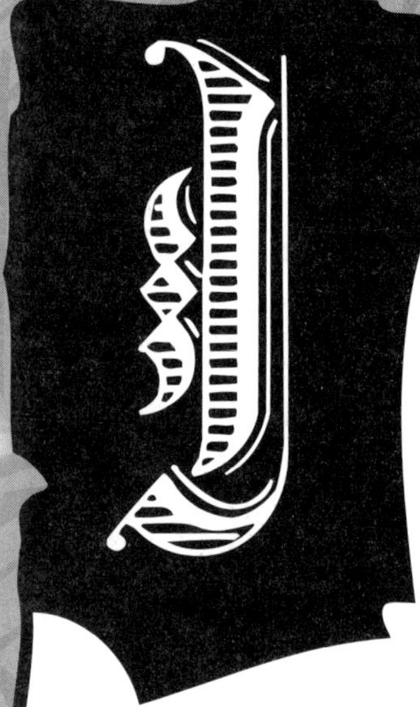

# nterconnectedness

*The energy of our lives connects us to everything and everyone in the universe—past, present, and future.*

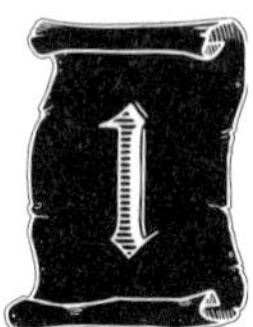

**Relationships create the fabric of our lives. They are the fibers that weave all things together.**

*—Eden Froust*

Reflection Questions

- *What people in your life are important to you?*
- *How does your life impact the people you see everyday?*
- *How does your life impact people you have never met?*

**As a kid I learned that my brother and I could walk forever on a railroad track and never fall off—if we just reached across the track and held each other's hand.**

*—Steve Potter*

Reflection Questions

- *How do you support the people in your life?*
- *How do you ask for support when you need it?*
- *What people in our society need a helping hand?*

**Individual commitment to a group effort—that is what makes a team work, a company work, a society work, a civilization work.**

*—Vince Lombardi*

Reflection Questions

- *When we think of teams we often think of sports. What other teams exist?*
- *What makes a good team?*
- *Why do people often try harder when they are part of a team?*

**No one can whistle a symphony. It takes an orchestra to play it.**

*—H.E. Luccock*

Reflection Questions

- *What things in life depend on people working together?*
- *What are you part of that is bigger than yourself?*
- *What do you share with others?*

**Man does not weave this web of life. He is merely a strand of it. Whatever he does to the web, he does to himself.**

*—Chief Seattle*

Reflection Questions

- *How are we interconnected with nature?*
- *What patterns can we find in nature that teach us about ourselves?*
- *Why do our decisions affect all living things?*

# Interconnectedness

◆ This we know. All things are connected like the blood which unites one family. All things are connected.
**—Chief Seattle**

◆ The true wonder of the world is available everywhere, in the minutest parts of our bodies, in the vast expanses of the cosmos, and in the interconnectedness of these and all things.
**—Michael Stark**

◆ Everything in nature contains all the power of nature. Everything is made of one hidden stuff.
**—Ralph Waldo Emerson**

◆ Each of us is connected to all living things whether we are aware of this beautiful fact or not. And should you ever begin to feel that you are becoming separated from the world, you are simply self-deceived, for you could no more do this than a wave could separate itself from the ocean and still be a wave.
**—Gerald Jampolsky**

◆ Four Laws of Ecology:
1) Everything is connected to everything else.
2) Everything must go somewhere.
3) Nature knows best.
4) There is no such thing as a free lunch.
**—Barry Commoner**

◆ When one tugs at a single thing in nature, he (she) finds it attached to the rest of the world.
**—John Muir**

◆ Live harmlessly.
**—Zen Maxim**

***Everything is connected … no one thing can change by itself.***
***—Paul Hawken***

◆ An act is not like a rock that one picks up and throws, and hits or misses and that's the end of it. When that rock is lifted, the earth is lighter; the hand that bears it is heavier. When it is thrown, the circuits of the stars respond, and where it strikes or falls the universe is changed.
**—Ursula K. LeGuin**

◆ When the oak is felled the forest echoes with its fall, but a hundred acorns are sown silently by an unnoticed breeze.
**—Thomas Carlyle**

◆ Every action in our lives touches on some chord that will vibrate in eternity.
**—Edwin Hubblel Chapin**

◆ We are all connected to everyone and everything in the universe. Therefore, everything one does as an individual affects the whole. All thoughts, words, images, prayers, blessings, and deeds are listened to be all that is.
**—Serge Kahili King**

◆ Today the network of relationships linking the human race to itself and to the rest of the biosphere is so complex that all aspects affect all others to an extraordinary degree. Someone should be studying the whole system, however crudely that has to be done, because no gluing together of partial studies of a complex nonlinear system can give a good idea of the behavior of the whole.
**—Murray Gell-Mann**

◆ Man (humankind) is a knot, a web, a mesh into which relationships are tied. Only those relationships matter.
**—Antoine de Saint-Exupery**

◆ My humanity is bound up in yours, for we can only be human together.
**—Archbishop Desmond Tutu**

◆ If you were all alone in the universe with no one to talk to, no one with which to share the beauty of the stars, to laugh with, to touch, what would be your purpose in life? It is other life, it is love, which gives your life meaning. This is harmony. We must discover the joy of each other, the joy of challenge, the joy of growth.
**—Mitsugi Saotome**

◆ Personal relationships are the fertile soil from which all advancement in real life grows.
**—Ben Stein**

◆ Our thoughts, our words and deeds are the threads of the net which we throw around ourselves.
**—Swami Vivekananda**

◆ It isn't intellect that connects us to other people; it is feeling.
**—Charles Fowler**

◆ Water, everywhere over the earth, flows to join together. A single natural law controls it. Each human is a member of a community and should work within it.
**—I Ching**

◆ We do not believe in ourselves until someone reveals deep inside us that something is valuable, worth listening to, worthy of our trust, sacred to our touch. Once we believe in ourselves we can risk curiosity, wonder, spontaneous delight or any experience that reveals the human spirit.
**—e.e. cummings**

◆ Each friend represents a world in us, a world possibly not born until they arrive, and it is only by this meeting that a new world is born.
**—Anaïs Nin**

◆ You think your pains and heartbreaks are unprecedented in the history of the world, but then you read. It was books that taught me that the things that tormented me were the very things that connected me with all the people who were alive, or who have ever been alive.
**—James Baldwin**

◆ We cannot live only for ourselves. A thousand fibers connect us with our fellow men; and among those fibers, as sympathetic threads, our actions run as causes, and they come back to us as effects.
**—Herman Melville**

◆ There is a destiny that makes us brothers. No one goes his way alone. What we send into the lives of others comes back into our own.
**—Edwin Markham**

◆ I believe every living thing carries its own energy force, and when we connect with the positive vibes in the air around us, we also infuse our aspirations with a breath of life.
**—Oprah Winfrey**

◆ People who deal with life generously and large-heartedly go on multiplying relationships to the end.
**—Arthur Christopher Benson**

***The best thing to hold on to in life is each other.***
***—Audrey Hepburn***

◆ When we choose actions that bring happiness and success to others, the fruit of our karma is happiness and success.
**—Deepak Chopra**

◆ The life I touch for good or ill will touch another life, and that in turn another, until who knows where the trembling stops or in what far place my touch will be felt.
**—Frederick Buechner**

◆ Do your little bit of good where you are; it's those little bits of good put together that overwhelm the world.
**—Archbishop Desmond Tutu**

◆ We are all affecting the world every moment, whether we mean to or not. Our actions and states of mind matter, because we're so deeply interconnected with one another.
**—Ram Dass**

◆ We are not going to be able to operate our Spaceship Earth successfully for much longer unless we see it as a whole spaceship and our fate as common. It has to be everybody or nobody.
**—R. Buckminster Fuller**

◆ A democracy is more than a form of government; it is primarily a mode of associated living, of conjoint communicated experience.
**—John Dewey**

◆ Nobody, but nobody, can make it out here alone.
**—Maya Angelou**

# 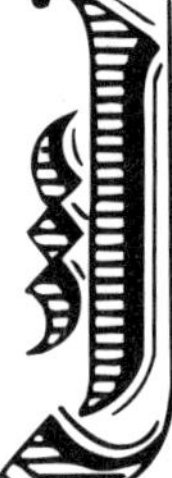nterconnectedness

◆ You can not sink someone else's end of the boat and still keep your own afloat.
**—Charles Bower**

◆ We are all in the same boat in a stormy sea, and we owe each other a terrible loyalty.
**—G. K. Chesterton**

◆ No one can go it alone. Somewhere along the line is the person who gives you faith that you can make it.
**—Grace Gil Oivarez**

◆ If you don't look out for others, who will look out for you?
**—Whoopi Goldberg**

◆ United we stand; divided we fall.
**—Aesop**

◆ It is in the shelter of each other that the people live.
**—Irish proverb**

◆ There can be hope only for a society which acts as one big family, not as many separate ones.
**—Anwar Sadat**

◆ We are so much less without each other.
**—Leo Buscaglia**

◆ Remember there's no such thing as a small act of kindness. Every act creates a ripple with no logical end.
**—Scott Adams**

◆ The miracle is this—the more we share, the more we have.
**—Leonard Nimoy**

◆ Shared joy is double joy. Shared sorrow is half sorrow.
**—Swedish proverb**

***There are plenty of teams in every sport that have great players and never win titles. Most of the time, those players aren't willing to sacrifice for the greater good of the team …. Talent wins games but teamwork and intelligence win championships.***
***—Michael Jordan***

◆ Appreciation is a wonderful thing: it makes what is excellent in others belong to us as well.
**—Voltaire**

◆ My biggest thrill came the night Elgin Baylor and I combined for seventy-three points in Madison Square Garden. Elgin had seventy-one of them.
**—Rod Hundley**

◆ To get the full value of joy you must have people to divide it with.
**—Mark Twain**

◆ The way is long—let us go together. The way is difficult—let us help each other. The way is joyful—let us share it.
**—Joyce Hunter**

◆ Good company in a journey makes the way seem shorter.
**—Izaak Walton**

◆ Surround yourself with people who believe you can.
**—Dan Zadra**

◆ Keep away from people who try to belittle your ambitions. Small people always do that, but the really great make you feel that you, too, can become great.
**—Mark Twain**

◆ To play and win together you must practice together.
**—Lewis Edwards**

◆ Teamwork requires that everyone's efforts flow in a single direction. Feelings of significance happen when a team's energy takes on a life of its own.
**—Pat Riley**

◆ It marks a big step in your development when you come to realize that other people can help you do a better job than you could do alone.
**—Andrew Carnegie**

◆ Light is the task when many share the toil.
**—Homer**

◆ None of us is as smart as all of us.
**—Ken Blanchard**

◆ We > I.
**—Spencer Kagan**

◆ Humans, as social beings, mature intellectually in reciprocal relationships with other people.
**—Art Costa**

◆ Alone we can do so little; together we can do so much.
**—Helen Keller**

◆ All communities have a culture. It is the climate of their civilization.
**—Walter Lippmann**

◆ One person may supply the idea for a company, community or nation, but what gives the idea its force is a community of dreams.
**—Andre Malraux**

◆ All human beings are also dream beings. Dreaming ties all mankind together.
**—Jack Kerouac**

◆ You can dream, create, design, and build the most wonderful idea in the world, but it requires people to make the dream a reality.
**—Walt Disney**

◆ It is social support from and accountability to valued peers that motivates committed efforts to succeed.
**—David & Roger Johnson**

◆ People must believe in each other, and feel that it can be done and must be done; in that way they are enormously strong. We must keep up each other's courage.
**—Vincent van Gogh**

◆ The first step in the evolution of ethics is a sense of solidarity with other human beings.
**—Albert Schweitzer**

◆ Real education should educate us out of self into something far finer; into a selflessness which links us with all humanity.
**—Nancy Astor**

***Great discoveries and achievements invariably involve the cooperation of many minds.***
***—Alexander Graham Bell***

◆ Whether for the individual or for the nation, self is best served by transcending self.
**—Senator Frank E. Moss**

◆ It seems ridiculous to have divisive things going on anywhere in the world.
**—Roberta Bondar**

◆ For behind all seen things lies something vaster; everything is but a path, a portal, a window opening on something more than itself.
**—Antoine de Saint-Exupery**

◆ I am done with great things and big plans, great institutions and big successes. I am for those tiny, invisible loving human forces that work from individual to individual, creeping through the crannies of the world like so many rootlets, or like the capillary oozing of water, which, if given time will rend the hardest monuments of pride.
**—William James**

◆ I believe we are here on the planet Earth to live, grow up and do what we can to make this world a better place for all people to enjoy freedom.
**—Rosa Parks**

◆ We must care about the world of our children and grandchildren, a world we may never see.
**—Bertrand Russell**

◆ Let us put our minds together and see what kind of life we can make for our children.
**—Sitting Bull**

◆ One generation plants the trees; another gets shade.
**—Chinese proverb**

◆ What cannot be achieved in one lifetime will happen when one lifetime is joined to another.
**—Harold Kushner**

◆ We are the ones we've been waiting for.
**—June Gordon**

◆ Within our bodies course the same elements that flame in the stars.
**—Susan Schiefelbein**

# Interconnectedness

**Relationships create the fabric of our lives. They are the fibers that weave all things together.**

**—Eden Froust**



Karen Kettle & Dr. Spencer Kagan: ***Inspirational Quotations***
Kagan Publishing • 1 (800) 933-2667 • www.KaganOnline.com

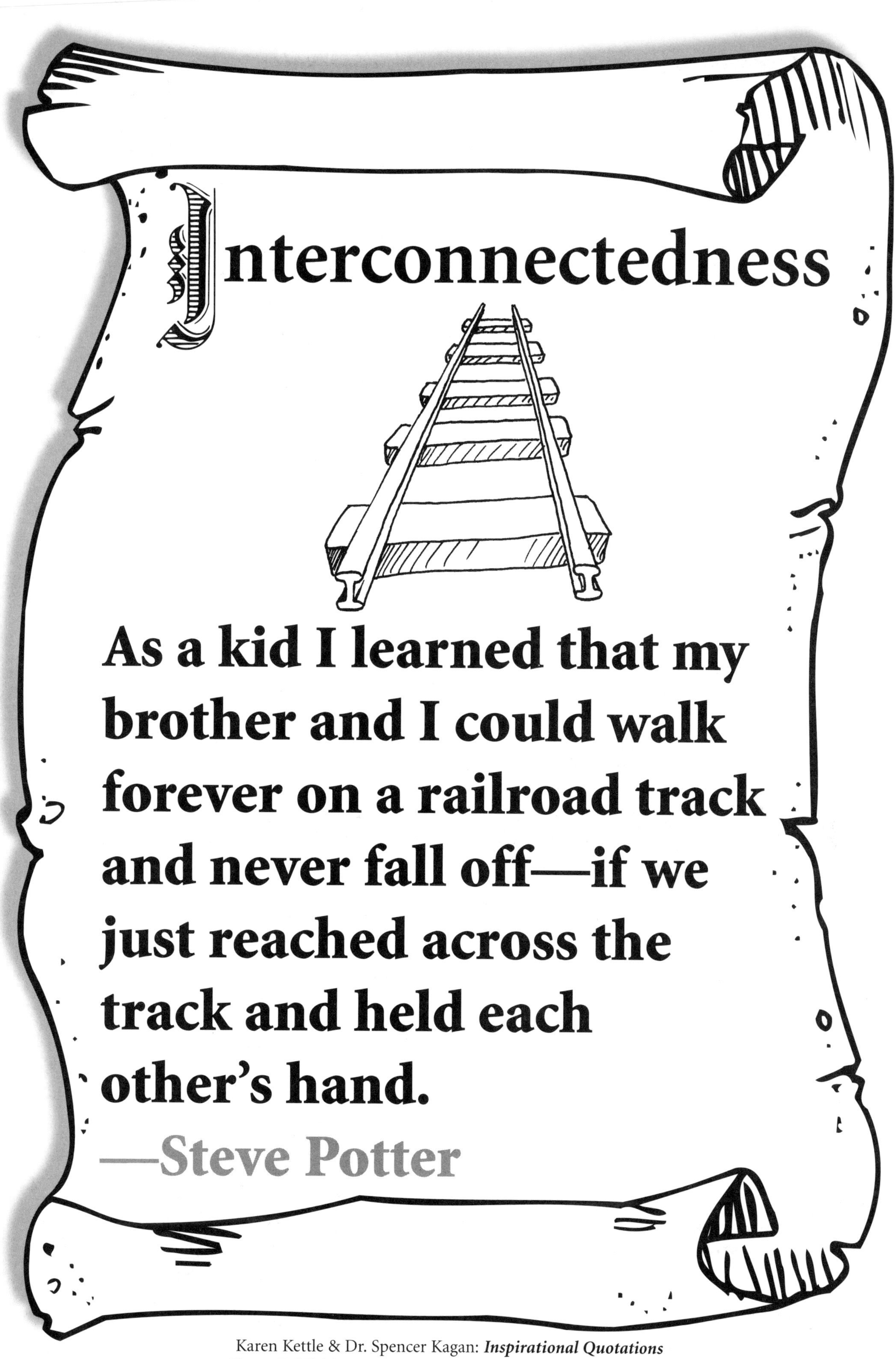

Interconnectedness
As a kid I learned that my brother and I could walk forever on a railroad track and never fall off—if we just reached across the track and held each other's hand.
—Steve Potter

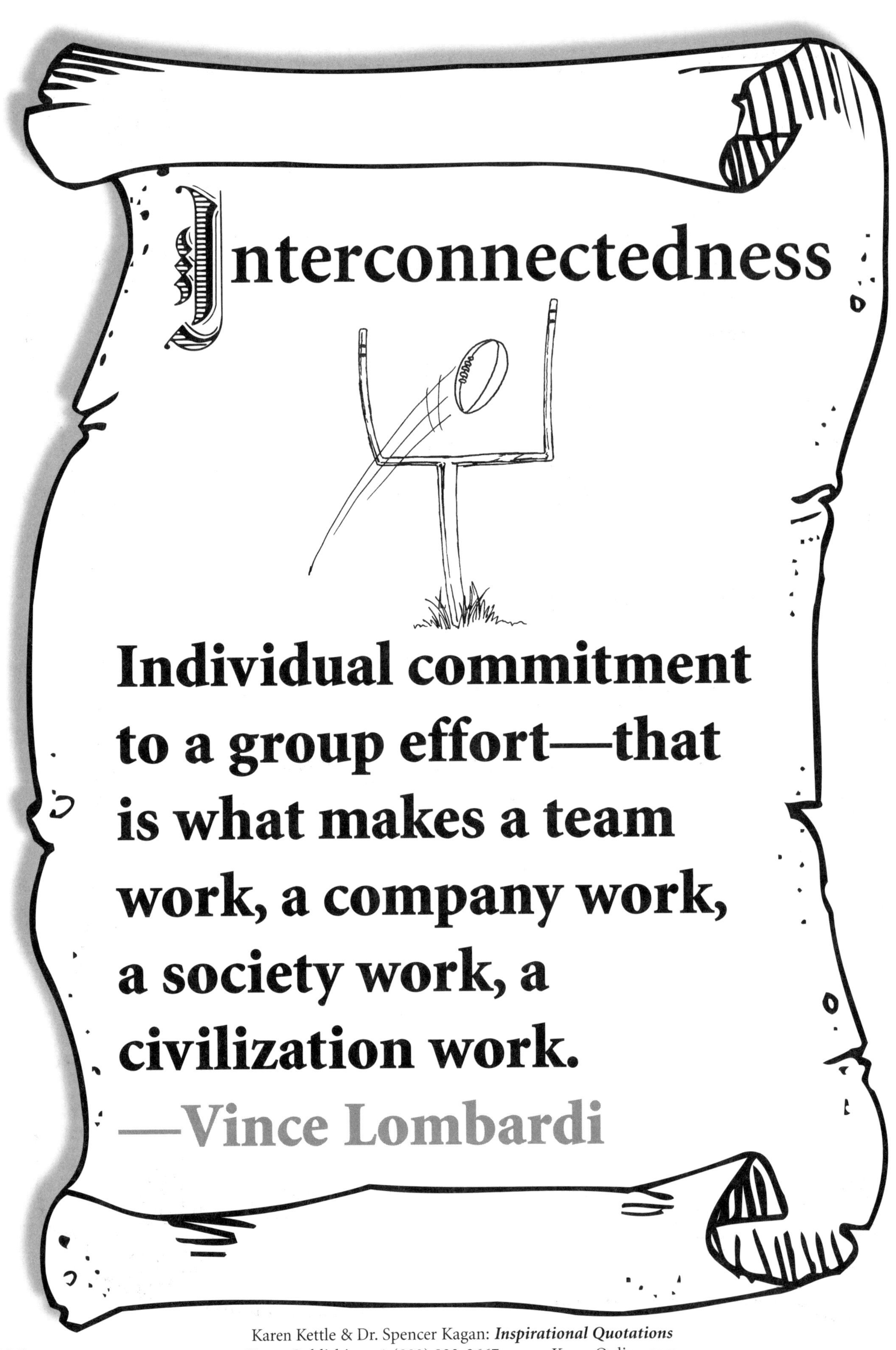
Interconnectedness
Individual commitment to a group effort—that is what makes a team work, a company work, a society work, a civilization work.
—Vince Lombardi

Karen Kettle & Dr. Spencer Kagan: *Inspirational Quotations*
Kagan Publishing • 1 (800) 933-2667 • www.KaganOnline.com

# Interconnectedness

**No one can whistle a symphony. It takes an orchestra to play it.**

**— H.E. Luccock**

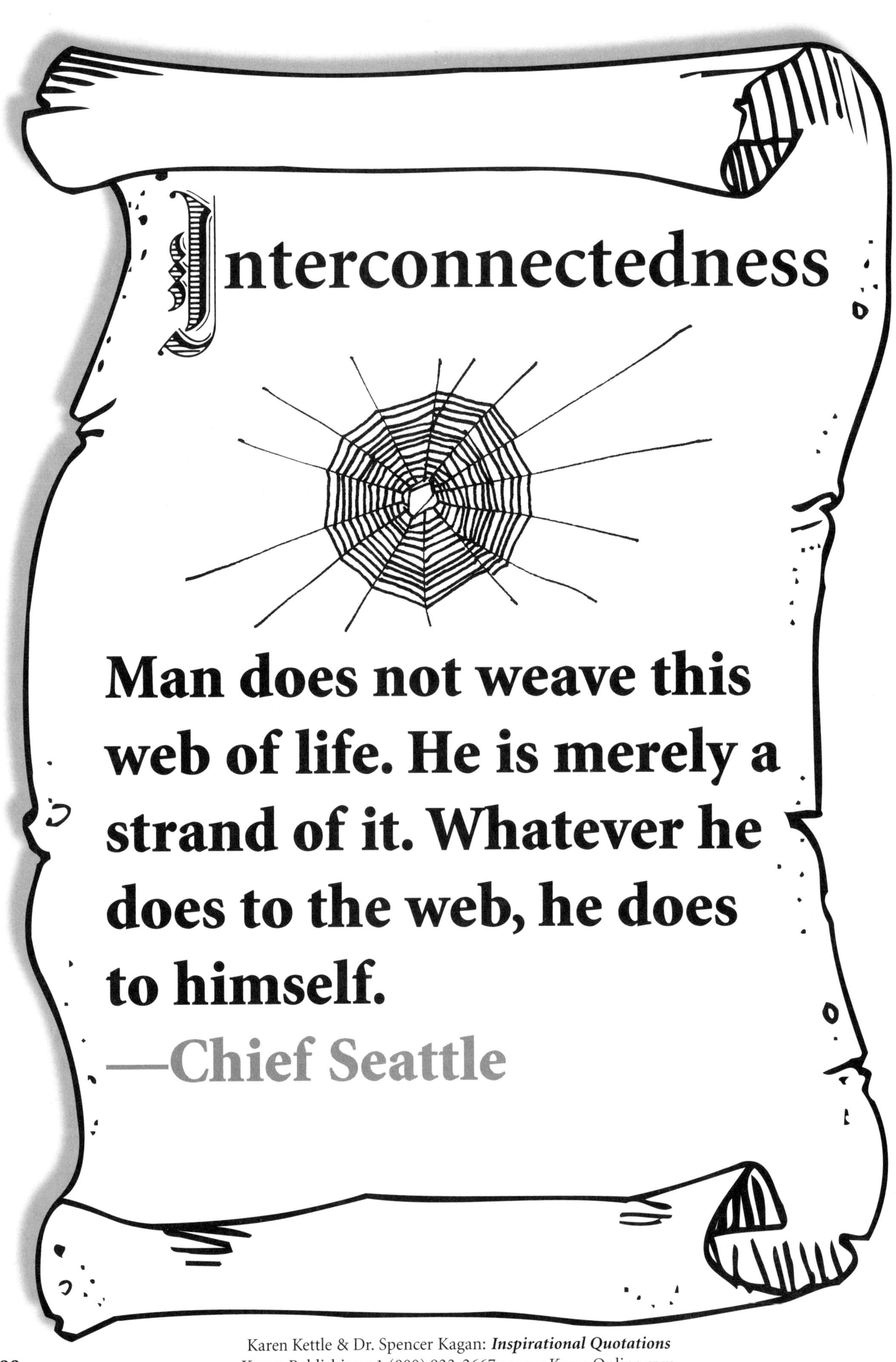
Interconnectedness
Man does not weave this web of life. He is merely a strand of it. Whatever he does to the web, he does to himself.
—Chief Seattle

Karen Kettle & Dr. Spencer Kagan: *Inspirational Quotations*
Kagan Publishing • 1 (800) 933-2667 • www.KaganOnline.com

Leadership

# Leadership

*Leaders guide us to our true selves: Who are we? What is our purpose? Where do we need to go? What principles will we embrace along our path?*

**Getting things done is not always what is most important. There is value in allowing others to learn, even if the task is not accomplished as quickly, efficiently, or effectively.**

*—R. D. Clyde*

Reflection Questions

- *Why is it important to help other people develop their skills?*
- *Why does it take us more time and energy to do something we are just learning?*
- *How do leaders serve and support their followers?*

**If you do not have the time to read, you do not have the time to lead.**

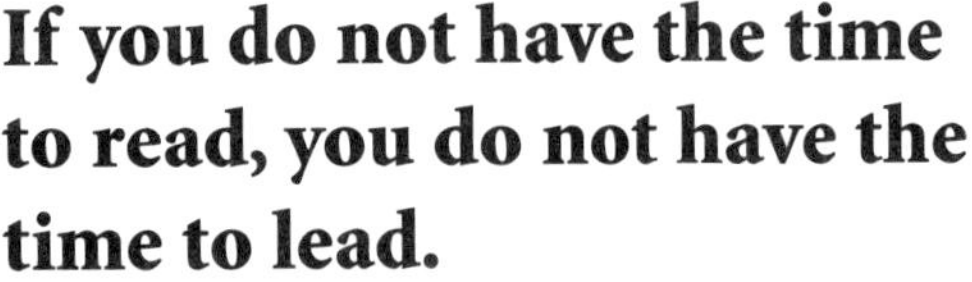

*—Phillip Schlechty*

Reflection Questions

- *What have you read lately?*
- *Why is it important that leaders continue to be learners?*
- *What should people in leadership positions be reading?*

**The great leaders are like the best conductors—they reach beyond the notes to reach the magic in the players.**

*—Blain Lee*

Reflection Questions

- *Who is the best leader you know?*
- *What qualities and skills do great leaders need?*
- *How do great leaders create meaning and commitment?*

**If you want to build a ship, don't drum up people to collect wood and don't assign them tasks and work, but rather teach them to long for the endless immensity of the sea.**

*—Antoine de Saint-Exupery*

Reflection Questions

- *Who inspires you?*
- *What do you long for? What are you willing to work toward?*
- *How do you motivate and engage others?*

**The only real training for leadership is leadership.**

*—Antony Jay*

Reflection Questions

- *When was a time in your life that you felt like a leader?*
- *What lessons have you already learned about leading others?*
- *What leadership roles would you like to step into in the future?*

# Leadership

◆ Leadership is not wielding authority—it's empowering people.
**—Becky Brodin**

◆ Leadership should be born out of the understanding of the needs of those who would be affected by it.
**—Marian Anderson**

◆ The very essence of all power to influence lies in getting the other person to participate.
**—Harry A. Overstreet**

◆ You will never be a leader unless you first learn to follow and be led.
**—Tiorio**

◆ There go my people. I must find out where they are going so that I can lead them.
**—Alexandre Ledru-Rollin**

◆ Everyone leads. Leadership is an action, not a position.
**—Donald H. McGannon**

◆ The function of leadership is to produce more leaders, not more followers.
**—Ralph Nader**

◆ Leadership and learning are indispensable to each other.
**—John F. Kennedy**

◆ The moment you stop learning, you stop leading.
**—Rick Warren**

◆ We should not only use the brains we have, but all that we can borrow.
**—Woodrow Wilson**

◆ A great leader must be an educator, bridging the gap between the vision and the familiar.
**—Henry Kissinger**

◆ Leader is synonymous with educator, and to me leadership in any context is an educational pursuit, unless we choose to confuse leadership with authority. Leadership is the practice of asking timely questions, raising contradictions to a level of awareness and wisely following.
**—John Hurt**

◆ The most successful leader of all is the one who sees another picture not yet actualized.
**—Mary Parker Follett**

***As we look ahead into the next century, leaders will be those who empower others.***
***—Bill Gates***

◆ Leadership is the capacity to translate vision into reality.
**—Warren Bennis**

◆ All leadership takes place through the communication of ideas to the minds of others.
**—Charles Cooley**

◆ The art of communication is the language of leadership.
**—James Humes**

◆ People are saying, "I want a company and a job that values me as much as I value it. I want something in my life not just to invest my time in, but to believe in."
**—Anita Roddick**

◆ "Come to the edge," he said. They said: "We are afraid." "Come to the edge," he said. They came. He pushed them, and they flew ….
**—Guillaume Apollinaire**

◆ All leadership is appreciative leadership. It's the capacity to see the best in the world around us, in our colleagues, and in the groups we are trying to lead.
**—David Cooperrider**

◆ Highlight my strengths and my weaknesses will disappear.
**—Maori proverb**


Karen Kettle & Dr. Spencer Kagan: ***Inspirational Quotations***
Kagan Publishing • 1 (800) 933-2667 • www.KaganOnline.com

◆ Outstanding leaders go out of the way to boost the self-esteem of their personnel. If people believe in themselves, it's amazing what they can accomplish.
**—Sam Walton**

◆ Successful people use their strength by recognizing, developing and utilizing the talents of others.
**—Zig Ziglar**

◆ A good objective of leadership is to help those who are doing poorly to do well and to help those who are doing well to do even better.
**—Jim Rohn**

◆ Treat people as they are, and they remain that way. Treat them as though they are already what they can be, and you help them become what they are capable of becoming.
**—Johann Wolfgang Von Goethe**

◆ The ultimate leader is one who is willing to develop people to the point that they eventually surpass him or her in knowledge and ability.
**—Fred A. Manske Jr.**

◆ A sense of humor is part of the art of leadership, of getting along with people, of getting things done.
**—Dwight D. Eisenhower**

◆ People will forget what you said, and people will forget what you did, but they will never forget how you made them feel.
**—Astraea**

◆ The one piece of advice which will contribute to making you a better leader, will provide you with greater happiness and will advance your career more than any other advice … and it doesn't call for a special personality or any certain chemistry … and any one of you can do it. And that advice is: You must care.
**—Lt. General Melvin Zais**

◆ A leader is a dealer in hope.
**—Napoleon Bonaparte**

◆ The first and last task of a leader is to keep hope alive—the hope that we can and will find our way through to a better world.
**—John W. Gardner**

***I suppose leadership at one time meant muscles; but today it means getting along with people.***
***—Indira Gandhi***

◆ A good head and a good heart are always a formidable combination.
**—Nelson Mandela**

◆ Heart, instinct, principles.
**—Blaise Pascal**

◆ Trust is the conviction that the leader means what he or she says. It is a belief in two old-fashioned qualities called consistency and integrity. Trust opens the door to change.
**—Peter Drucker**

◆ Trust is the emotional glue that binds followers and leaders together.
**—Warren Bennis & Bert Nanus**

◆ The supreme quality for a leader is unquestionably integrity. Without it, no real success is possible, no matter whether it is on a section gang, a football field, in an army or in an office.
**—Dwight D. Eisenhower**

◆ If anything goes bad, I did it. If anything goes semi-good, then we did it. If anything goes real good, then you did it. That's all it takes to get people to win football games for you.
**—Bear Bryant**

◆ It is amazing what you can accomplish if you do not care who gets the credit.
**—Harry S. Truman**

◆ My grandfather once told me that there were two kinds of people: those who do the work and those who take the credit. He told me to try to be in the first group; there was much less competition.
**—Indira Gandhi**

◆ Progress comes from caring more about what needs to be done than about who gets the credit.
**—Dorothy Height**

◆ A leader will only command the level of loyalty he or she is willing to give to others.
**—Winston Churchill**

◆ It is not fair to ask of others what you are not willing to do yourself.
**—Eleanor Roosevelt**

# Leadership

◆ Keep your fears to yourself, but share your courage with others.
**—Robert Louis Stevenson**

◆ I have cherished the idea of a democratic and free society in which all persons live together in harmony and with equal opportunities. It is an ideal which I hope to live for and to achieve. But, if needs be, it is an ideal for which I am prepared to die.
**—Nelson Mandela**

◆ Leadership is practiced not so much in words as in attitude and in actions.
**—Harold Geneen**

◆ One does not improve through argument but through examples … be what you wish to make others become.
**—Henri Frédéric Amiel**

◆ Practice what you preach.
**—English proverb**

◆ Example is not the main thing in influencing others. It is the only thing.
**—Albert Schweitzer**

◆ If you can't be a good example, then you'll just have to be a horrible warning.
**—Catherine Aird**

◆ I have learnt silence from the talkative, toleration from the intolerant, and kindness from the unkind; yet strangely, I am ungrateful to these teachers.
**—Kahlil Gibran**

◆ The role of the leader is to ensure that the organization develops relationships that help produce desirable results.
**—Michael Fullan**

◆ A learning organization is an organization in which people at all levels are collectively, continually enhancing their capacity to create things they really want to create.
**—Peter Senge**

***Management is doing things right; leadership is doing the right things.***
***—Peter Drucker***

◆ Successful leaders spend a lot of time creating the identity of the organization—what values are, what our mission is, what our purpose is, how we are going to act together as one.
**—Margaret Wheatley**

◆ If people are coming to work excited … if they're making mistakes freely and fearlessly …. If they're having fun … if they're concentrating on doing things, rather than preparing reports and going to meetings—then somewhere you have leaders.
**—Robert Townsend**

◆ Organizations intent on building shared visions continually encourage members to develop their personal visions. If people don't have their own vision, all they can do is "sign up" for someone else's. The result is compliance, never commitment. On the other hand, people with a strong sense of personal direction can join together to create a powerful synergy toward what I/we want.
**—Peter Senge**

◆ It is better to know some of the questions than all of the answers.
**—James Thurber**

◆ I make progress by having people around me who are smarter than I am and listening to them. And I assume that everyone is smarter about something than I am.
**—Henry J. Kaiser**

◆ I never got very far until I stopped imagining I had to do everything myself.
**—Frank W. Woolworth**

◆ The times do not allow anyone the luxury of waiting around for others to lead. All can lead and ought to be invited to do so.
**—Matthew Fox**

◆ The essence of intelligence would seem to be in knowing when to think and act quickly, and knowing when to think and act slowly.
**—Robert Sternberg**

◆ The art of being wise is the art of knowing what to overlook.
**—William James**

◆ Never tell people how to do things. Tell them what to do and they will surprise you with their ingenuity.
**—Gen. George Patton Jr.**

◆ The method of the enterprising is to plan with audacity and to execute with vigor.
**—Christian Bovee**

◆ Strategy is about marrying ideas and capabilities with intuition and daring.
**—J. Saul**

◆ Leadership has a harder job to do than just choose sides. It must bring sides together.
**—Jesse Jackson**

◆ To promote cooperation remember: People tend to resist that which is forced upon them. People tend to support that which they help to create.
**—Vince Pfaff**

◆ Do what you can, with what you have, where you are.
**—Theodore Roosevelt**

◆ Better to do a little well than a great deal badly.
**—Socrates**

◆ There are no office hours for leaders.
**—Cardinal Gibbons**

◆ You get nervous with no one supporting you. People don't always have the vision, and the secret for the person with the vision is to stand up. But it takes courage. You get lonely.
**—Natalie Cole**

◆ A real leader faces the music when he (she) doesn't like the tune.
**—Arnold H. Glassgow**

◆ Being in power is like being a lady. If you have to tell people you are, you aren't.
**—Margaret Thatcher**

***Mountaintops inspire leaders but valleys mature them.***
***—J. Phillip Everson***

◆ It is not enough that we do our best; sometimes we have to do what is required.
**—Winston Churchill**

◆ Leadership is about coping with change.
**—John Kotter**

◆ These days, doing nothing as a leader is a great risk, so you might as well take the risks worth doing.
**—Michael Fullan**

◆ Be assured that any worthwhile action will create change and attract support.
**—Philip Marvin**

◆ We have enough people who tell it like it is—now we could use a few who tell it like it can be.
**—Robert Orben**

◆ A leader takes people where they want to go. A great leader takes people where they don't necessarily want to go but ought to be.
**—Rosalynn Carter**

◆ The winds and waves are always on the side of the best navigators.
**—Edward Gibbon**

◆ Leaders achieve their effectiveness chiefly through the stories they relate …leaders present a dynamic perspective to their followers: not just a headline or snapshot, but a drama that unfolds over time, in which they—leader and followers—are the principal characters or heroes. Together, they have embarked on a journey in pursuit of certain goals, and along the way and into the future, they can expect to encounter certain obstacles or resistances that must be overcome.
**—Howard Gardner**

◆ If your actions inspire others to dream more, learn more, do more and become more, you are a leader.
**—John Quincy Adams**

◆ The final test of a leader is that he (she) leaves behind in other people the convictions and the will to carry on.
**—Walter Lippmann**

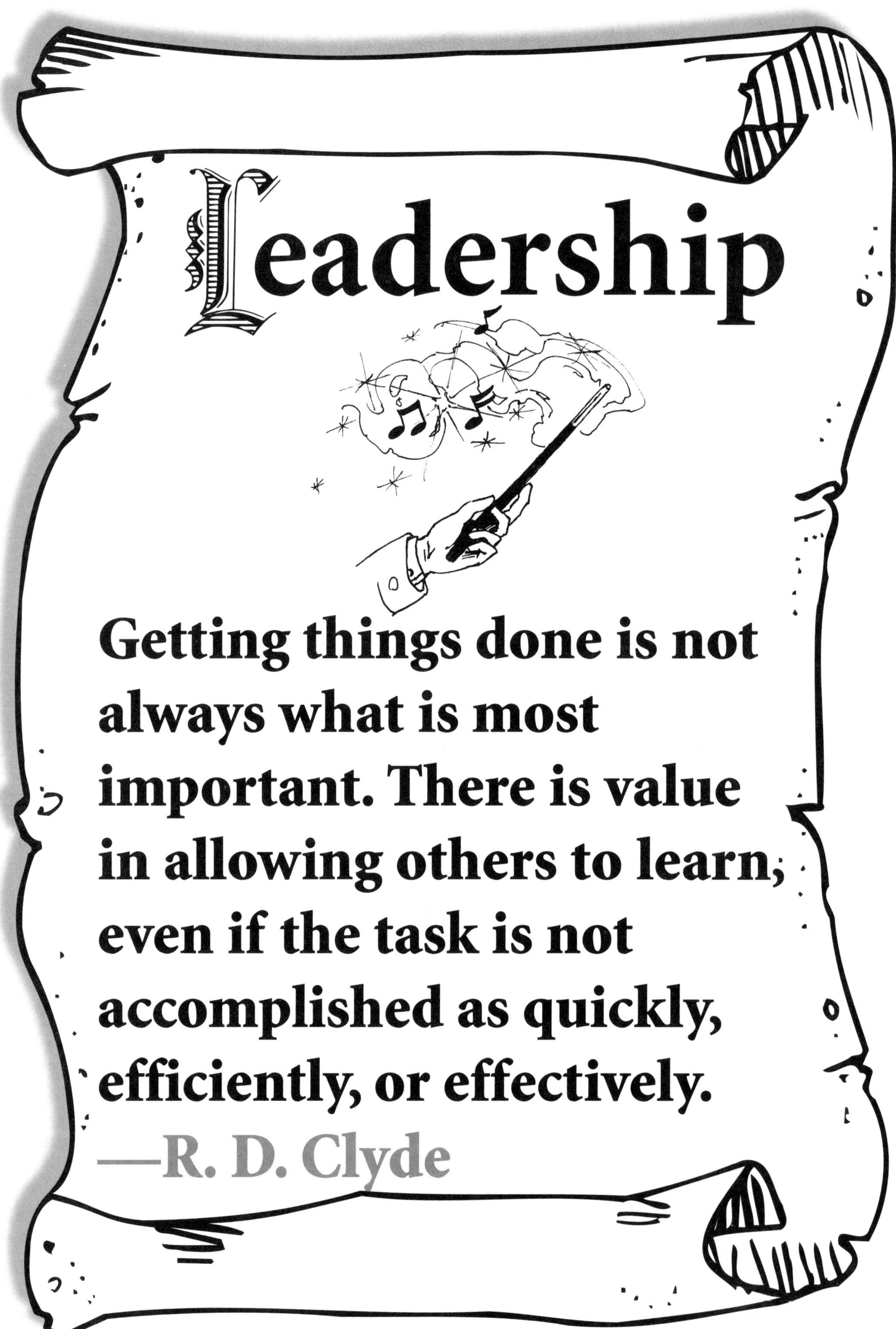
Leadership
Getting things done is not always what is most important. There is value in allowing others to learn, even if the task is not accomplished as quickly, efficiently, or effectively.
—R. D. Clyde

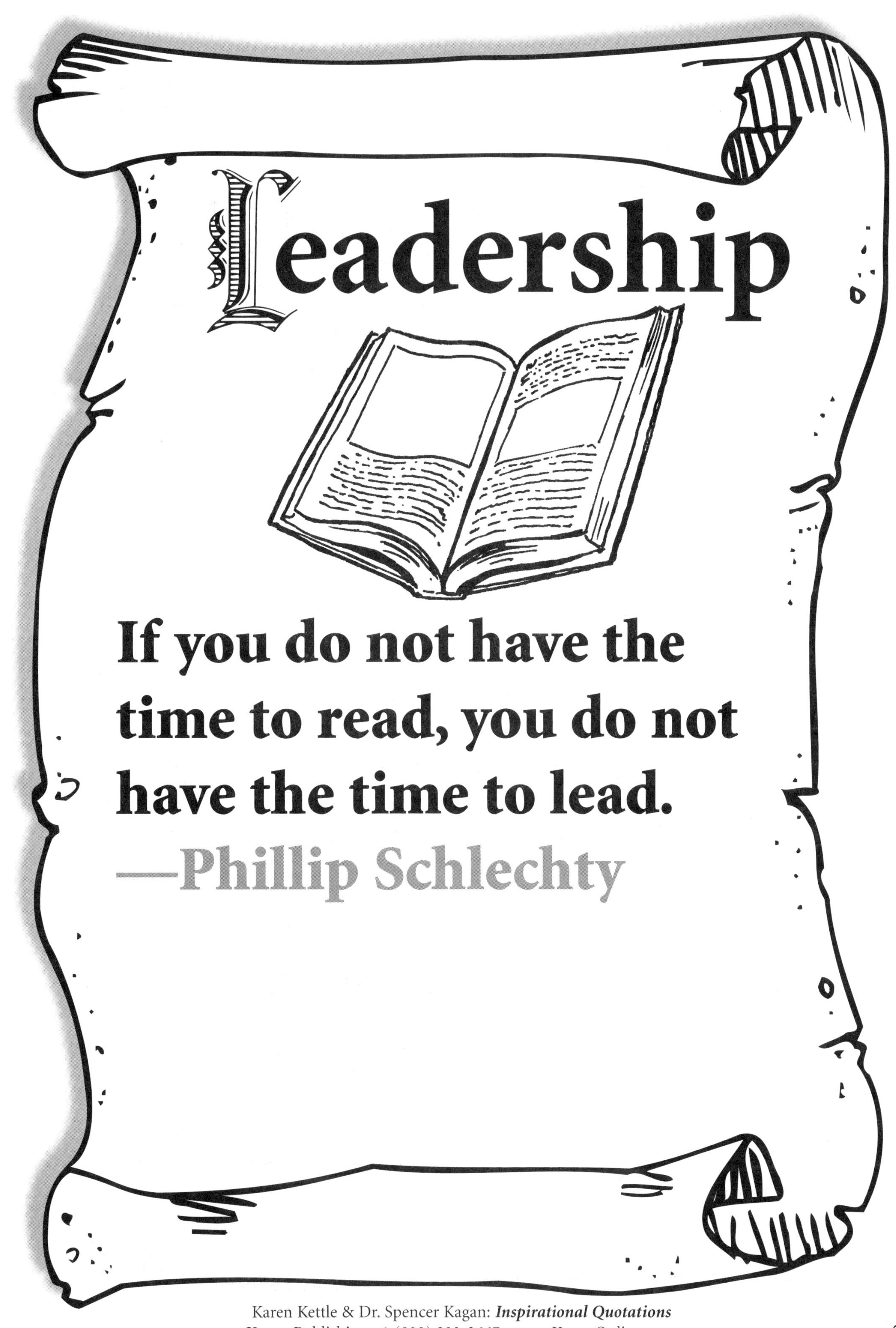
Leadership
If you do not have the time to read, you do not have the time to lead.
—Phillip Schlechty

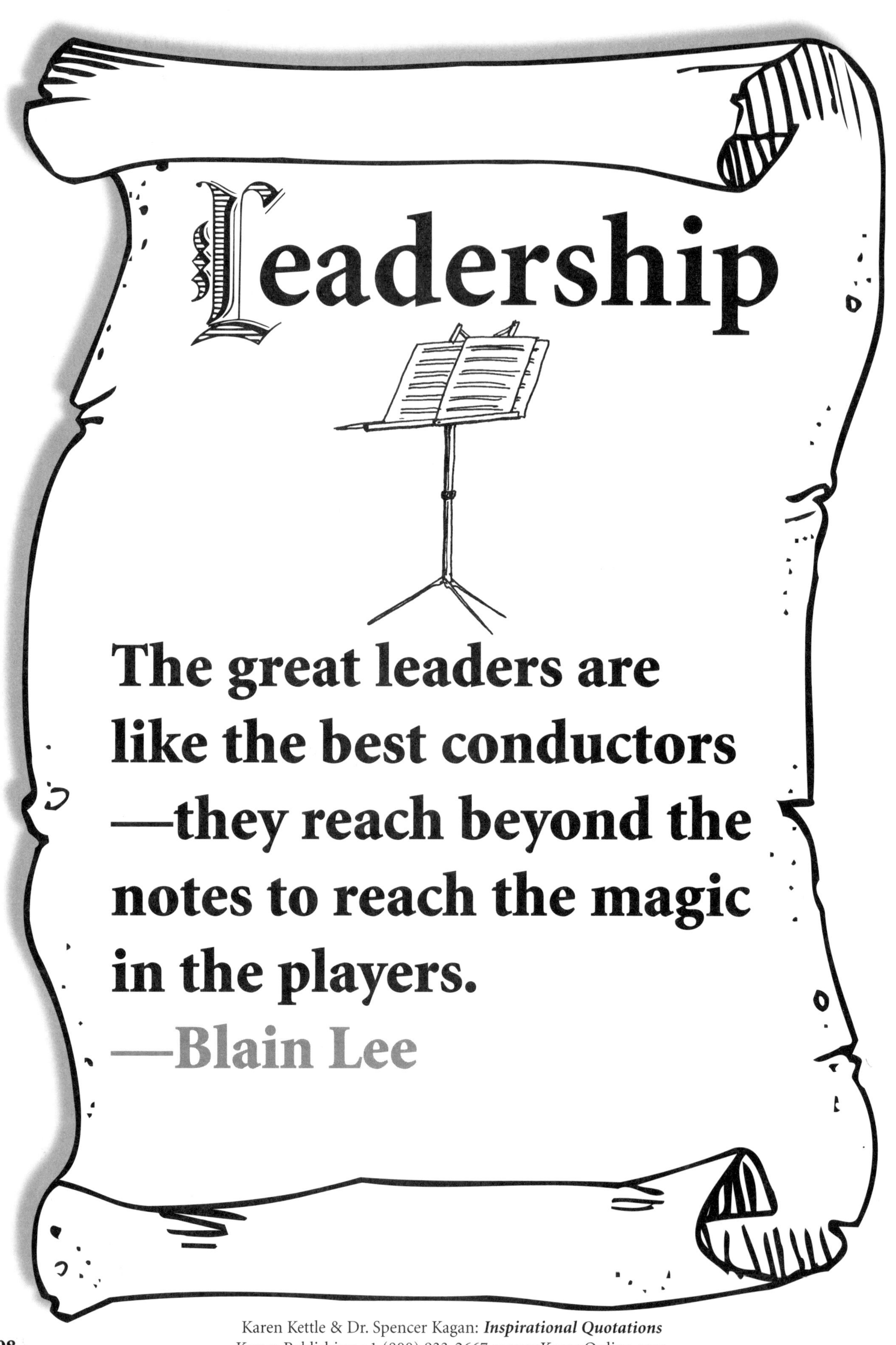

Leadership
The great leaders are
like the best conductors
—they reach beyond the
notes to reach the magic
in the players.
—Blain Lee

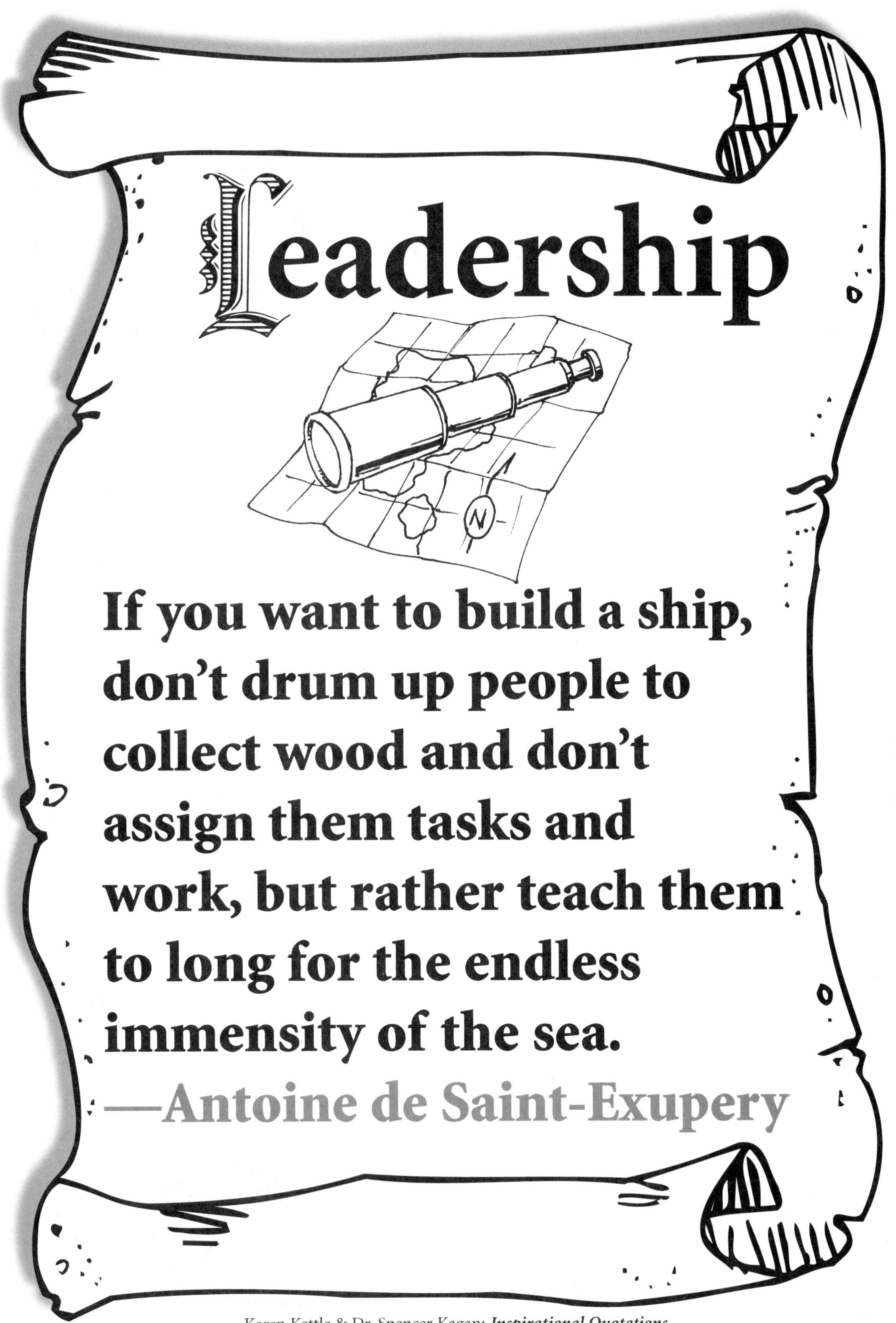
Leadership
N
If you want to build a ship, don't drum up people to collect wood and don't assign them tasks and work, but rather teach them to long for the endless immensity of the sea.
—Antoine de Saint-Exupery

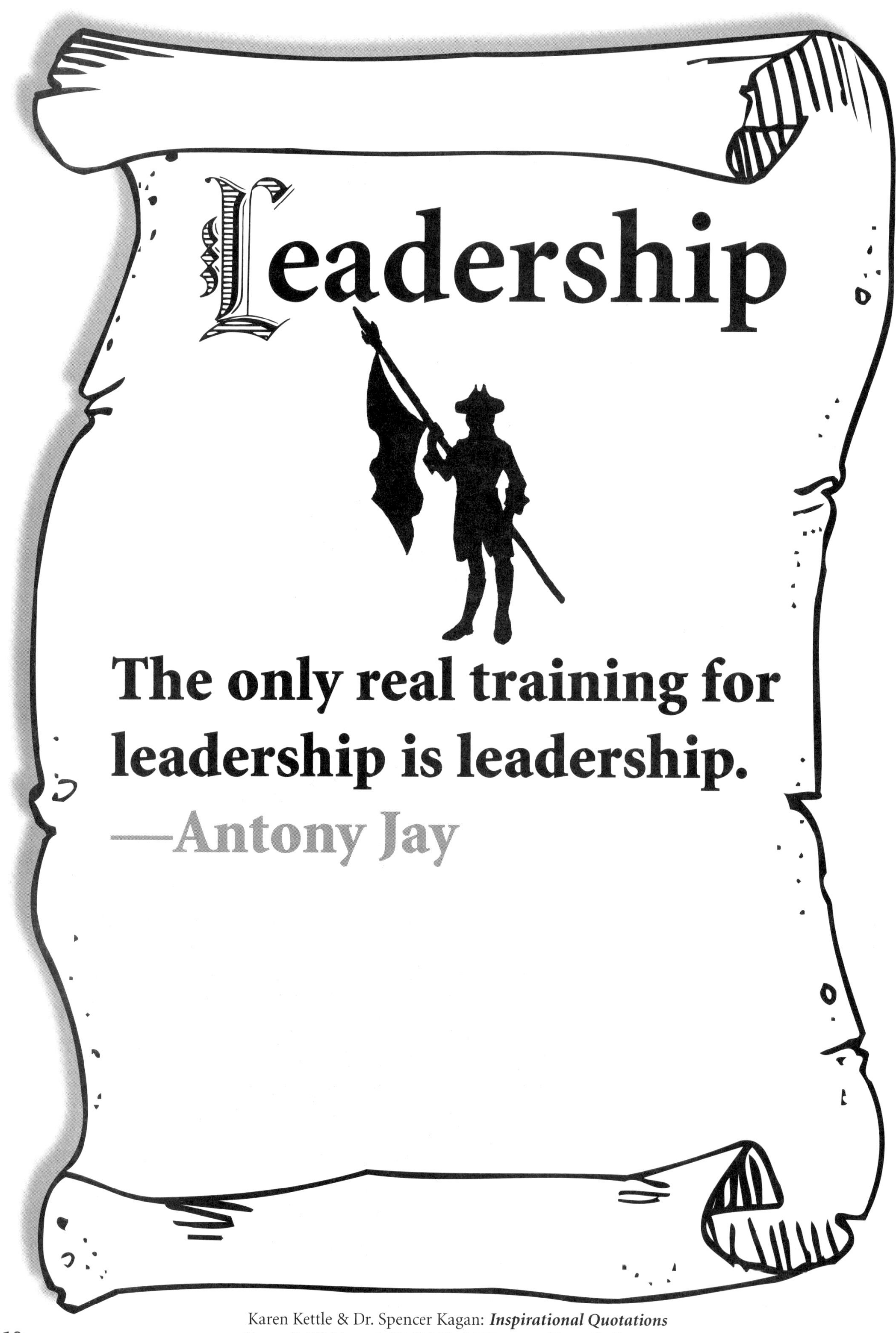
Leadership
The only real training for leadership is leadership.
—Antony Jay

Karen Kettle & Dr. Spencer Kagan: *Inspirational Quotations*
Kagan Publishing • 1 (800) 933-2667 • www.KaganOnline.com

# Learning

# Learning

*Learning makes us human. It allows us to make sense of the world and ourselves.*

**Ideas are like rabbits. You get a couple and learn how to handle them, and pretty soon you have a dozen.**

*—John Steinbeck*

Reflection Questions

- *What is the most interesting thing you have ever learned?*
- *How does one idea lead to another?*
- *Is it possible to stop learning? Why?*

**When starting a new project, try to make as many mistakes as rapidly as possible in order to learn as much as you can in the shortest period of time.**

*—Bob Moawad*

Reflection Questions

- *What have you learned from your mistakes?*
- *Why are people afraid to make mistakes if they help us learn?*
- *What kinds of mistakes do you make on purpose?*

**If I had influence with the good fairy who is supposed to preside over the christening of all children, I should ask that her gift to each child in the world be a sense of wonder so indestructible that it would last throughout life.**

*—Rachel Carson*

Reflection Questions

- *What did you wonder about as a child?*
- *What do you wonder about now?*
- *If you could grant a gift to each child in the world, what would it be?*

4

**I would be most content if my children grew up to be the kind of people who think decorating consists mostly of building enough bookshelves.**

*—Anna Quindlen*

### Reflection Questions

- *If you could fill a bookshelf in the school library, what would the books be about?*
- *What books do you think everyone your age should read? Why?*
- *Do we learn more from fiction or nonfiction? Why?*

**I am always doing that which I can not do, in order that I may learn how to do it.**

*—Pablo Picasso*

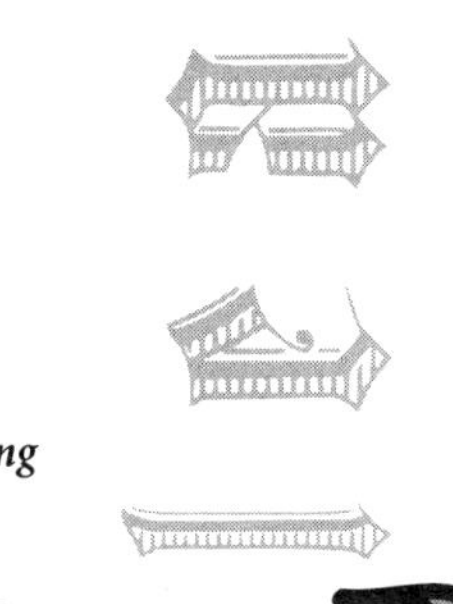

### Reflection Questions

- *What feelings do you have when you are learning something new?*
- *Do you find it easier to learn by yourself or with other people? Why?*
- *What would you like to learn how to do that you have never tried before?*

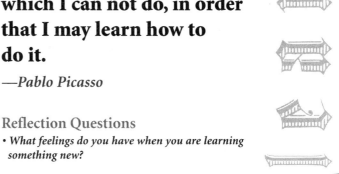

# Learning

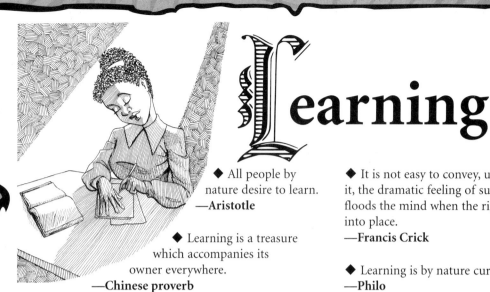

◆ All people by nature desire to learn.
—**Aristotle**

◆ Learning is a treasure which accompanies its owner everywhere.
—**Chinese proverb**

◆ It is not easy to convey, unless one has experienced it, the dramatic feeling of sudden enlightenment that floods the mind when the right idea finally clinches into place.
—**Francis Crick**

◆ Learning is by nature curiosity.
—**Philo**

◆ Learning is its own exceeding great reward.
—**William Hazlitt**

◆ A primary duty of education is to let curiosity rip.
—**Ivor Brown**

◆ All learning is in the learner, not in the teacher.
—**Plato**

***Anything will give up its secrets if you love it enough.***
***—George Washington Carver***

◆ Only the curious will learn and only the resolute overcome the obstacles to learning. The quest quotient has always excited me more than the intelligence quotient.
—**Eugene S. Wilson**

◆ They know enough who know how to learn.
—**Henry Adams**

◆ I have no special talents. I am only passionately curious.
—**Albert Einstein**

◆ When the student is ready … the lesson appears.
—**Gene Oliver**

◆ Whenever there are beginners and experts, old and young, there is some kind of learning going on, some kind of teaching. We are all pupils and we are all teachers.
—**Gilbert Highet**

◆ There is no difference between living and learning … it is impossible and misleading and harmful to think of them as being separate.
—**John Holt**

◆ By learning you will teach; by teaching you will learn.
—**Latin proverb**

◆ That is what learning is. You suddenly understand something, you've understood all your life, but in a new way.
—**Doris Lessing**

◆ I'm always looking like a child, for the wonders I know I'm going to find—maybe not every time, but every once in a while.
—**Richard Feynman**

◆ Learning is not attained by chance, it must be sought for with ardor and attended with diligence.
—**Abigail Adams**

◆ Learning without thought is labor lost.
—**Confucius**

◆ One can think effectively only when one is willing to endure suspense and to undergo the trouble of searching.
—**John Dewey**

◆ How sustained an episode a learner is willing to undergo depends upon what the person expects to get from his (her) efforts, in the sense of such external things as grades but also in the sense of a gain in understanding.
—**Jerome S. Bruner**

◆ We don't receive wisdom; we must discover it for ourselves after a journey that no one can take us or spare us.
**—Marcel Proust**

◆ Each artist was at first an amateur.
**—Ralph Waldo Emerson**

◆ It took me four years to paint like Raphael, but a lifetime to paint like a child.
**—Pablo Picasso**

◆ I think I am making progress!
**—Pablo Casals**
***(Response to reporter's question about why at 95 years of age he practiced the cello six hours a day)***

◆ Practice is the best of all instructors.
**—Pubilius Syrus**

◆ Learning is never done without errors and defeat.
**—Vladimir Lenin**

◆ You win some and you learn some.
**—Barry Johnson**

◆ Your most unhappy customers are your greatest source of learning.
**—Bill Gates**

◆ I learned more from the one restaurant that didn't work than from all the ones that were successes.
**—Wolfgang Puck**

◆ We learn something every day, and lots of times it's that what we learned the day before was wrong.
**—Billy Vaughn**

◆ Mistakes are the portals of discovery.
**—James Joyce**

◆ The road to wisdom? Well, it's plain and simple to express: Err and err and err again, but less and less and less.
**—Piet Hein**

◆ You've got to have a safe environment where people can make mistakes and learn from them. If we're not making mistakes, we're not going anywhere.
**—Gordon Forward**

***I hear and I forget. I see and I remember. I do and I understand.***
*—Confucius*

◆ Aim for success, not perfection. Never give up your right to be wrong, because then you will lose the ability to learn new things and move forward with your life.
**—David M. Burns**

◆ Unless you try to do something beyond what you have already mastered you will never grow.
**—Ronald E. Osborn**

◆ What a child can do in cooperation today, he (she) can do alone tomorrow. Therefore the only good kind of instruction is that which marches ahead of development and leads it; it must be aimed not so much at the ripe as the ripening action.
**—Lev Vygotsky**

◆ Learning is a social process that occurs through interpersonal interaction within a cooperative context. Individuals, working together, construct shared understandings and knowledge.
**—David Johnson, Roger Johnson, & Karl Smith**

◆ What children can do with the assistance of others might be in some sense even more indicative of their mental development than what they can do alone.
**—Lev Vygotsky**

◆ One must learn by doing the thing; for though you think you know it, you have no certainty, until you try.
**—Sophocles**

◆ All genuine learning is active, not passive. It involves the use of the mind, not just the memory. It is a process of discovery, in which the student is the main agents, not the teacher.
**—Mortimer J. Adler**

◆ Don't learn to do, but learn in doing. Let your falls not be on a prepared ground, but let them be bona fide falls in the rough and tumble of the world.
**—Samuel Butler**

◆ In the end we retain from our studies only that which we practically apply.
**—Johann Wolfgang Von Goethe**

# Learning

◆ To "learn from experience" is to make a backward and forward connection between what we do to things and what we enjoy or suffer from things in consequence. Under such conditions, doing becomes a trying; an experiment with the world to find out what it is like; the undergoing becomes instruction—discovery of the connection of things.
**—John Dewey**

◆ If students are not able to transform their lived experience into knowledge and to use the already acquired knowledge as a process to unveil new knowledge, they will never be able to participate rigorously in a dialogue as a process of learning and knowing.
**—Donald Macedo**

◆ It is important that students bring a certain ragamuffin, barefoot irreverence to their studies; they are not here to worship what is known, but to question it.
**—Jacob Bronowski**

◆ One of the first things I think young people, especially nowadays, should learn is how to see for yourself and listen for yourself and think for yourself.
**—Malcolm X**

◆ The important thing is not to stop questioning.
**—Albert Einstein**

◆ Good questions outrank easy answers.
**—Paul A. Samuelson**

◆ The shrewd guess, the fertile hypothesis, the courageous leap to a tentative conclusion—these are the most valuable coins of the thinker at work. But in most schools guessing is heavily penalized and is associated somehow with laziness.
**—Jerome S. Bruner**

◆ To every answer you can find a new question.
**—Yiddish proverb**

***There is a name for natural learning. It is called play. When play is divorced from learning, neither thrives.***
***—Spencer Kagan***

◆ The world is but a school of inquiry.
**—Michel de Montaigne**

◆ If we value independence, if we are disturbed by the growing conformity of knowledge, of values, of attitudes, which our present system induces, then we may wish to set up conditions of learning which make for uniqueness, for self-direction, and for self-initiated learning.
**—Carl Rogers**

◆ Self-initiated learning, once begun, develops its own momentum.
**—Ray Harjen**

◆ Long-lasting learning is generated by going "internal." We can take information in better when it's not forced on us by an outsider, and when we can process it in our own way.
**—Eric Jensen**

◆ The important thing is not so much that every child should be taught, as that every child should be given the wish to learn.
**—John Lubbock**

◆ All children have preparedness, potential, curiosity and interest in constructing their learning, in engaging in social interaction and in negotiating everything the environment brings to them.
**—Lella Gandini**

◆ Play gives children a chance to practice what they are learning .... They have to play with what they know to be true in order to find out more, and then they can use what they learn in new forms of play.
**—Fred Rogers**

◆ A positive learning climate in a school for young children is a composite of many things. It is an attitude that respects children. It is a place where children receive guidance and encouragement from the responsible adults around them. It is an environment where children can experiment and try out new ideas without the fear of failure. It is an atmosphere that builds children's self-confidence so they dare to take risks. It is an environment that nurtures a love of learning.
**—Carol B. Hillman**

◆ Extraordinariness is most likely to emerge if aspiring individuals are exposed to extraordinary models; ponder the lessons embodied in those models; and have the opportunity to enact critical practices in a relatively protected setting.
**—Howard Gardner**

◆ It is the quality of our experiences, the satisfaction, excitement or joy that we get or fail to get from them, that will determine how those experiences will change us—in short, what we learn.
**—John Holt**

***Children have more need of models than of critics.***
***—Joseph Joubert***

◆ There is no such thing as not paying attention; the brain is always paying attention to something.
**—Patricia Wolfe**

◆ If facts are the seeds that later produce knowledge and wisdom, then the emotions and the impressions of the senses are the fertile soil in which the seeds must grow.
**—Rachel Carson**

◆ All learning has an emotional base.
**—Plato**

◆ You cannot know what you do not feel.
**—Myra Mannes**

◆ Learning is a result of listening, which in turn leads to even better listening and attentiveness to the other person. In other words, to learn from the child, we must have empathy, and empathy grows as we learn.
**—Alice Miller**

◆ Learning first occurs as a part of emotional interactions; it involves the split-second initiatives that children take as they try to engage other people, interact with them, communicate and reason with them.
**—Stanley I. Greenspan**

◆ Happiness comes only when we push our brains and hearts to the farthest reaches of which we are capable.
**—Leo Rosten**

◆ What we learn with pleasure we never forget.
**—Louis Mercier**

◆ Just as eating against one's will is injurious to health, so study without a liking for it spoils the memory, and it retains nothing it takes in.
**—Leonardo da Vinci**

◆ There are three principal means of acquiring knowledge ... observation of nature, reflection, and experimentation. Observation collects facts; reflection combines them; experimentation verifies the result of that combination.
**—Denis Diderot**

◆ You can know the name of a bird in all the languages of the world, but when you're finished, you'll know absolutely nothing whatever about the bird .... So let's look at the bird and see what it's doing—that's what counts. I learned very early the difference between knowing the name of something and knowing something.
**—Richard Feynman**

◆ Knowledge is not a commodity to be traded between expert and novice. Rather, it is a construction of ideas negotiated by the learner in a social setting.
**—Rosamar Garcia**

◆ We have a hunger of the mind which asks for knowledge of all around us; and the more we gain, the more is our desire. The more we see, the more we are capable of seeing.
**—Maria Mitchell**

◆ I think the one lesson I have learned is that there is no substitute for paying attention.
**—Diane Sawyer**

◆ In completing one discovery we never fail to get an imperfect knowledge of others of which we could have no idea before, so that we cannot solve one doubt without creating several new ones.
**—Joseph Priestly**

◆ Doubt is the key to all knowledge.
**—Arabian proverb**

# Learning

◆ The greatest obstacle to discovering the shape of the earth, the continents, and the ocean was not ignorance but the illusion of knowledge.
**—Daniel J. Boorstin**

◆ It is what we think we know already that often prevents us from learning.
**—Claude Bernard**

◆ Belief gets in the way of learning.
**—Robert Heinlein**

◆ We don't know one millionth of one percent about anything.
**—Thomas Alva Edison**

◆ It is better to know nothing than to learn nothing.
**—Hebrew proverb**

◆ I try to learn as much as I can because I know nothing compared to what I need to know.
**—Muhammad Ali**

◆ I am not wise. Not knowing, and learning to be comfortable with not knowing, is a great discovery.
**—Sue Bender**

◆ The wisest mind has something yet to learn.
**—George Santayana**

◆ Where there is an open mind, there will always be a frontier.
**—Charles Kettering**

◆ Ignorance once dispelled is difficult to reestablish.
**—Laurence J. Peter**

◆ We can learn nothing except by going from the known to the unknown.
**—Claude Bernard**

◆ I was born not knowing and have had only a little time to change that here and there.
**—Richard Feynman**

***A mind once stretched by a new idea never regains its original dimension.***
***—Oliver Wendell Holmes***

◆ A love affair with knowledge will never end in heartbreak.
**—Michael Garrett Marino**

◆ The known is finite, the unknown infinite; intellectually we stand on an islet in the midst of an illimitable ocean of inexplicability. Our business in every generation is to reclaim a little more land.
**—Thomas H. Huxley**

◆ To learn means to accept the postulate that life did not begin at my birth. Others have been here before me, and I walk in their footsteps. The books I have read were composed by generations of fathers and sons, mothers and daughters, teachers and disciples. I am the sum total of their experiences, their guests. And so are you.
**—Elie Wiesel**

◆ When I got my library card, that's when my life began.
**—Rita Mae Brown**

◆ I find television very educating. Every time somebody turns on the set, I go into the other room and read a book.
**—Groucho Marx**

◆ Read not to contradict and confute, nor to believe and take for granted; but to weigh and consider.
**—Sir Francis Bacon**

◆ I suggest that the only books that influence us are those for which we are ready, and which have gone a little further down our particular path than we have gone ourselves.
**—E. M. Forster**

◆ The best of a book is not the thought which it contains, but the thought which it suggests; just as the charm of music dwells not in the tones but in the echoes of our hearts.
**—Oliver Wendell Holmes**

◆ Reading good books is like having a conversation with the most distinguished men of past ages.
**—René Descartes**

◆ Read every day something no one else is reading. Think every day something no one else is thinking. It is bad for the mind to be always part of unanimity.
**—Christopher Morley**

◆ The books that help you most, are those which make you think the most.
**—Theodore Parker**

◆ In the case of good books, the point is not how many of them you can get through, but rather how many can get through to you.
**—Mortimer J. Adler**

◆ You are the same today that you are going to be five years from now except for two things: the people with whom you associate and the books you read.
**—Charles Jones**

◆ Today a reader, tomorrow a leader.
**—W. Fusselman**

◆ Outside of a dog, a man's best friend is a book. Inside of a dog, it's too dark to read.
**—Groucho Marx**

◆ The essence of learning is the ability to manage change by changing yourself.
**—A. De Gues**

◆ Anyone who stops learning is old, whether at twenty or eighty. Anyone who keeps learning stays young.
**—Henry Ford**

◆ Nothing ages people like not thinking.
**—Christopher Morley**

◆ Wealth, if you use it, comes to an end. Learning if you use it, increases.
**—Swahili proverb**

***To learn is to change. Education is a process that changes the learner.***
*—George Leonard*

◆ I am convinced that it is of primordial importance to learn more every year than the year before.
**—Peter Ustinov**

◆ You must learn day by day, year by year, to broaden your horizon. The more things you love, the more you are interested in, the more you enjoy, the more you are indignant about, the more you have left when anything happens.
**—Ethel Barrymore**

◆ Study as if you were going to live forever; live as if you were going to die tomorrow.
**—Maria Mitchell**

◆ Whoever ceases to be a student has never been a student.
**—George Iles**

◆ Do not confine your children to your own learning, for they were born in another time.
**—Hebrew proverb**

◆ Do not believe what you have heard. Do not believe in tradition because it is handed down many generations. Do not believe in anything that has been spoken of many times. Do not believe because the written statements come from some old sage. Do not believe in conjecture. Do not believe in authority or teachers or elders. But after careful observation and analysis, when it agrees with reason and it will benefit one and all, then accept it and live by it.
**—Buddha**

◆ The illiterate of the 21st century will not be those who cannot read and write, but those who cannot learn, unlearn and relearn.
**—Alvin Toffler**

◆ What is important is to keep learning, to enjoy challenge, and to tolerate ambiguity. In the end there are no certain answers.
**—Martina Horner**

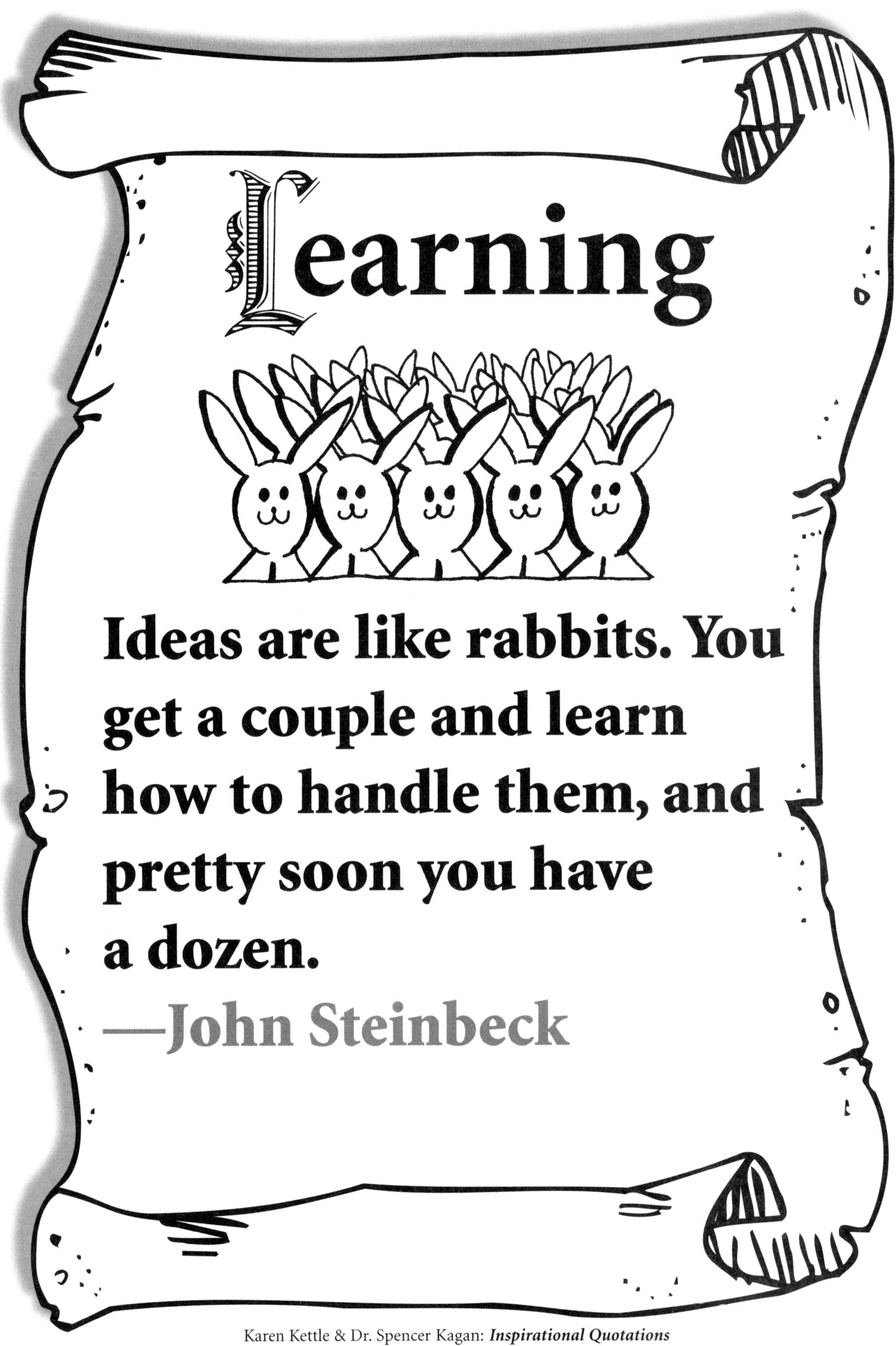
Learning
Ideas are like rabbits. You get a couple and learn how to handle them, and pretty soon you have a dozen.
—John Steinbeck

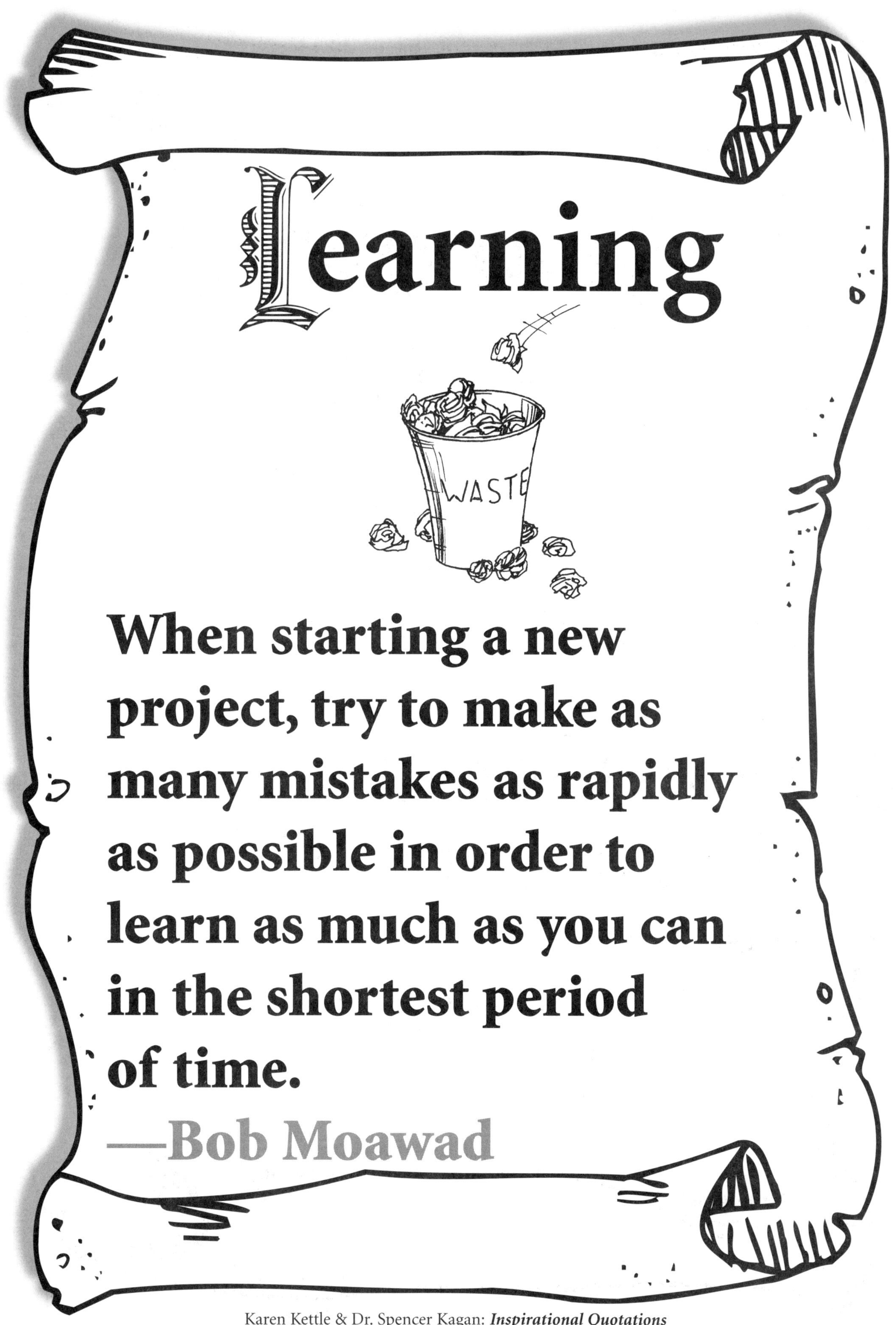
Learning
WASTE
When starting a new project, try to make as many mistakes as rapidly as possible in order to learn as much as you can in the shortest period of time.
—Bob Moawad

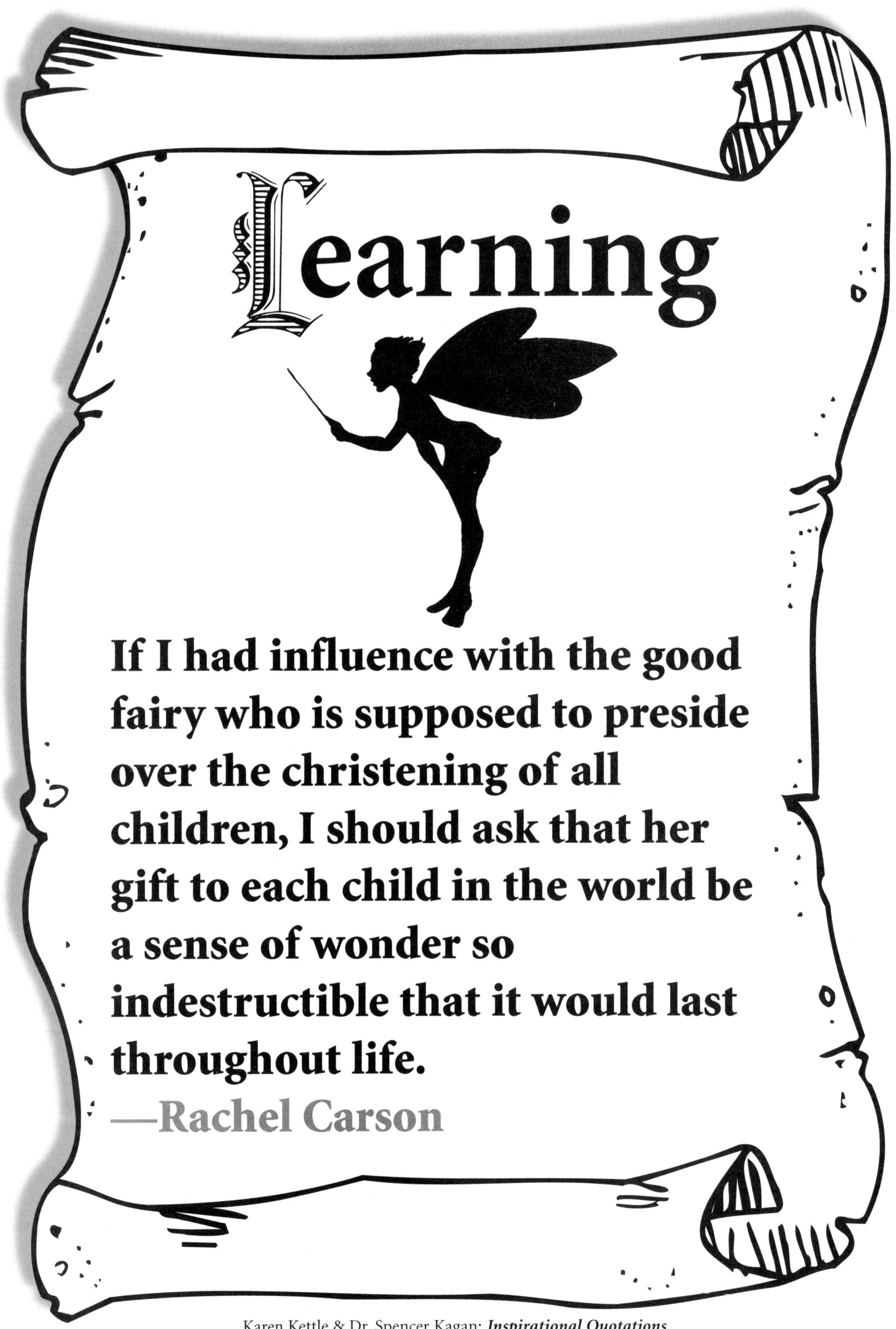
Learning
If I had influence with the good fairy who is supposed to preside over the christening of all children, I should ask that her gift to each child in the world be a sense of wonder so indestructible that it would last throughout life.
—Rachel Carson

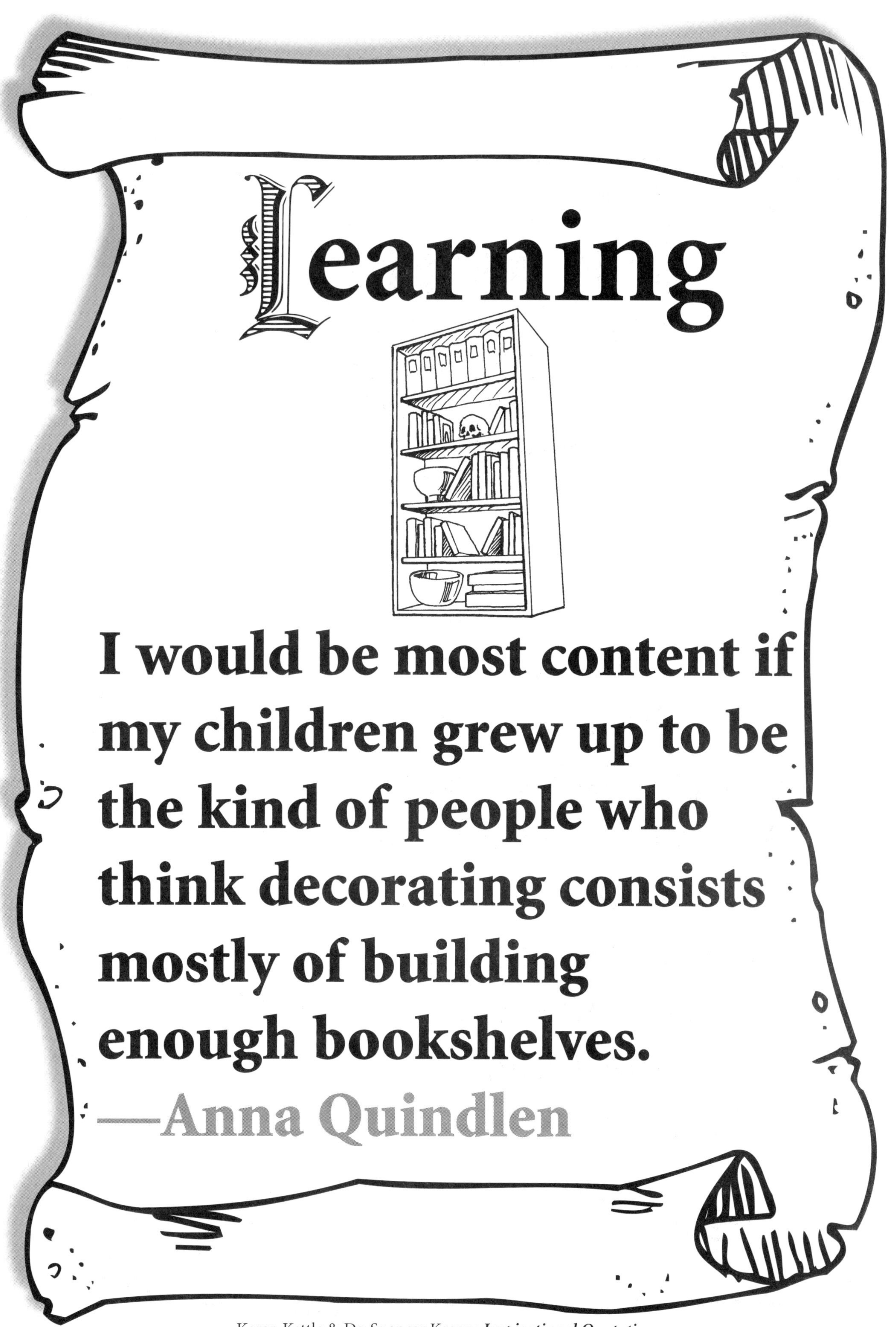
Learning
I would be most content if my children grew up to be the kind of people who think decorating consists mostly of building enough bookshelves.
—Anna Quindlen

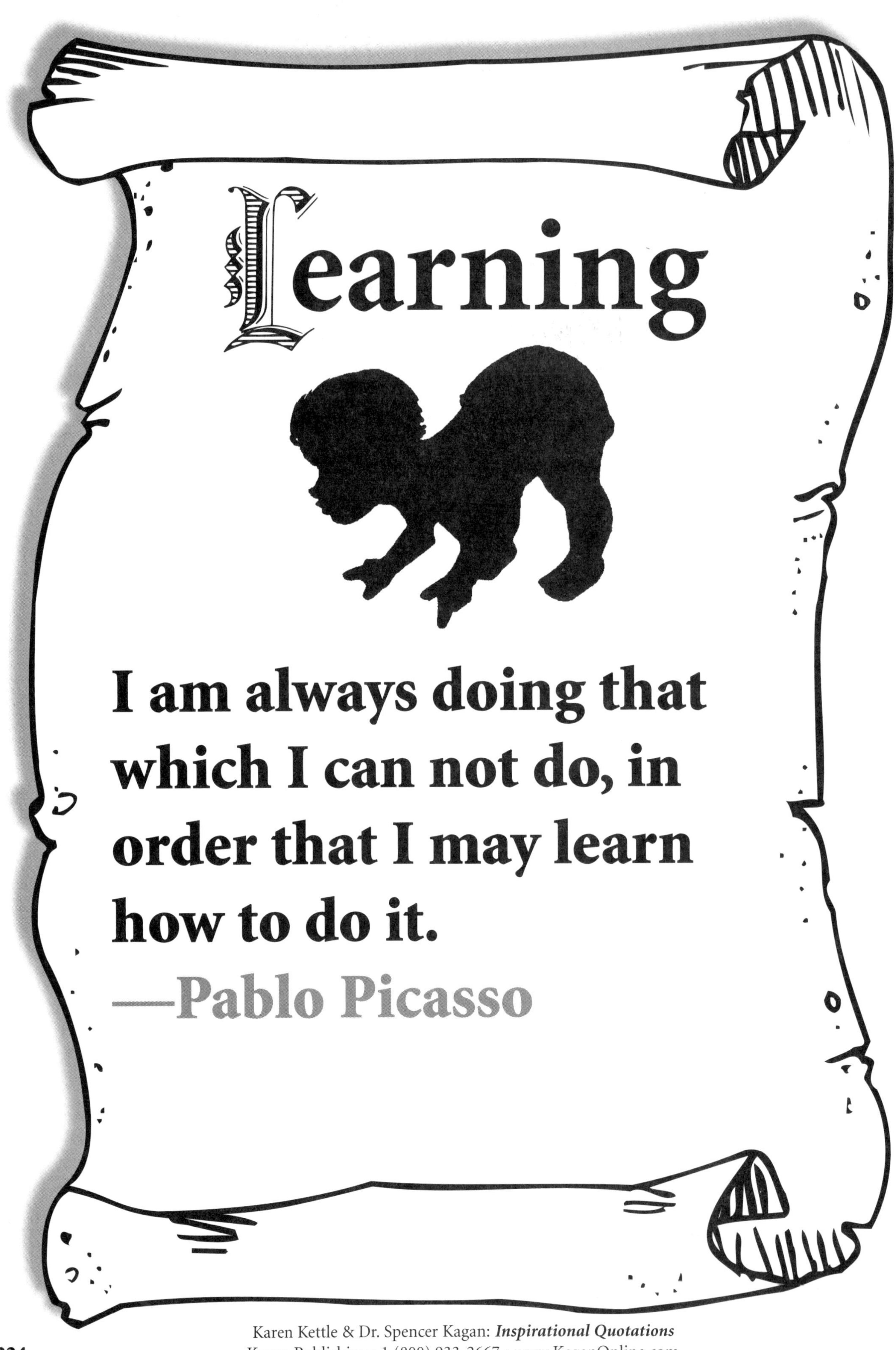
Learning
I am always doing that which I can not do, in order that I may learn how to do it.
—Pablo Picasso

Opportunity
OPPORTUNITY

# Opportunity

*Opportunities are all around us. They are chances to try something new or see something differently.*

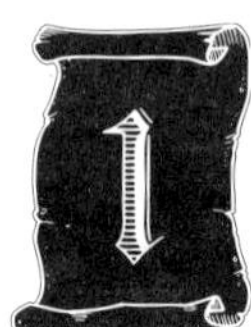

**Too often the opportunity knocks, but by the time you push back the chain, push back the bolt, unhook the two locks and shut off the burglar alarm, it's too late.**

*—Rita Coolidge*

Reflection Questions

- *What opportunities have you missed by being too cautious?*
- *What does an opportunity look like?*
- *How else do opportunities arrive other than "knocking at the door"?*

**Seize the moment. Remember all those women on the *Titanic* who waved off the dessert cart.**

*—Erma Bombeck*

Reflection Questions

- *Why is it scary to take a chance when a good opportunity comes along?*
- *When was a time in your life that you seized the moment?*
- *Why should we take advantage of the opportunities we have each day to do good things for other people?*

**Most look up and admire the stars; a champion climbs a mountain and grabs one.**

*—H. Jackson Brown Jr.*

Reflection Questions

- *What opportunities shine like stars for you?*
- *Why does everything worth doing require time, effort, and commitment?*
- *How is reaching your goal like climbing a mountain?*

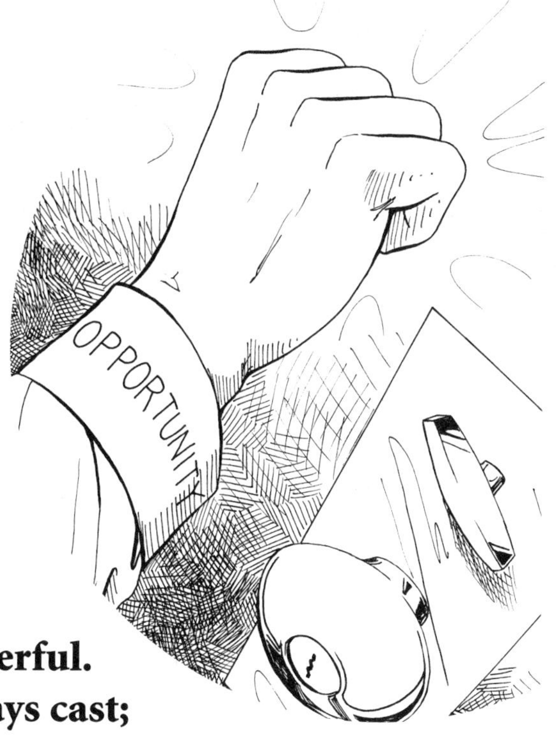


4

**Chance is always powerful. Let your hook be always cast; in the pool where you least expect it, there will be a fish.**

—*Ovid*

### Reflection Questions

- *What unexpected opportunities have appeared in your life?*
- *How could you increase the number of good opportunities coming your way?*
- *In what ways can you prepare yourself to take advantage of opportunities when they arise?*

**The most exciting phrase to hear in science, the one that heralds new discoveries, is not "Eureka!" (I found it!) but "That's funny …."**

—*Isaac Asimov*

### Reflection Questions

- *Why do mysteries provide interesting opportunities?*
- *What mysteries are scientists trying to solve?*
- *What do you find mysterious?*

# Opportunity

◆ There's always one moment in life when the door opens and lets the future in.
**—Graham Greene**

◆ People will try to tell you that all the great opportunities have been snapped up. In reality, the world changes every second, blowing new opportunities in all directions, including yours.
**—Ken Hakuta**

◆ Exhilaration of life can be found only with an upward look. This is an exciting world. It is cram-packed with opportunity. Great moments wait around every corner.
**—Richard M. Devos**

◆ If you are open to new possibilities in your life, then that alone will give you access to those possibilities—readiness is all.
**—Deepak Chopra**

◆ If you want to succeed in this world you don't have to be more clever than other people, you just have to be one day earlier.
**—Leo Szilard**

◆ Great opportunities to help others seldom come, but small ones surround us every day.
**—Sally Koch**

◆ Small opportunities are often the beginning of great enterprises.
**—Demosthenes**

◆ If I have ever made any valuable discoveries, it has been owing more to patient attention, than to any other talent.
**—Isaac Newton**

***By not listening to yourself, you deny yourself tremendous possibilities and glorious opportunity.***
***—Steven Spielberg***

◆ Your mind must remain open at all times. If you do not expect the unexpected, you will not find it.
**—Heraclitus**

◆ There's a fine line between fishing and standing on the shore like an idiot.
**—Steven Wright**

◆ Sometimes only a change of viewpoint is needed to convert a tiresome duty into an interesting opportunity.
**—Alberta Flanders**

◆ You have to recognize when the right place and the right time fuse and take advantage of that opportunity. There are plenty of opportunities out there. You can't sit back and wait.
**—Ellen Metcalf**

◆ People stumble over the truth from time to time, but most pick themselves up and hurry off as if nothing happened.
**—Winston Churchill**

◆ The sure way to miss success is to miss the opportunity.
**—Victor Charles**

◆ The chance will stand before you only once.
**—Sandra Day O'Connor**

◆ There's a big difference between seeing an opportunity and seizing an opportunity.
**—Jim Moore**

◆ Grab a chance and you won't be sorry for a might have been.
**—Arthur Ransome**

◆ As our knowledge is converted to wisdom, the door to opportunity is unlocked.
**—Barbara W. Winder**

◆ When one door closes, another opens; but we often look so long and so regretfully upon the closed door that we do not see the one which has opened for us.
**—Alexander Graham Bell**

◆ Even if you are on the right track, you'll get run over if you just sit there.
**—Will Rogers**

◆ Opportunity is missed by most people because it is dressed in overalls and looks like work.
**—Thomas Alva Edison**

◆ Opportunity follows struggle. It follows effort. It follows hard work. It doesn't come before.
**—Shelby Steele**

◆ I'm a great believer in luck, and I find the harder I work the more I have of it.
**—Thomas Alva Edison**

◆ Have the daring to accept yourself as a bundle of possibilities and undertake the game of making the most of your best.
**—Henry Emerson Fosdick**

◆ With increased opportunity comes increased stress. The stress comes from multiple conflicting demands and very little in the way of role models.
**—Madeline Hemmings**

◆ Life consists not in holding good cards but in playing those you do hold well.
**—Josh Billings**

◆ Make hay while the sun shines.
**—English proverb**

◆ In Chinese, the word *crisis* is *wei ji*, composed of the character wei, which means danger, and ji, which means opportunity.
**—Jan Wong**

◆ 1. Out of clutter, find simplicity.
2. From discord, find harmony.
3. In the middle of difficulty lies opportunity.
**—Albert Einstein**

◆ People are always blaming their circumstances for what they are. I don't believe in circumstances. The people who get on in this world are the people who get up and look for the circumstances that they want, and if they can't find them, make them.
**—George Bernard Shaw**

***I will study and get ready and someday my chance will come.***
***—Abraham Lincoln***

◆ To turn an obstacle to one's advantage is a great step towards victory.
**—French proverb**

◆ It is clear the future holds opportunities—it also holds pitfalls. The trick will be to seize the opportunities, avoid the pitfalls, and get back home by six o'clock.
**—Woody Allen**

◆ Don't say you don't have enough time. You have exactly the same number of hours per day that were given to Helen Keller, Pasteur, Michelangelo, Mother Teresa, Leonardo da Vinci, Thomas Jefferson, and Albert Einstein.
**—H. Jackson Brown Jr.**

◆ Don't sit down and wait for the opportunities to come; you have to get up and make them.
**—Madame C. J. Walker**

◆ It has long since come to my attention that people of accomplishment rarely sat back and let things happen to them. They went out and happened to things.
**—Elinor Smith**

◆ My philosophy is that not only are you responsible for your life, but doing the best at this moment puts you in the best place for the next moment.
**—Oprah Winfrey**

◆ I will study and get ready and someday my chance will come.
**—Abraham Lincoln**

◆ With opportunity comes responsibility.
**—Winston Churchill**

◆ The days come and go, but they say nothing, and if we do not use the gifts they bring, they carry them as silently away.
**—Ralph Waldo Emerson**

◆ Abundance is not something we acquire. It is something we tune into. There's no scarcity of opportunity to make a living at what you love. There is only a scarcity of resolve to make it happen.
**—Wayne W. Dyer**

◆ If not now, when? If not me, who?
**—Hillel**

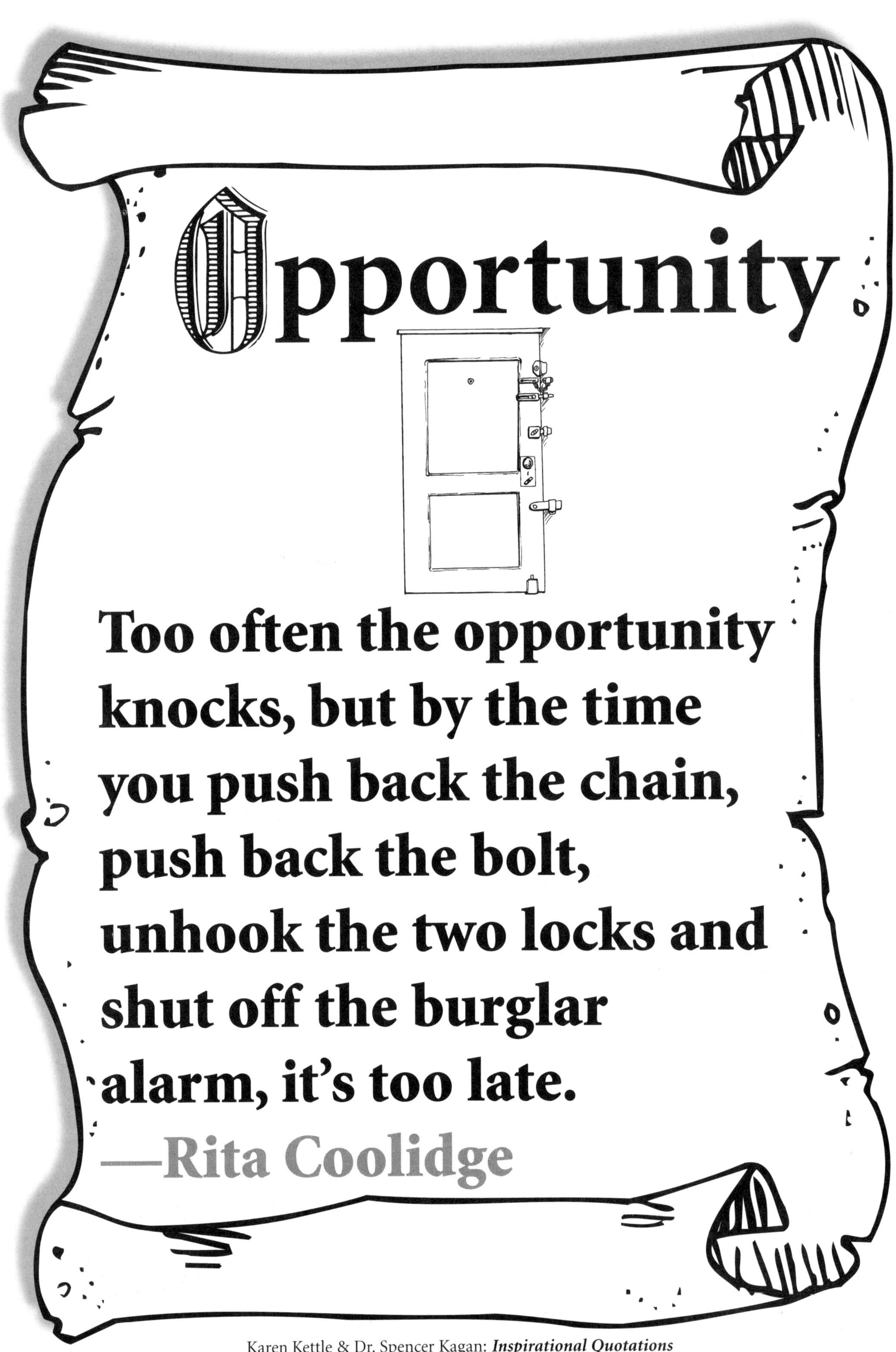
Opportunity
Too often the opportunity knocks, but by the time you push back the chain, push back the bolt, unhook the two locks and shut off the burglar alarm, it's too late.
—Rita Coolidge

Karen Kettle & Dr. Spencer Kagan: *Inspirational Quotations*
Kagan Publishing • 1 (800) 933-2667 • www.KaganOnline.com

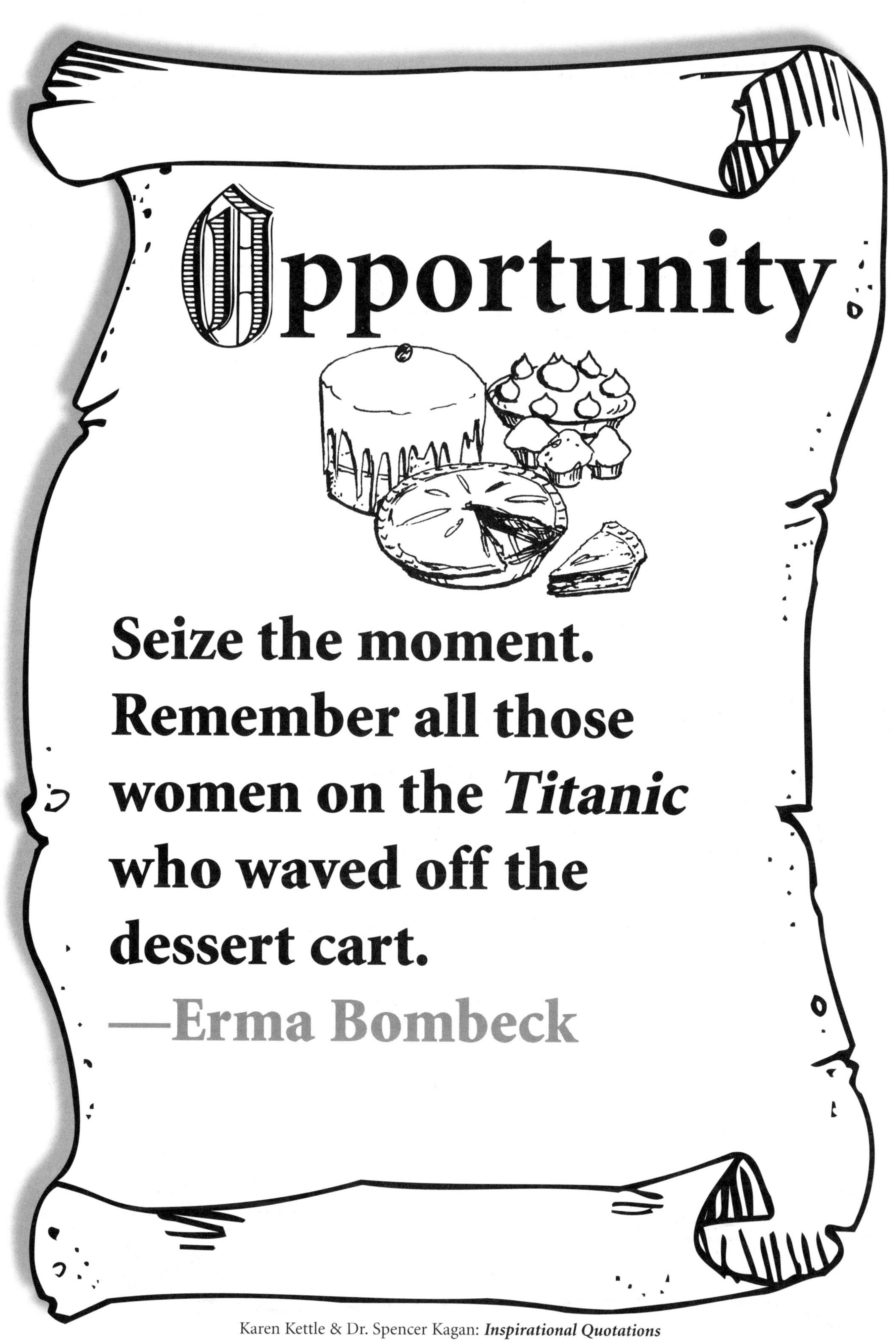
Opportunity
Seize the moment.
Remember all those
women on the *Titanic*
who waved off the
dessert cart.
—Erma Bombeck

Opportunity
Most look up and admire the stars; a champion climbs a mountain and grabs one.
—H. Jackson Brown Jr.

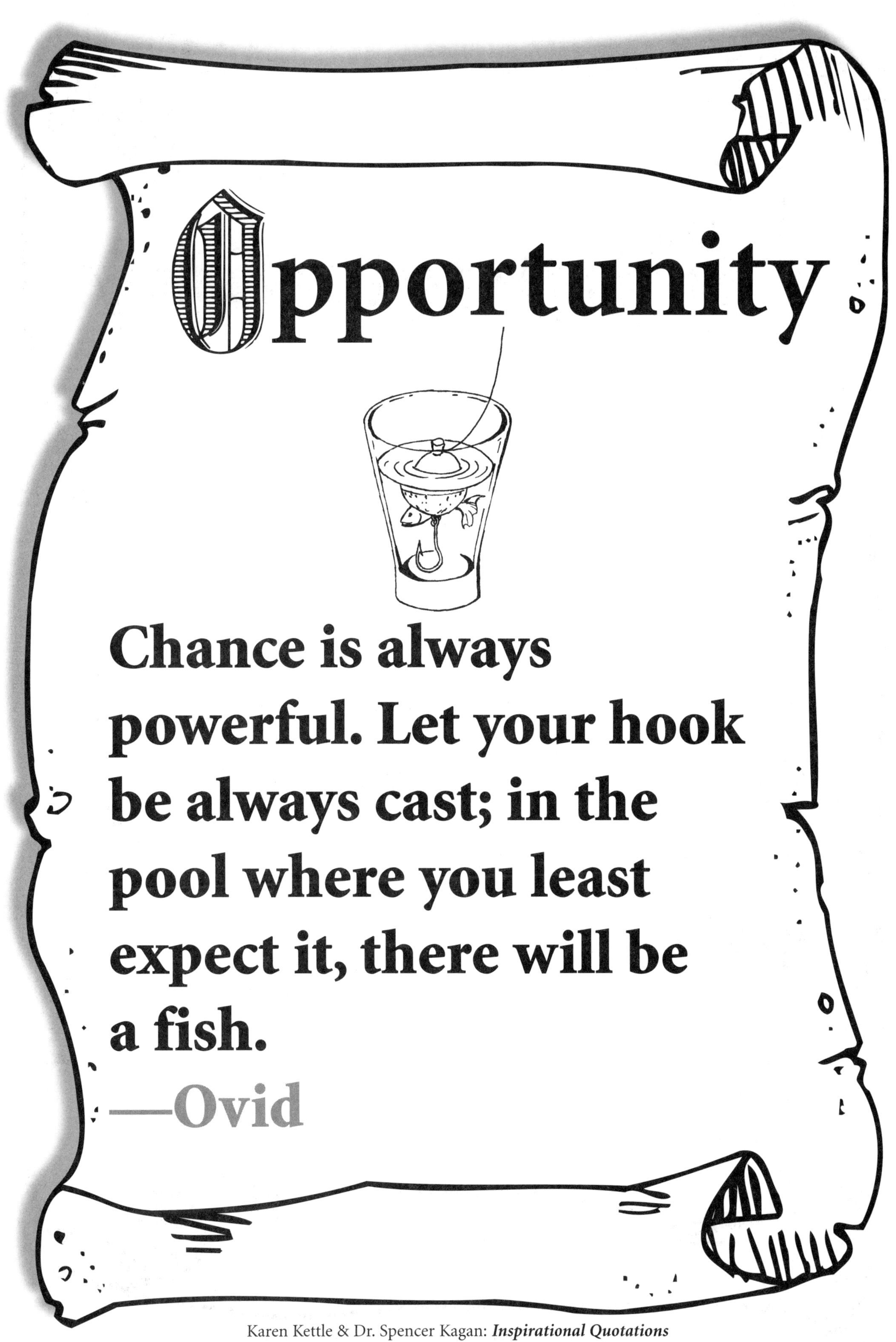

# Opportunity

**Chance is always powerful. Let your hook be always cast; in the pool where you least expect it, there will be a fish.**

**—Ovid**

Opportunity
LAB
The most exciting phrase to hear in science, the one that heralds new discoveries, is not "Eureka!" (I found it!) but "That's funny …."
—Isaac Asimov

# Perseverance

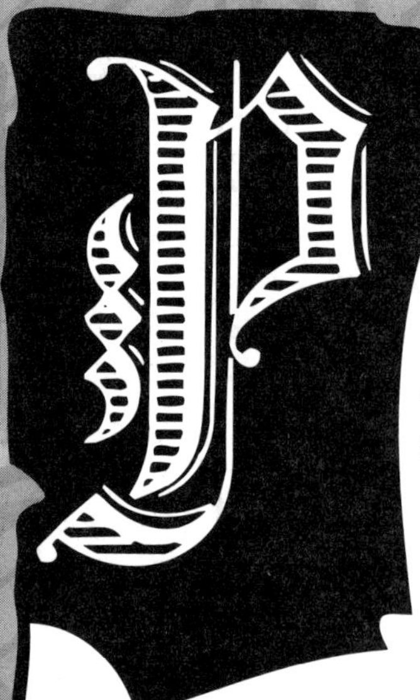

# Perseverance

***Perseverance is faith in action—faith that if we continue to do our best and refuse to give up, eventually we will succeed.***

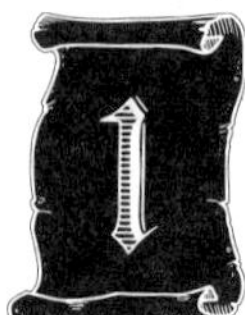

**A determined soul will do more with a rusty monkey wrench than a loafer will accomplish with all the tools in a machine shop.**

*—Robert Hughes*

Reflection Questions

- *What are you determined to do?*
- *When is a time in your life that you have succeeded against the odds?*
- *If you had to choose a historical figure to represent perseverance, who would it be? Why?*

**Persistence is not a long race; it is many short races one after another.**

*—Walter Elliott*

Reflection Questions

- *Why do you have to be persistent one minute at a time?*
- *What is the difference between being determined and being stubborn?*
- *When was a time when your persistence paid off?*

**When the morning's freshness has been replaced by the weariness of midday, when the leg muscles quiver under the strain, the climb seems endless, and, suddenly, nothing will go quite as you wish—it is then that you must not hesitate.**

*—Dag Hammarskjöld*

Reflection Questions

- *How do you motivate yourself to keep going when you are tired?*
- *What doubts creep into your mind that make you hesitate?*
- *Why is it better to keep moving forward slowly than to stand still?*

**In times of difficulty, you may feel that your problems will go on and on, but they won't. Every mountain has a top. Every problem has a life span. The question is, who is going to give in first, the frustration or you?**

*—Dr. Robert H. Schuller*

### Reflection Questions

- *What kinds of problems do you find the most frustrating?*
- *How do you know when you are starting to get frustrated?*
- *How do you fight through your frustration without giving up?*

**The Game isn't over till it's over.**

*—Lawrence Peter "Yogi" Berra*

### Reflection Questions

- *Why is it important not to give up in a game even if you are behind?*
- *What is a great "come from behind" story?*
- *Why do people like to see the "underdogs" win?*

# Perseverance

◆ Energy and persistence conquer all things.
**—Benjamin Franklin**

◆ Facing it—always facing it—that's the way to get through. Face it!
**—Joseph Conrad**

◆ Courage and perseverance have a magical talisman, before which difficulties disappear and obstacles vanish into air.
**—John Quincy Adams**

***There are many ways of going forward, but only one way of standing still.***
***—Franklin D. Roosevelt***

◆ Obstacles cannot crush me; every obstacle yields to stern resolve.
**—Leonardo da Vinci**

◆ I was taught that the way of progress is neither swift nor easy.
**—Marie Curie**

◆ History has demonstrated that the most notable winners usually encountered heartbreaking obstacles before they triumphed. They finally won because they refused to become discouraged by their defeats.
**—B. C. Forbes**

◆ We have all a few moments in life of hard glorious running; but we have days and years of walking—the uneventful discharge of small duties.
**—Alexander MacLaren**

◆ Decision and perseverance are the noblest qualities of man.
**—Johann Wolfgang Von Goethe**

◆ There are no secrets to success: Don't waste time looking for them. Success is the result of perfection, hard work, learning from failure, loyalty to those for whom you work, and persistence.
**—Colin Powell**

◆ Never give up. Never, never, never, never give up.
**—Winston Churchill**

◆ No one succeeds without effort. Those who succeed owe their success to their perseverance.
**—Ramana Maharshi**

◆ Hard work, dedication and desire don't guarantee you a thing, but without them you don't stand a chance.
**—Pat Riley**

◆ Genius is one per cent inspiration and ninety-nine per cent perspiration. As a result, a genius is often a talented person who has simply done all of his homework.
**—Thomas Alva Edison**

◆ Excellence in any art or profession is attained only by hard and persistent work.
**—Theodore Martin**

◆ If you want to leave footprints in the sands of time …. You had better wear work boots!
**—Thomas Alva Edison**

◆ Many people are inventive, sometimes cleverly so. But real creativity begins with the drive to work on and on and on.
**—Margueritte Harmon Bro**

◆ It takes twenty years to make an overnight success
**—Eddie Cantor**

◆ If people knew how hard I worked to get my mastery, it wouldn't seem so wonderful at all.
**—Michelangelo**

◆ You always pass failure on the way to success.
**—Mickey Rooney**

◆ The will to persevere is often the difference between failure and success.
**—David Sarnoff**

◆ Big shots are only little shots who kept on shooting.
**—Dale Carnegie**

◆ Hang in there. Many of life's failures are people who did not realize how close they were to success when they gave up.
**—Thomas Alva Edison**

◆ Don't be discouraged; it may be the last key in the bunch that opens the door.
**—Stonsifer**

◆ I have not failed. I've just found 10,000 ways that won't work.
**—Thomas Alva Edison**

◆ Nothing could be worse than the fear that one had given up too soon, and left one unexpended effort that might have saved the world.
**—Jane Addams**

◆ Desire is the key to motivation, but it's determination and commitment to an unrelenting pursuit of your goal—a commitment to excellence—that will enable you to attain the success you seek.
**—Mario Andretti**

◆ Hold on; hold fast; hold out. Patience is genius.
**—Comte De Buffon**

◆ A handful of patience is worth more than a bushel of brains.
**—Dutch proverb**

◆ Nothing takes the place of persistence. Talent will not. Nothing is more common than unsuccessful people with talent. Genius will not. Unrewarded genius is almost a proverb. Education will not. The world is full of educated derelicts. Persistence alone is omnipotent. The slogan "press on" has solved and always will solve the problems of the human race.
**—Calvin Coolidge**

◆ Genius is eternal patience.
**—Michelangelo**

◆ Patience is the key to paradise.
**—Armenian proverb**

◆ By perseverance the snail reached the ark.
**— Charles H. Spurgeon**

◆ People of mediocre ability sometimes achieve outstanding success because they don't know when to quit.
**—George Allen**

◆ You do what you can for as long as you can, and when you finally can't, you do the next best thing. You back up but you don't give up.
**—Chuck Yeager**

◆ I realized early on that success was tied to not giving up …. If you simply didn't give up, you would outlast the people who came in on the bus with you.
**—Harrison Ford**

◆ We are made to persist. That's how we find out who we are.
**—Tobias Wolff**

◆ On a journey of a hundred miles, ninety is but half way.
**—Chinese proverb**

◆ When you have gone so far that you can't manage one more step, then you've gone just half the distance you're capable of.
**—Greenland proverb**

◆ We conquer—not in any brilliant fashion—we conquer by continuing.
**—George Matheson**

◆ Life is not easy for any of us. But what of that? We must have perseverance and above all confidence in ourselves. We must believe that we are gifted for something, and that this thing, at whatever cost, must be attained.
**—Marie Curie**

◆ The best thing about the future is that it only comes one day at a time.
**—Abraham Lincoln**

***Have patience, all things are difficult before they become easy.***
***—Saadi***

◆ It is my belief that talent is plentiful, and that what is lacking is staying power.
**—Doris Lessing**

◆ I do the very best I know how—the very best I can; and I mean to keep doing so until the end. If the end brings me out all right, what is said against me won't amount to anything. If the end brings me out wrong, ten angels swearing I was right would make no difference.
**—Abraham Lincoln**

◆ Our greatest weakness lies in giving up. The most certain way to succeed is to always try one more time.
**—Thomas Alva Edison**

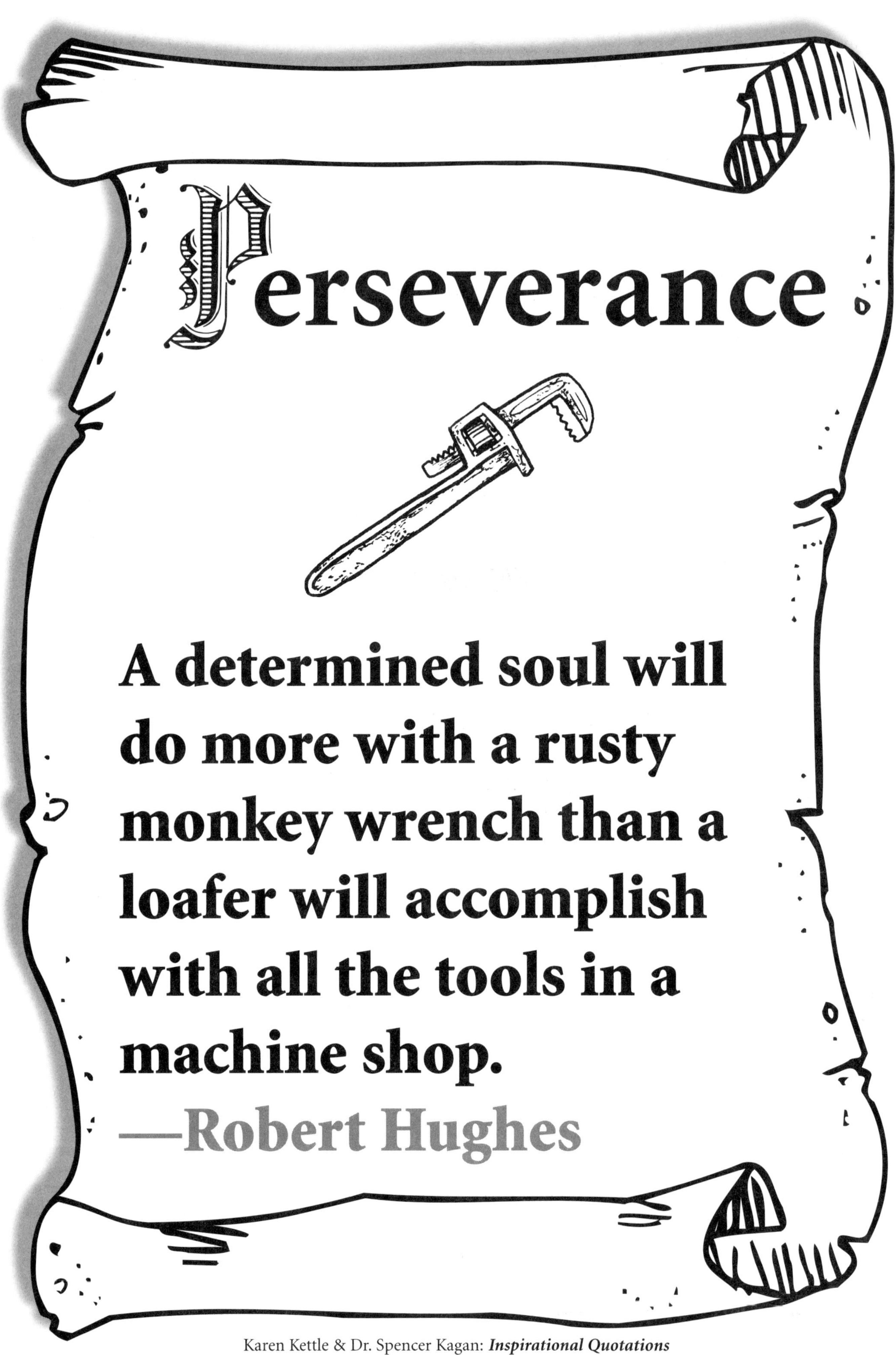
Perseverance
A determined soul will
do more with a rusty
monkey wrench than a
loafer will accomplish
with all the tools in a
machine shop.
—Robert Hughes

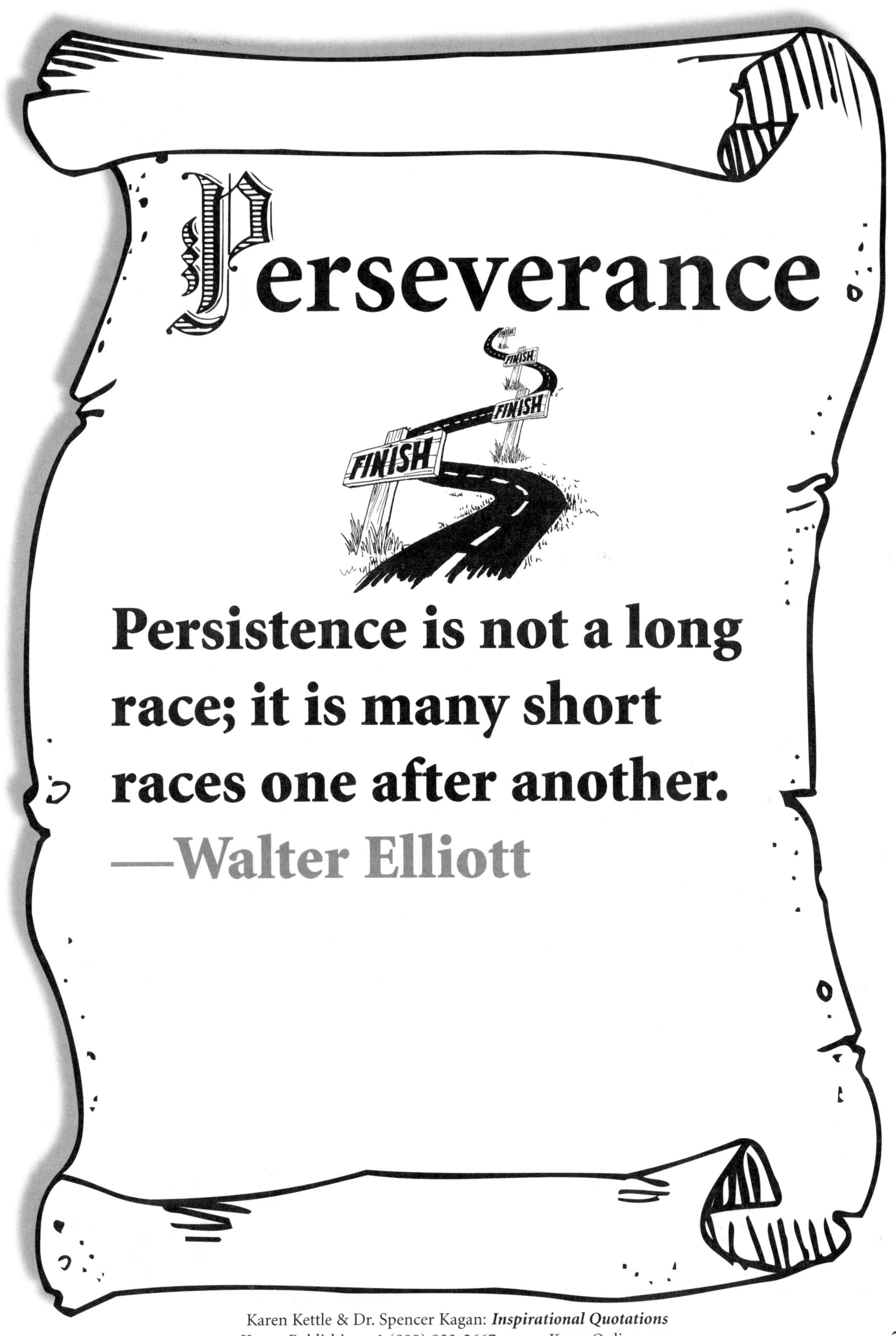


# Perseverance

**Persistence is not a long race; it is many short races one after another.**

**—Walter Elliott**

Perseverance
When the morning's freshness has been replaced by the weariness of midday, when the leg muscles quiver under the strain, the climb seems endless, and, suddenly, nothing will go quite as you wish—it is then that you must not hesitate.
—Dag Hammarskjöld

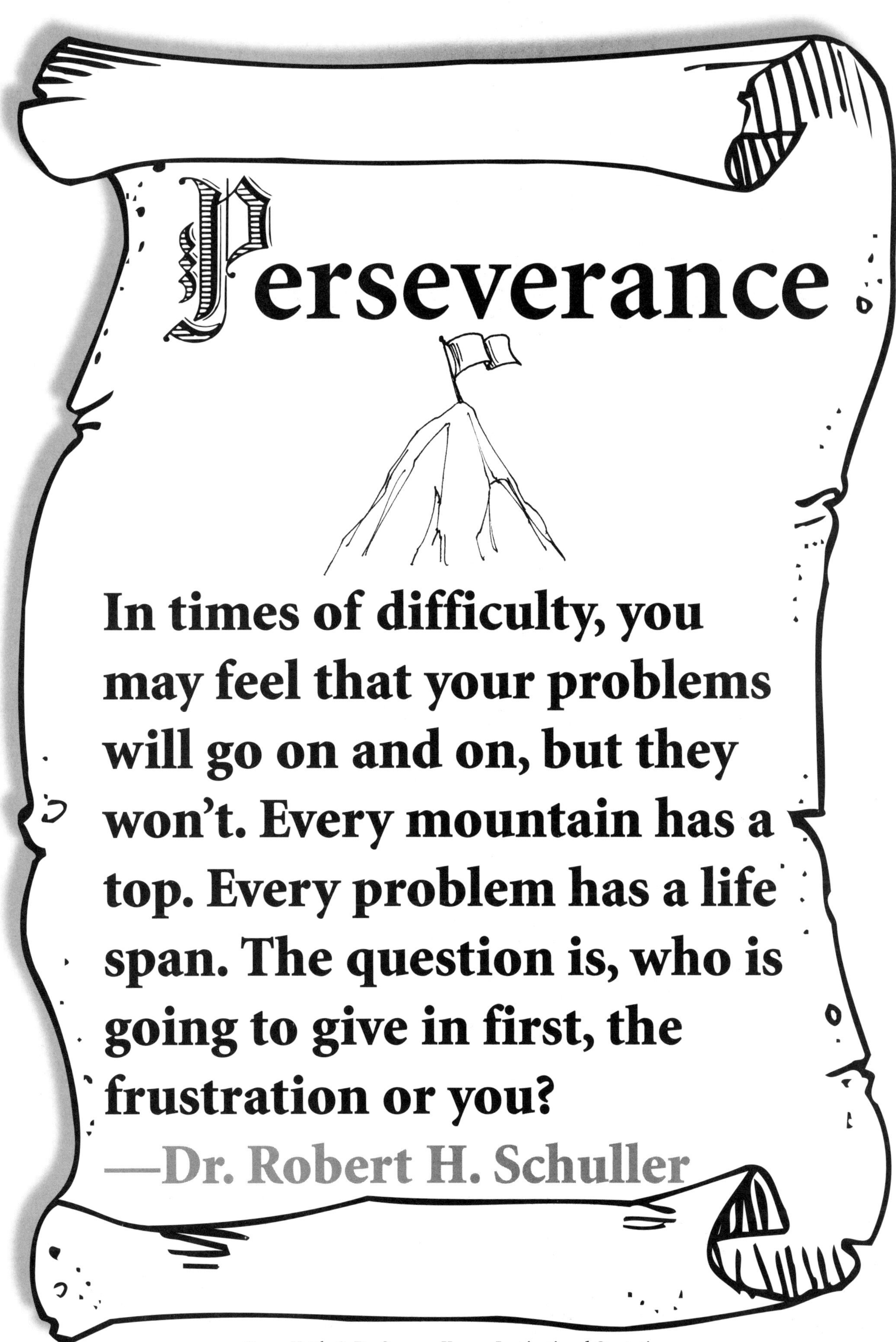
Perseverance
In times of difficulty, you may feel that your problems will go on and on, but they won't. Every mountain has a top. Every problem has a life span. The question is, who is going to give in first, the frustration or you?
—Dr. Robert H. Schuller

Perseverance
The Game isn't over till it's over.
—Lawrence Peter "Yogi" Berra

Risk

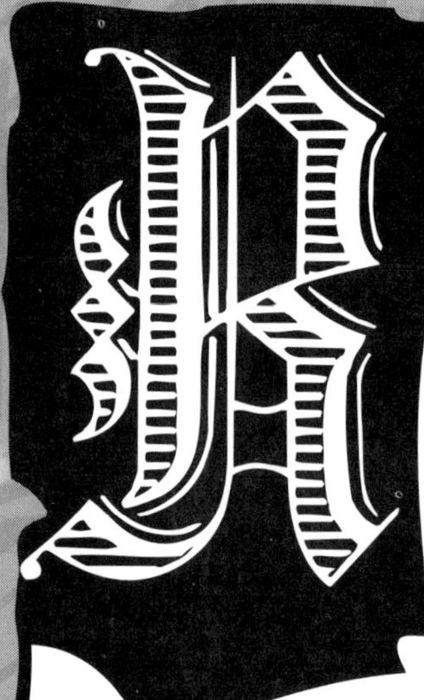

# Risk

*Risk represents promising possibilities and danger. It tests our judgment and our daring.*

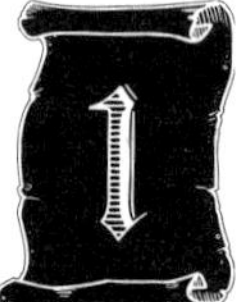

**Progress always involves risks. You can't steal second base and keep your foot on first.**

*—Fredrick B. Wilcox*

Reflection Questions

- *What makes something risky?*
- *What kinds of risks are worth taking?*
- *What would happen if you never took a risk?*

**Why not go out on a limb? Isn't that where the fruit is?**

*—Frank Scully*

Reflection Questions

- *What responsibility do you have for the risks you take?*
- *How can you reduce the danger that a risk presents?*
- *Why is it important not to put others at risk?*

**To dare is to lose one's footing momentarily; to not dare is to lose oneself.**

*—Søren Kierkegaard*

Reflection Questions

- *What connections can you make between taking a risk and growing?*
- *How is making a new friend an example of taking a risk?*
- *What is the difference between actual risks and imaginary ones?*

**Don't think there are no crocodiles because the water is calm.**

*—Malayan proverb*

Reflection Questions

- *What risks do we face at school?*
- *What risks do we face on the Internet?*
- *How do you decide if something is too risky to do?*

**One doesn't discover new lands without consenting to lose sight of the shore for a very long time.**

*—Andre Gide*

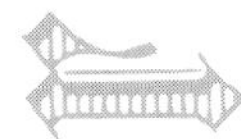

Reflection Questions

- *How do you feel when you venture into the unknown?*
- *How is every discovery like a voyage into the unknown?*
- *Why should you think twice before saying that something is impossible?*

# Risk

◆ There's no such thing as "zero risk."
—**William Driver**

◆ Yes, risk taking is inherently failure-prone. Otherwise, it would be called sure-thing-taking.
—**Tim McMahon**

◆ The distance doesn't matter; only the first step is difficult.
—**Madame du Deffand**

◆ If you're never scared or embarrassed or hurt, it means you never take any chances.
—**Julia Sorel**

◆ If you play it safe in life, you've decided that you don't want to grow anymore.
—**Shirley Hufstedler**

◆ Take chances, make mistakes. That's how you grow. Pain nourishes your courage. You have to fail in order to practice being brave.
—**Mary Tyler Moore**

◆ If you can walk, you can dance. If you can talk, you can sing.
—**Zimbabwean proverb**

◆ Don't stand shivering upon the bank; plunge in at once, and have it over with.
—**Sam Glick**

◆ They are ill discoverers that think there is no land, when they can see nothing but sea.
—**Sir Francis Bacon**

◆ A ship in port is safe, but that's not what ships are built for.
—**Grace Murray Hopper**

◆ Without risk there is no faith.
—**Søren Kierkegaard**

***If you wait until you're ready, you'll wait forever. —Will Rogers***

◆ It is easy to follow, but it is uninteresting to do easy things. We find out about ourselves only when we take risks, when we challenge and question.
—**Magdalena Abakanowicz**

◆ Unless you walk into the unknown, the odds of making a profound difference in your life are pretty low.
—**Tom Peters**

◆ If you want to succeed you should strike out on new paths rather than travel the worn paths of accepted success.
—**John D. Rockefeller**

◆ Live dangerously.
—**Friedrich Nietzsche**

◆ I'm in love with the potential of miracles. For me, the safest place is out on a limb.
—**Shirley MacLaine**

◆ If you're already walking on thin ice, why not dance?
—**Gil Atkinson**

◆ When choosing between two evils, I always like to try the one I've never tried before.
—**Mae West**

◆ The policy of being too cautious is the greatest risk of all.
—**Jawaharlal Nehru**

◆ And the trouble is, if you don't risk anything, you risk even more.
—**Erica Jong**

◆ If you wait for the perfect moment when all is safe and assured, it may never arrive. Mountains will not be climbed, races won, or lasting happiness achieved.
—**Maurice Chevalier**

◆ The only people who achieve much are those who want knowledge so badly that they seek it while the conditions are still unfavorable. Favorable conditions never come.
**—C. S. Lewis**

◆ Behold the turtle. He makes progress only when he sticks his neck out.
**—James B. Conant**

◆ Success is the child of audacity.
**—Benjamin Disraeli**

◆ What great thing would you attempt if you knew you could not fail?
**—Dr. Robert H. Schuller**

◆ How can you hesitate? Risk! Risk anything! Care no more for the opinion of others, for those voices. Do the hardest thing on earth for you. Act for yourself. Face the truth.
**—Katherine Mansfield**

***Those who dare to fail miserably, can achieve greatly.***
***—Robert Kennedy***

◆ Do the thing you fear and the death of fear is certain.
**—Ralph Waldo Emerson**

◆ Fear of failure brings fear of taking risks … and you're never going to get what you want out of life without taking some risks. Remember, everything worthwhile carries the risk of failure.
**—Lee Iacocca**

◆ Great deeds are usually wrought at great risks.
**—Herodotus**

◆ Anything I've ever done that ultimately was worthwhile … initially scared me to death.
**—Betty Bender**

◆ Our doubts are traitors, and make us lose the good we oft might win by fearing the attempt.
**—William Shakespeare**

◆ If we listened to our intellect, we'd never have a love affair. We'd never have a friendship. We'd never go into business, because we'd be cynical. Well, that's nonsense. You've got to jump off cliffs all the time and build your wings on the way down.
**—Ray Bradbury**

◆ All growth is a leap in the dark, a spontaneous unpremeditated act without the benefit of experience.
**—Henry Miller**

◆ There can be no vulnerability without risk; there can be no community without vulnerability; there can be no peace, and ultimately no life, without community.
**—M. Scott Peck**

◆ When you have come to the edge of all the light you know, and are about to step off into the darkness of the unknown, faith is knowing one of two things will happen: There will be something solid to stand on, or you will be taught to fly.
**—Barbara J. Winter**

◆ Part of the essence of mountain climbing is to push oneself to one's limits. Inevitably this involves risk, otherwise they would not be one's limits. This is not to say that you deliberately try something you know you can't do. But you do deliberately try something which you are not sure you can do.
**—Woodrow Wilson Sayre**

◆ I believe that courage is all too often mistakenly seen as the absence of fear. If you descend by rope from a cliff and are not fearful to some degree, you are either crazy or unaware. Courage is seeing your fear, in a realistic perspective, defining it, considering alternative, and choosing to function in spite of risks.
**—Leonard Zunin**

◆ Risk-taking is the essential first step in making decisions, crossing new frontiers of knowledge, accepting responsibility for discovering who we are and what we can do. The commonest and most difficult form of risk-taking is when you have to make a decision. No matter how carefully you prepare you will always find there is a gap between your present situation and your desired goal. Eventually you will have to decide whether to leap that gap or stay on your side of it. To venture is to risk anxiety, but not to venture is to lose oneself. Like happiness, security is elusive. To find it, you have to risk it.
**—John Lagman**

◆ Regret for the things we did can be tempered by time; it is regret for the things we did not do that is inconsolable.
**—Sydney J. Harris**

◆ What you risk reveals what you value.
**—Jeanette Winterson**

Risk

Progress always involves risks. You can't steal second base and keep your foot on first.
—Fredrick B. Wilcox

Karen Kettle & Dr. Spencer Kagan: *Inspirational Quotations*
Kagan Publishing • 1 (800) 933-2667 • www.KaganOnline.com

Risk
Why not go out on a limb? Isn't that where the fruit is?
—Frank Scully

Risk
To dare is to lose one's footing momentarily; to not dare is to lose oneself.
—Søren Kierkegaard

Karen Kettle & Dr. Spencer Kagan: *Inspirational Quotations*
Kagan Publishing • 1 (800) 933-2667 • www.KaganOnline.com

# Risk

**Don't think there are no crocodiles because the water is calm.**

**—Malayan proverb**

Risk
One doesn't discover new lands without consenting to lose sight of the shore for a very long time.
—Andre Gide

Karen Kettle & Dr. Spencer Kagan: *Inspirational Quotations*
Kagan Publishing • 1 (800) 933-2667 • www.KaganOnline.com

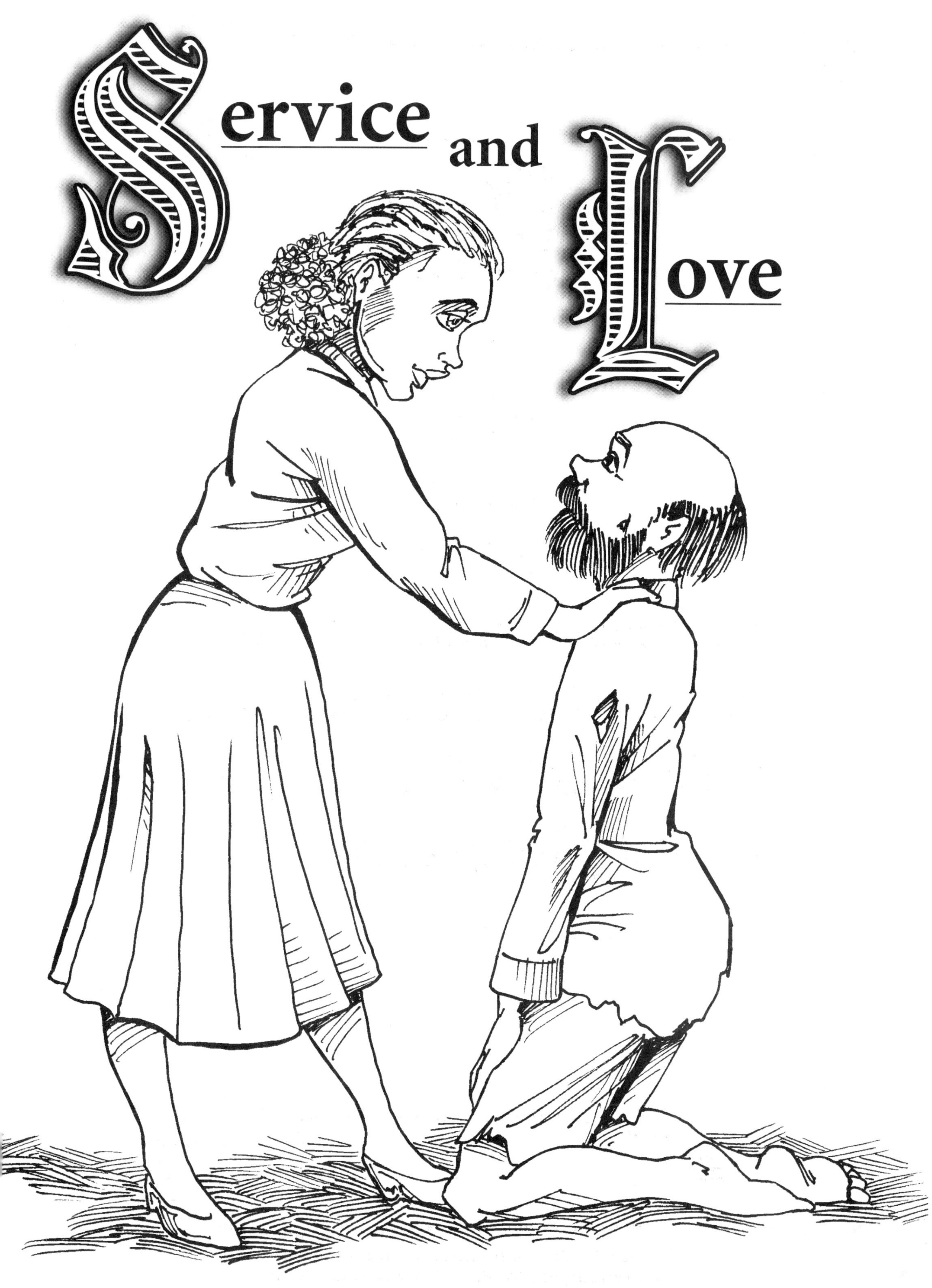
Service and Love

# ervice and Love

*Service is the ability to perceive the needs of others and the initiative to volunteer assistance. Service is love in action.*

**We cannot hold a torch to light another's path without brightening our own.**

*—Ben Sweetland*

Reflection Questions

- *How do you know that someone might benefit from your help?*
- *Why is it fun to do good deeds even when no one knows you did them?*
- *What jobs and volunteer agencies in our society provide community service?*

**Don't judge each day by the harvest you reap, but by the seeds you plant.**

*—Robert Louis Stevenson*

Reflection Questions

- *What are you thankful for?*
- *Who do you have a duty to serve? Who do you choose to serve?*
- *How is helping another person like planting a seed?*

**I don't know what your destiny will be, but one thing I do know: the only ones among you who will be really happy are those who have sought and found how to serve.**

*—Albert Schweitzer*

Reflection Questions

- *Why does it feel good to help others?*
- *What do you learn from helping others?*
- *Why do some people spend their lives in service to others?*

**Have I done any good in the world today? Have I cheered up the sad and made someone feel glad? If not I have failed indeed.**

*—Esther Peterson*

### Reflection Questions

- *What are some little ways that you serve others every day?*
- *How does serving others shift your priorities?*
- *How can random acts of kindness brighten someone's day?*

**I am convinced that my life belongs to the whole community, and as long as I live, it is my privilege to do for it whatever I can, for the harder I work the more I live.**

*—George Bernard Shaw*

### Reflection Questions

- *What are our responsibilities to our community?*
- *Why do you have to respect people in order to serve them?*
- *What can you do to help people in your community?*

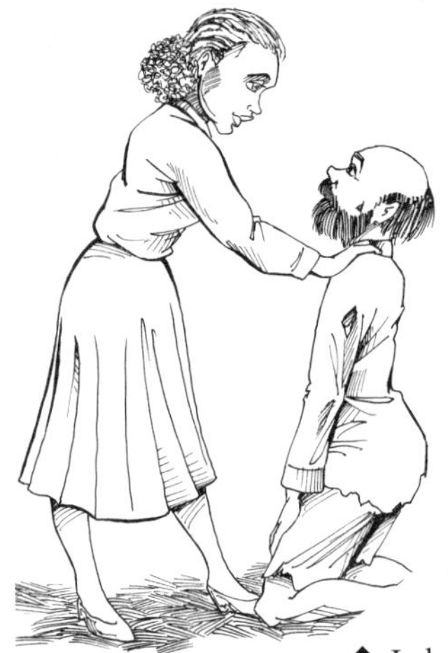

# Service and Love

◆ Life's most persistent and urgent question is: What are you doing for others?
**—Martin Luther King Jr.**

◆ I slept and dreamt that life was joy. I awoke and saw that life was service. I acted and behold, service was joy.
**—Rabindranath Tagore**

◆ There is joy in transcending self to serve others.
**—Mother Teresa**

◆ What is the essence of life? To serve others and to do good.
**—Aristotle**

◆ To care for anyone else enough to make their problems one's own, is ever the beginning of one's real ethical development.
**—Felix Adler**

◆ Compassion is the basis of all morality.
**—Arthur Schopenhauer**

◆ Only connect.
**—E. M. Forster**

◆ There are two kinds of people—those who come into a room and say, "Well here I am!" and those who come in and say, "Ah, there you are."
**—Fredrick L. Collins**

◆ Only a life lived for others is a life worthwhile.
**—Albert Einstein**

◆ We are here to add what we can to, not to get what we can from life.
**—Sir William Osler**

◆ Those who are happiest are those who do the most for others.
**—Booker T. Washington**

***We make a living by what we get. We make a life by what we give.***
***—Winston Churchill***

◆ Service is the rent that you pay for room on this earth.
**—Shirley Chisholm**

◆ The highest destiny of the individual is to serve rather than to rule.
**—Albert Einstein**

◆ The greatest source of happiness is forgetting yourself and trying seriously and honestly to be useful to others.
**—Millicent Fenwick**

◆ Joy can be real only if people look upon their life as a service, and have a definite object in life outside themselves and their personal happiness.
**—Leo Tolstoy**

◆ There is a wonderful mythical law of nature that the three things we crave most in life—happiness, freedom, and peace of mind—are always attained by giving them to someone else.
**—Peyton Conway March**

◆ You have not lived a perfect day, unless you have done something for someone who will never be able to repay you.
**—Ruth Smeltzer**

◆ We must serve consciously as caring role models, emphasizing the ethic of service, not consumption.
**—Marian Wright Edelman**

◆ If a free society cannot help the many who are poor, it cannot save the few who are rich.
**—John F. Kennedy**

◆ Those who give have all things; they who withhold have nothing.
**—Hindu proverb**

◆ Charity is, indeed, a great thing, a gift from God; for it is charity that makes the man.
**—St. John Chysostom**

◆ Charity is infinitely divisible. He (she) who has a little can always give a little.
**—Peter McArthur**

◆ The wise man does not lay up treasures. The more he gives, the more he has.
**—Chinese proverb**

◆ To give alms is nothing unless you give thought also. A little thought and a little kindness are often worth more than a great deal of money.
**—John Ruskin**

◆ It is a privilege to serve people, a privilege that must be earned, and once earned, there is an obligation to do something good with it.
**—Barbara Jordan**

***Make yourself necessary to somebody.***
***—Ralph Waldo Emerson***

◆ The best way to find yourself is to lose yourself in the service of others.
**—Mahatma Gandhi**

◆ Try to forget yourself in the service of others. For when we think too much of ourselves and our own interests, we easily become despondent. But when we work for others, our efforts return to bless us.
**—Sydney Powell**

◆ A nation, like an individual, to find itself must lose itself in the service of others.
**—W. L. Mackenzie King**

◆ The highest form of worship is service to humanity.
**—St. Vincent de Paul**

◆ We should love others truly, for their own sakes rather than our own.
**—St. Thomas Aquinas**

◆ Love is the immortal flow of energy that nourishes, extends and preserves. Its etermal goal is life.
**—Smiley Blanton**

◆ To feel the love of people whom we love is a fire that feeds our life.
**—Pablo Neruda**

◆ Love is the ultimate and highest goal to which one can aspire. The salvation of humanity is through love and in love.
**—Viktor Frankl**

◆ Just as a flower gives out its fragrance to whomever approaches, so love from within us radiates toward everybody and manifests as spontaneous service.
**—Swami Ramdas**

◆ What is important is that one be capable of love. It is perhaps the only glimpse that we are permitted of eternity.
**—Helen Hayes**

◆ Love thy neighbor as I have loved you. Love your enemies, bless them that curse you; do good unto them that hate you.
**—Jesus**

◆ Love builds bridges where there are none.
**—R. H. Delaney**

◆ Do all things with love.
**—Og Mandino**

◆ What you wish to experience, provide for another.
**—Dalai Lama**

◆ The love we give away is the only love we keep.
**—Elbert Hubbard**

◆ Lord, make me an instrument of thy peace. Where there is hatred, let me sow love. Where there is injury, pardon. Where there is despair, hope. Grant that I may not so much seek to be consoled as to console, to be loved as to love, for it is in the giving that we receive.
**—Saint Francis of Assisi**

◆ You don't have to have a college degree to serve. You don't have to make your subject and verb agree to serve. You only need a heart full of grace. A soul generated by love.
**—Martin Luther King Jr.**

◆ Life is short, and we have never too much time for gladdening the hearts of those who are traveling the dark journey with us. Oh, be swift to love, make haste to be kind!
**—Henri Frédéric Amiel**

# Service and Love

◆ Be of service. Whether you make yourself available to a friend or co-worker or you make time every month to do volunteer work, there is nothing that harvests more of a feeling of empowerment than being of service to someone in need.
**—Gillian Anderson**

◆ When we feel love and kindness toward others, it not only makes others feel loved and cared for, but it helps us also to develop inner happiness and peace.
**—Dalai Lama**

◆ So many gods, so many creeds, so many paths … while just the art of being kind is all the world needs.
**—Ella Wheeler Wilcox**

◆ Those who bring sunshine into the lives of others, cannot keep it from themselves.
**—James M. Barrie**

◆ Every day use your magic to be of service to others.
**—Marcia Wieder**

◆ If you were arrested for kindness, would there be enough evidence to convict you?
**—Unknown**

***What do we live for, if it is not to make life less difficult for each other?***
***—George Elliot***

◆ One of the most difficult things to give away is kindness, for it is usually returned.
**—Mark Ortman**

◆ Make happy those who are near, and those who are far will come.
**—Chinese proverb**

◆ Make one person happy each day, and in forty years you will have made 14,000 human beings happy for a time at least.
**—Charles Wiley**

◆ The place you are in needs you today.
**—Katherine Logan**

◆ Life begets life. Energy creates energy. It is by spending oneself that one becomes rich.
**—Sarah Bernhardt**

◆ I personally measure success in terms of the contributions an individual makes to her or his fellow human beings.
**—Margaret Mead**

◆ There is overwhelming evidence that the higher the level of self-esteem, the more likely one will be to treat others with respect, kindness, and generosity.
**—Nathaniel Branden**

◆ There is no more noble occupation in the world than to assist another human being—to help someone succeed.
**—Alan Loy McGinnis**

◆ You will find, as you look back upon your life, that the moments that stand out are the moments when you have done things for others.
**—Henry Drummond**

◆ If you're too busy to help those around you, you're too busy.
**—Bob Moawad**

◆ Doing nothing for others is the undoing of ourselves.
**—Benjamin Franklin**

◆ There is no exercise better for the heart than reaching down and lifting people up.
**—John Andrew Holmes**

◆ For this I bless you most: You give much and know not that you give at all.
**—Kahlil Gibran**

◆ Do all the good you can, to all the people you can, for as long as you can.
**—John Wesley**

◆ The most satisfying thing in life is to have been able to give a large part of one's self to others.
**—Pierre Teilhard de Chardin**

◆ One of the deep secrets of life is that all that is really worth the doing is what we do for others.
**—Lewis Carroll**

◆ What is the use of living if it be not to strive for noble causes and to make this muddled world a better place for those who will live in it after we are gone?
**—Winston Churchill**

◆ What we have done for ourselves alone dies with us; what we have done for others is immortal.
**—Albert Pike**

◆ I am only one. I cannot do everything but I can do something; and what I can do, that I ought to do; and what I ought to do, I shall do.
**—Edward Everett Hale**

◆ If you can't feed a hundred people, then feed just one.
**—Mother Teresa**

◆ It is the greatest of all mistakes to do nothing because you can only do a little. Do what you can.
**—Sydney Smith**

◆ Kindness in words creates confidence, kindness in thinking creates profoundness, kindness in feeling creates love.
**—Lao Tzu**

◆ If someone needs our help, it is our duty to provide it to the utmost of our power.
**—Marcus Tullius Cicero**

◆ The work of an individual still remains the spark that moves mankind forward.
**—Igor Sikorsky**

◆ Let no one come to you without leaving better.
**—Mother Teresa**

◆ Joy is not in things; it is in us.
**—Richard Wagner**

***Real generosity toward the future lies in giving all to the present.***
*—Albert Camus*

◆ No one is useless in the world who lightens the burden of it from anyone else.
**—Charles Dickens**

◆ It is better to light a candle than to curse the darkness.
**—Chinese proverb**

◆ When you've seen beyond yourself, then you may find, peace of mind is waiting there.
**—George Harrison**

◆ We are not here merely to make a living. We are here in order to enable the world to live more amply, with greater vision, with a finer spirit of hope and achievement. We are here to enrich the world, and we impoverish ourselves if we forget the errand.
**—Woodrow Wilson**

◆ Everybody can be great because everybody can serve.
**—Martin Luther King Jr.**

◆ How can I be useful, of what service can I be? There is something inside me, what can it be?
**—Vincent van Gogh**

◆ I wish to live because life has with it that which is good, that which is beautiful, and that which is love.
**—Lorraine Hansberry**

◆ In every community there is work to be done. In every nation, there are wounds to heal. In every heart there is the power to do it.
**—Marianne Williamson**

◆ Yesterday is gone. Tomorrow has not yet come. We have only today. Let us begin.
**—Mother Teresa**

Service and Love
We cannot hold a torch
to light another's path
without brightening
our own.
—Ben Sweetland

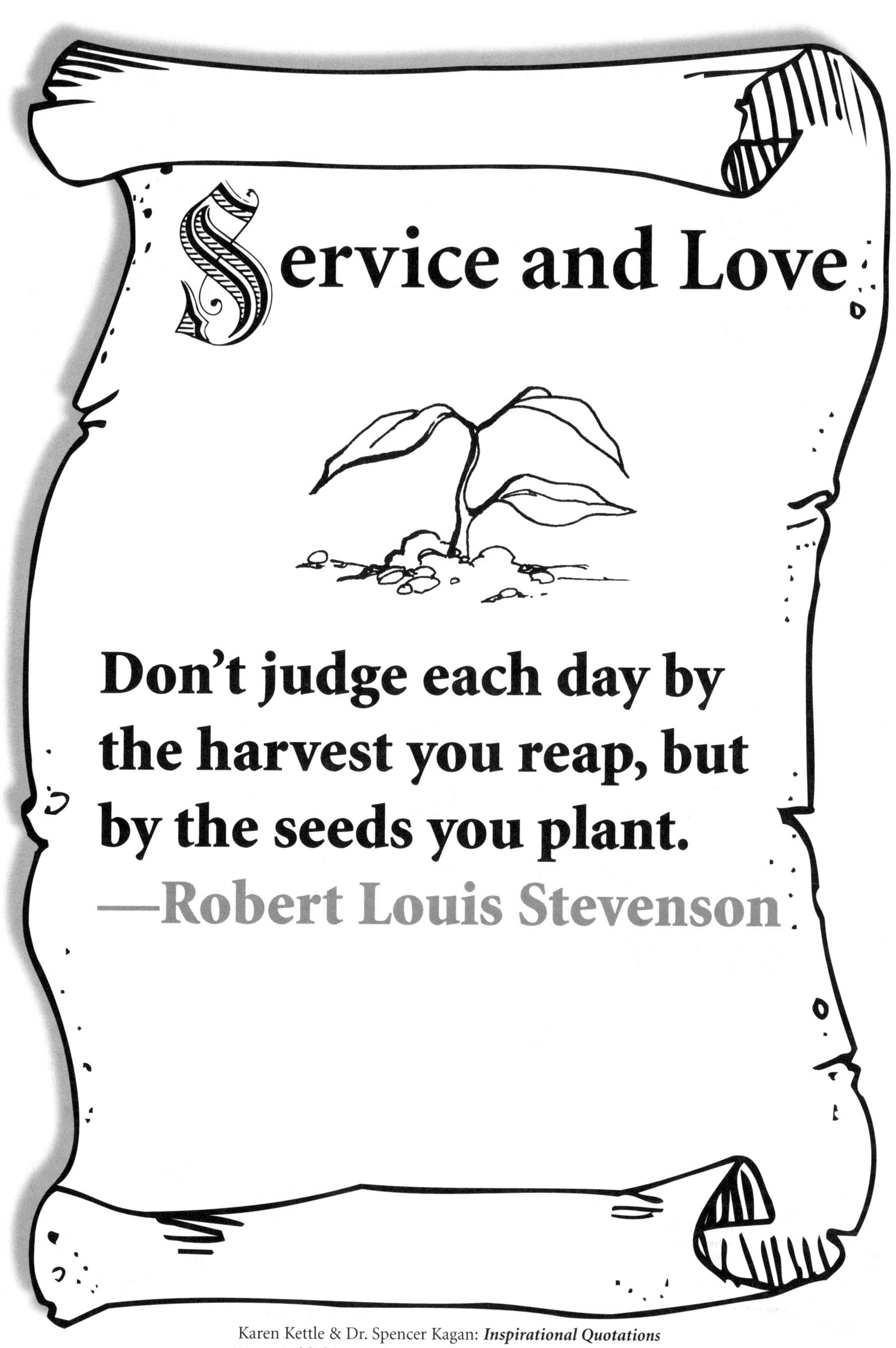
Service and Love
Don't judge each day by the harvest you reap, but by the seeds you plant.
—Robert Louis Stevenson

Service and Love
SHERIFF
I don't know what your destiny will be, but one thing I do know: the only ones among you who will be really happy are those who have sought and found how to serve.
—Albert Schweitzer

Karen Kettle & Dr. Spencer Kagan: *Inspirational Quotations*
Kagan Publishing • 1 (800) 933-2667 • www.KaganOnline.com

Service and Love
Have I done any good in the world today? Have I cheered up the sad and made someone feel glad? If not I have failed indeed.
—Esther Peterson

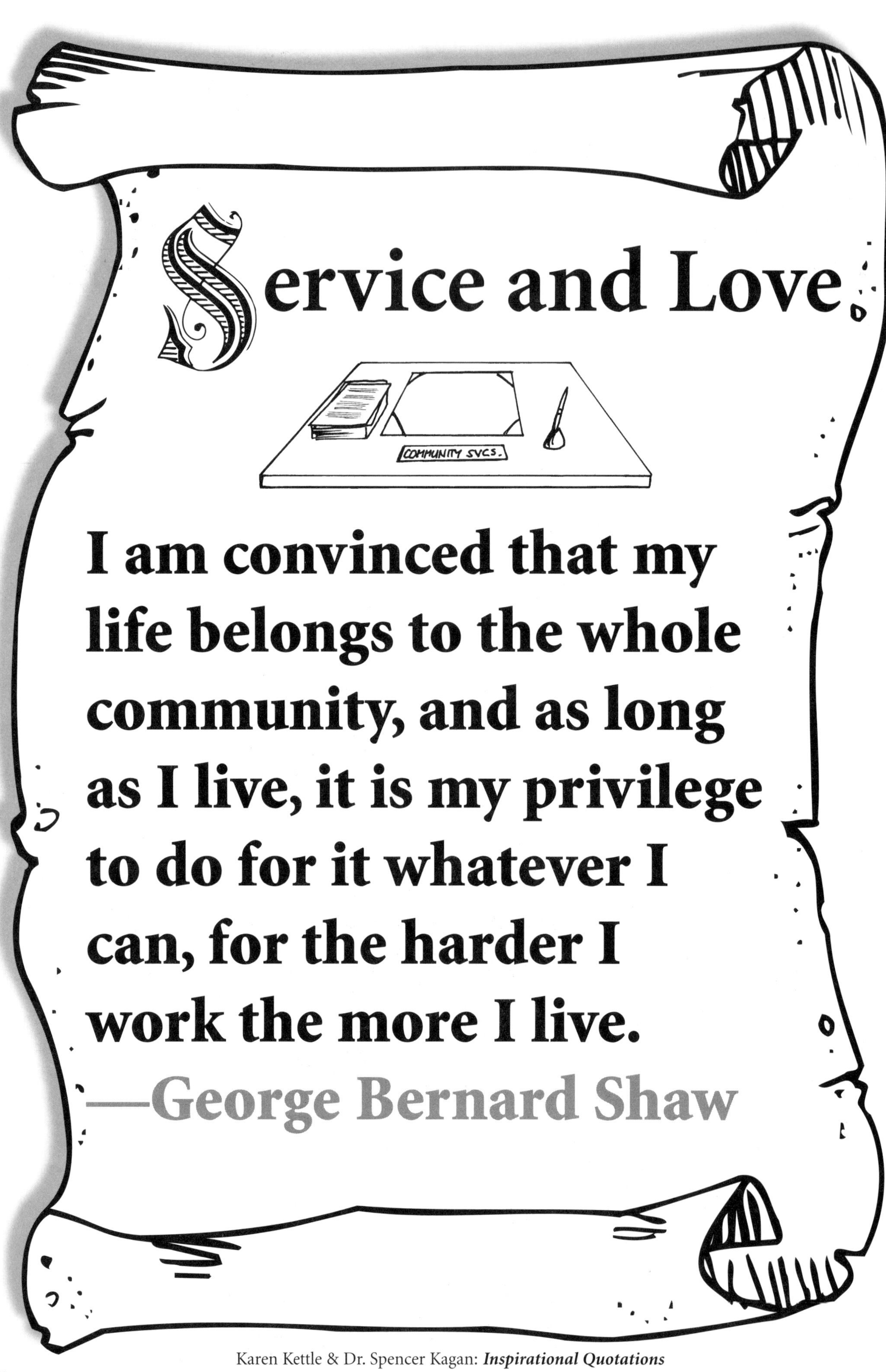


# Service and Love

**I am convinced that my life belongs to the whole community, and as long as I live, it is my privilege to do for it whatever I can, for the harder I work the more I live.**

**—George Bernard Shaw**

Success and Failure

# uccess and Failure

*Success and failure go hand in hand. Our ability to learn from our failures determines our capacity to succeed.*

**I succeed because I skate to where I think the puck will be.**

*—Wayne Gretzky*

Reflection Questions

- *How do you measure success?*
- *What do you need to do to help yourself succeed at school?*
- *What do you need to do to help yourself succeed beyond school?*

**Coming together is the beginning. Keeping together is progress. Working together is success.**

*—Henry Ford*

Reflection Questions

- *What does it take to be a good team member?*
- *What strategies can you use to help your teammates work together?*
- *What is the connection between success and treating other people well?*

**It is better to try and fail than fail to try.**

*—Spencer Kagan*

Reflection Questions

- *Why is it impossible to succeed if you fail to try?*
- *How does hard work turn failure into success?*
- *How do you maintain your dignity when you are disappointed?*

**Each success only buys an admission ticket to a more difficult problem.**

*—Henry Kissinger*

Reflection Questions

- *What are some of the most difficult problems people are trying to solve?*
- *What makes a problem difficult to solve?*
- *What is the advantage of seeing problems as opportunities rather than barriers?*

**Failure should challenge us to new heights of accomplishment, not pull us to new depths of despair. Failure is delay, but not defeat. It is a temporary detour, not a dead-end street.**

*—William Arthur Ward*

Reflection Questions

- *Why is failure temporary?*
- *How does your attitude affect your ability to learn from a failure?*
- *What temporary setback have you overcome?*

# Success and Failure

◆ Success is a journey, not a destination.
**—Ben Sweetland**

◆ It is good to have an end to journey towards; but it is the journey that matters in the end.
**—Ursula Le Guin**

◆ Success is not the key to happiness. Happiness is the key to success. If you love what you are doing, you will be successful.
**—Albert Schweitzer**

◆ Of course there is no formula for success, except perhaps an unconditional acceptance of life and what it brings.
**—Arthur Rubinstein**

◆ People spend a lifetime searching for happiness; looking for peace. They chase idle dreams, addictions, religions, even other people, hoping to fill the emptiness that plagues them. The irony is the only place they ever needed to search was within.
**—Ramona L. Anderson**

◆ Success is where preparation and opportunity meet.
**—Bobby Unser**

◆ Eighty percent of success is showing up.
**—Woody Allen**

◆ All my growth and development led me to believe that if you really do the right thing, and if you play by the rules, and if you've got good enough, solid judgment and common sense, that you're going to be able to do whatever you want to do with your life.
**—Barbara Jordan**

◆ I do not know anyone who has got to the top without hard work. That is the recipe. It will not always get you to the top, but it should get you pretty near.
**—Margaret Thatcher**

◆ Success supposes endeavor.
**—Jane Austen**

◆ In life you are given two ends, one to think with and the other to sit on. Your success in life depends on which end you use the most. Heads you win, tails you lose.
**—Conrad Burns**

***Success usually comes to those who are too busy to be looking for it.***
***—Henry David Thoreau***

◆ You can have unbelievable intelligence, you can have connections, you can have opportunities fall out of the sky. But in the end, hard work is the true, enduring characteristic of successful people.
**—Marsha Evans**

◆ The dictionary is the only place that success comes before work. Hard work is the price we must pay for success. I think you can accomplish anything if you're willing to pay the price.
**—Vince Lombardi**

◆ The problem with success is that its formula is the same as the one for ulcers.
**—Laurence J. Peter**

◆ I owe my success to having listened respectfully to the very best advice, and then going away and doing the exact opposite.
**—G. K. Chesterton**

◆ Success requires both urgency and patience. Be urgent about making the effort, and patient about seeing the results.
**—Ralph Marston**

◆ Always bear in mind that your own resolution to succeed is more important than any other thing.
**—Abraham Lincoln**

◆ It's a funny thing, the more I practice the luckier I get.
**—Arnold Palmer**

◆ The secret to success is constancy to purpose.
**—Benjamin Disraeli**

◆ We are what we repeatedly do. Excellence, then, is not an act, but a habit.
**—Aristotle**

◆ The secret of joy in work is contained in one word—excellence. To know how to do something well is to enjoy it.
**—Pearl S. Buck**

◆ Success is a little like wrestling a gorilla. You don't quit when you're tired—you quit when the gorilla is tired.
**—Robert Strauss**

◆ Your task it is, amid confusion, rush and noise, to grasp the lasting clam and meaningful and finding it anew, to hold and treasure it.
**—Paul Hindemith**

◆ Success is to be measured not so much by the position that one has reached in life as by the obstacles which he (she) has overcome while trying to succeed.
**—Booker T. Washington**

◆ If you want to increase your success rate, double your failure rate.
**—Thomas Watson**

◆ It is on our failures that we base a new and different and better success.
**—Havelock Ellis**

◆ You may be disappointed if you fail, but you are doomed if you don't try.
**—Beverly Sills**

◆ Success often comes from not knowing your limitations.
**—Frank Tyger**

◆ The young do not know enough to be prudent, and therefore they attempt the impossible—and achieve it, generation after generation.
**—Pearl S. Buck**

***Failure is the opportunity to begin again more intelligently.***
***—Henry Ford***

◆ Be bold. If you are going to make an error, make a doozy, and don't be afraid to hit the ball.
**—Billie Jean King**

◆ I'll match my flops with anybody's but I wouldn't have missed them. Flops are a part of life's menu and I've never been one to miss out on any of the courses.
**—Rosalind Russell**

◆ The mistakes are all there waiting to be made.
**—S. A. Tartakower (chess player)**

◆ It is not that I have confidence, but I believe if I fail, so what? Now I have the chance to try again.
**—Maya Angelou**

◆ Baseball teaches that errors are part of the game.
**—Ernest Kurtz**

◆ Failure is an event, never a person.
**—William D. Brown**

◆ Remember you will not always win. Some days the most resourceful individuals taste defeat. But there is, in this case, always tomorrow—after you have done your best to achieve success today.
**—Maxwell Maltz**

◆ My motto was always to keep swinging. Whether I was in a slump or feeling badly or having trouble off the field, the only thing to do was keep swinging.
**—Hank Aaron**

◆ In great attempts it is glorious even to fail.
**—Cassius Longinus**

◆ Good people are good because they've come to wisdom through failure. We get very little wisdom from success.
**—William Saroyan**

◆ I have learned throughout my life as a composer chiefly through my mistakes and pursuits of false assumptions, not my exposure to founts of wisdom and knowledge.
**—Igor Stravinsky**

◆ We learn wisdom from failure much more than from success. We often discover what will do by finding out what will not do; and probably he (she) who never made a mistake, never made a discovery.
**—Samuel Smiles**

# Success and Failure

◆ A person seldom makes the same mistake twice. Generally it's three times or more.
**—Marilyn Grey**

◆ Don't be discouraged by failure. It can be a positive experience. Failure is, in a sense, the highway to success, inasmuch as every discovery of what is false leads us to seek earnestly after what is true, and every fresh experience points out some form of error which we shall afterwards carefully avoid.
**—John Keats**

◆ An expert is a man (woman) who has made all the mistakes which can be made, in a narrow field.
**—Niels Bohr**

◆ Remember your past mistakes just long enough to profit by them.
**—Dan Mckinnon**

***We miss 100% of the shots we don't take.***
***—Wayne Gretzky***

◆ Honestly face defeat; never fake success.
Exploit the failure; don't waste it. Learn all you can from it. Never use failure as an excuse for not trying again.
**—Charles Kettering**

◆ We must accept finite disappointment, but we must never lose infinite hope.
**—Martin Luther King Jr.**

◆ Today is a new day; you'll get out of it just what you put into it. If you have made mistakes, even serious mistakes, you can make a new start whenever you choose. For the thing we call failure is not the falling down but the staying down.
**—Mary Pickford**

◆ Fall seven times, stand up eight.
**—Japanese proverb**

◆ The human spirit is never finished when it is defeated … it is finished when it surrenders.
**—Ben Stein**

◆ Failure comes only when we forget our ideals and objectives and principles.
**—Jawaharlal Nehru**

◆ You're gonna lose some ballgames and you're gonna win some ballgames, and that's about it.
**—Sparky Anderson**

◆ In the game of life it's a good idea to have a few early losses, which relieves you of the pressure of trying to maintain an undefeated season.
**—Billy Vaughn**

◆ I have missed more that 9,000 shots in my career. I have lost almost 300 games. On 26 occasions I have been entrusted to take the game-winning shot … and missed. I have failed over and over again in my life. And that is why I succeed.
**—Michael Jordan**

◆ We are all failures … at least, all the best of us are.
**—J. M. Barrie**

◆ Success is all about going from failure to failure without losing your enthusiasm.
**—Winston Churchill**

◆ Even a stopped clock is right twice every day. After some years, it can boast of a long series of successes.
**—Marie Von Ebner-Eschenbach**

◆ Success is never final and failure is never fatal. It's courage that counts.
**—Jules Ellinger**

◆ Courage allows the successful person to fail—and to learn powerful lessons from the failure—so that in the end, it was not a failure at all.
**—Maya Angelou**

◆ If your success is not on your own terms, if it looks good to the world but does not feel good in your heart, it is not success at all.
**—Anna Quindlen**

◆ You have reached the pinnacle of success as soon as you become uninterested in money, compliments or publicity.
**—Thomas Wolfe**

◆ It's not a successful climb unless you enjoyed the journey.
**—Dan Benson**

◆ Failures are few among people who have found a work they enjoy enough to do it well. You invest time in your work; invest love in it too.
**—Clarence Flynn**

◆ An aim in life is the only fortune worth finding.
**—Jacqueline Kennedy**

◆ Work for something because it is good, not just because it stands a chance to succeed.
**—Vaclav Havel**

◆ What is the recipe for successful achievement? To my mind there are just four essential ingredients: Choose a career you love; give it the best there is in you; seize your opportunities; and be a member of the team.
**—Benjamin F. Fairless**

◆ It is only when we develop others that we permanently succeed.
**—Harvey S. Firestone**

◆ If everyone is moving forward together; then the success takes care of itself.
**—Henry Ford**

◆ People are not motivated by failure; they are motivated by achievement and recognition.
**—F. F. Fournies**

◆ Success breeds confidence.
**—Beryl Markham**

◆ I know the price of success: dedication, hard work, and an unremitting devotion to the things you want to see happen.
**—Frank Lloyd Wright**

***Yesterday I dared to struggle. Today I dare to win.***
***—Bernadette Devlin***

◆ The good we secure for ourselves is precarious and uncertain until it is secured for all of us and incorporated into our common life.
**—Jane Addams**

◆ How far you go in life depends on your being tender with the young, compassionate with the aged, sympathetic with the striving and tolerant of the weak and strong. Because someday in life you will have been all of these.
**—George Washington Carver**

◆ The purpose of life is not to be happy—but to matter, to be productive, to be useful, to have it make a difference that you lived at all.
**—Leo Rosten**

◆ Don't ask yourself what the world needs—ask yourself what makes you come alive, and then go do it. Because what the world needs is people who have come alive.
**—Harold Thurman Whitman**

◆ I don't want to get to the end of my life and find that I just lived the length of it. I want to have lived the width of it as well.
**—Diane Ackerman**

◆ The art of living successfully consists of being able to hold two opposite ideas in tension at the same time: first, to make long-term plans as if we were going to live forever; and second, to conduct ourselves daily as if we were going to die tomorrow.
**—Sydney J. Harris**

◆ If I have been of service, if I have glimpsed more of the nature and essence of ultimate good, if I am inspired to reach wider horizons of thought and action, if I am at peace with myself, it has been a successful day.
**—Alex Noble**

◆ Love the moment. Flowers grow out of dark moments. Therefore, each moment is vital. It affects the whole. Life is a succession of such moments and to live each, is to succeed.
**—Corita Kent**

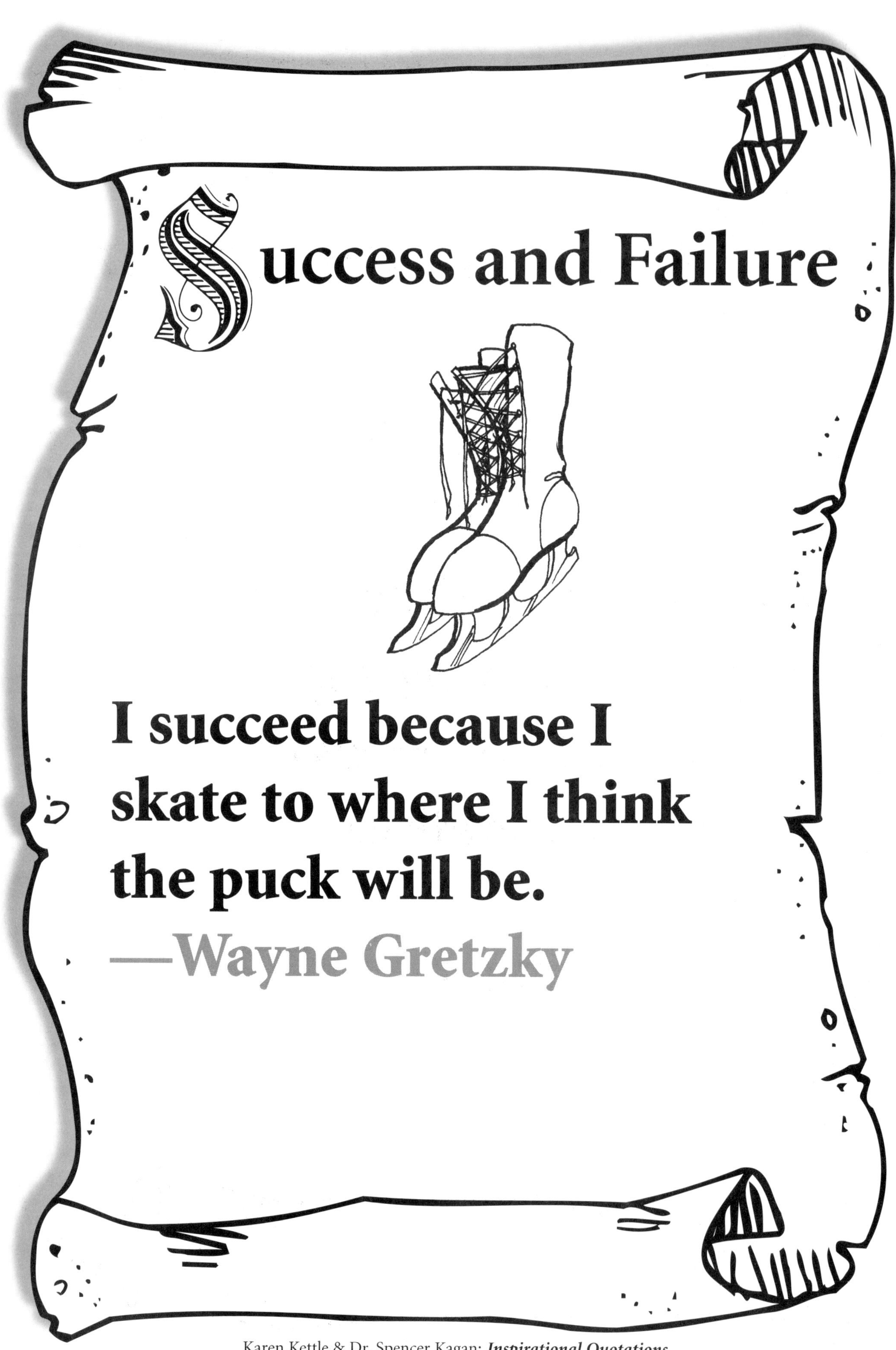
Success and Failure
I succeed because I
skate to where I think
the puck will be.
—Wayne Gretzky

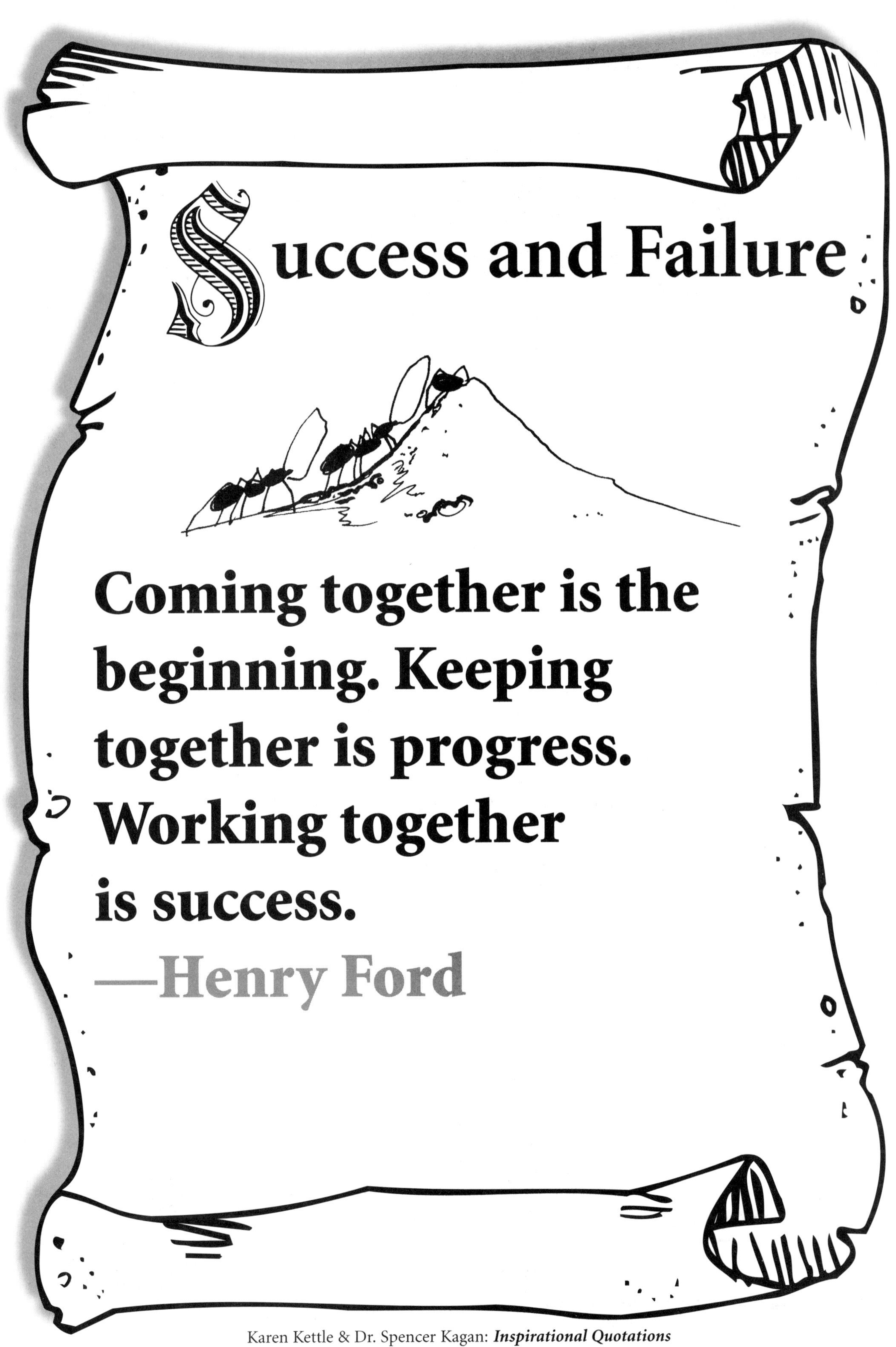

Success and Failure
Coming together is the beginning. Keeping together is progress. Working together is success.
—Henry Ford

# Success and Failure

**It is better to try and fail than fail to try.**

**—Spencer Kagan**

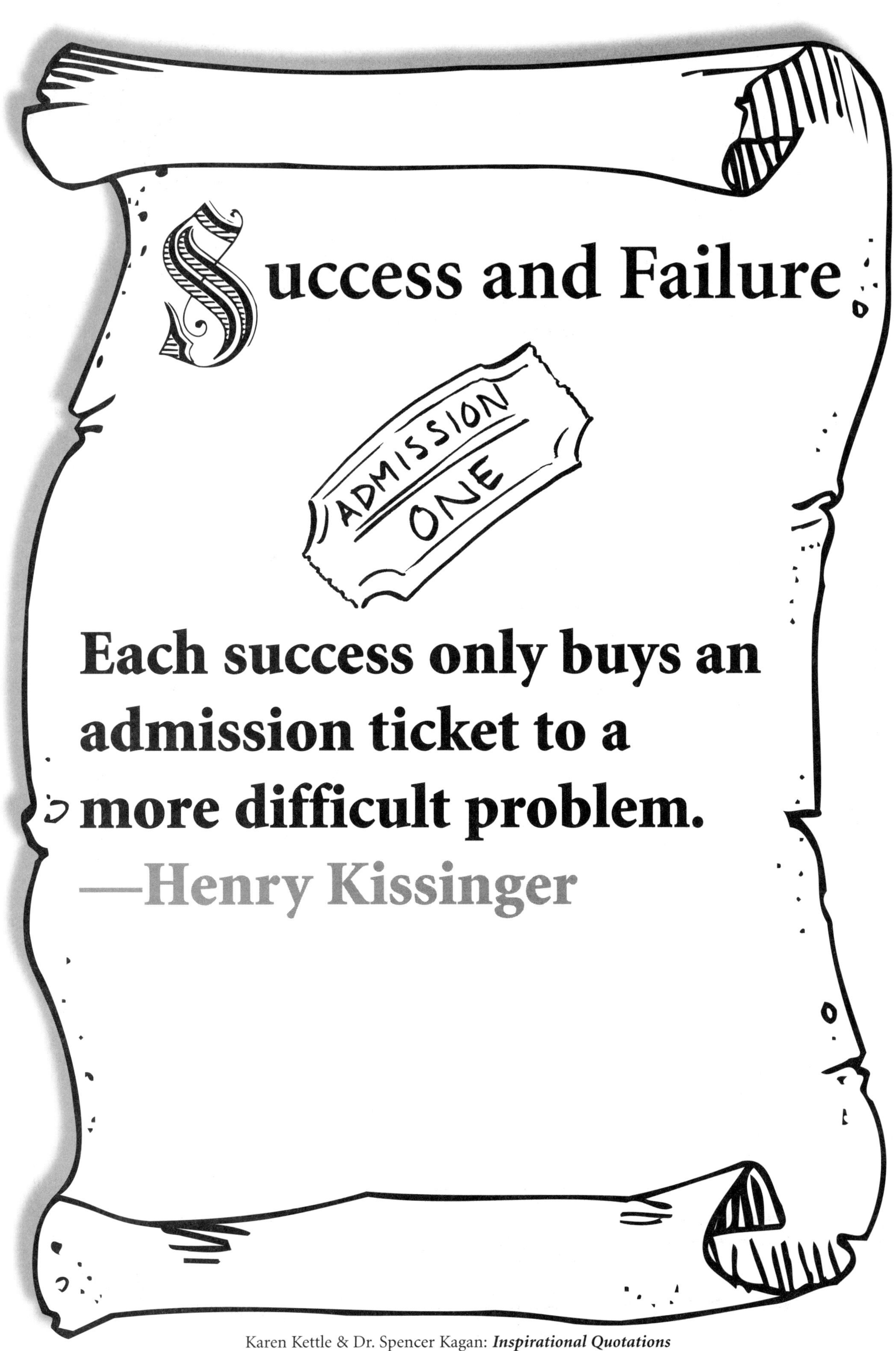


# Success and Failure

**Each success only buys an admission ticket to a more difficult problem.**

**—Henry Kissinger**

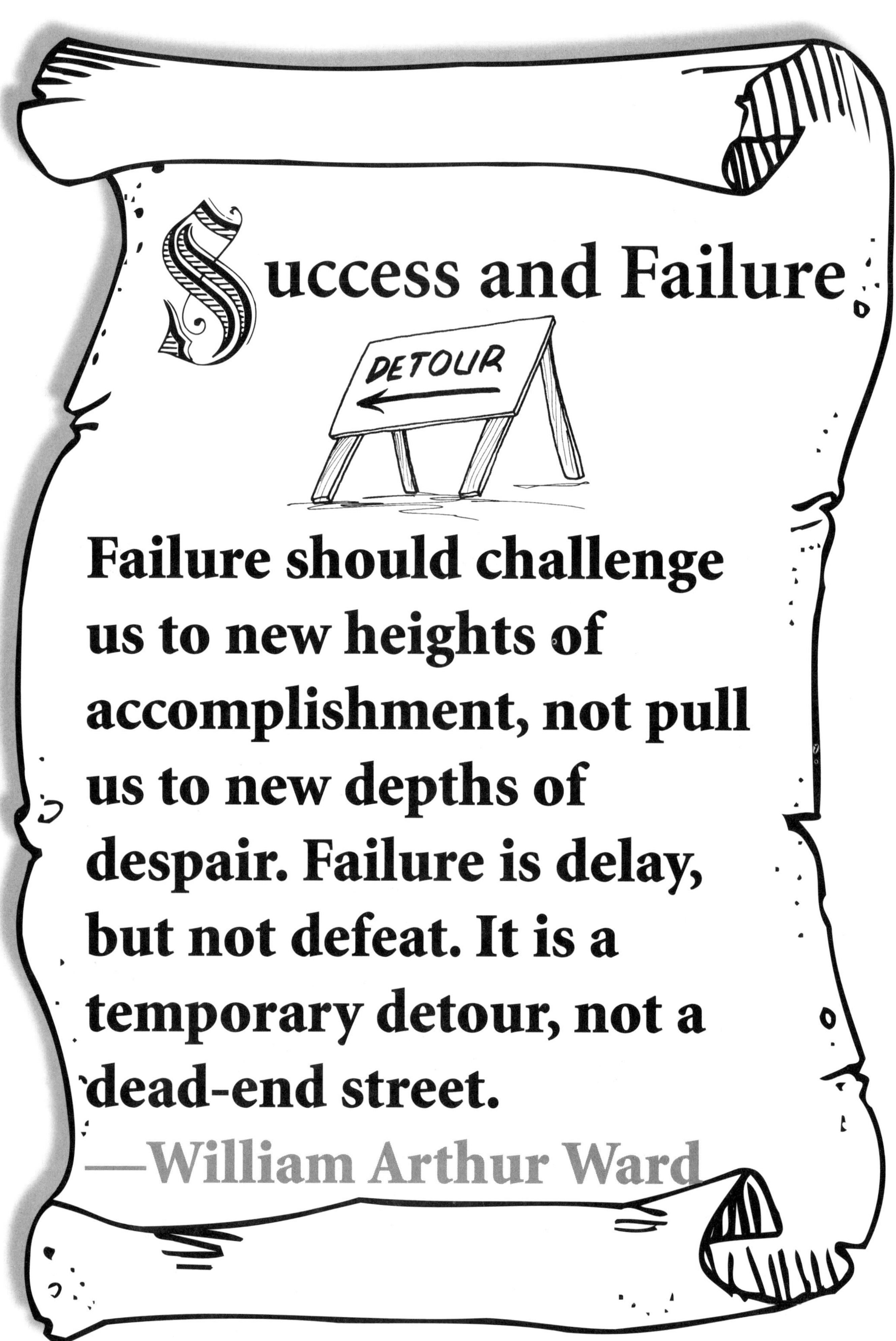
Success and Failure
DETOUR
Failure should challenge us to new heights of accomplishment, not pull us to new depths of despair. Failure is delay, but not defeat. It is a temporary detour, not a dead-end street.
—William Arthur Ward

# Teaching

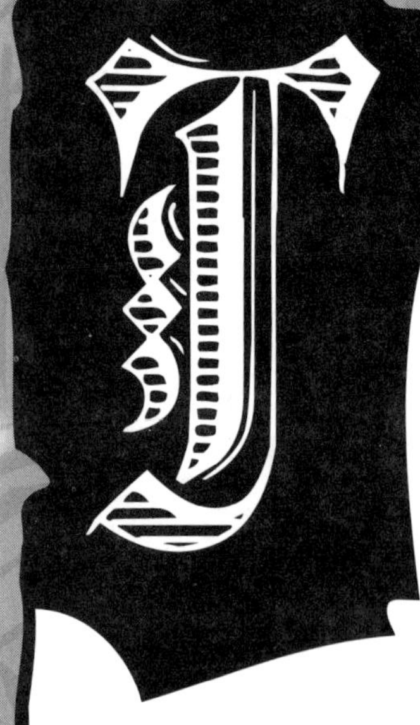

# Teaching

***Memorable teachers touch our hearts as well as our minds. They help us discover who we are and inspire us to fulfill our dreams.***

1

**Too often we give children answers to remember rather than problems to solve.**

*—Roger Lewis*

Reflection Questions

- *How do you like to learn?*
- *Do you learn in the same way in and out of school? Explain.*
- *What is the most interesting problem or challenge you have solved?*

**To love what you do and feel that it matters—how could anything be more fun?**

*—Katharine Graham*

Reflection Questions

- *What do you love to do that is important to you?*
- *How do you know when teachers love what they are doing?*
- *When do you think teaching would be fun and when would it not be fun?*

**Thought flows in terms of stories—stories about events, stories about people, and stories about intentions and achievements. The best teachers are the best story tellers. We learn in the form of stories.**

*—Frank Smith*

Reflection Questions

- *How do you make a story interesting?*
- *What qualities make someone a good storyteller?*
- *Who tells stories worth hearing?*



Karen Kettle & Dr. Spencer Kagan: ***Inspirational Quotations***
Kagan Publishing • 1 (800) 933-2667 • www.KaganOnline.com

**Too often we underestimate the power of a touch, a smile, a kind word, a listening ear, an honest compliment, or the smallest act of caring, all of which have the potential to turn a life around.**

*—Leo Buscaglia*

Reflection Questions

- *What is a simple thing that you have done to help someone else?*
- *Why is it important that teachers show their students that they care?*
- *When has a teacher made a positive difference in your life?*

**It is difficult to connect general principles with such thoroughly concrete things as little children.**

*—John Dewey*

Reflection Questions

- *What advice would you like to give your teachers?*
- *How do teachers make complicated things easier to understand?*
- *When has a teacher helped you do your best?*

# Teaching

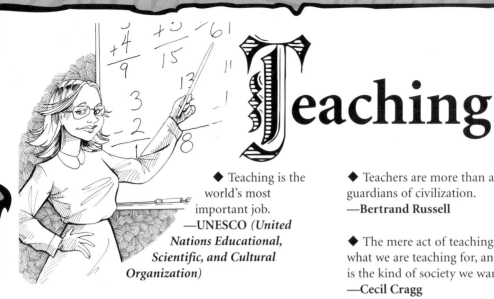

◆ Teaching is the world's most important job.
**—UNESCO *(United Nations Educational, Scientific, and Cultural Organization)***

◆ In a completely rational society, the best of us would aspire to be teachers and the rest of us would have to settle for something less, because passing civilization along from one generation to the next ought to be the highest honor and the highest responsibility anyone could have.
**—Lee Iacocca**

◆ But let us never forget that the true heroes of our society are not to be found on a movie screen or football field. They are to be found in our classrooms.
**—Elizabeth Dole**

◆ Teaching seems to me beyond doubt the greatest of the professions.
**—Theodore Brameld**

◆ Teachers can change lives with just the right mix of chalk and challenges.
**—Joyce A. Myers**

◆ What office is there which involves more responsibility, which requires more qualifications, and which ought, therefore, to be more honorable, than that of teaching?
**—Harriet Martineau**

◆ To be allowed to teach children should be the sign of the final approval of society.
**—G. Brock Chisholm**

◆ The most creative and emotionally engaged teachers see themselves not just as educating learners and workers, but as developing citizens.
**—Andy Hargreaves and Michael Fullan**

***Teaching is the highest form of understanding.***
***—Aristotle***

◆ Teachers are more than any other class the guardians of civilization.
**—Bertrand Russell**

◆ The mere act of teaching is rather secondary to what we are teaching for, and what we are teaching for is the kind of society we want to create.
**—Cecil Cragg**

◆ No calling in society is more demanding than teaching; no calling in our society is more selfless than teaching; and no calling is more central to the vitality of a democracy than teaching.
**—Roger Mudd**

◆ Teachers, I believe, are the most responsible and important members of society because their professional efforts affect the fate of the earth.
**—Helen Caldicott**

◆ Teaching is the greatest act of optimism.
**—Colleen Wilcox**

◆ Teachers are like flowers: they spread their beauty throughout the world. Their love of learning touches the hearts of their students, who then carry that sense of wonder with them wherever they may go. Teachers, with their words of wisdom, awaken the spirit within us all and lead us down the roads of life.
**—Deanna Beisser**

◆ Acquire new knowledge whilst thinking over the old, and you may become a teacher of others.
**—Confucius**

◆ It is a luxury to learn; but the luxury of learning is not to be compared with the luxury of teaching.
**—R. D. Hitchcock**

◆ A teacher is … a very special person who uses his or her creativity and loving, inquiring mind to develop the rare talent of encouraging others to think, to dream, to learn, to try, to do!
**—Beverly Conklin**

◆ Teachers teach because they care. Teaching young people is what they do best. It requires long hours, patience, and care.
**—Horace Mann**

◆ The work of a teacher—exhausting, complex, idiosyncratic, never twice the same—is at its heart, an intellectual and ethical enterprise. Teaching is the vocation of vocations, a calling that shepherds a multitude of other callings, It is an activity that is intensely practical and yet transcendent, brutally matter-of-fact, and yet fundamentally a creative act. Teaching begins in challenge and is never far from mystery.
**—William Ayres**

◆ Teaching is a daily exercise in vulnerability.
**—Parker Palmer**

◆ If a doctor, lawyer, or dentist had 40 people in his/her office at one time, all of whom had different needs, and some of whom didn't want to be there and were causing trouble, and the doctor, lawyer, or dentist, without assistance had to treat them all with professional excellence for nine months then he/she might have some conception of the classroom teacher's job.
**—Donald D. Quinn**

◆ A poor surgeon hurts 1 person at a time. A poor teacher hurts 130.
**—Ernest Boyer**

◆ Only the brave should teach. Only those who love the young should teach. Teaching is a vocation. It is as sacred as priesthood; as innate a desire, as inescapable as the genius which compels a great artist. If he (she) has not the concern for humanity, the love of living creatures, the vision of the priest and the artist, he (she) must not teach.
**—Pearl S. Buck**

◆ I have come to believe that a great teacher is a great artist and that there are as few as there are any other great artists. Teaching might even be the greatest of the arts since the medium is the human mind and spirit.
**—John Steinbeck**

***You cannot have students as continuous learners and effective collaborators, without teachers having the same characteristics.***
***—Michael Fullan***

◆ No one should teach who is not in love with teaching.
**—Margaret E. Sangster**

◆ Who dares to teach, must never cease to learn.
**—John Cotton Dana**

◆ The teachers who get "burned out" are not the ones who are constantly learning, which can be exhilarating, but those who feel they must stay in control and ahead of the students at all times.
**—Frank Smith**

◆ The good teacher, the proper teacher, must be ever-living in faith and ever-renewed in creative energy to keep the sap packed in herself, himself, as well as the work.
**—Sylvia Plath**

◆ Teaching is a process of becoming that continues throughout life, never completely achieved, never completely denied. This is the challenge and the fun of being a teacher—there is no ultimate end to the process.
**—Frances Mayforth**

◆ This is the road I have tried to follow as a teacher: living my convictions; being open to the process of knowing and sensitive to the experience of teaching as an art; being pushed forward by the challenges that prevent me from bureaucratizing my practice; accepting my limitations, yet always conscious of the necessary effort to overcome them and aware that I cannot hide them because to do so would be a failure to respect both my students and myself as a teacher.
**—Paolo Freire**

◆ I'm not a teacher: only a fellow-traveller of whom you asked the way. I pointed ahead—ahead of myself as well as you.
**—George Bernard Shaw**

◆ If you have knowledge, let others light their candles at it.
**—Margaret Fuller**

◆ It is by teaching that we teach ourselves, by relating that we observe, by affirming that we examine, by showing that we look, by writing that we think, by pumping that we draw water into the well.
**—Henri-Frédéric Amiel**

# Teaching

◆ I was still learning when I taught my last class.
**—Claude M. Fuess**

◆ To show a child what once delighted you, to find the child's delight added to your own, this is happiness.
**—J. B. Priestley**

◆ We teach what we like to learn and the reason many people go into teaching is vicariously to reexperience the primary joy experienced the first time they learned something they loved.
**—Stephen Brookfield**

◆ The special power of teachers to infect others with the virus of their own passion for learning often gives teachers more power than they either realize or want.
**—Marshall Gregory**

◆ The art of teaching is the art of assisting discovery.
**—Mark Van Doren**

◆ The dream begins with a teacher who believes in you, who tugs and pushes and leads you to the next plateau, sometimes poking you with a sharp stick called "truth."
**—Dan Rather**

◆ The student is infinitely more important than the subject-matter.
**—Nel Noddings**

◆ I will teach things that are not in books. For instance, I believe that children will be better students if they like each other and themselves better.
**—Ennis Cosby**

◆ Every child's life is like a piece of paper on which every person leaves a mark.
**—Chinese proverb**

***It's not what is poured into a student that counts, but what is planted.***
***—Linda Conway***

◆ As teachers we must believe in change, must know it is possible, or we wouldn't be teaching—because education is a constant process of change. Every single time you "teach" something to someone, it is ingested, something is done with it, and a new human emerges.
**—Leo Buscaglia**

◆ When the uncapped potential of a student meets the liberating art of a teacher, a miracle unfolds.
**—Mary Hatwood Futrell**

◆ Better than a thousand days of diligent study is one day with a great teacher.
**—Japanese proverb**

◆ Teachers and learners are correlates one of which was never intended to be without the other.
**—Jonathan Edwards**

◆ To create and sustain for children the conditions for productive growth without those conditions existing for educators is virtually impossible.
**—Seymour Sarason**

◆ Teachers open the door. You enter by yourself.
**—Chinese proverb**

◆ A teacher is ... one of the most special people in the world, for who else could spend day after day giving of themselves to someone else's children?
**—Deanna Beisser**

◆ Good teaching comes not from behind the desk but from behind the heart.
**—Elizabeth Andrew**

◆ Most of us end up with no more than five or six people who remember us. Teachers have thousands of people who remember them for the rest of their lives.
**—Andrew A. Rooney**

◆ In teaching you cannot see the fruit of a day's work. It is invisible and remains so, maybe for twenty years.
**—Jacques Barzum**

◆ I owe a lot to my teachers and mean to pay them back someday.
**—Stephen Leacock**

◆ Students don't separate method from ethos, and they are quite right not to do so. To students, we are what we do.
**—Marshall Gregory**

◆ In the end, you can only teach the things that you are.
**—Max Learner**

◆ If we don't model what we teach, we are teaching something else.
**—Abraham Maslow**

◆ One looks back with appreciation to the brilliant teachers, but with gratitude to those who touched our human feelings. The curriculum is so much necessary raw material, but warmth is the vital element for the growing plant and the soul of the child.
**—Carl Jung**

◆ Young people need much more to be demanded of them. They need to be needed, they need to give, they need opportunities to show love, courage, sacrifice. They need to be part of a cause that is larger than the sum of their individual appetites. They need to believe in something.
**—Thomas Sobol**

◆ Every child, every person needs to know that they are a source of joy; every child, every person needs to be accepted.
**—Jean Vanier**

◆ As a teacher I possess tremendous power to make a child's life miserable or joyous. I can be a tool of torture or an instrument of inspiration. I can humiliate or humor, hurt or heal. In all situations it is my response that decides whether a crisis will be escalated or de-escalated, and a child is humanized or de-humanized.
**—Haim Ginott**

◆ Ideally, school is supposed to provide a setting where our performance has fewer esteem-threatening consequences than in the "real world," presumably in the interest of encouraging the learner to "try things out."
**—Jerome Bruner**

◆ We ought to regard the breaking of a child's spirit as a sin against humanity.
**—Erik Erikson**

◆ We worry about what a child will be tomorrow, yet we forget that he or she is someone today.
**—Stacia Tausher**

◆ As teachers, we must constantly try to improve schools and we must keep working at changing and experimenting and trying until we have developed ways of reaching every child.
**—Albert Shanker**

◆ If the child is not learning the way you are teaching, then you must teach in the way the child learns.
**—Rita Dunn**

◆ The conflict between the need to belong to a group and the need to be seen as unique and individual is the dominant struggle of adolescence.
**—Jeanne Elium**

◆ Children of the middle years do not do their learning unaffected by attendant feelings of interest, boredom, success, failure, chagrin, joy, humiliation, pleasure, distress and delight. They are whole children responding in a total way, and what they feel is a constant factor that can be constructive or destructive in any learning situation.
**—Dorothy H. Cohen**

***Once children learn how to learn, nothing is going to narrow their minds. The essence of teaching is to make learning contagious, to have one idea spark another.***
***—Marva Collins***

◆ The most significant word in teacher is *each.*
**—Robert DeBruyn**

◆ All students can learn and succeed, but not on the same day in the same way.
**—William G. Spady**

◆ There is, in fact, no teaching without learning.
**—Paolo Freire**

◆ The best learners … often make the worst teachers. They are, in a very real sense, perceptually challenged. They cannot imagine what it must be like to struggle to learn something that comes so naturally to them.
**—Stephen Brookfield**

# Teaching

◆ Be patient and sympathetic with the type of mind that cuts a poor figure in examinations. It may, in the long examination which life sets us, come out in the end in better shape than the glib and ready reproducer, its passion being deeper, its purposes more worthy, its combining power less commonplace, and its total mental output consequently more important.
**—William James**

◆ We must teach our children to dream with their eyes open.
**—Harry Edwards**

◆ The teacher is one who makes two ideas grow where only one grew before.
**—Elbert Hubbard**

◆ I like a teacher who gives you something to take home to think about besides homework.
**—Lily Tomlin**

***Teaching should be such that what is offered is perceived as a valuable gift and not as a hard duty.***
***—Albert Einstein***

◆ The task of the excellent teacher is to stimulate "apparently ordinary" people to unusual effort. The tough problem is not in identifying winners: it is in making winners out of ordinary people.
**—K. Patricia Cross**

◆ The good teacher makes the poor student good and the good student superior. When our students fail, we, as teachers, too, have failed.
**—Marva Collins**

◆ My heart is singing for joy this morning. A miracle has happened! The light of understanding has shone upon my little pupil's mind. And behold, all things are changed.
**—Anne Sullivan**

◆ The greatest sign of success for a teacher is to be able to say, "The children are now working as if I did not exist."
**—Maria Montessori**

◆ The task of the best teacher is to balance the difficult juggling act of becoming vitally, vigorously, creatively, energetically, and inspiringly unnecessary.
**—Gerald O. Grow**

◆ The most important knowledge teachers need to do good work is a knowledge of how students are experiencing learning and perceiving their teacher's actions.
**—Stephen Brookfield**

◆ Teaching is human communication and like all communication, elusive and difficult … we must be wary of the feeling that we know what we are doing in class. When we are most sure of what we are doing, we may be closest to being a bore.
**—John Holt**

◆ We should not be speaking to, but with. That is second nature to any good teacher.
**—Noam Chomsky**

◆ Any teacher can study books, but books do not necessarily bring wisdom, nor that human insight essential to consummate teaching skills.
**—Bliss Perry**

◆ Learn your theories as well as you can, but put them aside when you touch the miracle of the living soul. Not theories but your own creative individuality alone must decide.
**—Carl Jung**

◆ Human activity consists of action and reflection: it is praxis; it is transformation of the world. And as praxis, it requires theory to illuminate it. Human activity is theory and practice; it is reflection and action. It cannot be reduced to either verbalism or activism.
**—Paolo Freire**

◆ Teaching is an instinctual act, mindful of potential, craving of realizations, a pausing, seamless process, where one rehearses constantly while acting, sits as a spectator at a play one directs, engages every part in order to keep the choices open and the shape alive for the student, so that the student may enter in and begin to do what the teacher has done: make choices.
**—A. Bartlett Giamatti**

◆ The best teachers give their pupils both a sense of order, discipline, control; and a powerful stimulus which urges them to take their destinies in their own hands, kick over rules, and transgress all boundaries.
**—Gilbert Highet**

◆ The teacher who is indeed wise does not bid you to enter the house of his (her) wisdom but rather leads you to the threshold of your mind.
**—Kahlil Gibran**

◆ For good teaching rests neither in accumulating a shelf full of knowledge nor in developing a repertoire of skills. In the end, good teaching lies in a willingness to attend and care for what happens in our students, ourselves, and the space between us. Good teaching is a certain kind of stance, I think. It is a stance of receptivity, of attunement, of listening.
**—Laurent A. Daloz**

◆ The more you prepare outside of class, the less you perspire in class. The less you perspire in class, the more you inspire the class.
**—Ho Boon Tiong**

◆ Teachers who cannot keep students involved and excited for several hours in the classroom should not be there.
**—John Roueche**

◆ A teacher, like a playwright, has an obligation to be interesting or, at least brief. A play closes when it ceases to interest audiences.
**—Haim Ginott**

◆ When I give a lecture, I accept that people look at their watches, but what I do not tolerate is when they look at it and raise it to their ear to find out if it stopped.
**—Marcel Archard**

***The whole art of teaching is only the art of awakening the natural curiosity of young minds for the purpose of satisfying it afterwards.***
***—Anatole France***

◆ There are two kinds of teachers: the kind that fill you with so much quail shot that you can't move, and the kind that just gives you a little prod behind and you jump to the skies.
**—Robert Frost**

◆ To teach is not to transfer knowledge but to create the possibilities for the production or construction of knowledge.
**—Paolo Freire**

◆ In teaching, it is the method and not the content that is the message … the drawing out, not the pumping in.
**—Ashley Montague**

◆ A teacher who can arouse a feeling for one single good action, for one single good poem, accomplishes more than he (she) who fills our memory with rows and rows of natural objects, classified with name and form.
**—Johann Wolfgang Von Goethe**

◆ I have a theory about the human mind. A brain is a lot like a computer. It will only take so many facts, and then it will go into overload and blow up.
**—Erma Bombeck**

◆ The mediocre teacher tells. The good teacher explains. The superior teacher demonstrates. The great teacher inspires.
**—William Arthur Ward**

◆ It is not the answer that enlightens, but the question.
**—Eugene Ionesco**

◆ Socrates didn't have an overhead projector. He asked questions that bothered people and 3,500 years later people are still talking about him.
**—Hanoch McCarty**

◆ A teacher who is attempting to teach, without inspiring the pupil with a desire to learn, is hammering on cold iron.
**—Horace Mann**

◆ Not only is there an art in knowing a thing, but also a certain art in teaching it.
**—Marcus Tullius Cicero**

# Teaching

◆ It is the supreme art of the teacher to awaken joy in creative expression and knowledge.
**—Albert Einstein**

◆ Good teaching is one-fourth preparation and three-fourths theater.
**—Gail Godwin**

◆ Do not teach too many subjects. What you teach, teach thoroughly.
**—Alfred North Whitehead**

◆ Breadth and depth, like freedom and discipline, are not mutually exclusive, though one will incline more toward one at one time, and toward the other at another.
**—Kenneth Eble**

***Events in our classrooms today will prompt world events tomorrow.***
***—J. Lloyd Trump***

◆ It is only by introducing the young to great literature, drama and music, and to the excitement of great science that we open to them the possibilities that lie within the human spirit—enable them to see visions and dream dreams.
**—Eric Anderson**

◆ Learning and teaching should not stand on opposite banks and just watch the river flow by; instead, they should embark together on a journey down the water. Through an active, reciprocal exchange, teaching can strengthen learning how to learn.
**—Loris Malaguzzi**

◆ I am not a teacher, but an awakener.
**—Robert Frost**

◆ Awaken people's curiosity. It is enough to open minds, do not overload them. Put there just a spark.
**—Anatole France**

◆ To know how to suggest is the great art of teaching.
**—Henri-Frédéric Amiel**

◆ Part of teaching is helping students learn how to tolerate ambiguity, consider possibilities, and ask questions that are unanswerable.
**—Sara Lawrence Lightfoot**

◆ Teachers should guide without dictating, and participate without dominating.
**—C. B. Neblette**

◆ How to tell students what to look for without telling them what to see is the dilemma of teaching.
**—Lascelles Abercrombie**

◆ I cannot teach anybody anything. I can only make them think.
**—Socrates**

◆ We only think when we are confronted with a problem.
**—John Dewey**

◆ Teaching consists of causing people to go into situations from which they cannot escape, except by thinking. Do not handicap your children by making their lives easy.
**—Robert Heinlein**

◆ A large part of the art of instruction lies in making the difficulty of new problems large enough to challenge thought, and small enough to that, in addition to the confusion naturally attending the novel elements, there shall be luminous familiar spots from which helpful suggestions may spring.
**—John Dewey**

◆ The most important part of teaching is to teach what it is to know.
**—Simone Weil**

◆ Just think of the tragedy of teaching children not to doubt.
**—Clarence Darrow**

◆ The difficulty is to try and teach the multitude that something can be true and untrue at the same time.
**—Arthur Schopenhauer**

◆ How can we help students to understand that the tragedy of life is not death; the tragedy is to die with commitments undefined and convictions undeclared and service unfulfilled?
**—Vachel Lindsay**

◆ The mere act of teaching is rather secondary to what we are teaching for, and what we are teaching for is the kind of society we want to create.
**—Cecil Cragg**

◆ The educator must above all understand how to wait; to reckon all effects in the light of the future, not of the present.
**—Ellen Key**

◆ The teachers of this country, one may say, have its future in their hands.
**—William James**

◆ Any genuine teaching will result, if successful, in someone's knowing how to bring about a better condition of things than existed earlier.
**—John Dewey**

◆ The future is in the hands of those who can give tomorrow's generations valid reasons to live and hope.
**—Pierre Teilhard de Chardin**

◆ In the lifetimes of our children our brightest inventions will become outdated. But the love we give them today will live on forever: those they touch will touch others.
**—Spencer Kagan**

***There comes that mysterious meeting in life when someone acknowledges who we are and what we can be, igniting the circuits of our highest potential.***
***—Rusty Berkus***

◆ In the end we will conserve only what we love. We will love only what we understand. We will understand only what we are taught.
**—Baba Dioum**

◆ Whoever touches the life of the child touches the most sensitive point of a whole which has roots in the most distant past and climbs toward the infinite future.
**—Maria Montessori**

◆ Light tomorrow with today.
**—Elizabeth Barrett Browning**

◆ To believe in a child is to believe in the future. Through their aspirations they will save the world. With their combined knowledge the turbulent seas of hate and injustice will be calmed. They will champion the causes of life's underdogs, forging a society without class discrimination. They will supply humanity with music and beauty as it has never known. They will endure. Towards these ends I pledge my life's work. I will supply the children with tools and knowledge to overcome the obstacles. I will pass on the wisdom of my years and temper it with patience. I shall impact in each child the desire to fulfill his or her dream. I shall teach.
**—Henry James**

◆ There are only two lasting bequests we can hope to give our children. One of these is roots; the other, wings.
**—Hodding Carter**

◆ I touch the future, I teach.
**—Christa McAuliffe**

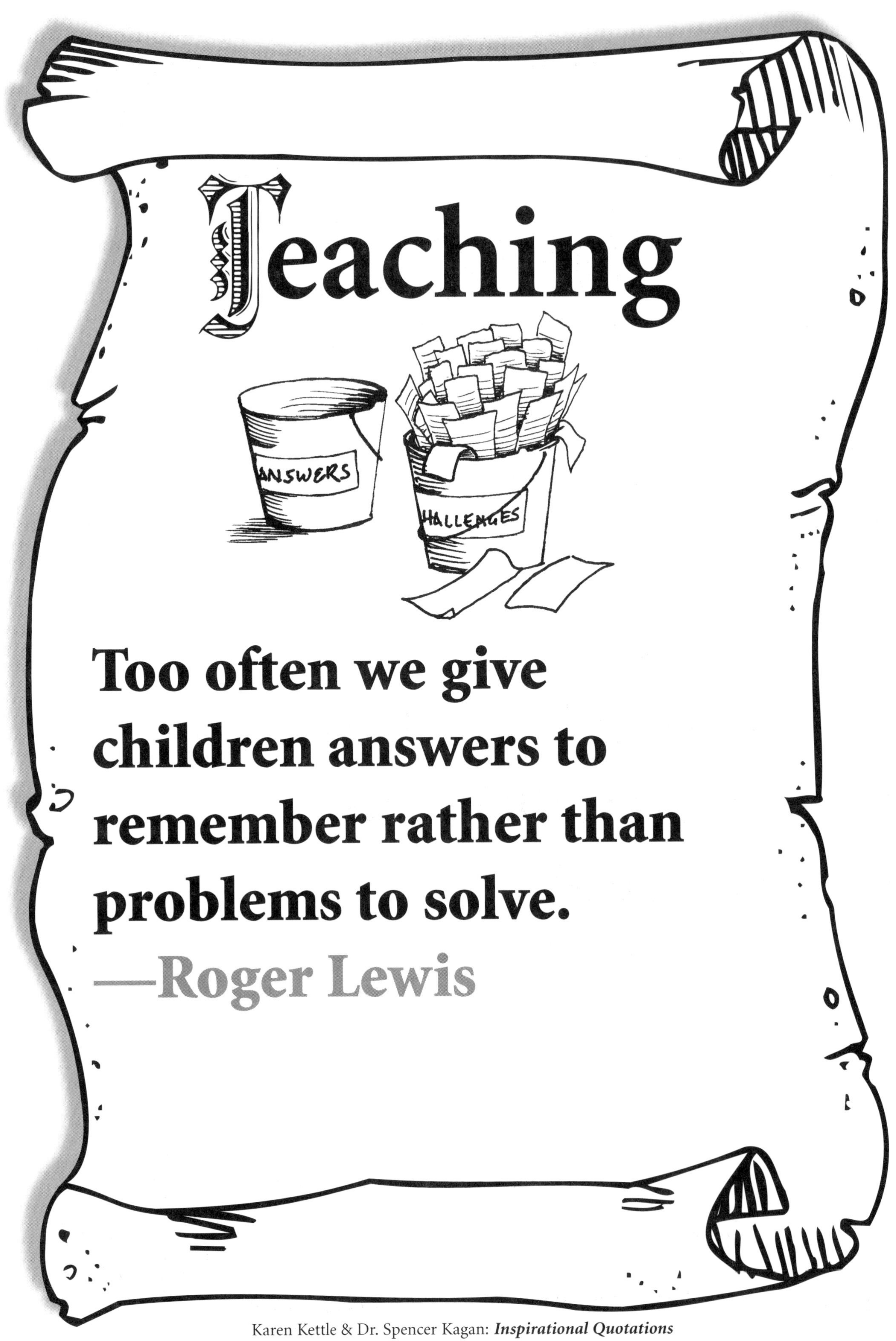
Teaching
NSWERS
HALLENGES
Too often we give children answers to remember rather than problems to solve.
—Roger Lewis

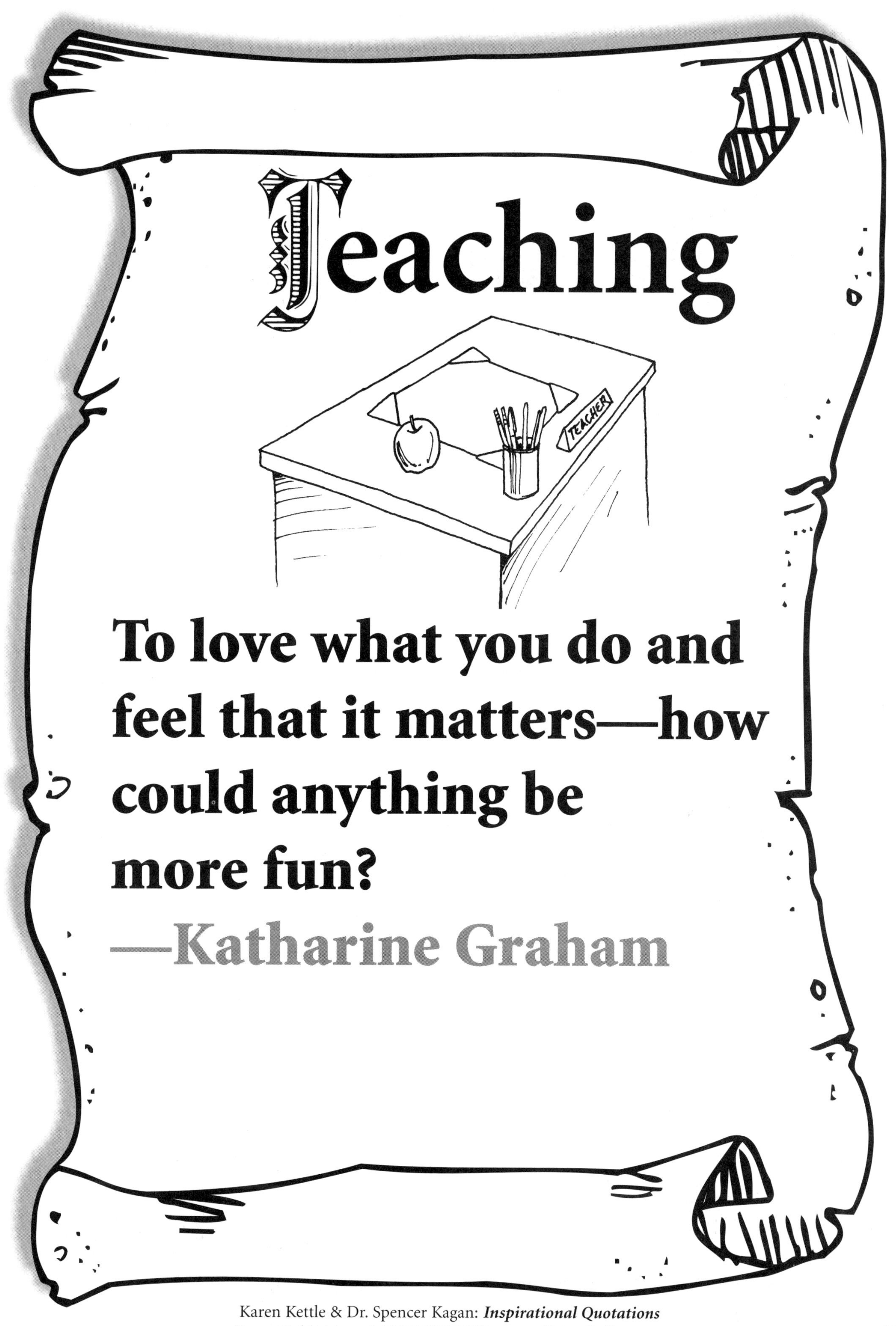
Teaching
TEACHER
To love what you do and feel that it matters—how could anything be more fun?
—Katharine Graham

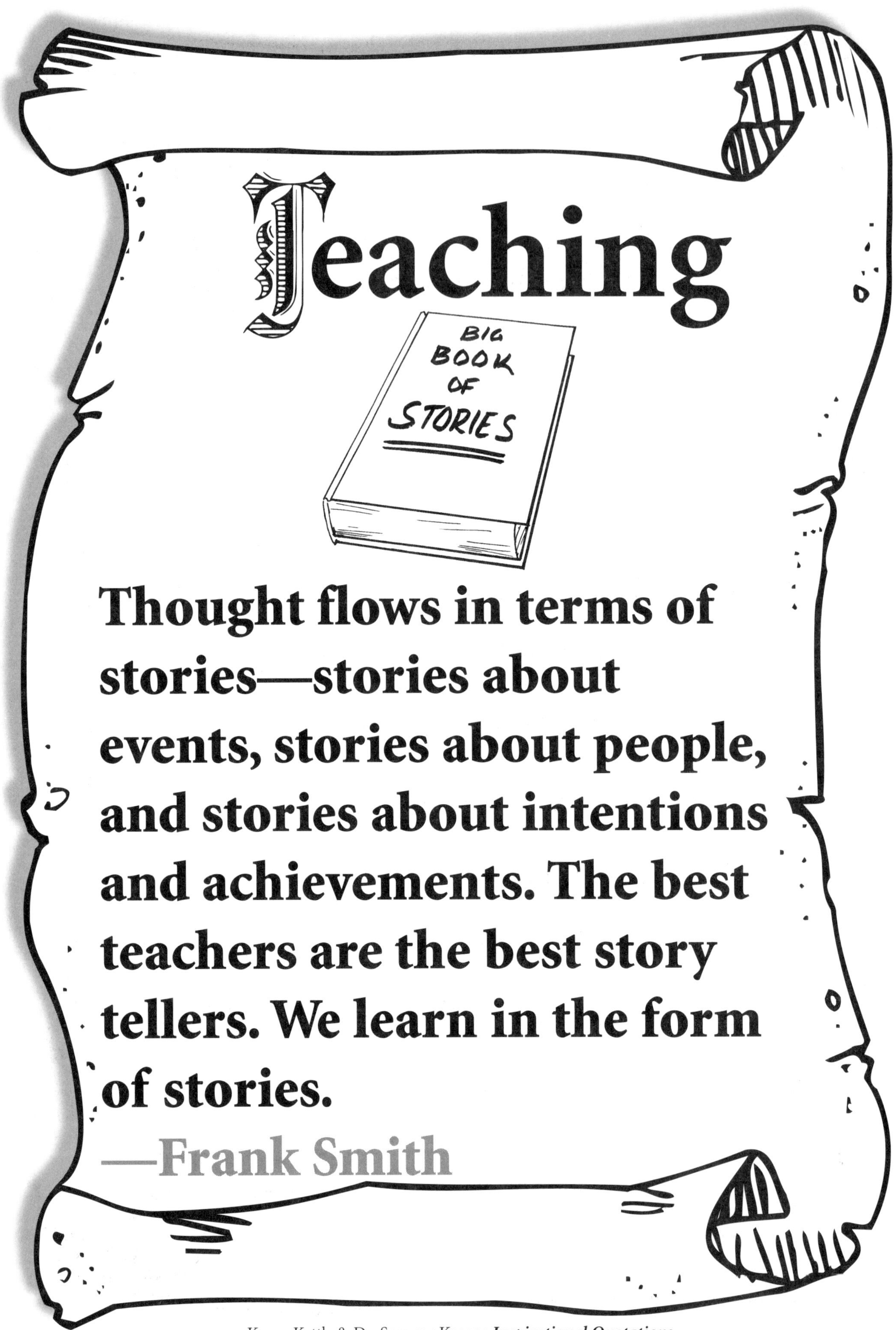


# Teaching

**Thought flows in terms of stories—stories about events, stories about people, and stories about intentions and achievements. The best teachers are the best story tellers. We learn in the form of stories.**

**—Frank Smith**

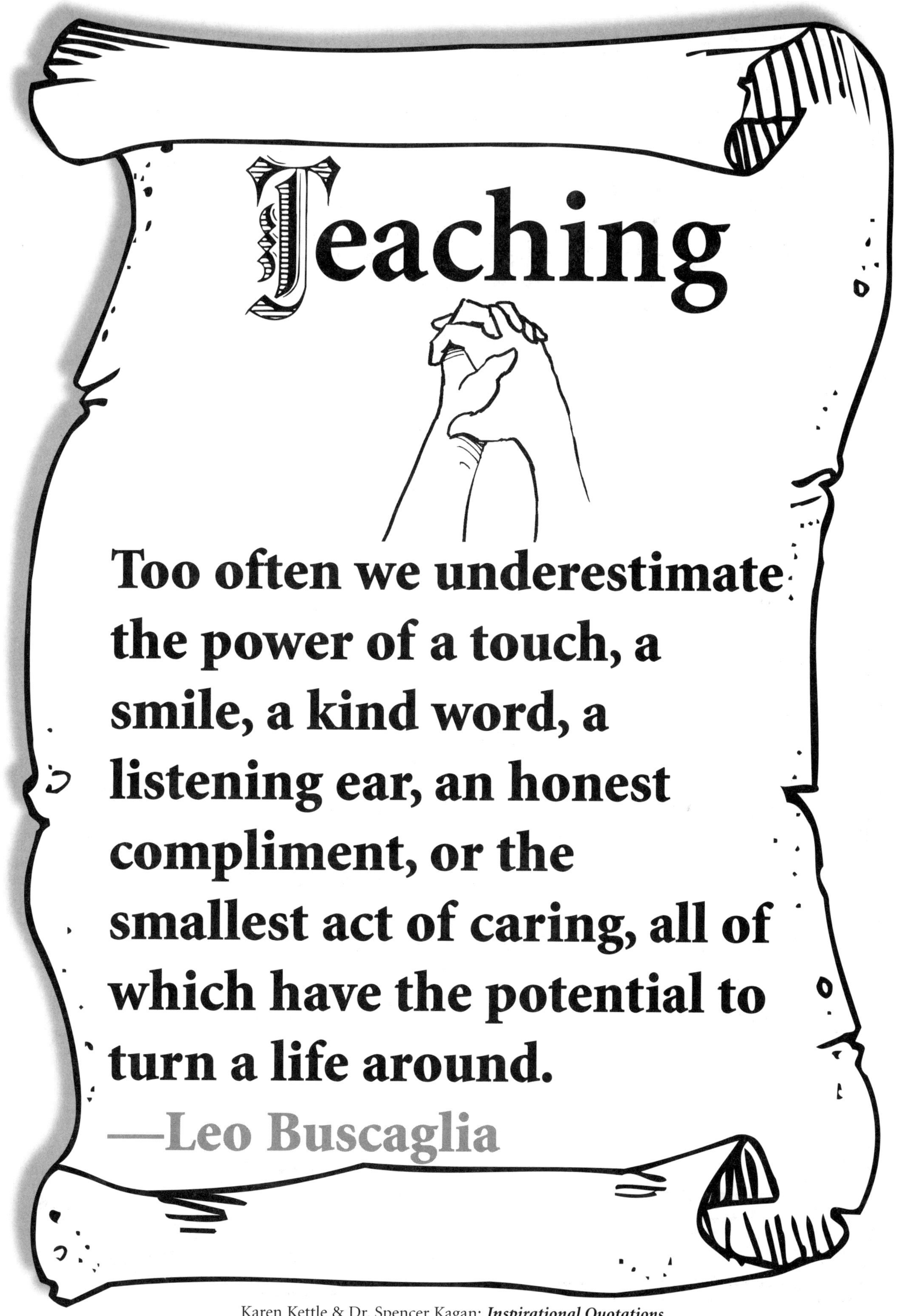
Teaching
Too often we underestimate the power of a touch, a smile, a kind word, a listening ear, an honest compliment, or the smallest act of caring, all of which have the potential to turn a life around.
—Leo Buscaglia

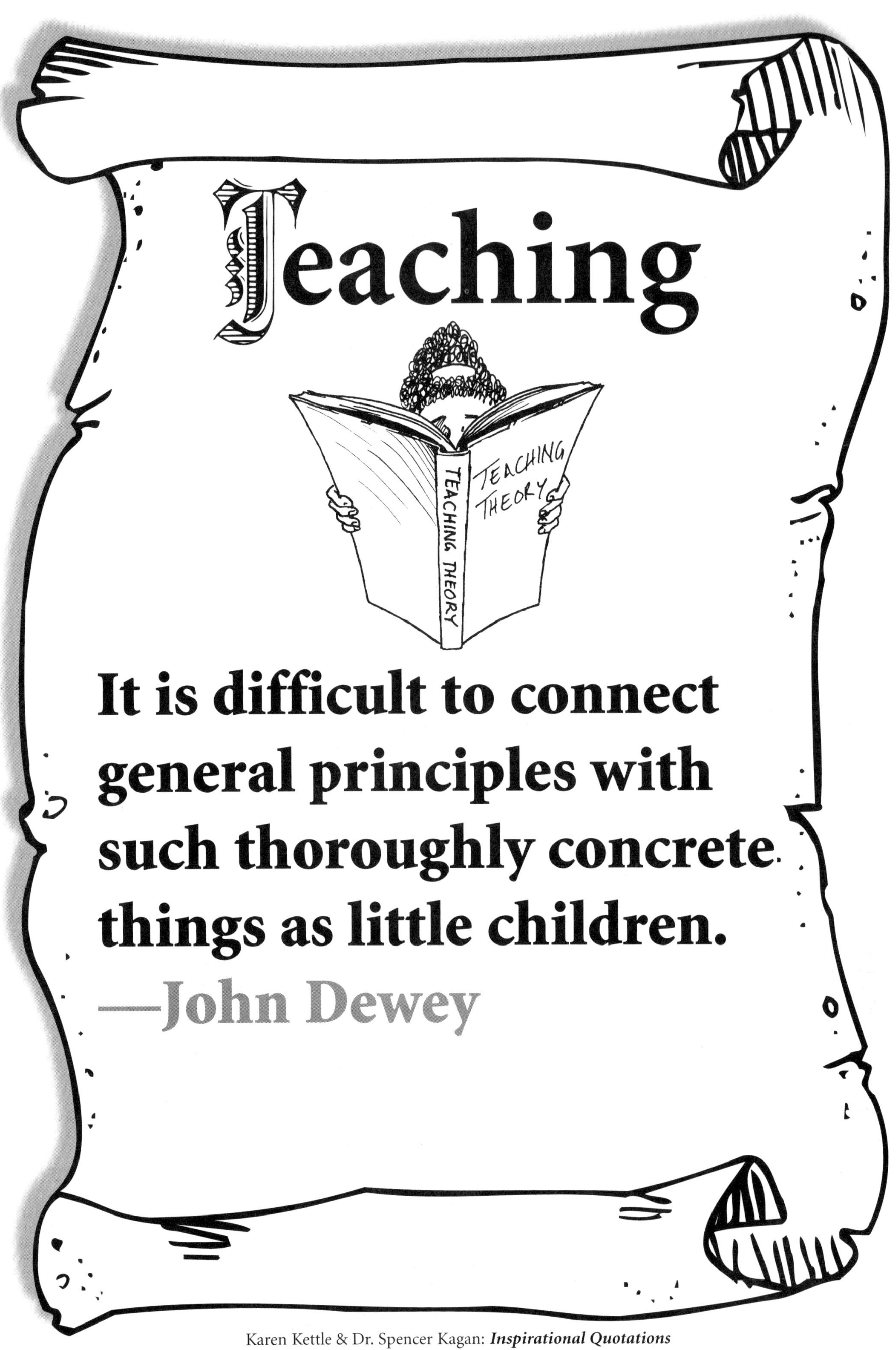
Teaching
TEACHING THEORY
TEACHING THEORY
It is difficult to connect general principles with such thoroughly concrete things as little children.
—John Dewey

Vision and Goals

# ision and Goals

*Vision is the ability to see the world the way we would like to make it. Our goals are signposts along the way.*

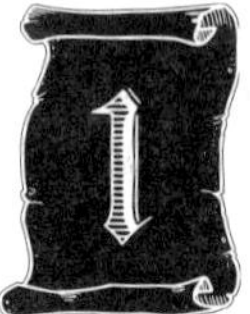

**Begin challenging your own assumptions. Your assumptions are your windows on the world. Scrub them off every once in awhile, or the light won't come in.**

*—Alan Alda*

### Reflection Questions

- *When you meet someone for the first time how do you decide what to think of him or her?*
- *Why can first impressions be misleading?*
- *What is a stereotype? How do stereotypes limit our vision?*

**Vision is the art of seeing things invisible.**

*—Jonathan Swift*

### Reflection Questions

- *What do you see yourself doing ten years from now?*
- *What plans do you have to help you make that vision a reality?*
- *What evidence will you gather to let you know you are on the right track?*

**The starting point for a better world is the belief that it is possible.**

*—Norman Cousins*

### Reflection Questions

- *How would you like to make the world better?*
- *What positive changes in the world do you think are possible?*
- *What makes something possible or impossible?*

4

**Dreams come in a size too big so that we can grow into them.**

*—Josie Bisset*

### Reflection Questions

- *What do you dream of doing?*
- *Why is your dream currently beyond your reach?*
- *What will you need to do to grow into your dream?*

**What do you pack to pursue a dream, and what do you leave behind?**

*—Sandra Sharpe*

### Reflection Questions

- *As you pursue your dream, what knowledge, skills and attitudes will you need?*
- *As you grow and mature, what ideas and attitudes will you leave behind?*
- *How can you ensure that you never stop reaching for your dreams?*

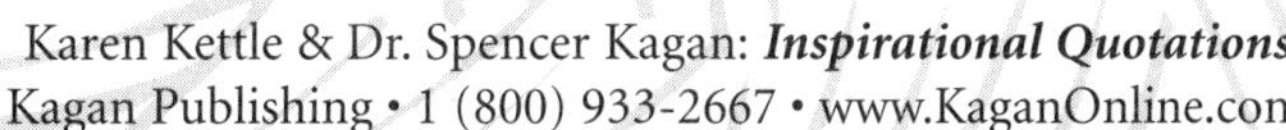

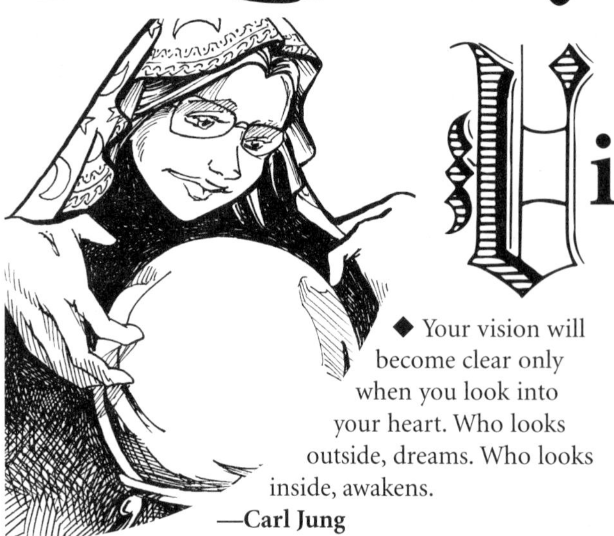

# Vision and Goals

◆ Your vision will become clear only when you look into your heart. Who looks outside, dreams. Who looks inside, awakens.
**—Carl Jung**

◆ See things as you would have them be, instead of as they are.
**—Robert Collier**

◆ The search for meaning is intrinsic to human nature. As thinking creatures, we want to understand why we find ourselves on this road and where the journey is taking us … we are wanderers, searching and striving for end and aim, for purpose and connection.
**—William J. Bennett**

◆ Life is a path that you beat while you walk it.
**—Machado**

◆ The very act of seeking set something in motion to meet us; something in the universe or in the unconscious responds as if to an invitation.
**—Jean Shinoda Bolen**

◆ To will is to select a goal, determine a course of action that will bring one to that goal, and then hold to that action till the goal is reached. The key is action.
**—Michael Hanson**

◆ The key to motivation is having a motive—having a why.
**—Stephen Covey**

◆ Beware of what you want—for you will get it.
**—Ralph Waldo Emerson**

◆ What we must decide is perhaps how we are valuable, rather than how valuable we are.
**—F. Scott Fitzgerald**

***Your work is to discover your work and then with all your heart follow it.***
***—Buddha***

◆ Plant the seeds of expectation in your mind; cultivate thoughts that anticipate achievement. Believe in yourself as being capable of overcoming all obstacles and weaknesses.
**—Norman Vincent Peale**

◆ If you are working on something exciting that you really care about, you don't have to be pushed. The vision pulls you.
**—Steve Jobs**

◆ Far and away the best prize that life offers is the chance to work hard at work worth doing.
**—Theodore Roosevelt**

◆ It is not enough to be busy, so are the ants. The question is, what are we busy about?
**—Henry David Thoreau**

◆ It's not so much how busy you are, but why you are busy. The bee is praised; the mosquito is swatted.
**—Marie O'Conner**

◆ Far away there in the sunshine are my highest aspirations. I may not reach them, but I can look up and see their beauty, believe in them and try to follow their lead.
**—Louisa May Alcott**

◆ Keep your eyes on the stars and your feet on the ground.
**—Theodore Roosevelt**

◆ To become what we are capable of becoming is the only end of life.
**—Spinoza**

◆ The greatest use of life is to spend it for something that outlasts it.
**—William James**

◆ It's time to start living the life we've imagined.
**—Henry James**

◆ Form the habit of saying "Yes" to your good ideas. Then write down all the reasons why they will work. There will always be plenty of people around to tell you why they won't work.
**—Gil Atkinson**

◆ We are what we think. All that we are arises with our thoughts. With our thoughts we make the world.
**—Buddha**

◆ Of all of the beautiful truths pertaining to the soul which have been restored and brought to light in this age, none is more gladdening or fruitful of divine promise and confidence than this—that you are the master of thought, the molder of your character, and the maker and shaper of condition, environment and destiny.
**—James Allen**

◆ If my mind can conceive it, and my heart can believe it, I know I can achieve it.
**—Jesse Jackson**

◆ You'll see it when you believe it.
**—Wayne W. Dyer**

***The future belongs to those that believe in the beauty of their dreams.***
***—Eleanor Roosevelt***

◆ There is nothing in a caterpillar that tells you it's going to be a butterfly.
**—R. Buckminster Fuller**

◆ To see things in the seed, that is genius.
**—Lao Tzu**

◆ Imagination is more important than knowledge, for knowledge is limited, while imagination embraces the entire world.
**—Albert Einstein**

◆ If we are going to do anything significant with life, we sometimes have to move away from it—beyond the usual measurements. We must occasionally follow visions and dreams.
**—Bede Jarrett**

◆ What happens to a dream deferred? Does it dry up like a raisin in the sun?
**—Langston Hughes**

◆ The poor man is not he who is without a cent, but he who is without a dream.
**—Harry Kemp**

◆ Lord, grant that I may always desire more than I can accomplish.
**—Michelangelo**

◆ Some men see things as they are and say "Why?" I dream things that never were, and say, "Why not?"
**—George Bernard Shaw**

◆ Dare to dream things never seen; then align your decisions with your visions.
**—Spencer Kagan**

◆ Nothing happens unless first a dream.
**—Carl Sandburg**

◆ If you can dream it, you can do it.
**—Walt Disney**

◆ Without leaps of imagination, or dreaming, we lose the excitement of possibilities. Dreaming, after all, is a form of planning.
**—Gloria Steinem**

◆ Dreams and dedication are a powerful combination.
**—William Longgood**

◆ Dreams are the touchstones of our characters.
**—Henry David Thoreau**

◆ Cherish your visions and your dreams as they are the children of your soul; the blue prints of your ultimate achievements.
**—Napoleon Hill**

◆ Keep true to the dreams of thy youth.
**—Johann Friedrich Von Schille**

◆ A goal is a dream that has an ending.
**—Duke Ellington**

◆ There are no impossible dreams, just our limited perception of what is possible.
**—Beth Mende Conny**

◆ The limits of the possible can only be defined by going beyond them into the impossible.
**—Arthur C. Clarke**

◆ We must not allow other people's limited perceptions to define us.
**—Virginia Satir**

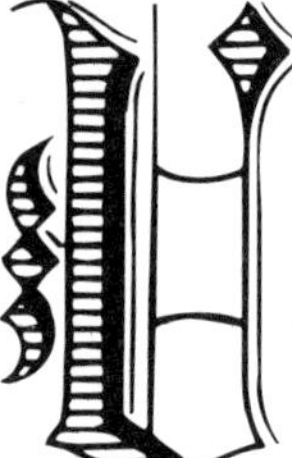

# Vision and Goals

◆ The bravest are surely those who have the clearest vision of what is before them, glory and danger alike, and yet notwithstanding, go out to meet it.
**—Thucydides**

◆ Turn your face to the sun and the shadows fall behind you.
**—Maori proverb**

◆ The great tragedy of life doesn't lie in failing to reach your goals. The great tragedy lies in having no goals to reach.
**—Benjamin E. Mays**

◆ If you don't know where you're going you will end up somewhere else.
**—Lawrence Peter "Yogi" Berra**

◆ It is more important to know where you are going than to get there quickly. Do not mistake activity for achievement.
**—Mabel Newcomer**

◆ When I got cut from the varsity team as a sophomore in high school, I learned something. I knew I never wanted to feel that bad again. I never wanted to have that taste in my mouth, that hole in my stomach. So I set a goal of becoming a starter on the varsity.
**—Michael Jordan**

◆ The first step toward getting somewhere is to decide that you are not going to stay where you are.
**—J. Pierpont Morgan**

◆ In life, the first thing you must do is decide what you really want. Weigh the costs and the results. Are the results worthy of the costs? Then make up your mind completely and go after your goal with all your might.
**—Alfred A Montapert**

◆ Those who are unwilling to invest in the future haven't earned one.
**—H. W. Lewis**

***Go as far as you can see. When you get there, you can see farther.***
***—B. J. Marshal***

◆ Goals are dreams with deadlines.
**—Diana Scharf Hunt**

◆ We can only survive when we have a goal—a passionate purpose which bears upon the public interest.
**—Margaret E. Kuhn**

◆ In the long run you only hit what you aim at. Therefore, though you should fail immediately, you had better aim at something high.
**—Henry David Thoreau**

◆ We aim above the mark to hit the mark.
**—Ralph Waldo Emerson**

◆ A soul without a high aim is like a ship without a rudder.
**—Eileen Caddy**

◆ The very essence of leadership is that you have to have a vision.
**—Theodore Hesburgh**

◆ Your goal should be out of reach but not out of sight.
**—Anita DeFrantz**

◆ Live your life each day as you would climb a mountain. An occasional glance toward the summit keeps the goal in mind, but many beautiful scenes are to be observed from each new vantage point. Climb slowly, steadily, enjoying each passing moment, and the view from the summit will serve as a fitting climax for the journey.
**—Harold V. Melchert**

◆ You must have long term goals to keep you from being frustrated by short term failures.
**—Charles C. Noble**

◆ Great minds have purposes, others have wishes.
**—Washington Irving**

◆ We are made wise not be the recollecting of our past but by the responsibility for our future.
**—George Bernard Shaw**

◆ Cautious, careful people, always casting about to preserve their reputation and social standing, never can bring about a reform. Those who are really in earnest must be willing to be anything or nothing in the world's estimation, and publicly and privately, in season and out, avow their sympathy with despised and persecuted ideas and their advocates, and bear the consequences.
**—Susan B. Anthony**

◆ I see only my goal; the obstacles must give way.
**—Napoleon Bonaparte**

◆ Be larger than your task.
**—Orison Swett Marden**

◆ To tend, unfailing, unflinchingly, towards a goal, is the secret to success.
**—Anna Pavolva**

◆ Every physical creation begins as a mental creation—as a thought, a plan, a perception or a motive. Visualizing something organizes one's ability to accomplish it.
**—Stephen R. Covey**

◆ The secret of achievement is to hold a picture of a successful outcome in mind.
**—Henry David Thoreau**

◆ Visualize winning.
**—Gary Player**

◆ Formulate and stamp indelibly on your mind a mental picture of yourself as succeeding. Hold this picture tenaciously. Never permit it to fade. Your mind will seek to develop the picture .... Do not build up obstacles in your imagination.
**—Norman Vincent Peale**

◆ A vision foretells what may be ours. With a great mental picture in mind we begin to go from one accomplishment to another, using the materials about us only as stepping stones to that which is higher, better, and more satisfying.
**—Katherine Logan**

◆ If you want to move people, it has to be toward a vision that's positive for them, that taps important values, that gets them something they desire, and it has to be presented in a compelling way that they feel inspired to follow.
**—Martin Luther King Jr.**

◆ It is difficult to say what is impossible for us. The dream of yesterday is the hope of today and the reality of tomorrow.
**—Robert Goddard**

◆ There is nothing like a dream to create the future.
**—Victor Hugo**

◆ Cherish your visions, your ideals, the music that stirs in your heart. If you remain true to them, your world will at last be built.
**—James Allen**

◆ I like the dreams of the future better than the history of the past.
**—Thomas Jefferson**

***The only limits are, as always, those of vision.***
***—James Broughton***

◆ Our awesome responsibility to ourselves, to our children, and to the future is to create ourselves in the image of goodness, because the future depends on the nobility of our imaginings.
**—Barbara Grizzuti Harrison**

◆ The empire of the future are empires of the mind.
**—Winston Churchill**

◆ The greatest thing in this world is not so much where we are, but in what direction we are moving.
**—Oliver Wendell Holmes**

◆ I have great hope for tomorrow. My hope lies in three things—truth, youth, and love.
**—R. Buckminster Fuller**

◆ Yesterday is but a dream, tomorrow is only a vision. But today well lived makes every yesterday a dream of happiness and every tomorrow a vision of hope. Look well, therefore, to this day, for it is life, the very life of life.
**—Sanskrit proverb**

◆ In the absence of a vision, there can be no clear and consistent focus. In the absence of a dream, there can be no renewal of hope. In the absence of a philosophy, there is no real meaning to work and to life itself.
**—Joe Batten**

◆ So many worlds, so much to do. So little done, such things to be.
**—Alfred Lord Tennyson**

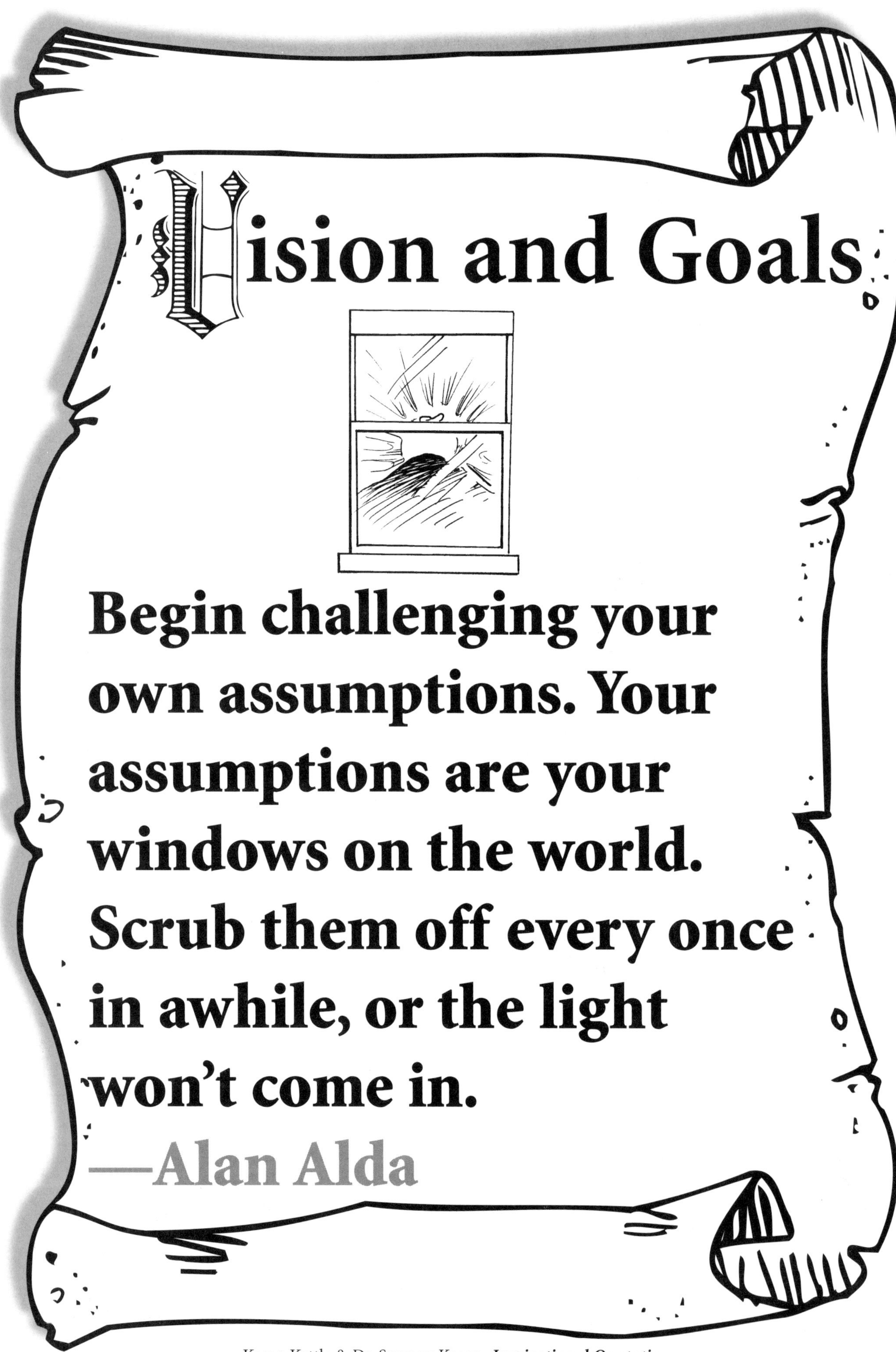
Vision and Goals
Begin challenging your own assumptions. Your assumptions are your windows on the world. Scrub them off every once in awhile, or the light won't come in.
—Alan Alda

Karen Kettle & Dr. Spencer Kagan: *Inspirational Quotations*
Kagan Publishing • 1 (800) 933-2667 • www.KaganOnline.com

Vision and Goals
Vision is the art of seeing things invisible.
—Jonathan Swift

Vision and Goals
NEW & IMPROVED
The starting point for a better world is the belief that it is possible.
—Norman Cousins

Vision and Goals
Dreams come in a size too big so that we can grow into them.
—Josie Bisset

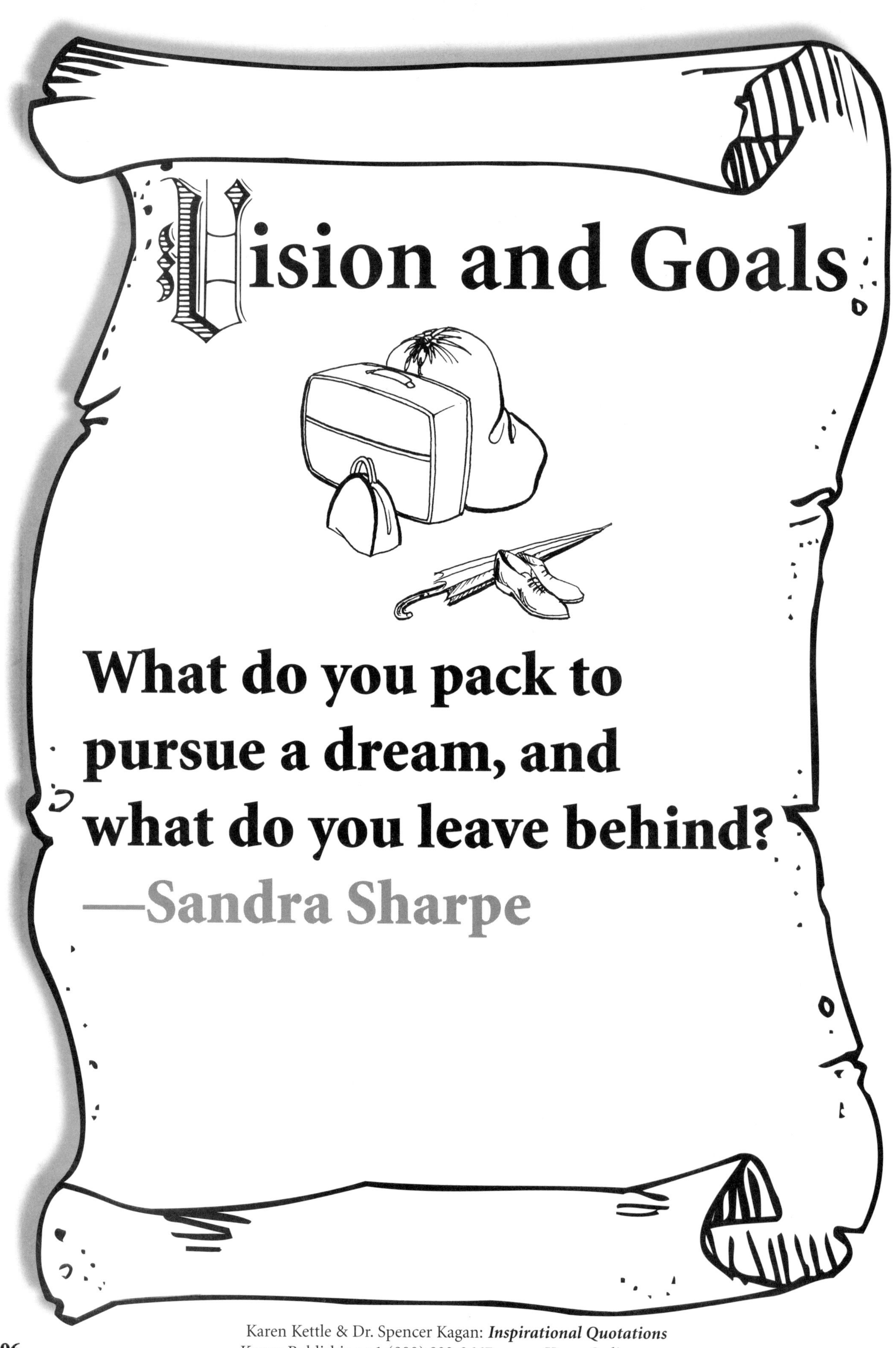

# Vision and Goals

**What do you pack to pursue a dream, and what do you leave behind?**

**—Sandra Sharpe**



Karen Kettle & Dr. Spencer Kagan: *Inspirational Quotations*
Kagan Publishing • 1 (800) 933-2667 • www.KaganOnline.com

# Inspirational Quotations Index


Aaron, Hank ............................271
Aaronovitch, Ben ......................120, 128
Abakanowicz, Magdalena .........248
Abercrombie, Lascelles.............288
Ackerman, Diane......................273
Adams, Abigail .........................78, 214
Adams, Douglas .......................169, 170
Adams, George M. ..................159
Adams, Henry ..........................214
Adams, John ............................147
Adams, John Quincy................205, 238
Adams, Scott............................110, 192
Addams, Jane...........................134, 239, 273
Adler, Felix...............................258
Adler, Mortimer J. ...................145, 147, 215, 219
Aesop .......................................157, 192
Aird, Catherine.........................204
Albright, Herm.........................44
Alcott, Louisa May ...................298
Alda, Alan ................................111, 296, 302
Ali, Muhammad.......................135, 218
Alinsky, Saul ............................98, 104
Allen, George...........................239
Allen, James ............................299, 301
Allen, Woody...........................229, 270
Althoff, Jim..............................180
Amiel, Henri Frédéric..............54, 124, 204, 259, 283, 288
Anderson, Eric.........................288
Anderson, Gillian .....................260
Anderson, Marian ....................202
Anderson, Ramona L. .............270
Anderson, Sparky.....................272
Andreas, Brian.........................111, 112
Andretti, Mario ........................69, 239
Andrew, Elizabeth ....................284
Angelou, Maya .........................17, 18, 44, 62, 71, 80, 110, 113, 132, 134, 136, 159, 169, 191, 271, 272
Anthony, Susan B. ...................78, 301
Apollinaire, Guillaume ............202
Apple, Fiona ............................156
Aquinas, St. Thomas ................259
Archard, Marcel........................287
Arendt, Hannah .......................144
Aristotle ...................................44, 81, 123, 144, 157, 214, 258, 271, 282
Ash, Mary Kay..........................54, 91
Ashe, Arthur ............................80
Asimov, Isaac...........................29, 64, 227, 234
Astor, Nancy ............................193
Astraea ....................................203
Atkinson, Gil ...........................109, 118, 248, 299
Auden, W. H. ..........................181
Aurelius, Marcus ......................157
Austen, Jane .............................270
Aweida, Jesse............................124
Ayres, William .........................283
Azikiwe, Nnamdi......................111
Bacon, Sir Francis ....................168, 218, 248
Bach, Richard ..........................171
Bagehot, Walter ........................68
Baldwin, Christina ...................64
Baldwin, James ........................66, 67, 90, 191
Baldwin, Monica ......................169

Bandura, Albert........................35, 147
Barr, Amelia E. ........................90
Barrett, Colleen C. ..................44
Barrick, Marilyn C. .................158
Barrie, J. M. ............................272
Barrie, James M. ......................260
Barrymore, Ethel......................180, 219
Barton, Bruce ..........................65, 79
Barzum, Jacques.......................284
Bateson, Mary Catherine..........159, 168
Batten, Joe................................301
Beaumarchais, Pierre ...............101
Beecher, Henry Ward...............80, 181
Beethoven ................................113
Beisser, Deanna ........................282, 284
Bell, Alexander Graham...........229
Bell, Chip R. ............................146
Bender, Betty ...........................249
Bender, Sue ..............................218
Bengis, Ingrid ..........................90
Bennett, Robert ........................122
Bennett, William J. ..................298
Bennis, Warren & Bert Nanus..203
Bennis, Warren ........................125, 202
Benson, Arthur Christopher.....44, 191
Benson, Dan ............................273
Bentley, Timothy ......................101
Bergson, Henri .........................64
Berkus, Rusty...........................289
Berle, Milton............................180
Bernard, Claude .......................218
Bernard, Jami ..........................90
Bernhardt, Sarah ......................260
Bernikow, Louise......................181
Berr, Wendell ...........................171
Berra, Lawrence Peter "Yogi"....237, 244, 300
Bestor, Arthur..........................17, 134
Bethune, Mary McLeod...........158
Billings, Josh ............................229
Bird, Tom.................................69
Birmingham, Carolyn..............180, 181
Birney, Earle ............................110
Bisset, Josie ..............................297, 305
Bittle, Less................................90
Blair, Tony................................123
Blake, Edward..........................124
Blanchard, Ken ........................193
Blanton, Smiley ........................259
Blessing, Leo ............................79
Block, Francesca Lia.................156
Bohr, Niels ...............................272
Bok, Derek...............................146
Bolen, Jean Shinoda .................298
Bolton-Holifield, Ruthie..........20, 42
Bombeck, Erma........................155, 164, 226, 231, 287
Bonaparte, Napoleon...............203, 301
Bondar, Roberta .......................193
Boorstin, Daniel J. ...................218
Boreham, R. W. .......................122
Borge, Victor............................178, 182
Boswell, Nelson ........................44
Bottome, Phyllis .......................54
Bourne, Randolph....................168
Bovee, Christian .......................205
Bower, Charles..........................112, 192
Boyer, Ernest............................283
Bradbury, Ray..........................249
Brameld, Theodore ..................282
Brand, Stewart..........................65
Brande, Dorothea.....................45
Branden, Nathaniel ..................260
Brenan, Gerald .........................67
Brendel, Alfred ........................91
Bridges, Madeline.....................81
Bro, Margueritte Harmon ........238
Brodin, Becky ..........................202
Bronowski, Jacob......................216
Bronte, Charlotte .....................156
Brookfield, Stephen..................284, 285, 286
Brooks, Garth ..........................100
Brooks, Mel .............................181
Brougham, Lord.......................147
Broughton, James.....................301
Brown, A. Whitney...................181
Brown, Ivor..............................214
Brown, Rita Mae ......................16, 90, 111, 142, 150, 181, 218
Brown, Sarah ...........................54
Brown, William D. ..................271
Brown Jr., H. Jackson...............79, 226, 229, 232
Browning, Elizabeth Barrett.....289
Brueau, Beatrice .......................68
Bruner, Jerome S. ....................214, 216, 285
Bryan, William Jennings..........125
Bryant, Bear.............................52, 56, 159, 203
Buck, Pearl S. ..........................110, 156, 271, 283
Buddha ....................................89, 96, 159, 171, 219, 298, 299
Buechner, Frederick .................191
Bull, Sitting..............................193
Burbank, Luther.......................67
Burnett, Carol...........................68
Burns, Conrad..........................270
Burns, David M. ......................215
Burns, George...........................65
Buscaglia, Leo ..........................91, 147, 181, 192, 281, 284, 293
Butler, Nicholas Murray ..........43

Butler, Samuel ............166, 173, 215
Byrd, Richard E. ............67
Byron, Lord ............180
Caddy, Eileen ............300
Cadman ............168
Caldicott, Helen ............282
Campbell, G. ............90
Camus, Albert ............168, 261
Cantor, Eddie ............238
Capra, Frank ............112
Carlyle, Thomas ............190
Carman, Bliss ............110
Carnegie, Andrew ............192
Carnegie, Dale ............43, 101, 158, 238
Carr, Emily ............110
Carroll, Lewis ............111, 261
Carson, Johnny ............67
Carson, Rachel ............171, 212, 217, 222
Carter, Hodding ............289
Carter, Jimmy ............134
Carter, Rosalynn ............205
Carver, George Washington ......144, 214, 273
Casals, Pablo ............146, 215
Cassou, Michell ............113
Castaneda, Carlos ............156
Cather, Willa ............100
Cezanne, Paul ............113, 156
Channing, William Ellery ............100, 169
Chapin, Edwin Hubblel ............190
Charles, Victor ............228
Chesterton, G. K. ............ 65, 145, 169, 192, 270
Chevalier, Maurice ............248
Ching, I ............191
Ching, Tao Te ............101
Chisholm, G. Brock ............282
Chisholm, Shirley ............258
Cho, Margaret ............157
Cholomondeley, Mary ............171
Chomsky, Noam ............147, 286
Chopra, Deepak ............191, 228
Churchill, Winston ............18, 44, 54, 81, 123, 203, 205, 228, 229, 238, 258, 261, 272, 301
Chysostom, St. John ............259
Cicero, Marcus Tullius ............261, 287
Clark, Frank ............181
Clark, Karen Kaiser ............64
Clark, Ramsay ............100
Clarke, Arthur C. ............299
Claudel, Paul ............112
Cleaver, Eldridge ............100
Clinton, Hillary Rodham ............134
Clyde, R. D. ............200, 206
Cody, Frank ............78
Cohen, Alan ............64, 81
Cohen, Dorothy H. ............285
Colao, Flora ............180
Cole, Natalie ............205
Coleridge, Samuel Taylor ............113, 157
Colette ............43
Collier, Robert ............298
Collins, Fredrick L. ............258
Collins, Marva ............285, 286
Coloroso, Barbara ............27, 159
Colton, Charles Caleb ............124
Commager, Henry Steele ............147
Commoner, Barry ............190
Conant, James B. ............249
Confucius ............16, 18, 80, 144, 214, 215, 282
Conklin, Beverly ............282
Conny, Beth Mende ............299
Conrad, Joseph ............238
Conway, Linda ............284
Cook, Mary Lou ............31, 110
Cooley, Charles ............202
Coolidge, Calvin ............239
Coolidge, Rita ............226, 230
Cooperrider, David ............202
Coppola, Sophia ............90
Corey, Irwin ............64
Cosby, Bill ............181
Cosby, Ennis ............284
Coser, Lewis A. ............100
Costa, Art ............193
Cousins, Norman ............296, 304
Covey, Stephen ............68, 123, 298, 301
Cragg, Cecil ............282, 289
Crane, Frank ............123
Crane, George W. ............91
Crichton, Lyle Samuel ............171
Crick, Francis ............214
Crosby, Philip ............124
Cross, K. Patricia ............286
Crowley, Mary ............158
Csikszentmihalyi, Mihaly ............42, 88, 92, 110
cummings, e.e. ............ 79, 191
Curie, Marie ............238, 239
Cusack, John ............125
da Vinci, Leonardo ............217, 238
Dale, Abbie M. ............122
Daloz, Laurent A. ............21, 145, 287
Dana, John Cotton ............283
Darrow, Clarence ............100, 288
Darwin, Charles ............64
Dass, Ram ............191
Davenport, Russell ............81
Davies, Robertson ............146

DaVinci, Leonardo ....................68
Davis Jr., Sammy ......................180
De Bono, Edward .....................110, 111, 180
De Buffon, Comte ....................239
de Chardin, Pierre Teilhard ......261, 289
De Gues, A. ..............................69, 219
De La Bruyere, Jean..................159
de La Rochefoucauld, Francois..91
De Mille, Agnes ........................113, 122
de Montaigne, Michael .............134, 156, 216
de Paul, St. Vincent ..................259
De Pree, Max ............................65
de Saint-Exupery, Antoine........190, 193, 201, 209
de Sales, Saint Francis ..............157, 170
DeBruyn, Robert .......................285
DeFrantz, Anita ........................300
Delaney, R. H. ..........................259
DeMille, Cecil B. .....................113
Demosthenes ............................228
Denning, W. Edwards ..............64
Descartes, René ........................219
Devlin, Bernadette ...................273
Devos, Richard M. ..................91, 228
Dewey, John..............................100, 111, 122, 142, 146, 147, 149, 168, 169, 170, 191, 214, 216, 281, 288, 289, 294
Dickens, Charles.......................157, 261
Dickinson, Emily......................154, 160
Diderot, Denis ..........................217
Didion, Joan ............................157
Dinesen, Isak ............................32, 55
Dioum, Baba ............................289
Disney, Walt.............................113, 193, 299
Disraeli, Benjamin ...................68, 122, 156, 168, 249, 271
Dole, Elizabeth .........................124, 282
Douglas, William O. ................55
Drayton, William .....................67
Driver, William.........................248
Drucker, Peter...........................19, 91, 123, 124, 203, 204
Drummond, Henry..................260
Du Bos, Charles........................68
Dubos, Rene .............................135
du Deffand, Madame ...............248
Dunn, Rita ................................285
Durant, Will .............................145
Dyer, Wayne W. .......................229, 299
Earhart, Amelia ........................169
Eble, Kenneth ...........................288
Edelman, Marian Wright..........69, 144, 258
Edinborough, Arnold...............143, 151
Edison, Thomas Alva ...............218, 229, 238, 239
Edwards, Harry ........................286
Edwards, Jonathan ...................284
Edwards, Lewis .........................192
Edwards, Tyron ........................78
Ehrmann, Max .........................135
Einstein, Albert.........................16, 65, 90, 112, 113, 146, 168, 171, 214, 216, 229, 258, 286, 288, 299
Eisenhower, Dwight D. ...........203
Eliot, George.............................79, 81, 122, 147
Elium, Jeanne ...........................285
Ellinger, Jules ...........................272
Ellington, Duke ........................299
Elliot, George...........................260
Elliott, Walter ...........................236, 241
Ellis, Havelock ..........................271
Ellison, Ralph ...........................144
Emerson, Ralph Waldo ............43, 45, 81, 91, 100, 124, 147, 169, 170, 190, 215, 229, 249, 259, 298, 300
Epictetus ..................................45, 54, 91
Erikson, Erik.............................285
Esbensen, Barbara J. ................169
Escher, M. C. ............................113
Evans, Marsha ..........................270
Evans, Noela .............................52, 57
Everson, J. Phillip .....................205
Ewig, Sam ................................77, 85
Fairless, Benjamin F. ...............273
Fallon, Jimmy ...........................112
Fenwick, Millicent....................258
Ferguson, Marilyn....................62, 70
Feynman, Richard....................214, 217, 218
Field, Charles............................180
Firestone, Harvey S. ................273
Fischer, John.............................17, 135
Fitzgerald, Ella..........................44
Fitzgerald, F. Scott ....................101, 298
Fitzwater, P. B. .........................78
Fizgerald, Zelda ........................157
Flanders, Alberta ......................228
Fleishman, Jerome P. ...............159
Flynn, Clarence ........................273
Follett, Mary Parker .................134, 202
Forbes, B. C. ............................43, 54, 238
Forbes, Malcolm.......................43, 135
Ford, Harrison..........................239
Ford, Henry ..............................41, 50, 219, 268, 271, 273, 275
Forster, E. M. ...........................218, 258
Forward, Gordon .....................215
Fosdick, Henry Emerson ..........229
Foster, Willa A. ........................123
Fournies, F. F. ..........................273
Fowler, Charles.........................191
Fox, Matthew............................204
France, Anatole.........................66, 145, 147, 287, 288

Frank, Anne ............................. 135
Frankl, Viktor ............................. 45, 259
Franklin, Benjamin ............................. 44, 145, 157, 238, 260
Franklin, John Hope ............................. 167, 175
Franklin, Ursula ............................. 144
Freire, Paolo ............................. 15, 21, 90, 101, 283, 285, 286, 287
Freud, Anna ............................. 157
Freud, Sigmund ............................. 112
Frisch, Max ............................. 81
Fritz, Robert ............................. 123
Fromm, Erich ............................. 67, 110, 112, 147
Frost, Robert ............................. 81, 125, 144, 145, 287, 288
Froude, James A. ............................. 78
Froust, Eden ............................. 188, 194
Fuess, Claude M. ............................. 284
Fulghum, Robert ............................. 180
Fullan, Michael ............................. 29, 65, 66, 68, 123, 124, 134, 204, 205, 283
Fuller, Margaret ............................. 283
Fuller, R. Buckminster ............................. 112, 191, 299, 301
Fusselman, W. ............................. 219
Futrell, Mary Hatwood ............................. 284
Gabriel, Peter ............................. 68
Galbraith, John Kenneth ............................. 67
Gallagher, Robert C. ............................. 64
Galsworth, John ............................. 111
Gandhi, Indira ............................. 28, 135, 203
Gandhi, Mahatma ............................. 69, 79, 81,132, 137, 159, 259
Gandini, Lella ............................. 216
Garcia, Rosamar ............................. 217
Gardner, Howard ............................. 205, 217
Gardner, John W. ............................. 203
Garner, James ............................. 42
Gates, Bill ............................. 202, 215
Gawain, Shakti ............................. 54
Gell-Mann, Murray ............................. 190
Geneen, Harold ............................. 204
George, David Lloyd ............................. 120, 126
Gere, Richard ............................. 156
Ghandi, Indira ............................. 99, 106
Giamatti, A. Barlett ............................. 21, 287
Gibbon, Edward ............................. 205
Gibbons, Cardinal ............................. 205
Gibran, Kahlil ............................. 158, 204, 260, 287
Gide, Andre ............................. 166, 172, 247, 254
Gilbert, Arland ............................. 44
Gilbertson, Joan ............................. 65
Ginott, Haim ............................. 21, 285, 287
Girzartis, Loretta ............................. 154, 161
Glasgow, Arnold ............................. 180
Glasgow, Ellen ............................. 65, 67
Glassgow, Arnold H. ............................. 205
Glick, Sam ............................. 248
Goddard, Robert ............................. 301
Godwin, Gail ............................. 288
Goldberg, Whoopi ............................. 192
Goldman, Emma ............................. 144
Goodall, Jane ............................. 68, 135
Gordon, James ............................. 67
Gordon, June ............................. 193
Gould, Glenn ............................. 91
Gould, Stephen Jay ............................. 158
Graffito ............................. 45
Graham, Katharine ............................. 280, 291
Graham, Martha ............................. 135
Grant, W. Lee ............................. 181
Gray, John ............................. 54
Greene, Graham ............................. 157, 228
Greenspan, Stanley I. ............................. 217
Greer, Germaine ............................. 55
Gregory, Marshall ............................. 284, 285
Gretzky, Wayne ............................. 268, 272, 274
Grey, Marilyn ............................. 44, 272
Groch, Judith ............................. 146
Grow, Gerald O. ............................. 286
Grubman, Jack B. ............................. 100
Hahn, Kurt ............................. 78, 81, 168
Hakuta, Ken ............................. 228
Hale, Edward Everett ............................. 261
Hale, Nancy ............................. 113
Half, Robert ............................. 100
Hall, Doug ............................. 180
Hamilton, Edith ............................. 145
Hamilton, Scott ............................. 42
Hammarskjöld, Dag ............................. 236, 242
Hammond, John Hays ............................. 79
Hancock, John ............................. 42
Hanks, Tom ............................. 80
Hansberry, Lorraine ............................. 261
Hanson, Michael ............................. 298
Hargreaves, Andy and Michael Fullan ............................. 69, 145, 146, 282
Harjen, Ray ............................. 216
Harris, Lawren ............................. 111
Harris, Sydney J. ............................. 145, 249, 273
Harrison, Barbara Grizzuti ............................. 301
Harrison, Elizabeth ............................. 159
Harrison, George ............................. 261
Hart, Leslie ............................. 147
Hathaway, Katherine Butler ............................. 125
Hautzig, Esther ............................. 156
Havel, Vaclav ............................. 45, 135, 273
Hawken, Paul ............................. 190
Hay, Louise ............................. 156
Hayes, Frederick ............................. 66
Hayes, Helen ............................. 259
Hazlitt, William ............................. 55, 214

Height, Dorothy........................203
Hein, Piet..................................215
Heine, Heinrich........................169
Heinlein, Robert........................125, 218, 288
Hemingway, Ernest ...................91
Hemmings, Madeline ...............229
Henderson, Hazel......................69
Hendrix, Harville ......................100
Hendrix, Jimi............................100
Henry, Robert...........................159
Hepburn, Audrey ......................191
Heraclitus .................................64, 78, 170, 228
Herbert, George ........................100
Herodotus.................................249
Hesburgh, Theodore.................300
Highet, Gilbert ..........................214, 287
Hill, Napoleon...........................125, 299
Hillel ........................................229
Hillman, Carol B. ....................217
Hindemith, Paul.......................271
Hirsch, Mary ............................179, 185
Hitchcock, R.D. .......................282
Hoffer, Eric...............................29, 63, 74
Hoffman, Eva ...........................181
Holdcroft, L. Thomas ...............42
Holland, J. G. ...........................54
Holmes, John Andrew ..............260
Holmes, Oliver Wendell...........91, 112, 123, 218, 301
Holt, John.................................81, 168, 214, 217, 286
Homer.......................................193
Hooker, Richard .......................66
hooks, bell ................................90, 135, 144
Hoover, J. Edgar ........................80
Hope, Bob.................................179, 186
Hopper, Grace Murray.............67, 248
Horace ......................................157
Horner, Martina........................36, 219
Houston, Jean...........................180
Howard, Vernon........................67
Howe, Gordie ...........................55
Hubbard, Elbert .......................45, 123, 259, 286
Hufstedler, Shirley....................248
Hughes, Charles Evans.............134
Hughes, Langston.....................170, 299
Hughes, Robert ........................236, 240
Hugo, Victor .............................69, 79, 301
Hull, Bobby ..............................98, 102
Humbert, Phil ...........................122
Hume, David ............................53, 59
Humes, James...........................28, 202
Humphrey, Hubert H. .............158
Hundley, Rod ...........................192
Hunt, Diana Scharf...................300
Hunt, H. L. ..............................123
Hunter, Joyce ............................192
Hurt, John ................................202
Huxley, Aldous ..........................65, 76, 83, 168, 169
Huxley, Thomas H. .................81, 101, 125, 218
Iacocca, Lee...............................54, 90, 249, 282
Iles, George ...............................66, 219
Ionesco, Eugene.........................287
Irving, Washington ..................66, 300
Isaksen, Scott ............................112
Jackson, Andrew........................124
Jackson, Jesse ............................28, 69, 158, 205, 299
James, Henry ............................168, 289, 298
James, William..........................42, 67, 193, 205, 286, 289, 298
Jameson, Storm ........................171
Jampolsky, Gerald ....................190
Jarrett, Bede ..............................157, 299
Jay, Antony................................201, 210
Jefferson, Thomas ....................79, 100, 157, 301
Jensen, Eric ...............................216
Jerrold, Douglas ........................181
Jesus .........................................259
Jobs, Steve.................................298
Johnson, Barry .........................16, 215
Johnson, David & Roger..........193
Johnson, David, Roger Johnson, & Karl Smith...215
Johnson, Lyndon B. .................122, 145
Johnson, Samuel ......................69, 124
Jones, Charles ...........................219
Jones, Franklin P. .....................168
Jones, William ..........................170
Jong, Erica ................................66, 248
Joplin, Janis...............................79
Jordan, Barbara ........................259, 270
Jordan, Michael ........................192, 272, 300
Joubert, Joseph .........................217
Joyce, James ..............................215
Jung, Carl..................................100, 112, 156, 285, 286, 298
Kagan, Spencer .........................63, 64, 67, 74, 122, 159, 193, 216, 268, 276, 289, 299
Kaiser, Henry J. ........................204
Kay, Allan..................................68
Keats, John...............................170, 272
Keightley, Alan..........................69
Keller, Helen ............................42, 43, 44, 78, 80, 145, 169, 193
Kemp, Harry.............................299
Kennedy, Florynce.....................123
Kennedy, Jacqueline .................273
Kennedy, John F. .....................11, 65, 144, 145, 147, 202, 258
Kennedy, Robert........................249
Kent, Corita .............................273

Kerouac, Jack ............................193
Kettering, Charles ....................66, 125, 218, 272
Key, Ellen .................................289
Keynes, John Maynard.............67
Kierkegaard, Søren...................55, 246, 248, 252
Kimball, Barbara ......................135
King, Billie Jean........................271
King, Serge Kahili.....................190
King, W. L. Mackenzie .............259
King Jr., Martin Luther ............76, 78, 81, 82, 101, 132, 138, 258, 259, 261, 272, 301
Kingsley, Charles ......................43
Kingston, Maxine Hong ...........111
Kissinger, Henry.......................202, 269, 277
Koch, Sally ...............................228
Koestler, Arthur........................110
Korda, Michael .........................80
Kossuth, Louis ..........................54
Kotter, John .............................205
Kozol, Jonathan........................123
Krishnamurti, Jiddu.................158, 159
Kubler-Ross, Elisabeth .............78, 122
Kuhn, Margaret E. ...................300
Kuhn, Thomas..........................68
Kurtz, Ernest............................271
Kushner, Harold.......................193
Kyi, Aung San Suu....................145
L'Engle, Madeleine ...................54, 111
Lagman, John ..........................249
Lama, Dalai .............................259, 260
Langer, Susanna K. ..................156
Laurence, Margaret ..................159
Law, Vernon Sanders................169
Lawrence, D. H. .......................65
Lazear, Jonathon.......................125
Le Carré, John .........................169
Leacock, Stephen......................147, 285
Learner, Max............................285
Ledru-Rollin, Alexandre ...........202
Lee, Blain ................................200, 208
LeGuin, Ursula K. ...................171, 190, 270
Lenin, Vladimir........................215
Leno, Jay .................................181
Leonard, George.......................219
Lerner, Max .............................78
LeShan, Eda .............................159
Lessing, Doris ..........................214, 239
Lewis, C. S. .............................249
Lewis, H. W. ...........................300
Lewis, Roger ............................280, 290
Lightfoot, Sara Lawrence..........288
Lin, Maya.................................100, 110
Lincoln, Abraham ....................42, 79, 144, 170, 229, 239, 270
Lindbergh, Anne Morrow.........29, 64, 89, 95, 135
Lindsay, Vachel ........................289
Linkletter, Art ..........................45
Lippmann, Walter ....................134, 193, 205
Logan, Katherine......................260, 301
Lois, George.............................112
Lombardi, Vince.......................188, 196, 270
Longfellow ...............................125
Longgood, William ..................299
Longinus, Cassius.....................271
Loren, Sophia ..........................168
Lorimer, George H. .................79
Lowell, James R. ......................67
Lubbock, John .........................43, 216
Luccock, H. E. ........................189, 197
Lucretius .................................81
Luther, John.............................78
Luther, Martin .........................40, 47, 180
Macedo, Donald.......................216
Machado .................................298
MacLaine, Shirley.....................134, 248
MacLaren, Alexander ...............238
Madwed, Sidney ......................68
Maharshi, Ramana ..................238
Malaguzzi, Loris ......................288
Malle, Louis .............................156
Malraux, Andre .......................193
Maltz, Maxwell........................271
Mandela, Nelson ......................147, 203, 204
Mandino, Og ...........................43, 259
Manley, John ...........................101
Mann, Horace ..........................146, 283, 287
Mannes, Myra .........................217
Mansfield, Katherine................249
Manske Jr., Fred A. .................203
March, Peyton Conway............258
Marden, Orison Swett..............301
Margaret, Mead .......................134
Marino, Michael Garrett...........218
Markham, Beryl .......................273
Markham, Edwin .....................191
Markins, Philip.........................43
Marshal, B. J. ...........................300
Marshall, Peter..........................55
Marston, Ralph.........................270
Martin, Theodore.....................238
Martineau, Harriet...................282
Marvin, Philip .........................205
Marx, Groucho.........................218, 219
Masai, J. ..................................156
Maslow, Abraham ....................285
Mason, Andrew .......................178, 184
Matheson, George ....................239
Matsushita, Konosuke..............124
Matthews, William ...................55

Maugham, W. Somerset............181
Maurer, R. ................................100
Maxim, Zen ..............................190
Maxwell, Elaine .........................122
Maxwell, Elsa............................180
Maxwell, John...........................67
May, Rollo................................90, 110, 111, 125
Mayforth, Frances ....................283
Mays, Benjamin E. ..................300
McArthur, Peter........................259
McAuliffe, Christa ....................289
McCarthy, Eugene....................135
McCarty, Hanoch .....................287
McGannon, Donald H. ............202
McGinnis, Alan Loy .................260
Mckinnon, Dan ........................272
McMahon, Tim ........................248
McNight, Mike .........................157
Mead, Margaret........................69, 158, 260
Meanwell, Clive ........................68
Melchert, Harold V. .................300
Melville, Herman .....................191
Menninger, William .................78
Menton, Thomas......................170
Mercier, Louis...........................16, 217
Metcalf, Ellen............................228
Michelangelo ...........................238, 239, 299
Michener, James A. .................78
Mill, John Stuart ......................90, 100
Miller, Alice .............................217
Miller, Henry............................69, 249
Miller, John R. .........................170
Miller, Margaret .......................91
Milne, A. A. .............................112
Mitchell, Maria.........................170, 217, 219
Moawad, Bob ...........................212, 221, 260
Montague, Ashley.....................287
Montana, Joe ............................181
Montapert, Alfred A. ...............300
Montessori, Maria....................146, 147, 286, 289
Montgomery, Lucy Maud........43
Moore, Isabel...........................41, 49
Moore, Jim................................228
Moore, Mary Tyler...................248
Morely, Christopher.................91
Morgan, J. Pierpont .................300
Morland, Miles.........................124
Morley, Christopher.................101, 219
Moses .......................................79
Moses, Grandma ......................20, 42
Moss, Senator Frank E. ............193
Moyers, Bill..............................31, 110
Mozart, Wolfgang Amadeus.....112
Mudd, Roger............................282
Muir, John ...............................171, 190
Muncy, Dunc...........................180
Munson, Gorham.....................54
Murrow, Edward R. .................80
Muskie, Edmund......................90
Myers, Joyce A. ........................282
Nachmanovitch, Stephen..........110, 112
Nader, Ralph............................202
Napoleon .................................123
NASA Motto............................40, 46
Nash, Ogden ............................43
Nathan, David .........................180
Nathanson, Jerome...................134
Neblette, C. B. ..........................288
Needham, Richard J. ...............124, 158
Nehru, Jawaharlal.....................17, 134, 248, 272
Neruda, Pablo...........................259
Newcomer, Mabel ....................300
Newhart, Bob ...........................181
Newton, Howard W. ...............158
Newton, Isaac...........................228
Newton, Joseph F. ...................45
Nicklaus, Jack ..........................157
Nidetch, Jean ...........................25, 122
Niebuhr, Reinhold....................66
Nietzsche, Friedrich .................170, 248
Nimoy, Leonard .......................192
Nin, Anaïs................................80, 191
Noble, Alex ..............................273
Noble, Charles C. ....................300
Noddings, Nel .........................17, 135, 284
Noe, John.................................79
Nolan, Michael.........................108, 116
Norris, Kathleen.......................65
Northrop, Ann..........................135
O'Conner, Marie ......................298
O'Connor, Sandra Day ............228
O'Faolain, Sean ........................68
Ogden, Frank............................64
Oivarez, Grace Gil....................192
Oliver, Gene.............................214
Olivier......................................166, 174
Orben, Robert ..........................205
Ortman, Mark..........................260
Osborn, Ronald E. ...................215
Osler, Sir William.....................67, 168, 258
Osmond, Marie ........................181
Overstreet, Harry A. ................202
Ovid .........................................54, 227, 233
Owens, Jesse ............................43
Paddleford, Clementine...........79
Pajares, Frank ..........................91
Palmer, Arnold ........................271
Palmer, Parker .........................283

Pandit, Vijaya Lakshmi ............145
Papyrus ....................................43
Parker, Dorothy ........................55
Parker, Theodore ......................219
Parks, Rosa ...............................80, 193
Parr, Ellen ................................112
Parton, Dolly ............................40, 48, 64
Pascal, Blaise ............................203
Pater, Walter .............................113
Paterson, Katherine ..................142, 148
Patton Jr., Gen. George ............205
Pauling, Linus ...........................108, 115
Pavolva, Anna ...........................301
Peale, Norman Vincent ............34, 43, 44, 68, 298, 301
Pearce, Joseph Chilton .............111
Pearson, Lester B. ....................101
Peck, M. Scott ...........................91, 169, 249
Penn, William ...........................158
Penney, Alexandria ...................101
Perry, Bliss ...............................286
Peter, Laurence J. .....................123, 218, 270
Peters, Margaret .......................158
Peters, Tom ...............................123, 159, 248
Peterson, Esther ........................257, 265
Pfaff, Vince ...............................205
Phillips, Jan ...............................65
Philo ..........................................214
Picasso, Pablo ...........................213, 215, 224
Pickert, Doris ...........................98, 103
Pickford, Mary .........................272
Pierson, Frank R. .....................90
Pike, Albert ...............................261
Pirsig, Robert M. .....................79
Planck, Max ..............................67
Plath, Sylvia ..............................283
Plato ..........................................76, 84, 146, 214, 217
Player, Gary ..............................301
Plomer, William .......................31, 110
Poincare, Henri ........................111
Poole, Mary Pettibone .............101, 181
Pope John XXIII .......................158
Porter, Irene ..............................65
Potter, Steve .............................188, 195
Powell, Colin ............................238
Powell, John ..............................19, 91
Powell, Sydney ..........................259
Priest, Ivy Baker ........................65
Priestley, J. B. ...........................284
Priestly, Joseph .........................217
Pritchard, Michael .....................181
Prochnow, Herbert V. .............124
Proust, Marcel ..........................170, 215
Proverb, Afghan .......................158
Proverb, African .......................145
Proverb, American ...................181
Proverb, Arabian .......................91, 217
Proverb, Armenian ...................239
Proverb, Assyrian .....................81
Proverb, Chinese ......................64, 122, 124, 157, 167, 170, 176, 181, 193, 214, 239, 259, 260, 261, 284
Proverb, Dutch .........................239
Proverb, English .......................79, 204, 229
Proverb, French ........................55, 66, 229
Proverb, German ......................64
Proverb, Greek ..........................134
Proverb, Greenland ..................239
Proverb, Hebrew ......................218, 219
Proverb, Hindu .........................258
Proverb, Indian .........................44
Proverb, Irish ............................147, 192
Proverb, Italian .........................79
Proverb, Japanese .....................100, 101, 111, 169, 272, 284
Proverb, Jewish .........................124
Proverb, Kurdish ......................79
Proverb, Latin ...........................68, 214
Proverb, Malayan .....................247, 253
Proverb, Maori .........................202, 203, 300
Proverb, Nigerian .....................134
Proverb, Russian .......................144
Proverb, Sanskrit ......................301
Proverb, Sioux ..........................67
Proverb, Spanish ......................79, 101, 169
Proverb, Swahili ........................219
Proverb, Swedish ......................159, 170, 192
Proverb, Turkish .......................124
Proverb, Welsh ..........................81
Proverb, Yiddish .......................16, 180, 216
Proverb, Zimbabwean ..............248
Puck, Wolfgang .........................215
Pusey, Nathan M. ....................146
Pythagoras ................................90, 123
Quindlen, Anna ........................65, 213, 223, 272
Quinn, Donald D. ...................283
Radner, Gilda ............................45
Ramdas, Swami ........................259
Ramirez, Carlos ........................101
Rand, Ayn .................................54
Ransome, Arthur .......................228
Rather, Dan ...............................55, 284
Reagan, Nancy ..........................20, 42
Reardon, Daniel L. ..................45
Redford, Robert .........................101
Redmoon, Ambrose ..................18, 80
Reese, Betty ...............................154, 162
Reeve, Christopher ....................55, 121, 130
Reiner, Carl ...............................181
Repplier, Agnes .........................181
Ride, Sally .................................54

Ridge, Julie....66
Riley, Pat....192, 238
Robbins, Tom....135
Roberts, Jane....156
Robinson, James Harvey....66
Robinson, Parkes....44
Rochlin, Harriet....180
Rockefeller, John D. ....248
Roddick, Anita....202
Roethke, Theodore....159, 170
Rogers, Carl....42, 68, 91, 145, 216
Rogers, Fred....216
Rogers, Will....134, 229, 248
Rohn, Jim....203
Rooney, Andrew A. ....284
Rooney, Mickey....238
Roosevelt, Eleanor....20, 45, 55, 88, 94, 135, 146, 169, 203, 299
Roosevelt, Franklin D. ....101, 147, 238
Roosevelt, Theodore....42, 54, 55, 124, 205, 298
Rorty, Richard....19, 90
Rosenberg, Marshall B. ....33, 156, 159
Rossetti, Christina....53, 60
Rosten, Leo....80, 217, 273
Roueche, John....287
Rubin, Theodore Isaac....112, 158
Rubinstein, Arthur....270
Rukeyser, Muriel....88, 93
Runbeck, Margaret Lee....43
Rusk, Dean....91
Ruskin, John....79, 259
Russel, David....168
Russell, Bertrand....65, 124, 193, 282
Russell, Rosalind....271
Saadi....239
Sadat, Anwar....192
Sagan, Carl....111, 113
Saint Francis of Assisi....259
Salzberg, Sharon....69
Samsel, R. C. ....79
Samuelson, Paul A. ....216
Sandburg, Carl....299
Sangster, Margaret E. ....283
Santayana, George....55, 218
Saotome, Mitsugi....191
Sarason, Seymour....284
Sarnoff, David....238
Sarnoff, Dorothy....91
Saroyan, William....271
Sartre, Jean-Paul....122
Satir, Virginia....44, 299
Saul, J. ....205
Sawyer, Diane....217
Saying, Seneca....78
Saying, Taoist....171
Sayre, Woodrow Wilson....249
Schabacker, Ann....42
Schaef, Anne Wilson....180
Schein, Edgar....67
Schiefelbein, Susan....193
Schiefer, Eli J. ....157
Schlechty, Phillip....200, 207
Schopenhauer, Arthur....64, 67, 258, 288
Schuller, Dr. Robert H. ....54, 122, 123, 237, 243, 249
Schulz, Charles M. ....26, 144, 180
Schweitzer, Albert....28, 30, 54, 157, 158, 193, 204, 256, 264, 270
Scott, Zachary....125
Scully, Frank....246, 251
Seattle, Chief....189, 190, 198
Seeger, Pete....168
Selleck, Tom....78
Seneca, Lucius Annaeus....55
Senge, Peter....204
Sergiovanni, Thomas J. ....157, 159
Seuss, Dr. ....100, 134, 181
Shackleton, Ernest....170
Shakespeare, William....249
Shanker, Albert....285
Sharpe, Sandra....297, 306
Shaw, George Bernard....19, 65, 91, 171, 229, 257, 266, 283, 299, 300
Sheehan, George....42
Shinn, Florence....42
Shoemaker, Samuel....157
Shokansai, Iizuka....156
Shore, Dinah....158
Siegfried....110
Sikorsky, Igor....261
Sills, Beverly....271
Sinetar, Marsha....66
Singer, Isaac....111
Sizer, Theodore R. ....146
Skinner, B.F. ....144
Slim, W. J. ....125
Smeltzer, Ruth....258
Smiles, Samuel....271
Smith, Betty....43
Smith, Elinor....229
Smith, Frank....280, 283, 292
Smith, Sydney....261
Sobol, Thomas....285
Socrates....68, 81, 205, 288
Solomon, Muriel....155, 163
Sophocles....215
Sorel, Julia....248
Spady, William G. ....285
Spielberg, Steven....228
Spinoza....298

Spurgeon, Charles H. ...............239
Stafford, William ......................90, 171
Stark, Michael..........................190
Steele, Shelby ..........................229
Stein, Ben ................................191, 272
Steinbeck, John........................125, 212, 220, 283
Steinberg, Saul.........................111
Steinem, Gloria ........................299
Sternberg, Robert .....................205
Stevenson, Robert Louis ..........55, 203, 256, 263
Stockdale, James B. ..................145
Stone, Clement .........................123
Stonsifer ..................................239
Strauss, Robert .........................30, 271
Stravinsky, Igor.........................271
Streisand, Barbara ....................135
Strode, Muriel ..........................170
Stuttelle, Rebecca .....................157
Sullivan, Anne ..........................286
Swaim, Alice Mackenzie...........80
Sweetland, Ben .........................256, 262, 270
Swift, Jonathan .........................296, 303
Swindonoll, Charles .................45
Syrus, Pubilius ..........................101, 215
Szent-Gyorgyi, Albert ..............111
Szilard, Leo ...............................228
Tagore, Rabindranath ...............258
Talmud......................................44
Tapp, June ................................64
Tartakower, S.A. ......................271
Tausher, Stacia ..........................285
Taylor, Elizabeth .......................80
Taylor, Harold...........................81
Teague, Junior...........................90
Tennyson, Alfred Lord .............170, 301
Teresa, Mother..........................91, 99, 105, 158, 258, 261
Thackeray .................................180
Thatcher, Margaret...................124, 205, 270
Thompson, William Irving.......108, 114
Thoreau, Henry David.............91, 113, 169, 270, 298, 299, 300, 301
Thorndike.................................5
Thucydides ...............................300
Thurber, James .........................170, 181, 204
Thurman, Howard ...................81
Tillich, Paul...............................122
Tiong, Ho Boon .......................287
Tiorio .......................................202
Toffler, Alvin ............................24, 64, 125, 143, 152, 219
Tolstoy, Leo ..............................258
Tomlin, Lily ..............................286
Townsend, Robert ....................204
Trudeau, Pierre E. ....................69, 101
Truman, Harry S. .....................203
Truman, Henry.........................43
Trump, J. Lloyd.........................288
Tutu, Archbishop Desmond.....190, 191
Twain, Mark ............................44, 67, 79, 80, 90, 113, 123, 124, 146, 169, 181, 192
Tyger, Frank..............................91, 271
Tzu, Lao ...................................80, 261, 299
Ueland, Brenda.........................113
UNESCO .................................282
Unknown .................................260
Unser, Bobby ............................270
Ustinov, Peter ...........................43, 219
Valery, Paul ...............................66
Van Buren, Abigail ...................169
Van Doren, Mark .....................284
Van Dyke, Henry......................109, 117
van Gogh, Vincent ...................55, 193, 261
Vanier, Jean ..............................285
Vaughn, Billy ............................215, 272
Veeck, Bill ................................120, 127
Virgil ........................................54
Viscott, David ...........................158
Vivekananda, Swami ................135, 168, 191
Voltaire.....................................101, 192
Von Braun, Werner ..................111
Von Ebner-Eschenbach, Marie..101, 272
Von Goethe, Johann Wolfgang..43, 65, 78, 122, 123, 134, 169, 203, 215, 238, 287
Von Oech, Roger ......................113, 123
Von Schille, Johann Friedrich ..299
Vonnegut Jr., Kurt ....................156
Vonnegut, Kurt.........................77, 86
Vygotsky, Lev ...........................215
Wagner, Richard .......................261
Walker, Madame C. J. .............229
Walker, Mort.............................180
Walker, Phillipa ........................178, 183
Walton, Izaak............................192
Walton, Sam .............................44, 203
Ward, C. M. .............................68
Ward, Don ...............................123
Ward, William Arthur..............91, 269, 278, 287
Warhol, Andy ...........................69
Warren, Rick.............................202
Washington, Booker T. ...........30, 81, 258, 271
Washington, George.................80
Washington, Martha ................42
Watson, Thomas ......................271
Watts, Alan ...............................68
Wauneka, Annie .......................80
Wayne, John .............................80
Weil, Simone ............................122, 288
Welch, Jack ...............................65
Wells, H.G. ...............................147
Wesley, John .............................260

West, Mae ....248
Wharton, Edith ....168
Wheatley, Margaret....62, 64, 72, 113, 204
White, Sabina ....180
Whitehead, Alfred North....112, 288, 65
Whitman, Harold Thurman....273
Whitman, Walt....101
Whitney Jr., King....66
Whittemore, Flora....121, 129
Wieder, Marcia ....260
Wiesel, Elie ....218
Wilcox, Colleen ....282
Wilcox, Ella Wheeler....260
Wilcox, Fredrick B. ....246, 250
Wilde, Oscar....65, 145, 169
Wiley, Charles....260
Wilkie, Wendell L. ....144
Wilkins, Roger....17, 133, 140
Williams, Ella ....54
Williams, Montel....159
Williamson, Marianne....261
Wilson, Eugene S. ....214
Wilson, Mary J. ....44
Wilson, Woodrow ....65, 202, 261
Winder, Barbara W. ....228
Winfrey, Oprah ....52, 58, 191, 229
Winter, Barbara J. ....249
Winterson, Jeanette....249
Wolfe, Patricia ....217
Wolfe, Thomas ....273
Wolff, Tobias....239
Wollstoncraft, Mary....125
Wong, Jan ....229
Woodman, Cousin....168
Woodson, Carter G. ....144
Woolf, Virginia....111, 113
Woolworth, Frank W. ....204
Wosmek, Frances....146
Wright, Frank Lloyd....273
Wright, Steven....228
X, Malcolm....66, 145, 216
Yamada, Kobi....42, 157
Yeager, Chuck....239
Yeats, William Butler....144
Young, Brigham ....144
Young, Vash ....45, 55, 133, 139, 192
Zais, Lt. General Melvin ....203
Zarlenga, Peter Nivio ....113
Ziglar, Zig ....203
Zunin, Leonard ....249